SERVING THE ELDERLY

MODERN APPLICATIONS OF SOCIAL WORK

An Aldine de Gruyter Series of Texts and Monographs

SERIES EDITOR

James K. Whittaker

Ralph E. Anderson and Irl Carter, **Human Behavior in the Social Environment: A Social Systems Approach** (fourth edition)

Richard P. Barth and Marianne Berry, **Adoption and Disruption: Rates, Risks, and Responses**

Larry K. Brendtro and Arlin E. Ness, **Re-Educating Troubled Youth: Environments for Teaching and Treatment**

Kathleen Ell and Helen Northen, **Families and Health Care: Psychosocial Practice**

Marian Fatout, **Models for Change in Social Group Work**

Mark Fraser, Peter J. Pecora, and David Haapala (eds.), **Families in Crisis: The Impact of Intensive Family Preservation**

James Garbarino, **Children and Families in the Social Environment**

James Garbarino, Patrick E. Brookhouser, Karen J. Authier, and Associates, **Special Children—Special Risks: The Maltreatment of Children with Disabilities**

James Garbarino, Cynthia J. Schellenbach, Janet Sebes, and Associates, **Troubled Youth, Troubled Families: Understanding Families At-Risk for Adolescent Maltreatment**

Roberta Greene, **Social Work with the Aged and Their Families**

Roberta R. Greene and Paul H. Ephross, **Human Behavior Theory and Social Work Practice**

Jill Kinney, David Haapala, and Charlotte Booth, **Keeping Families Together: The Homebuilders Model**

Paul K. H. Kim (ed.), **Serving the Elderly: Skills for Practice**

Robert M. Moroney, **Shared Responsibility: Families and Social Policy**

Robert M. Moroney, **Social Policy and Social Work**

Peter J. Pecora and Mark Fraser, **Evaluating Family Preservation Services**

Peter J. Pecora, James K. Whittaker, Anthony N. Maluccio, Richard P. Barth, and Robert D. Plotnick, **The Child Welfare Challenge: Policy, Practice, and Research**

Steven P. Schinke (ed.), **Behavioral Methods in Social Welfare**

Albert E. Trieschman, James K. Whittaker, and Larry K. Brendtro, **The Other 23 Hours: Child-Care Work with Emotionally Disturbed Children in a Therapeutic Milieu**

Deborah Valentine and Patricia G. Conway, **Guide for Helping the Natural Healer**

Harry H. Vorrath and Larry K. Brendtro, **Positive Peer Culture** (second edition)

Betsy Vourlekis and Roberta R. Greene (eds.), **Social Work Case Management**

Heather B. Weiss and Francine H. Jacobs (eds.), **Evaluating Family Programs**

James K. Whittaker and James Garbarino, **Social Support Networks: Informal Helping in the Human Services**

James K. Whittaker, Jill Kinney, Elizabeth M. Tracy, and Charlotte Booth (eds.), **Reaching High-Risk Families: Intensive Family Preservation in Human Services**

James K. Whittaker and Elizabeth M. Tracy, **Social Treatment, 2nd Edition: An Introduction to Interpersonal Helping in Social Work Practice**

Hide Yamatani, **Applied Social Work Research: An Explanatory Framework**

SERVING THE ELDERLY
Skills for Practice

Paul K. H. Kim

Editor

ALDINE DE GRUYTER
New York

About the Editor

Paul K. H. Kim, DSW, is Clinical Professor of Medicine and Codirector of the Louisiana Geriatric Education Center at the Louisiana State University School of Medicine. He is also Professor and Chair of the MSW/Aging Concentration at the School of Social Work, Louisiana State University. Among his research interests, reflected in numerous previous books, journal articles, and funded projects, are the mental health problems of the elderly and the situation of the rural elderly.

ALDINE DE GRUYTER
A division of Walter de Gruyter, Inc.
200 Saw Mill River Road
Hawthorne, New York 10532

The paper used in this publication meets the minimum requirements of American National Standard for Information Sciences—Permanence of Paper for Printed Library Materials, ANSI Z39.48-1984.   ∞

Library of Congress Cataloging-in-Publication Data
Serving the elderly : skills for practice / Paul K. H. Kim, editor.
    p.   cm. — (Modern applications of social work)
    Includes bibliographical references and index.
    ISBN 0-202-36073-3 (alk. paper). — ISBN 0-202-36074-1 (pbk. : alk. paper)
    1. Aged—Services for—United States. 2. Social work with the aged—United States.   I. Kim, Paul K. H.   II. Series.
HV1461.S46   1991
362.6'0973—dc20   91-19923
                                                                     CIP

Manufactured in the United States of America
10 9 8 7 6 5 4 3 2 1

Dedicated to our parents

Yong Nak Kim, Mying Soo Woo, Dong Kyu Kim,
and Jong Soo Lee

CONTENTS

LIST OF CONTRIBUTORS

Marion L. Beaver	University of Pittsburgh
Naomi Feil	Edward Feil Productions
Leon H. Ginsberg	University of South Carolina
Joan Hashimi	University of Missouri, St. Louis
Jon Hendricks	Oregon State University
Paul K. H. Kim	Louisiana State University
Cynthia A. Leedham	University of Kentucky
Nancy Lohmann	University of West Virginia
Roger Lohmann	University of West Virginia
Susan Massa	Florida State University
Eloise Rathbone-McCuan	University of Kansas
Maxie C. Maultsby, Jr.	Howard University
Frank B. Raymond, III	University of South Carolina
Steven R. Rose	Louisiana State University
Bruce A. Thyer	University of Georgia
Kim Thyer	University of Georgia
R. O. Washington	University of New Orleans

FOREWORD

Despite an explosion in services available to the aging population of this country, we continue attempts to define what may be undefinable. Experts do not agree as to the boundaries of the group we categorize as aged. Is it composed of persons who are 65 or over (the definition of senior citizens developed by some airlines for discounted fares), 50 and over (the age at which one is eligible to join the American Association of Retired Persons, better known as AARP), or 40 and over (the age at which one receives certain governmental protection against discrimination as an "older worker")?

To suggest that we can define the aged population on the basis of self-definition creates still other problems. There are countless individuals in their sixties and seventies who would never classify themselves as "aged" as exemplified in the 74-year-old widow who helps to care for the "old people" in her community. Health and vitality cannot be used as a criterion except possibly for the old–old in their eighties and nineties. Even retirement age is no longer a good measure as employment now extends far beyond the "gold watch" standard age of 65. Lacking precise definitions of the cohort we serve, we nevertheless have witnessed and participated in creating a myriad of programs, structures, and agencies to meet the needs of this group.

Despite the inability to decide who belongs to the group we serve, we have had to cope with those who, too glibly, suggest that services to the elderly are essentially assistance to the frail. Part of our services are indeed directed to those who need to be assisted in daily living tasks and may even require institutional care. Yet many older persons are not in need of this kind of assistance, but rather wish to continue being productive and active. Some may require the specialized setting that senior centers offer—a place where they can develop friendships, participate in classes and hobbies, and learn new skills, while having needs such as meal preparation, housekeeping, and transportation provided. Still others faced with the loss of a spouse or gainful employment may need counseling in addition to communal living arrangements. Still others will want to maintain their status as active workers and seek support against discrimination of present or potential employers.

The point being made is that the aged represent a vast, though not exactly defined, population that is as diverse as any other age segment. For instance, services to children must also be broad and involve a huge variety of services aimed at different elements of that group.

It is not surprising, therefore, that the providers of services to the aged are not based on any one profession, but rather include social workers, psychologists, sociologists, educators, occupational and physical therapists, recreational therapists, physicians and nurses, dentists, lawyers, architects, and dozens of other professions and occupations. To this conglomerate we must add volunteers of all kinds, including daughters and daughters-in-law, other older persons who are spouses or friends, service groups, etc. They bring various skills to those whom they seek to help, and that is as it should be. Therefore, to work with such a diverse population and varied service providers requires a variety of knowledge and skills. Moreover, it is possible to advance the notion that all these providers of services can share some core knowledge about aging, and more importantly can and *must* share a common set of attitudes that, in our view, is an essential aspect of their work.

The values that guide our work are based on both our religious and democratic traditions. They have been incorporated in the codes of conduct developed in many of the helping professions. As one who was trained in, and has spent monumental time developing indispensable aspects of my professional work, they include, inter alia, the empowerment of the client and a need to maintain the maximum independence and autonomy of the person seeking help; the rejection of case management if it becomes a bureaucratic control system over the client; containment as an essential practice mode that avoids the imposition of the worker's cultural values on the client; and the willingness to advocate on behalf of the client and to seek policy changes and systemic changes. These examples of concepts that guide my practice can be taught to all who provide services to the aged. The identification and development of such seminal ideas are relatively simple. It is the implementation of the concepts in real life situations that is difficult and will create value conflicts and dilemmas for the practitioner.

The struggle to develop effective services that are based on a view of man that grants dignity, independence, and choice to the aged person is challenging and exhilarating. It makes up for the frustrations of low budgets, long hours, and the lack of public recognition.

Serving the aged is attracting some wonderful and highly dedicated persons who exude an element of crusade in their work. They do not accept the myths that are communicated about old people. They know that ageism is a form of discrimination as evil as sexism and racism.

Within the chapters of this book, students and readers will find rich material to guide them in examining a wide variety of interventive service strategies to a diverse population that is growing substantially each year. And what is more exciting is that, in time, they will write their own chapters, adding to the knowledge of this vast field and to the improvement in lives of older Americans.

Dr. Daniel Thursz, President
The National Council on the Aging

PREFACE

A major American discovery in both the fields of science and humanities is indeed the reality of old age. This American phenomenon has been contributed to by the quagmire of incessantly developing knowledge and related technologies of all scientific disciplines and professions (particularly in the field of health science and human services, which have resulted in prolonged human longevity), and, albeit insignificant in number, by the influx of "new immigrants."

Aging Americans, who have acquired age 65, account for about 12.5%, or 31 million of the total population today, and by the turn of the century that figure is projected to rise to about 15%, or 35 to 40 million in number. By virtue of the steadily increasing life expectancy and resultant in numbers, the aging population may be classified into three subgroups: young–old (age 65–74), old (age 75–84), and old–old (age 85 and older).

Unfortunately, however, the advancement of human aging is destined to accompany a human dilemma, that is a series of problems in living, characterized by poor health and mental health, income insecurity, under- and/or unemployment, substandard housing and inadequate living arrangements, and the lack of creative opportunity, mobility, human services, etc. In fact, the third group, the old–old, is the fastest growing segment of the American population, and has been empirically documented as the most vulnerable and dependent group of people.

Human service disciplines, primarily such professions as social work, health services administration, medicine, psychiatry, dentistry, nursing, allied health, pharmaceutics, clinical counseling, law, public administration, religion, as well as relevant biological and behavioral sciences, have independently responded to the needs facing the elderly. Their intervention strategies basically include two approaches: clinical (or micro) and indirect (or macro) practices. The former focuses on an individualized service impact essentially through dyadic relationships between the professional and client (or clients in case of a small therapeutic group), whereas the latter emphasizes a broader impact on organizations and/or communities that are designed to serve the elderly. Although gerontological human service providers may establish and be involved in respective application of their primary practice skill(s), these approaches are never meant to be mutually exclusive, but interdependent. There exists a relationship of bilateral reinforcement between them, implying that the clinical gerontologist should not only be fully aware of the eminence of macro practice that facilitates effective and efficient clinical services for the elderly, but also be a responsible participant in the macro approach to problem-solving. Likewise, the macro practitioner should not only be knowledgeable about, but also capable of providing clinical services as an effective and efficient manager, administrator, planner, and/or program evaluator. He/she should have a full perception of the idiosyncracy pertaining to clinical approaches and subsequently integrate that knowledge into practice.

This book is designed to bring together unique and appropriate skills for the field of gerontological human services, beginning with generational theories of aging that are explicit guides to seven clinical or micro skills, i.e., Counseling, Family Therapy, Reminiscent Therapy, Validation Therapy, Behavioral Therapy, Rational Self-Help Counseling, and Small Group Approach; and five macro skills, i.e., Social Planning, Management and Administration, Program Evaluation, Consultation, and Fund Raising.

The editor is deeply indebted for the dedicated indulgence of contributing authors, without which this long overdue text is beyond realization. To say the least, it certainly is a humbling experience to have them as close professional colleagues who devote themselves to the same cause, that is, serving the elderly, and to solicit superb chapters written by a number of rightfully established experts in the field of gerontological human services. On behalf of the contributing authors, sincere gratitude is extended to Dr. Daniel Thursz who accords the eminence of professional values and ethics within human service practice.

P.K.H.K.

Theories of Aging Implications for Human Services[1]

JON HENDRICKS and CYNTHIA A. LEEDHAM

This book concerns the importance for human services to understand the elderly and their lifeworld in a societal context. Social policies and programs affect actors' life chances as they age. The elderly themselves are social actors, capable of helping to shape the community of which they are members. An understanding of this dialectic is obviously crucial to macro practice skills, such as program management and community development. To be effective, clinical practices also must be cognizant of the limitations and opportunities afforded by social structure. The goal of human service practice with the elderly, as with people of all ages, is to enhance the autonomy of clients, drawing on their strengths—with due respect for the needs, strengths, and weaknesses of their families. An exclusive focus on individual-level factors can lead to "blaming the victim" for problems with social roots, and to a sense of learned helplessness as people strive to solve structural problems using individual solutions. Enshrining structural imperatives as immutable can imperil individual initiative, and discourage people from questioning social arrangements.

Explanatory frameworks or theories can broaden one's vision, or act as blinders, limiting one's perspectives and insulating one from new information. Theory can segment structure form individual lives, or reveal the dynamic interplay between the two. Theory can focus on the narrow interests and viewpoints of a particular group, or set group interests in relationship to the wider society. Ideally, theory opens new vistas, pointing to unanticipated connections. This chapter will provide an overview of the development of gerontological theory, focusing on the ways in which theoretical perspectives enhance or obscure the vision. The chapter begins by considering elements essential to emancipatory theories conducive to practice styles that respect the elderly's autonomy. These criteria will then be used in a critical analysis of the development of gerontological theory, and potential contributions of particular theories to human service practice. In conclusion, implications of gerontological theory for human services are summarized.

Features of an Emancipatory Gerontological Theory

A fundamental question for human service practice at both the clinical (micro) and the macro level is the extent to which gaining is socially constructed and therefore modifiable. Which factors constitute limiting constraints to be dealt with as best people can? Which can be modified to enhance quality of life and increase chances of self-fulfillment? How can people respond creatively to the immutable? Answering these questions implies understanding the dynamic interplay between social structure, culture, psychology, and biology. Social institutions shape patterns of aging for individuals, yet may themselves be amenable to community or political action. Although physiology may present limiting factors, there is growing evidence that the physiology of "usual aging" is shaped by socially determined access to resources, and stresses across the life-course. "Normal aging," unhampered by negative environmental influences, may be very different (Rowe & Kahn, 1987). Control over one's environment and access to resources are affected by a variety of factors, including gender, race, and class. Awareness of the differences they imply is crucial to understanding the opportunities and constraints affecting aging individuals, and to determining when to work for personal change and when to contest limits. Cultural diversity in interaction with social structure should also be taken into account. The meanings of aging and associated life changes vary greatly between groups. Gibson (1987, 1988), for instance, suggests that mainstream distinctions between work and retirement may not be meaningful for Blacks with interrupted work histories who are forced by economic necessity to continue working into advanced old age. Historical factors, too, powerfully affect the resources and liabilities particular cohorts bring to the aging process. Having lived through particular epochs, the Great Depression, the Vietnam War, the social protests of the 1960s, has long-term repercussions in terms of the way people look at their world, their ability to accumulate financial resources for later life, and their attitudes about aging.

Theories cannot be all embracing, and they obviously vary in scope. Yet, even when focusing on a particular facet of aging, a sound theory will be sensitive to the complexity of the aging process, and will not actively deny the importance of any of its aspects. Theories of aging operate at many levels, and entail underlying assumptions about the process itself. How far is it physiologically, socially, or psychologically determined? Is there such a thing as normal aging? Theories may propose general explanations of particular aspects of aging. What factors best predict retirement satisfaction in the United States? Or they may seek to explain why a particular occurrence is just so and not otherwise. Why was the Medicare Catastrophic Illness Act passed then repealed? Why do workers in a particular industry or sector of the economy tend to withdraw from the labor force early? Confusion between these levels can lead to undesirable consequences for human service practice. Broad applications of theories drawn from limited situations, as general theories of aging, can prejudice people's thinking, blinding them to individual differences. An awareness of how problem definition affects professionals' approaches to problem solving is vital to effective human service practice.

Theories of Aging

Although such a schematization obviously does not do justice to the complexities and contributions of individual theories, it is useful to conceptualize the evolution of gerontological theories in social gerontology in terms of three generations, representing thesis, antithesis, and synthesis (Hendricks & Leedham, 1987; Hendricks & Hendricks, 1986). Broadly speaking this development represents a move toward increasing awareness of the complex, dynamic, variable, and socially constructed nature of aging. Early theories in social gerontology tended to focus on individual factors, taking structure for granted. They asked how the aging individual could best adapt to circumstances. Second generation theories shifted the emphasis to structure, downplaying culture and individual intentionality in their search for universal imperatives. Third generation synthetic theories seek to explore dynamic interactions between individuals and social structure. They examine the social construction of societal institutions. They ask how people react to resultant constraints, and how they can affect them (Marshall, 1981, 1986). Whose interests are served by social policies? How are those policies shaped? How do they impact diverse groups of elderly (Estes, Swan, & Gerard, 1982; Estes, 1986)? Recent critical theories of aging take this line of thinking even further, challenging assumptions and norms of exchange in which policy is grounded.

Early theories are, on the whole, too narrow in scope to be taken as comprehensive. To do so would be prejudicial to practice. Institutional problems and variations in individual capacities and needs would be denied. An uncritical acceptance of disengagement theory, for instance, could lead to development of programs to foster individual adjustment to retirement, rather than questioning of company policies that force out competent and motivated older workers. Rigid adherence to early varieties of activity theory may mean pushing people to participate in organized activities regardless of their preferences and needs. Yet, there is much to be learned from early theoretical developments. Proponents of early theories addressed criticisms raised against them, laying the foundations for the development of more synthetic process oriented theories. In this section, the authors will briefly survey the major developments in gerontological theory, highlighting their strengths and weaknesses. Clearly only a summary account of each theory is possible.

First Generation Theories

The first generation, deriving from functionalist and symbolic interactionist perspectives in sociology, concentrated on individual reactions to the circumstances of aging. Generally speaking the idea was to identify individual characteristics that promoted or impeded successful aging. This wave of theorizing includes disengagement, activity, and, subsequently, subcultural, and continuity theory. In all instances, social structure is taken as given. The quest is for universals affecting people's adjustment independent of situational variations, on the basis of data derived from relatively limited groups.

Disengagement Theory. As the first explicitly formulated model in social gerontology, disengagement theory (Cumming & Henry, 1961) had the merit of focusing attention on underlying assumptions about aging. It grew out of a cross-sectional study of 275 Kansas City resident aged 50 to 90, all of whom were physically and financially self-sufficient. Its basic tenet is that as people age a process of mutual withdrawal ensures continuity in the social system and personal satisfaction for the old. Disengagement is seen as integral to society and human nature, and therefore independent of individuals' wills. It is inevitable and universal. It is portrayed as fostering social equilibrium by removing older people, no longer as dependable as they were, and more susceptible to sudden death, from crucial positions. Individuals are seen as being released form responsibility as their capacities diminish and the time left to them dwindles. Adjustment difficulties are viewed as due to lack of synchronization between individual readiness for disengagement and societal demands. Once an individuals adapt their priorities to the new situation, morale will improve (Cumming & Henry, 1961; Hendricks & Hendricks, 1992).

A major difficulty with disengagement theory is that it derived a general theory of aging from a cross-sectional study of a limited group. It met with immediate criticism centering on the assumptions of inevitability and intrinsicality. As early as 1965, the Duke longitudinal studies began to show that social status is more predictive of relevant differences than is age (Maddox, 1964, 1987). Analysts asked whether withdrawal is always functional for either individuals or society. They also critiqued the apparent lack of attention to personality factors and their role in the process (Maddox, 1964; Atchley, 1971). Hochschild (1976) noted logical flaws in the way the theory was derived from the data. Disengagement theory is virtually unfalsifiable since non-withdrawers are described as "unsuccessful adjusters," "off-time disengagers," or members of an elite. The implicit assumption that the elderly are not fit to participate in the crucial affairs of society has decidedly ageist implications (Hendricks & Hendricks, 1992).

In the face of controversy and criticism, both Cumming and Henry modified their positions (Henry, 1965; Cumming, 1963, 1975). Henry (1965) in particular came to acknowledge individual personality differences and earlier life experiences, thus foreshadowing activity and continuity theories. He maintained that earlier experiences influence personal coping strategies and degrees of inferiority. Those who customarily dealt with stress by turning inward will probably be disengaged during old age. Those with more socially oriented styles will probably remain engaged in one form or another of social interaction until the end (Hendricks & Hendricks, 1992).

Activity Theory. Activity theory contends that continued activity is vital to morale. Initially it was simply an unformulated assumption that active old people are more satisfied with life (Cavan et al., 1949; Havighurst & Albrecht, 1953). Later formulations in response to disengagement theory drew on symbolic interactionism, holding that the importance of activity derives from "consensual validation"—affirmation by others of the personal worth and integrity of the elderly as they perform socially acceptable roles (Cavan, 1962). The identity crisis resulting from relinquishment of mid-life roles may be resolved through adoption of compensatory activities (Blau, 1973). In response to critics' assertions that pastimes geared to presumed age-related declines in ability may be poor substitutes for the socially meaningful roles of middle age (Phillips, 1957; Gubrium, 1973), later researchers sought to refine the theory. Studies by Longino and Kart (1982) and Liang et al. (1980) indicate meaningful activity and interaction improve morale, while ritualistic and highly structured activities have the opposite effect. These findings may be compared to later studies that demonstrate that enhancing people's subjective sense of control results in significant gains in well-being (Labouvie-Vief, 1985; Shupe, 1985). Activity theory did not, however, question social arrangements that tend to isolate some elderly from the mainstream (Hendricks & Hendricks, 1992).

Subcultural Theory. Like activity theory, subcultural theory utilizes symbolic interactionism. Its primary focus, however, is not on activity per se but on how self-concept derives from interpersonal relations. Positive interaction is held to enhance in positive self-esteem, while negative interaction undermines it. Unlike activity theory, however, subcultural theory holds that old people are served better by developing their own standards and their own subculture than by continuing to remain involved with the wider culture of their middle years. Rose (1965), the initial advocate of subcultural theory, asserted subcultures are generated whenever members of one category interact more with each other than with outsiders. He argued that an identifiable aged subculture was developing as a result of various demographic and social trends. These included increasing numbers of individuals 65 and over, still healthy and mobile enough to interact, and the growth of inner-city aged ghettoes, planned retirement communities, and concentrations of rural elderly left behind when younger people migrate to urban areas. Retirement policies segregating older people from the labor force and social services designed to assist the aging were also seen as enhancing the likelihood of group identification. Rose further pointed to the role of biological changes, differences in socialization, and the way the general population perceives older people (Hendricks & Hendricks, 1992).

Subculture theory has the merit of viewing the elderly as proactive, capable of organizing and influencing social policy. Rose cites the creations of age-activist groups, the Gray Panthers and the American Association of Retired Persons (AARP) among others, as indicative of an aged subculture. Yet the elderly as a group do not fit traditional definitions of minority groups and some research indicates they do not demonstrate group consciousness with regard to voting patterns, attitudes, or values (Streib, 1965, 1985; Rosow, 1967; Hochschild, 1973; Allen & von de Vliert, 1984). Subculture theory underestimates diversity among the elderly, and the strength of class, race, and gender-based differences etched out through life. The evidence indicates people become more dissimilar rather than more alike as they age, and that there are greater difference between old people than between the old and the young (Hendricks & Hendricks, 1992).

Continuity Theory. Rejecting the idea of a gulf between old age and the rest of life, continuity theorists focus on precisely that continuity of development across the lifecourse that makes old people so very different from each other, rejecting the idea of a gulf between old age and the rest of life. A major strand of the theory sees continuity in terms of personality variables rather than as resulting from enduring socio-economic status. Personality is defined as an individual's characteristic values, ways of feeling, interpreting events, and coping mechanisms, arising from an interplay of biological, psychological, and social factors. Nonwork roles, relationships, and orientations continue from mid-life into the later years, and personal stability is seen as springing from enduring ties in face of the emerging realities of old age. Yet, stable though they may be, coping mechanisms are also dynamic, allowing for gradual developmental change as new circumstances evolve (Havighurst, 1968; Neugarten, Havighurst, & Tobin, 1968; Fox, 1981–1982; Atchley, 1989). Research appears to support both continuity in personality (George, 1980; McCrae & Costa, 1984), and developmental change in response to new challenges even into late old age (Ryff, 1984; Hendricks & Hendricks, 1992).

More sociologically oriented versions of continuity theory focus on modes of social participation learned through lifelong involvements. Some even note that the ability to maintain continuity varies with an individual's social resources, health, emotional attachment to roles, and opportunities. Dynamic continuity perspectives such as Breytspraak (1984) and Atchley (1989) raise questions about the interaction between structurally and environmentally imposed constraints and coping styles, thus presaging third generation models (Hendricks & Hendricks, 1992).

Second Generation Theories

Second generation theories maintain individual level models of socialization are too reductionist. Society is more than the sum of its parts. Aging must be examined as a consequence of structural arrangements. In doing so, however, they deemphasize individual intentionality. This is particularly true of modernization theory with its tendency to operate as a grand theory at the structural level. Even the age stratification model did not succeed in making explicit the crucial nexus between individual intentionality and societal structure, despite calling attention to the interplay between human lives and changing social structures (Dowd, 1987; Riley, 1987).

Modernization Theory. Modernization theory focuses explicitly on structural influences on the status of the elderly. It contends their standing declines proportionately to the degree of modernization of a society, at least during the early stages (Cowgill, 1974, 1986; Cowgill & Holmes, 1972; Palmore & Manton, 1974). In Parsons' formulation, modernization was seen as a universal, structurally autonomous process, through which societies move toward administrative bureaucracies, money-market economies, and rational-scientific worldviews, fostering societal integration and efficiency. As a result of these changes, people come to be judged by their economic contributions more than on any other basis (Parsons, 1964; Hendricks, 1982). Although less insistent than Parsons on the universal autonomous nature of the process, Cowgill's definition of modernization shares many features with Parsons' perspective. According to Cowgill (1974), modernization brings

> a transformation of a total society from a relatively rural way of life based on animate power, limited technology, relatively undifferentiated institutions, parochial and transitional outlook and values, toward a predominantly urban way of life based on inanimate sources of power, highly developed scientific technology, highly differentiated institutions matched by segmented individual roles, and a cosmopolitan outlook which emphasizes efficiency and progress. (p. 127)

Research within the modernization paradigm seems to indicate that loss of prestige among the elderly is associated with loss of control over information, the means of production, and other resources vital to daily life (Maxwell & Silverman, 1980; Maxwell, 1980; Press & McKool, 1980; Hendricks & Hendricks, 1992).

Modernization theory has been criticized for ethnocentrism since it models world development on theorists' views on Western history (Tipps, 1973; Williamson, Evans, & Powell, 1982; Cowgill, 1986). Assuming that evolution toward economic and scientific rationality is universal and uniformly desirable, slights ways in which diverse cultures lead people to seek disparate ends as they encounter modern technology (Hendricks & Leedham, 1987; Stearns & Van Tassel, 1986). Cultural values are crucial in mediating the effects of modernization for the elderly (Rhoads, 1984). Most importantly, there are problems with extrapolating the results of comparisons between contemporary developing and industrialized societies to the historical process of modernization. Social historians have debunked the idea that the elderly enjoyed universal esteem in preindustrial societies with extensive critiques of the "golden age of age" myth of the past (Laslett, 1976, 1985; Cohn, 1982; Gratton, 1986). Historical documents provide evidence of old people's need to protect themselves from ill treatment. A critical problem with modernization theory for present purposes, however, is that its insistence on universal structural imperatives obscures the impact on aging of differences in culture, race, class, and gender. The impact on aging of the modernization process will surely be very different for members of a ruling elite than for peasant farmers. Modernization theory does, however, make a significant contribution by drawing attention to the role of social structure and control over resources in shaping life in the later years (Hendricks & Hendricks, 1992).

Age Stratification Theory.   Since its appearance in the early 1970s, age stratification theory has been highly influential. Its basic tenet is that age strata or categories are used in assigning roles and resources. The age strata of societies include infancy, childhood, youth, mid-life, old age, and any number of intermediate points. Cohorts, or groups born at the same time, move together through a socially patterned sequence of age grades used to allocate roles. Each successive cohort will experience its own distinctive patterns of aging as a result of changing historical circumstances, structurally imposed constraints and opportunities, and the biological composition of the cohort itself (Riley, Johnson, & Foner, 1972; Foner & Kertzer, 1979). Social change affects people's experiences giving rise to new socially sanctioned age-typical patterns and regularities of behavior, which in turn transform patterns of aging for those who follow (Riley et al., 1972; Riley, 1987). The baby-boom cohort is encountering very different labor market conditions from those experienced by previous generations, and those that will face the birth–dearth cohort of the 1960s. Effects of age may also be alloyed by a multifaceted hierarchy, including ethnicity, gender, socioeconomic status, and so on (Dowd, 1987; Ragan & Wales, 1980; Hendricks & Hendricks, 1992).

Age stratification brought conceptual and methodological tools of mainstream sociology to social gerontology. Its most noted contributions are the concepts of cohort and cohort flow, stressing the importance of historical and social factors in explaining aging. Recognition of dissimilarities in experiences of successive cohorts led to discrimination of cohort differences from intrinsic developmental processes of aging. What were formerly thought to be age-related declines have been recognized as differences in levels of education and experience between cohorts (Passuth & Bengston, 1988). Age stratification has called attention to the interplay between human lives and changing social structures, and the interdependence of sociological, psychological, and biological concerns, thus placing age in broader perspective (Riley, 1987). Yet concern has been expressed about the appropriateness of portraying age as a social stratifier in the same sense as class, race, and gender (Cain, 1987; Dowd, 1987). Age does not result in a relatively permanent distribution of wealth, income, and life chances. Overemphasizing the role of age strata in the allocation of resources may fan the flames of the intergenerational equity debate (Foner, 1984; Cain, 1987). Downplaying class, race, and gender obscures structurally determined differences in patterns of resource distribution and opportunity within cohorts, and issues of social justice that cut across all generations. Age stratification has also been criticized for its lack of attention to individual meanings and intentions (Dowd, 1987). Its exclusive emphasis on social roles has been seen as slighting individual autonomy and implying a form of cultural determinism. What is needed is a reconceptulization of the crucial nexus joining individuals and societal structures (Dowd, 1987; Passuth & Bengtson, 1988; Hendricks & Hendricks, 1992).

Third Generation Theories

Exploration of this nexus lies at the heart of third generation theories. Their point of departure is an integrative view of the elderly's situation as developing from their ongoing relationship with society. Old people age differently in part because of the way material and social resources are allocated. Different futures could be invented by altering social patterns of allocations (Maddox, 1987). The elderly themselves are intentional actors implicated in creating their own lives and shaping social policies. Since the mid-1970s, gerontological theory has become more dynamic, recognizing how policy not only molds the lifeworld of individuals, but is also at the same time socially created by the people it affects (Hendricks & Leedham, 1989). Theories grounded in political economy (Estes et al., 1982) concentrate on the shaping of social institutions by individual and corporate actors and resultant socioeconomic constraints on individuals. Social psychological perspectives examine how people deal with the impacts of social structure. Taken together these perspectives draw people's attention to the interweaving of societal constraints, cultural meanings, individual meaning-giving, and social power in the fabric of their daily lives. Rather than positing a universal grand theory, they provide a conceptual framework within which discipline and situation-specific theories may be developed. Yet neither social psychological nor political economic theories specify a paradigm for articulating the dynamics of the interplay between individual and structure. This challenge is taken up by recent attempt to develop a moral and political economy of old age (Hendricks & Hendricks, 1992; Hendricks & Leedham, 1991; Minkler & Estes, 1991).

Social Psychological Perspectives. The social psychological stream examines the effects of social factors, including policy, on individuals and their capacity for action and social change. It specifically looks at self-creating aspects of aging within biological and structural constraints (Kenyon, 1988). Three broad trends may be identified within recent thinking: social environmental and social breakdown theories, focusing on interactions between people and their social and physical environments; exchange theory; and models that highlight the importance of policy and social structure (Hendricks & Hendricks, 1992).

Social environmental perspectives emphasize the functional contexts of people's daily lives. Aging is seen, not as isolation, but as growing out of situations in which people have long lived. Values, beliefs, and structural constraints are treated as backdrops against which older people test their ability and personal worth. Adaptation and self-fulfillment are active and reactive, negotiated and renegotiated as people attempt to master situations (Huyck, 1979; Marshall, 1980). Social environmental models examine the degree of correspondence between three basic dimensions: normative expectations operating in particular circumstances, individual capacity for interaction, and self-perceived competence for dealing with the demands of the specific situation. A sense of well-being results from a realistic expectation that one is capable of dealing with situational demands. Environments that are insufficiently challenging and stimulating, or that present demands beyond people's capacities, are seen as detrimental to functioning. Continued adjustment depends on maintaining a relatively supportive environment and the resources to meet any challenges it may present (Gubrium, 1973, 1974; Lawton, 1983). Social policy plays an important part in both shaping the environment of the elderly's lives and their access to resources to deal with it (Hendricks & Hendricks, 1992).

Social breakdown theory originated from the social breakdown syndrome model developed by Zusman (1966) to explain how negative feedback leads to a cycle of deterioration in people already susceptible to psychological problems. Meeting with criticism for poor performance, people lose confidence so their performance declines, thus drawing further criticism. Gerontologists argue that a similar phenomenon affects older people who are forced out of the workforce and other mid-life roles, and treated as incompetent and dependent (Kuypers & Bengtson, 1973; Breytspraak, 1984). As a result of these changes, people may lose their self-confidence and reach out for reassurance. This uncertainty is taken as a sign of failing capacity, and responded to in a way that encourages dependence. Providing opportunities for older people to demonstrate and enhance their abilities may replace social breakdown with a "reconstruction syndrome" in which competence is reaffirmed (Kuypers & Bengtson, 1973). Although the model was initially targeted at practical interventions on a clinical level, it does have broader social policy implications (Hendricks & Hendricks, 1992). Labor market and social service policies may treat the elderly as autonomous and resourceful, or foster withdrawal and dependency. In the face of an aging labor force, utilizing the capacities of the elderly to the full will become increasingly important, not only for their self-image, but for society as a whole (McLaughlin, 1989a, b; Schrank & Waring, 1989; McAuliffe, 1990).

Exchange theory originated from an individualistic neoclassical sociological theory that held that people seek to maximize rewards from interactions while minimizing costs. Social contacts will continue only as long as benefits outweigh liabilities (Homans, 1961; Blau, 1964). Early gerontological versions of exchange theory posited that diminishing financial resources, worsening health, and obsolescent skills decrease old people's bartering power in social relations (Blau, 1973; Dowd, 1975, 1980; Bengtson and Dowd, 1980). Hendricks and Hendricks (1986) identify three overlapping dimensions of resources that influence the degree of control older people have over their environment: health, or "personal-physiological" resources; social support systems, the "social familiar" dimension; and material goods or the fiduciary dimension. Later forms of exchange theory turn to issues of distributive justice, asking whether the elderly receive rewards proportional to their contributions (Dowd, 1978; Cheal, 1984; Hendricks, 1987; Hendricks & Hendricks, 1992).

There are inherent problems with exchange theory. The assumption that all people are uniquely motivated by the prospect of interpersonal gain has been criticized as ethnocentric in that it constitutes what may be seen as a norm of contemporary American culture into a universal facet of human nature (Passuth & Bengtson, 1988; Hendricks, 1987). The view of aging as uniform loss and decline implicit in some early statements of exchange theory contains hints of ageism. Yet exchange theory does point toward policy considerations by its suggestion that structures of opportunity may affect people's access to resources and therefore their negotiating power. This is particularly evident in later forms of the theory that focus on issues of distributive justice (Hendricks & Hendricks, 1992).

Social psychological models with a structural focus concentrate on the elderly as social actors. They restore the dimension of individual intentionality, rejecting the view of the elderly as passively adapting to structural imperatives. Yet they also emphasize the role of economic and historical factors in limiting their options, and the ways in which diversity results from differing structures of opportunity. Social structures themselves are seen as socially created, not natural objects, and therefore modifiable. True, they have a logic of their own that renders change difficult, but they are not immutable (Hendricks & Hendricks, 1992).

Marshall (1981, 1986) sees social structure as both created by and creating individuals. He identifies a constant tension between stability flowing from structural constraints and social consensus and instability flowing from human intentionality. The emphasis is on understanding connections between personal, individual, and structural levels to identify how "personal troubles" of the elderly actually stem from "public issues' limiting access to opportunities (Marshall, 1981, 1986; Mills, 1959). A similar focus is evident in Rowe and Kahn's (1987) exploration of ways in which socially determined environmental factors negatively affect the physiology of aging through, for instance, workplace stress and lack of access to vital resources (Hendricks & Hendricks, 1992).

A variety of other theorists seek to affirm the importance of autonomous individual activity and the mutability of social structures while acknowledging the pervasive and sometimes negative effects of social structural arrangements. Dowd (1987) argues that Western economic organization curtails opportunities for self-development thereby heightening the likelihood of alienation during old age. With Séve (1978), he contends that "the human essence is the ensemble of social relations in which men not only produce their means of subsistence, but are themselves produced" (p. 141; Dowd, p. 327). Dannefer (1989) criticizes exclusively structuralist descriptions of aging and normative lifecourse development models for normalizing particular culturally specific patterns as if they were incontrovertible. He calls for longitudinal studies highlighting individual intentionality and the plasticity of social structure. Others turn their attention to social conditions for human emancipation, calling for a critique of ideology to identify ways the organization of work, gender roles, age stereotypes, and political arrangements delimit possibilities throughout life (Moody, 1988; Clark, 1989; Habermas, 1971; Hendricks & Hendricks 1992).

The Political Economy of Aging. Political economic approaches scrutinized the role of social policies, institutions, and group interests in shaping patterns of aging. They tap many levels, from involvement in the world of work to international factors. The basic contention is that aging never occurs in isolation. Values, public policy, political priorities, and material conditions influence an individual's economic and psychosocial resources. Labor markets provide differential opportunities for saving or accruing pension rights that affect patterns of individual adjustment. Location in the labor market and accompanying advantages or disadvantages are influenced by a number of factors, notably gender, race, and class. The impact of governmental policies varies by social group, with profound effects on individuals and families across the lifecourse (Hendricks & Hendricks, 1992). Dependency theory uses political economic approaches in examining how politically influenced inequalities in exchanges between developed and developing countries affect the quality of life for the elderly in the Third World (Hendricks, 1982; Tigges & Cowgill, 1981; Neysmith & Edwardh, 1984; Hendricks & Hendricks, 1986). Internal colonialism examines the effects of unequal development and geographic and cultural domination within particular countries (Hendricks, 1982; Hendricks & Hendricks, 1986). Here, however, the focus will be on use of political economy in examining aging in contemporary United States society.

The impetus for the development of political economic perspectives came in the late 1970s and early 1980s. Estes (1979) undertook a critical analysis of the role of policies and services in segregating old people from the mainstream. Walker (1980) began to outline the role of age-based policies in creating dependency among older people in Great Britain. Olson (1982) examined how the negative effects of market, class, gender, and race relations across the lifecourse engender even more adverse conditions during old age. From these beginnings, more systematic statements of a political economy of aging were subsequently developed by Estes and Walker (Estes, 1986; Estes et al., 1982; Walker, 1980; Hendricks & Hendricks, 1992).

The central challenge for political economy, according to Estes (1986), is to move beyond mere critique to develop an understanding of the character and import of variations in the treatment of the aged, and how these relate to policy, economy and society. There are two major facets to the political economy of aging: Investigation of how social location affects patterns of aging, and analysis of the dynamic, ever-changing relationship between distribution of power and forms of economic organization as various groups strive to attain and maintain a measure of control (Hendricks & Leedham, 1991). The "structured dependence of the elderly" (Townsend, 1981) comes about because of changing perceptions of their utility as producers and consumers due to shifts in the economy and the relations of production. The old are deprecated not merely because they are elderly, but because they are believed to embody traditional, particularistic values potentially inimical to the impersonal efficiency demanded by a market economy. Their experiences must be considered in the context of world and national economics, the state, labor market conditions, class, race, gender, and age divisions. The status and resources of different groups of elderly are conditioned by their social location (Estes et al., 1982; Townsend, 1981; Hendricks & Hendricks, 1992; Hendricks & Leeham, 1991).

Like so many other components of human life, aging reflects modes of economic organization. Fiscal austerity, cost-cutting, reemerging federalist rejection of national responsibility for basic human needs, deregulation, market competition, and the rise of the medical–industrial complex with its market model of health care affect the way people age. Hardy's (1988) focus on retirement policies, how these create dependency by limiting economic access, and the impact of class and labor-market differences on control over the nature and timing of retirement is but one example of a political economy perspective. Baron and Bielby (1985) and Minkler and Stone (1985) also point to ways in which labor market segmentation and other factors exacerbate economic risks for women across the lifecourse, thereby resulting in feminization of poverty during old age. Hess (1985) analyzes gender biases in retirement and health policy. Zones, Estes, and Binney (1987), among others, consider how the situation of the oldest old, who are primarily women, results from the impact of historical factors throughout life. Dressel (1988) calls attention to the need to broaden gender-based perspectives to examine the complex interplay of race and class with gender in creating patterns of poverty in old age (Hendricks & Leedham, 1991; Hendricks & Hendricks, 1992).

Notwithstanding Passuth and Bengtson's (1988) charge that political economy shortchanges individual interpretation, many writing within the political economic tradition share Marshall's (1981, 1986) concern with the links between structure and individual life worlds. They seek to show that "the personal is political" and its parameters are subject to change (Harrison, 1983; Zones et al., 1987; Hendricks & Hendricks, 1992). Yet neither political economy nor social psychological perspectives explicitly articulate the links between social structure and individual intentionality so vital to understanding possibilities for empowerment. The most recent development is gerontological theory attempts to do just that.

The Moral and Political Economy of Aging. The moral and political economy of aging focuses on the assumptions underlying policy formation in order to identify avenues for empowerment of the elderly. Two theoretical traditions are tapped in this analysis: Gramsci's concept of hegemony as a pervasive widely shared worldview permitting economic activity, politics, and civil society; and E. P. Thompson's idea of moral economy or norms of reciprocity (Gramsci, 1971; Bocock, 1988; Thompson, 1971).

The implicit assumptions constituting hegemony result in active consent to existing forms of leadership and social organization. Sometimes this has the effect of normalizing dominance of one group over another into the culture. In this case, active consent is based on a misapprehension of the situation, and thus is similar to the Marxian idea of false consciousness. People accept as legitimate conditions that lead to their own exploitation. Women, for instance, might accept lower wages and benefits throughout the lifecourse and resultant impoverishment in old age as the norm. Although concerned with ways in which hegemony might reinforce dominance, Gramsci also aspired to a new moral and philosophical leadership, a state of hegemony to which people could give full and informed consent as being in their own long-term best interest. Such a state would be grounded in a fundamental, common, freely shared set of ideals and values constituting a basic notion of what is appropriate. Failure of hegemony opens the way for competition between a variety of groups to advance their own narrow, economic corporatist interest, which may not be in the best interest of the majority. Alternatively, absence of hegemony may lead to domination—

maintenance of order through sheer force, always difficult to sustain in the long run (Bocock, 1988; Hendricks & Leedham, 1991). Hegemony in the first sense may create dependency among the elderly, by normalizing their exclusion from the mainstream. An understanding of the dynamics of hegemony as false consciousness may serve as a first step toward empowerment of the elderly by affording insight into the mechanics of their disempowerment. Gramsci's idea of a new hegemony calling for free assent serves as a stimulus to conceptualizing principles of social organization to which people could consent as maximizing their chances for a decent life at all ages. As political economy has amply demonstrated, the effects of economic factors on individual lifechances are of central importance. Fundamental to emancipatory hegemony is the form of moral economy in which it is grounded (Hendricks & Leedham, 1991).

Thompson (1971) and Claeys (1987) argue that eighteenth-century moral economy, protecting the rights of the poor through the idea of a just price, has been replaced by a new ideology of political economy in which rulers and capital unite in the interests of profit. Proponents of the moral and political economy of aging (Hendricks & Leedham, 1991; Minkler & Cole, 1991; Kohli, 1991) argue rather that earlier forms of moral economy have been replaced by forms reflecting advanced industrial society and its political economy. Thompson's (1971) form of moral economy, in its concern for human welfare, may be compared to Marx's concept of production for use value, and has been replaced by a moral economy grounded in exchange value, focusing on production for the market (Marx, 1964, 1967, 1970). The path toward empowerment of the elderly, and indeed of all generations, lies in the adoption of a moral economy grounded in use value appropriate to advanced industrial society (Hendricks & Leedham, 1991).

The driving force of moral economies grounded in exchange value is the maximization of profit. They are rigid in their imposition of economic rationality. Goods and persons are judged in market-oriented monetary terms. In its individualistic version, moral economy grounded in exchange value feeds into interest group politics and failure of hegemony by conceptualizing the public good as the right of each individual or group to maximize their own subjectively defined interests (House, 1980). By focusing on isolated interactions, exchange value prevents the young and middle-aged from realizing their own interest in creating a system of economic security that will persist into their own old age. Such thinking is manifest in the intergenerational equity debate. In its structuralist manifestation, exchange value defines the public good as maximizing satisfactions measured in terms of global economic indicators, such as the gross national product, in society at large (House,

1980). This is prejudicial to elderly excluded from the labor market. It also ignores uneven distribution of wealth and life chances within generations and productive contributions outside the labor market. It is hegemonic in the sense of perpetuating exploitation, since increased productivity in terms of profits may be bought at the expense of the economically marginal (Hendricks & Leedham, 1991).

A new universalistic hegemony calls for a moral economy grounded in use value—the meeting of human need—attentive to the long-term interplay of social structure and individual lifeworlds. Moral economy grounded in use value conceptualizes the public good as a negotiated rule structure to which people adhere even when it runs contrary to their own immediate interests, because it maximizes the chance of a decent human life for all members of society, themselves included (House, 1980). Enhancing productivity is crucial to meet human needs, not as an end in itself. The key question is not how to allocate resources between competing generations, but what resources would people judge appropriate for themselves at various times in the lifecourse (Clark, 1985), and how to weigh health and welfare against other budgetary concerns. Attention is given to inequities within generations, and to ensuring a decent minimum standard of living for all. In a spirit of true hegemony, the elderly and those of all generations are seen not as passive consumers, but as productive citizens with an active role in the policy process (Ladd, 1973; Hendricks & Leedham, 1991).

Clark's fourfold scheme of empowerment in old age and across the lifecourse is consistent with a moral economy grounded in use value. The first of Clark's (1989) four dimensions is social goods and political activism. It "does little good to speak of personal empowerment without at least some initial consideration of the need to provide sufficient social resources to enable individuals to exercise choice in their lives" (Clark, 1989, p. 271). Acknowledging both the role of social policy in patterning life choices and the need to involve people in the policy process is a first step. Second, empowerment is effective deliberation: the ability to think consciously about complex actions. This means treating people as autonomous, giving them access to adequate information about key decisions and policies, and, where necessary, education in decision-making. By raising the question of their real long-term interests as members of a social community, moral economy can provide a framework for effective deliberation. Third, Clark emphasizes long-term nature of rempowerment. The conditions of dependency and its grounding in social policy stretch across life rather than beginning fresh in old age. Finally, Clark sees empowerment as balance and interdependence, an ability to come to terms with the realities of one's own personal history, present situation, and needs for support and assistance while maintaining a measure of freedom and independence. It calls for a balancing of needs and visions of one's own generation and those of other within existing resource constraints. This is precisely the challenge posed by moral economy grounded in use value (Hendricks & Leedham, 1987).

Implications of Gerontological Theory for Human Services

Gerontological theory focuses attention on current assumptions regarding aging and the elderly in the wider society and in human service practices. Over the course of its evolution, it has come to a richer understanding of the interactive effects of social policy, socioeconomic status, culture, history, and individual initiative on patterns of aging. It has provided human service professionals with conceptual tools for understanding the dynamics of aging. A basic challenge for clinical practice skills is to identify the role of hegemony in disempowering the elderly. Does acceptance of taken-for-granted assumptions result in practice styles that foster dependence? How can Clark's (1989) paradigm for empowerment be implemented in service practice with the elderly, as they struggle with decisions and crucial turning points in their lives? Clark calls for empowerment and involvement of the elderly in the consideration of concrete decisions, such as possible nursing home placement, as well as in wider social policy.

At the macro-practice level, the Gramscian ideal of a new hegemony challenges practitioners to involve the elderly and other interested parties in formulating policies and programs affecting their lives—to treat them as active moral agents, rather than passive consumers of social policy (Ladd, 1973). In program evaluation, use value points toward criteria of cost effectiveness—how well do programs use available resources to meet needs—rather than cost efficiency formulated in exclusively financial terms. A basic problem with recent approaches to cost control in health and social services is not their focus on resource use, but the reliance on market models that conceptualize health and social services in primarily economic terms. At the level of social policy and budgetary concerns, the question is not competition for fixed health and welfare dollars, but how allocation of resources in the total budget contributes to meeting human needs. How to capitalize on the productivity of all generations is crucial. The concept of use value draws attention to issues of distributive justice, the plight of the elderly poor, and its roots earlier in life. Social justice is evaluated in terms of adequacy of results and what it takes to make possible a decent minimum standard of living rather than quantitatively equal benefits for all. A moral economy grounded in use value provides a means of transcend-

ing the intergenerational equity debate by replacing competition between generations for resources with the question of how to utilize them
to provide an acceptable standard of living throughout life. This implies
balancing a modicum of income security for both present and future
generations of elderly with the exigencies of mid-life and the need to
educate a viable workforce for the future (Hendricks & Leedham, 1991).
The crucial challenge for policy advocacy is not a matter of pitting the
needs of the elderly against those of other generations, but of how to
create a livable society based on a moral economy grounded in use
value. Human service practitioners are in a unique position to appreciate
the links between personal troubles and public issues (Mills, 1959). In
fact, human service practice is in a unique position to change the way
aging is perceived and lived out.

Note

1. Portions of this chapter will be appearing in Hendricks, J. & Hendricks,
C. D. (1992). *Aging in mass society: Myths and realities* (4th edn.). New York:
Harper Collins; and portions have already appeared in Hendricks, J., &
Leedham, C. A. (1991). Dependency or empowerment? Toward a moral and
political economy of aging. In M. Minkler & C. L. Estes (Eds.), *Critical perspectives on aging*. Amityville, NY: Baywood Publishing Co. (Authors are listed
alphabetically.)

References

Allen, V. L., & van de Veiert, E. (1984). *Role transformations: Exploration and
explanations*. New York: Plenum.
Atchley, R. C. (1971). Disengagement among professors. *Journal of Gerontology,
26*, 476–480.
Atchley, R. C. (1989). A continuity theory of normal aging. *The Gerontologist, 29*,
183–190.
Baron, J. H., & Bielby, W. T. (1985). Organizational barriers to gender equality:
Sex segregation of jobs and opportunities. In A. S. Rossi (Ed.), *Gender and
the lifecourse* (pp. 233–251). New York: Aldine.
Bengtson, V. L., & Dowd, J. J. (1980). Sociological functionalism, exchange
theory and life cycle analysis. *International Journal of Aging and Human
Development, 12*, 55–73.
Blau, P. M. (1964). *Exchange and power in social life*. New York: Wiley.
Blau, Z. S. (1973). *Old age in a changing society*. New York: New Viewpoints, a
Division of Franklyn Watts, Inc.
Bocock, R. (1988). *Hegemony*. London: Tavistock Publications.
Breytspraak, L. M. (1984). *The development of self in later life*. Boston: Little,
Brown.

Cain, L. D., Jr. (1987). Theoretical observations on applied behavioral science. *The Journal of Applied Behavioral Science, 23,* 277–294.

Cavan, R. S. (1962). Self and role in adjustment during old age. In A. M. Rose (Ed.), *Human behavior and social processes* (pp. 526–536). Boston: Houghton Mifflin.

Cavan, R. S., Burgess, E. W., Havighurst, R. J., & Goldhamer, H. (1949). *Personal adjustment in old age.* Chicago: Science Research Associates.

Cheal, D. J. (1984). Transactions and transformation models. In N. K. Denzen (Ed.), *Studies in symbolic interaction* (pp. 141–151). Greenwich, CT: JAI Press.

Claeys, G. (1987). *Machinery and the millennium: From moral economy to socialism 1815–1860.* Cambridge, England: Polity Press.

Clark, P. G. (1985). The social allocation of health care resources: Ethical dilemmas in age-group competition. *The Gerontologist, 25,* 119–125.

Clark, P. G. (1989). The philosophical foundation of empowerment. *Journal of Aging and Health, 1,* 267–285.

Cohn, R. M. (1982). Economic development and status change of the aged. *American Journal of Sociology, 87,* 1105–1161.

Cowgill, D. O. (1974). Aging and modernizations: A revision of the theory. In Gubrium (Ed.), *Late life: Communities and environmental policy* (pp. 54–67). Springfield, IL: Charles C Thomas.

Cowgill, D. O. (1986). *Aging around the world.* Belmont, CA: Wadsworth.

Cowgill, D. O., & Holmes, I. D. (1972). *Aging and modernization.* New York: Appleton-Century-Crofts.

Cumming, E. (1963). Further thoughts on the theory of disengagement. *International Social Science Journal, 15,* 377–393.

Cumming, E. (1975). Engagement with an old theory. *Aging and Human Development, 6,* 187–191.

Cumming, E., & Henry, W. E. (1961). *Growing old: The process of disengagement.* New York: Basic Books.

Dannefer, D. (1989). Human action and its place in theories of aging. *Journal of Aging Studies, 3,* 1–20.

Dowd, J. J. (1975). Aging as exchange: A preface to theory, *Journal of Gerontology, 30,* 584–594.

Dowd, J. J. (1978). Aging as exchange: A test of the distributive justice proposition. *Pacific Sociological Review, 21,* 351–375.

Dowd, J. J. (1980). *Stratification among the aged.* Monterey, CA: Brooks/Cole.

Dowd, J. J. (1987). The reification of age: Age stratification theory and the passing of the autonomous subject. *Journal of Aging Studies, 1,* 317–335.

Dressel, P. L. (1988). Gender, race and class: Beyond the feminization of poverty in later life. *The Gerontologist, 28,* 177–180.

Estes, C. L. (1979). *The aging enterprise.* San Francisco: Jossey-Bass.

Estes, C. L. (1986). The politics of aging in America. *Ageing and Society, 6,* 121–134.

Estes, C. L., Swan, J., and Gerard, L. (1982). Dominant and competing paradigms in gerontology: Toward a political economy of ageing. *Ageing and Society, 2,* 151–164.

Foner, A., & Kertzer, D. (1979). Intrinsic and extrinsic sources of change in life-course transitions. In M. W. Riley (Ed.), *Aging from birth to death* (pp. 121–136). Boulder, CO: Westview Press.

Foner, N. (1984). *Ages in conflict: A Cross-cultural perspective between old and young.* New York: Columbia University Press.

Fox, J. H. (1981–1982). Perspectives on the continuity perspective. *International Journal of Aging and Human Development, 14,* 97–115.

George, L. K. (1980). *Role transition in later life.* Monterey, CA: Brooks/Cole.

Gibson, R. C. (1987). Reconceptualizing retirement for black Americans. *The Gerontologist, 27,* 691–698.

Gibson, R. C. (1988). The work, retirement and disability of black Americans. In J. S. Jackson (Ed.), *The black elderly: Research on physical and psychosocial health* (pp. 304–324). New York: Springer.

Gramsci, A. (1971). *Selections from the prison notebooks.* In Q. Hoare and G. Nowell Smith (Ed. & Trans.) London: Lawrence and Wishart.

Gratton, B. (1986). The new history of the aged: A Critique. In D. Van Tassel & P. N. Stearns (Eds.), *Old age in a bureaucratic society* (pp. 3–29). Westport, CT: Greenwood Press.

Gubrium, J. F. (1973). *The myth of the golden years: A socio-environmental theory of aging.* Springfield, IL: Charles C Thomas.

Gubrium, J. F. (1974). Toward a socio-environmental theory of aging. *The Gerontologist, 12,* 281–284.

Habermas, J. (1971). *Knowledge and human interests* (Trans. J. J. Shapiro). Boston: Bacon Press.

Hardy, M. (1988). Vulnerability in old age: The issue of dependency in American society. *Journal of Aging Studies, 2,* 311–320.

Harrison, J. (1983). Women and ageing: Experience and implications. *Ageing and Society, 3,* 209–233.

Havighurst, R. J. (1968). *Social psychological perspectives on aging. The Gerontologist, 8,* 67–71.

Havighurst, R. J., & Albrecht, R. (1953). *Older people.* New York: Longmans Green.

Hendricks, J. (1982). The elderly in society: Beyond modernization. *Social Science History, 6,* 321–345.

Hendricks, J. (1987). Exchange theory in aging. In G. L. Maddox et al. (Eds.), *The encyclopedia of aging* (pp. 238–239). New York: Springer.

Hendricks, J., & Hendricks, C. D. (1986). *Aging in mass society: Myths and realities,* 3rd ed. Boston: Little, Brown.

Hendricks, J., & Hendricks, C. D. (1992). *Aging in mass society: Myths and realities,* 4th ed. New York: Harper Collins.

Hendricks, J., & Leedham, C. A. (1987). Making sense of literary aging: Relevance of recent gerontological theory. *Journal of Aging Studies, 1,* 187–208.

Hendricks, J., & Leedham, C. A. (1989). Creating psychological and societal dependency in old age. In P. S. Fry (Ed.), *Psychological perspectives of helplessness and control in the elderly* (pp. 369–394). Amsterdam: Elsevier Science Publishers B. V. (North-Holland).

Hendricks, J., & Leedham, C. A. (1991). Dependency or empowerment: Toward amoral and political economy of aging. In M. Minkler & C. L. Estes (Eds.), *Critical perspectives on aging*. Amityville, NY: Baywood Publishing Co. In press.

Henry, W. E. (1965). Engagement and disengagement: Toward a theory of adult development. In R. Kastenbaum (Ed.), *Contributions to the psychobiology of aging* (pp. 19–35). New York: Springer.

Hess, B. B. (1985). Aging policies and old women: The hidden agenda. In A. S. Rossi (Ed.), *Gender and the lifecourse* (pp. 319–331). New York: Aldine.

Hochschild, A. (1970). Disengagement theory: A critique and proposal. *American Sociological Review, 40*, 553–569.

Hochschild, A. (1973). *The unexpected community*. Englewood Cliffs, NJ: Prentice-Hall.

Hochschild, A. (1975). Disengagement theory: A critique and proposal. *American Sociological Review, 40*, 553–569.

Hochschild, A. (1976). Disengagement theory: A logical, empirical, and phenomenological critique. In J. F. Gubrium (Ed.), *Time, roles, and self in old age* (pp. 53–87). New York: Human Sciences Press.

Homans, G. C. (1961). *Social behavior: Its elementary forms*. New York: Harcourt, Brace Jovanovich.

House, E. R. (1980). *Evaluating with validity*. Beverly Hills, CA: Sage.

Huyck, M. G. (1979). Psychological perspective on adaptation in later life. In H. Orimo, D. Shimada, M. Iriki, & D. Maeda (Eds.), *Recent advances in gerontology* (pp. 643–648). Amsterdam: Excerpta Medica.

Kenyon, G. M. (1988). Basic assumptions in theories of human aging. In J. E. Birren & V. L. Bengtson (Eds.), *Emergent theories of aging* (pp. 3–18). New York: Springer.

Kohli, M. (1991). Retirement and the moral economy: An historical interpretation of the German case. In M. Minkler & C. L. Estes (Eds.), *Critical perspectives in aging*. Amityville, NY: Baywood Publishing Co. In press.

Kuypers, J. A. & Bengtson, V. L. (1973). Social breakdown and competence: A model of normal aging. *Human Development, 26*, 181–201.

LaBouvie-Vief, G. (1985). Intelligence and cognition. In J. E. Birren & V. L. Bengtson (Eds.), *Handbook of the psychology of aging*, 2nd ed. (pp. 502–543). New York: Van Nostrand Reinhold.

Ladd, J. (1973). Policy studies and ethics. *Policy Studies Journal, 2*, 38–43.

Laslett, P. (1976). Societal development and aging. In R. H. Binstock & E. Shanas (Eds.), *Handbook of aging and social sciences* (pp. 3–34). New York: Van Nostrand Reinhold.

Laslett, P. (1985). Societal development and aging. In R. H. Binstock and E. Shanas (Eds.), *Handbook of aging and social sciences* (pp. 199–230). New York: Van Nostrand Reinhold.

Lawton, M. P. (1983). Environment and other determinants of well-being in older people. *The Gerontologist, 23*, 349–357.

Liang, J., Dvorkin, L., Kahana, E., & Mazian, F. (1980). Social integration and morale: A reexamination. *Journal of Gerontology, 35*, 746–757.

Longino, C. F., & Kart, C. S. (1982). Explicating activity theory: A formal replication. *Journal of Gerontology, 37,* 713–722.

Maddox, G. L. (1964). Disengagement theory: A critical evaluation. *The Gerontologist, 4,* 80–82.

Maddox, G. L. (1965). Fact and artifact: Evidence bearing on disengagement from the Duke Geriatrics Project. *Human Development, 8,* 117–130.

Maddox, G. L. (1987). Aging differently. *The Gerontologist, 27,* 557–564.

Marshall, V. W. (1980). No exit: A symbolic interactionist perspective on aging. In J. Hendricks (Ed.), *Being and becoming old* (pp. 20–32). Farmingdale, NY: Baywood Publishing Company.

Marshall, V. W. (1981). Societal toleration of aging: Sociological theory and social response to population. *Adaptability and Aging, 1,* 85–104. Paris: International Center of Social Gerontology, 1981.

Marshall, V. W. (1986). Dominant and emerging perspectives in the social psychology of aging. In V. Marshall (Ed.), *Later life: The social psychology of aging* (pp. 9–31). Beverly Hills, CA: Sage.

Marx, K. (1964). *The economic and philosophic manuscripts of 1898.* ed. D. J. Struik (pp. 110–112). New York: International Publishers.

Marx, K. (1967). *Capital* (Vol. 1), ed. F. Engels. New York: International Publishers.

Marx, K. (1970). *The German ideology,* (pp. 54–56, 68–77), ed. C. J. Arthur. New York: International Publishers.

Maxwell, R. J. (1980). The changing status of elders in Polynesian society. In J. Hendricks (Ed.), *In the country of the old* (pp. 57–66). Farmingdale, NY: Baywood Publishing Company.

Maxwell, R. J., & Silverman, P. (1980). Information and esteem: Cultural considerations in the treatment of the aged. In J. Hendricks (Ed.), *In the country of the old* (pp. 3–34). Farmingdale, NY: Baywood Publishing Company.

McAuliffe, D. W. (1990). Unretiring seniors. *Sky, 19,* 100–107.

McCrae, R. R., & Costa, P. T. (1984). *Emerging lives, enduring dispositions.* Boston: Little, Brown.

McLaughlin, A. (1989a). *Labor market shortages.* Washington, DC: U.S. Department of Labor.

McLaughlin, A. (1989b). *Older worker task force: Key policy issues for the future.* Washington, DC: U.S. Department of Labor.

Mills, C. W. (1959). *The sociological imagination.* New York: Oxford University Press.

Minkler, M., & Cole, T. G. (1991). Moral and political economy: Not such strange bedfellows. In M. Minkler & C. L. Estes (Eds.), *Critical perspectives on aging.* Amityville, NY: Baywood Publishing Co. In press.

Minkler, M., & Estes, C. L. (Eds.) (1991). *Critical perspectives on aging.* Amityville, NY: Baywood Publishing Co.

Minkler, M., & Stone, R. (1985). The feminization of poverty and older women. *The Gerontologist, 25,* 351–357.

Moody, H. R. (1988). Toward a critical gerontology: The contribution of the humanities to theories of aging. In J. E. Birren & V. L. Bengtson (Eds.), *Emerging theories of aging* (pp. 19–40). New York: Springer.

24   Jon Hendricks and Cynthia A. Leedham

Neugarten, B. L.; Havighurst, R. J.; & Tobin, S. S. (1968). Personality and patterns of aging. In B. L. Neugarten (Ed.), *Middle age and aging* (pp. 173–177). Chicago: University of Chicago Press.

Neysmith, S., & Edwardh, J. H. (1984). Economic dependency in the 1980's: Its impact on Third World elderly. *Ageing and Society, 4*, 21–44.

Olson, L. K. (1982). *The political economy of aging: The state, private power, and social welfare*. New York: Columbia University Press.

Palmore, E., & Manton, K. (1974). Modernization and the status of the aged: International correlations. *Journal of Gerontology, 29*, 205–210.

Parsons, T. (1964). Evolutionary universals. *American Sociological Review, 29*, 339–357.

Passuth, P. M., & V. L. Bengtson. (1988). Sociological theories of aging: Current perspectives and future directions. In J. E. Birren & V. L. Bengtson (Eds.), *Emergent theories of aging* (pp. 333–355). New York: Springer.

Phillips, B. S. (1957). A role theory approach to adjustment in old age. *American Sociological Review, 22*, 212–227.

Press, I., & McKool, M. (1980). Social structure and the status of the aged: Toward some valid cross-cultural generalizations. In J. Hendricks (Ed.), *In the country of the old* (pp. 47–56). Farmingdale, NY: Baywood Publishing Company.

Ragan, P. K., & Wales, J. B. (1980). Age stratification and the life course. In J. E. Birren & R. B. Sloane (Eds.), *Handbook of mental health and aging* (pp. 377–399). Engelwood Cliffs, NJ: Prentice-Hall.

Rhoads, E. C. (1984). Reevaluation of the aging and modernization theory: The Samoan evidence. *The Gerontologist, 24*, 243–250.

Riley, M. W. (1987). On the significance of age in sociology. *American Sociological Review, 52*, 1–14.

Riley, M. W., Johnson, M., & Foner, A. (1972). *Aging and society*, Vol. 3: A *Sociology of Age Stratification*. New York: Russell Sage Foundation.

Rose, A. M. (1965). The subculture of aging: A framework in social gerontology. In A. M. Rose & W. A. Peterson (Eds.), *Older people and their social world* (pp. 3–16). Philadelphia: F.A. Davis.

Rosow, L. (1967). *Social stratification of the aged*. New York: The Free Press.

Rowe, J. W., & Kahn, R. L. (1987). Human aging: Usual and successful. *Science, 237*, 143–149.

Ryff, C. D. (1984). Personality development from the inside: The subjective experience of change in adulthood and aging. In P. B. Baltes & O. G. Brim, Jr. (Eds.), *Life-span development and behavior* (pp. 244–248). New York: Academic Press.

Schrank, H. R., & Waring, J. M. (1989). Older workers, ambivalence and interventions. *The Annals of the American Academy of Political and Social Science, 503*, 113–126.

Séve, L. (1978). *Man in Maxist theory and the psychology of personality*. Atlantic Highlands, NJ: Humanities Press.

Shupe, D. R. (1985). Perceived control, helplessness and choice. In J. E. Birren & J. Lovingston (Eds.), *Cognition, stress and aging* (pp. 174–197). Englewood Cliffs, NJ: Prentice-Hall.

Stearns, P. N. & Van Tassel, D. (1986). Introduction: Themes and prospects in old age history. In D. Van Tassel & P. N. Stearns (Eds), *Old age in a bureaucratic society* (pp. ix–xxx). Westport, CT: Greenwood Press.

Streib, G. F. (1965). Are the aged a minority group? In A. W. Gouldner & S. M. Miller (Eds.), *Applied sociology* (pp. 321–328). New York: The Free Press.

Streib, G. F. (1985). Social stratification and aging. In R. Binstock & E. Shanas (Eds.), *Handbook of aging and social science* (pp. 339–368). New York: Van Nostrand Reinhold.

Thompson, E. P. (1971). The moral economy of the English crowd in the eighteenth century. *Past and Present, 50,* 76–136.

Tigges, L., & Cowgill, D. (1981). *Aging from a world systems perspective: An alternative modernization theory.* Paper presented to the Gerontological Society of America.

Tipps, D. C. (1973). Modernization theory and the comparative study of societies: A critical perspective. *Comparative Studies in Society and History, 15,* 199–226.

Townsend, P. (1981). The structured dependency of the elderly. *Ageing and Society, 1,* 5–28.

Walker, A. (1980). The social creation of poverty and dependency in old age. *Journal of Social Policy, 9,* 49–75.

Williamson, J. B., Evans, L., & Powell, L. A. (1982). *The politics of aging: Power and policy.* Springfield, IL: Charles C Thomas.

Zones, J. S., Estes, C. L., & Binney, E. A. (1987). Gender, public policy and the oldest old. *Ageing and Society, 7,* 275–302.

Zusman, J. (1966). Some exploration of the changing appearance of psychotic patients: Antecedents of the social breakdown syndrome complex. *The Millbank Memorial Fund Quarterly, 44,* 363–374.

I

CLINICAL PRACTICE IN
GERONTOLOGICAL HUMAN SERVICES

Introduction

PAUL K. H . KIM

Clinical gerontology is a burgeoning practice in the field of human services, for the aging and aged require individualized attention, due in part to the vastness of problems in living that they face. The professional and the client or a small group of clients enter into professional relationships including the provision of caring and support services, and counseling and/or therapeutic situations. Social, health, and educational agencies provide such services, as well as clinical private sectors. Professionals in geriatric private practice have formed a national organization called the National Association of Private Geriatric Care Mangers, whose office is located in Dayton, Ohio.

Authors who contribute to the following clinical chapters are well established, experienced educators and practitioners. Two of them should be specifically noted for the fact that they are founders of age-appropriate therapeutic modalities: Naomi Feil and Maxie C. Maultsby are originators of Validation Therapy and Rational Self-Counseling, respectively.

Counseling is a supportive and reeducative psychotherapy, according to Joan Hashimi (see Chapter 1), that focuses on healthy, mentally nonimpaired and/or drug-free older adults and their problems in living. On the other hand, therapy is a remedial approach primarily directed to the elderly who are physically unhealthy and/or mentally perplexed (though possibly medication induced). Therefore, the objective of geriatric counseling is to increase the problem-coping skills of the elderly within their physical and mental limitations. Without any form of prejudice against older adults and with a greater level of appreciation of their life experiences and present situational "givens," the professional begins the counseling process with an assessment of the problem(s) presented by the client. Choice of intervention strategies should depend on the client's self-determination and be contingent on available resources in the client's environment. Termination of geriatric counseling does not imply any form of ending the service but the counselor's preparedness and readiness for returning of the client due to the fact that he/she is bound to cope with the predestination of facing new problems in life or the old problem revived.

Unlike traditional and conventional family therapy, Eloise Rathbone-McCuan (known rather well as Lee McCuan) (see Chapter 2) contends with family counseling, which closely accords with the general systems theory. In view of increasing longevity, the number of "aging families" and "multigenerational families" is multiplying. Consequently, in addition to problems in living contributed to by declining health and limited social and economic resources, the adaptation in the multigenerational family has become an unavoidable life anticipation particularly for women who are being pulled by both dependent groups, namely, children and aging parents.

Therefore, McCuan articulates family counseling in terms of the perspectives of nonpathology, structures of social and family support, interaction of family members, and larger systems in the context of family. Family counseling is rather versatile; more so than usual family therapeutic approaches in that it can be easily adapted in almost all situations in which the elderly person may be found. Nonetheless, being an emerging approach in the field of clinical gerontology, research on family counseling is needed, and thus gerontological human service professionals are called on to share knowledge about their responsible participation in this venture.

Marion L. Beaver (see Chapter 3) clearly explicates life review or reminiscent therapy. To reminisce life events in retrospect means "the progressive return to consciousness of past experiences" through self-critique and analysis, and implies the continuous growth potential of the reminiscing person either through a series of jubilees or through feelings of pain, disappointment, and frustration. Depending on the life events with which elderly person is preoccupied, he/she experiences either integrated happiness or painful disparity. Nonetheless, the past life is his/her indispensable property, perhaps the only wealth and power under absolute possession and control.

Life review process is primarily a mental mechanism of the elderly individual who reminisces primarily prompted and facilitated by his/her own life stories, family albums, diaries, yearbooks, old letters, and other memorabilia. The recovery of memories can be expedited by the therapist's good rapport with the client, and empathy toward and appreciation of the client's reliving through reminiscing. Moreover, the therapist may capitalize the client's life review process and transofrm it into an effective curative means.

After experiencing a lesser degree of success and satisfaction with conventional therapeutic approaches, Naomi Feil (see Chapter 4) has developed Validation Therapy, which is being widely used in the field of clinical gerontology, working with nursing home residents in particular. She expands her theoretical notion beyond Erikson's eighth stage of development; and explicates the stages beyond integrity, "Resolution vs. Vegetation," the ninth stage of human development. The four discrete, progressive substages of the final resolution–vegetation encounter are Malorientation, Time Confusion, Repetitive Motion, and Vegetation.

In addition to behavioral characteristics of individuals at various substages, Feil specifically points out how to validate the client's expression. Of the four subgroups, however, the time confused benefit most from validation therapy, while those in repetitive motion are better served by individual rather than group validation. The therapy is intended to improve the quality of life during the validation time, but not designed to deter the progressive deterioration after onset of disease or dimentia.

Bruce A. Thyer and his colleagues (see Chapter 5) identify an emerging interdisciplinary field of behavioral gerontology. The learning theory is the basis of the approach, which includes respondent conditioning, operant conditioning, and observational learning. Each component subapproach is theoretically explicated with specific procedures and case examples.

Rational Self-Counseling (RSC) was developed and perfected by Maxie C. Maultsby (see Chapter 6) during the 1970s. RSC is rooted in the assumption that the human mind (consisting of beliefs and attitudes) influences the brain via the sincere words that are "entirely real symbolic stimuli." This therapeutic modality is very effective with emotionally distressed elderly (1) by teaching the client a healthy concept of rational, (2) through daily rational bibliotherapeutic reading, and (3) with subsequent weekly follow-up sessions, either dyadic or in group, to monitor the previous two steps.

Steven R. Rose (see Chapter 7) summarizes the purpose and process of small therapeutic groups, including prevention and education. A small group process can be used for all counseling and therapeutic approaches discussed earlier except perhaps one, Rational Self-Counseling. In addition, it combines discussion, psychodrama and sociodrama, activity therapy, the arts and art therapy, creative writing, autobiography, oral history, poetry, dance and movement therapy, drama, and music. Its technique include sensory retraining, reality orientation, and remotivation. Nonetheless, inclusion of the physically, socially, and emotionally weak and fragile elderly in any form of small group therapuetic situations should be carefully considered prior to the implementation of group process.

1

Counseling Older Adults

JOAN HASHIMI

Why is there a need to address counseling of the elderly as a topic separate from counseling of any other adult? It seems clear that no one suddenly becomes a different person because he/she has passed some critical birthday. Rather, over time each person tends to see him/herself in the same way; identity is not so much age linked as it is linked to an individuals' sense of self, to his/her work, or family, to his/her place within the community.

What is different about this group of adults is the greater probability of decline of health and vigor, health-related loss of control over his/her life, losses of friends and family, a deferent social milieu or historical context during earlier life, and the different resources that are available to meet the changing daily needs of an older adult.

Counseling with elders, therefore, is seen as therapeutic activity rather much like counseling with any other adult. The emphasis within this chapter, will be to see the elder client as an adult first and their circumstances, which include age, second (Kaufman, 1986; Schlossberg, 1990).

Defining Terms

Counseling is used in this chapter synonymously with individual psychotherapy, but assumes some limitations on scope. Counseling suggests limits on the methods or goals of the intervention. Campbell (1989) defines counseling as "a type of psychotherapy of the supportive or re-educative variety" (p. 161). In addition to these suggested limitations on method this chapter will narrow focus to those clients with problems in living rather than individuals with long standing severe psychiatric disturbances or those with organic mental disorders.

Working with these special populations calls for greater attention to
medical interventions, provision of support services, environmental
modification, and care provider support and education, rather than on
direct individual intervention with the mentally disabled older adult. To
the extent that counseling is provided for those more severely disabled
clients, counseling goals are limited to helping clients develop coping
skills and set realistic goals with their significant limitations. In nursing
homes or other long-term care settings counselors may help reduce
aggressive behavior that makes patient care difficult or threaten other
residents (Ganote, 1990). In these situations one should exercise care to
separate those situations that call for client change from those in which
environmental change may be more appropriate. A hazard of counseling in long-term or medical settings is to focus exclusively on client
change when environmental change is necessary.

Stereotypes and Stigmas

Older adults often are unlikely to define themselves as old. A great
many national and local political and business leaders and artistic mas-
ters are over 65 years of age but are not classified as "old." "Old" has
come to mean an individual who is frail, sickly, and unable to adequately manage his/her affairs. Thus the vast majority of people over 65
are not old by that definition. Neugarten (1982) reminds human service
professionals of the difference by using the terms young–old and old–
old. The young–old are the majority of vigorous and active older adults;
the old–old suffer major mental, physical, and social losses that require a
range of supportive and restorative services. The use of the term old–old
focuses on the double meaning of the word "old" and may help point
out the confusion that exists.

Kaufman (1986) addresses the problem of how to view the older client:

> I have observed that when they talk about who they are and how their
> lives have been, they do not speak of being old as meaningful in itself. To
> the contrary, when old people talk about themselves, they express a sense
> of self that is ageless—an identity that maintains continuity despite the
> physical and social changes that come with old age. (p. 7)

Matthews (1979) supports this same view. When discussing obstacles
in data gathering on aging she notes:

> The conversations that occur . . . are infrequently related to oldness . . . A
> designation of themselves as old is refuted by many old people. (p. 25)
> Being old is like playing a character role. Inside you're just the same.
> (p. 76)

Although the client may not define him/herself as old or cannot be best understood if primarily viewed as old, there are programs and services that are provided on the basis of chronological age, and there is knowledge specific to aging as a process that is helpful as background information to enrich one's understanding of the older client. Age-related stereotypes are so pervasive and ageism so common in mental health settings that gerontological specialists are needed to ensure older clients access to the full range of services needed. Paradoxically, it appears that to avoid being cast as old and the stereotypic assumptions of younger people some older people prefer age-segregated environments (Matthews, 1979). The reasoning appears to be that in an age-segregated community or setting one can forget about age as a defining characteristic. At the same time other older people avoid age-segregated facilities for the same reasons.

There is yet another stigma to be concerned about in providing mental health services, that is the stigma of mental disorder. This stigma is likely to be even stronger among older adults making it less likely for them to see their problems defined as mental disorder and to seek out mental health services. It may well be that extensive use of stress terminology, e.g., Stress Clinics, Stress Response, Posttraumatic Stress Disorder (PTSD), will make seeking mental health services and admitting to problems in everyday living more acceptable. Even the term counselor rather than psychologist or clinical social worker has a more benign connotation.

One needs to help elders understand the nature of their symptoms in a way that can help define them more accurately and to demystify what is entailed in working with mental health professionals. It goes without saying that professional education must also train counselors to respond more helpfully to elders and to help the older client better understand the helping process.

Outreach in both age-specific and general social settings may help to overcome the reticence of many to seek help in resolving problems and issues in their lives (Gurian, 1982). If this outreach were carried out through a family service or similar agency not associated with stigmatizing labels, the services might be more attractive. The outreach could take the form of workshops, discussion groups, or services in churches, health clinics (Lustbader, 1990), senior centers (Grady, 1990), and even department stores. (In St. Louis there is a regular series of lectures and discussions geared to older adults located in department stores.) Peer counseling can be provided through neighborhood organizations that train older neighborhood residents to contact and provide assistance for those elders who are isolated and refer particularly needful cases back to the agency for professional intervention.

Mental health clinics can and do provide services to many older adults

(Kent, 1990). However, counselors must go beyond the traditional sources of mental health out-patient services and provide a broader range of settings to enhance their ability to introduce a wary population group to traditional services.

Mental Health Needs of Older Adults

Although 12% of the U.S. population is over 65, only 4% of services of mental health clinics are directed to them and only 2% of private psychiatric clinics have patients who are over 65 years of age (Dagon, 1982). The extent of need for mental health services is unclear. Much of the literature on the mental health needs of older adults reports that the rates of mental disorder rise with increasing age (Butler & Lewis, 1982). An extensive National Institute of Mental Health (NIMH) community study, however, indicates the rates of functional disorder among the elderly are significantly lower than other age cohorts. Only when organic mental disorder is included, does one see equivalent rates (Myers et al., 1984; Robins et al., 1984). The finding of these lower rates does not explain the very high rate of suicide among the elderly. They account for 25% of all suicides. This statistic suggests that either the mental health data gathered are inaccurate, that there is a grater propensity for suicide among elders with mental health disorders than other age groups, or that suicides in this age group are not solely a product of mental disorder but a personal decision and response to the disabilities associated with aging, that is "rational suicide." Organic mental disorders, because of the basic physical health dimension, are more often seen within physical health settings. Although there may be need for counseling for these individuals, it is not the primary component for service, nor is it needed for all who have organic disorder.

The lack of clarity on rates of functional disorder among older adults, as compared to other age groups, affects the counselor's understanding of their utilization of mental health services. An NIMH study (as mentioned above) found mixed evidence among reporting sites; data tended to refute the assumption of comparative underutilization (Shapiro et al., 1984). Whether there is a greater reluctance for elders to use mental health resources is thus unanswered. What is shown is that there is a reluctance in all age groups to use mental health services. One could say that the underutilization of mental health services of this age cohort is similar to that of other adults. One must also be aware that health insurance, particularly Medicare, offers rather limited reimbursement for mental health services. This precludes many older adults from seeking service unless they are provided at a nominal cost.

Although services to older adults are often suggested as a response to their increased support and resource needs resulting from failing health, the older client has mental health needs that go beyond the need for tangible services and finding ways to deal with the losses associated with old age. To some extent these other needs are little different than the rest of the adult population. Older people have marital problems, disputes and estrangements with their adult children, and/or self-doubts about decisions made in the past. Older clients often come to the counselor with symptoms and manifestations of psychopathology indistinguishable from those of younger adults. For some, age adds an additional burden to a more general need for treatment (Chodorkoff, 1990).

If one is, therefore, to describe the older client and their issues and needs, he/she must not lose the focus on their essential selves. It is a disservice to the client to view them through a lens of group identity. It is quite a different matter to identify problems that the client has after the initial interviews, rather than to assume anything based on his or her age.

The typical client within the narrowed focus as defined earlier is quite likely to be an older person who has not successfully met the stressors associated with aging, because the demands placed on them by these events have overwhelmed their resources and functional capacity. The result is to reawaken lifelong patterns of defensive responses or anxiety.

Understanding the Client

Older adults face an increasing number of stressors that do not yield to neat solutions. There are deaths of close family members, increasingly fragile health, and an evermore complex system of resources to meet health, finance, and residential needs. Although counselors in the field of mental health service have long used this rise in stressors in later life as the foundation for supporting the provision of mental health services to elders, research evidence provides mixed support for this view (Neugarten, 1976; Vaux & Meddin, 1987). It appears that events that one might expect to occur such as retirement or loss of spouse do not in themselves have long-term effects. Retirement from work is an expected and commonplace event; there are an ample number of models to follow to prepare for and accommodate the life changes that will be necessary. The adjustment period may cause some disequilibrium as the retiree and other family members seek to restabilize life with this new element, but for most this will not produce any particular difficulty. Professionals do not find clients within their caseload with uncomplicated retirement as the issue. Nor should one. Those persons unable to adjust to these events are the exceptions. Therefore, professional must look for special circumstances, what meaning work had in their lives, the adequacy of their retirement income, the existence of friends with whom the retiree can spend time.

Those stressors with greater impact are the ones that act as triggers for a host of unexpected, continuing, or highly negative consequences. Most elders who lose their spouse will grieve the loss, but within a year equilibrium returns to their lives; although they may always have moments of sadness, they are unlikely to develop debilitating mental or physical disorder as a result. They may be helped through a grieving period with understanding from support groups, family, or church, but specific mental health treatments are unlikely to be desired or needed. It is inappropriate to define normal grieving over a significant loss as pathological or something that can or should be avoided with mental health intervention. It is the support of those who are close that is needed.

Response to stressors is a complex process. An event becomes stressful only if it is perceived as such by the affected person. Whether an event is seen as stressful depends on prior experience with similar event, special psychological meaning of the event, possible personal consequences of the event, and personal and community resources that may make the event less overwhelming. Thus even loss of a spouse will be understood quite differently if the relationship was abusive for the survivor, or when the deceased had been ill for a long time and needed extensive care. A burden may have lifted but a complete reordering of life is needed (Lazarus & Folkman, 1984). Most stressors are resolved by the affected persons who use their own resources and the supports of family and friends. Many older adults seem to have developed a mental hardiness or perhaps resigned acceptance of the events of aging, which may be why some studies show the incidence of functional disorder so much lower in this group.

Continuing problems result when the individual lacks the resources to meet the added demand or pressures. One can view intervention through counseling therefore as helping an individual better assess personal or community resources to resolve the problems the client faces.

Counseling Process

Are there theoretical models of intervention that are more useful with older clients? The emphasis in this chapter has been on viewing the older client first as a person with a problem and only secondarily as older. In that same spirit it seems appropriate to assume that choice of intervention is dependent on each client's particular circumstances and needs rather than on their age. As a general statement, however, the older client is less likely to be accepting of lengthy, esoteric models of intervention that do not directly deal with immediate problems. But then one might add many younger clients are also issue or specific problem oriented. Psychotherapy directed at basic personality change may be counterproductive for the older adult whose developmental tasks are directed to self-validation. (For example, see Chapter 4, Validation Therapy.) The focus is on maintaining the self rather than developing a new self (Tobin & Gustafson, 1987).

There are regularities to all individual intervention regardless of the counselor's theoretical point of view and chosen therapeutic strategy. These regularities include assessment, intervention, and termination and evaluation.

Assessment

All counseling beings with assessment. The purpose of assessment is to understand the client, his/her circumstances, strengths and weaknesses, and problems. What makes this process different in a dyad that includes an older client is the extent to which age-related issues confound the exchange and the added range of resources that is available to older clients. It is important during initial contact to note client/counselor issues and resolve them early.

The older client's response to the counseling setting is likely to be colored by beliefs about mental health problems and mental health professionals, and by an unclear understanding of what he/she may encounter in this exchange. The counselor should begin by defining how he/she can help the client, what the client can expect from the counselor, and what will be expected from the client. Essentially the counselor seeks to demystify the process. Although the tenor of the interview should be warm and informal, proper care should be taken to be professional and respectful.

It is particularly important to seek an accurate understanding of the client's strengths and capabilities. The counselor tends to underestimate the functional abilities of older persons when they simply want more information on what they are to do or are reluctant to follow suggestions for their own unstated reasons. Sometimes relatives, in making referrals or providing information, tend to understate the client's functioning ability because they feel more comfortable if the client were to go to a more restrictive and protective residence. They are fearful of the health risks for the elder living alone. They seem to feel a responsibility to first consider safety whether or not this is a high priority of the elder. For the elder, the highest priority seems to be on maintaining quality of life.

That includes remaining in their own home, often times in a familiar neighborhood, and being in control (Lewin, 1990). This need may ever mean not telling family members of problems they are having, simply to avoid their children's initiatives for placement. Many elders fear social services or mental health professional because they believe control over their life will be lost to them. This fear may cause an elder to be less than candid in responding to inquiries on their functioning.

A focus on functioning abilities is more appropriate for old–old adults rather than the majority of young–old, but these concerns come up frequently in practice. The counselor is more likely to have in his/her practice older adults who are frail or "near" frail, i.e., those who fall in the gray area between frail and healthy. The focus on issues of control are more universal for all elders, for "of all the things that might explain the social patterns of distress, one stands out as central: The sense of control over one's own life" (Mirowsky & Ross, 1989, p. 167).

It would be difficult to overstate the importance of such basic principles as respecting the dignity and intelligence of the client, respecting the client's right to self-determination, understanding the issue from the client's point of view, and respecting the client's competency and strengths as demonstrated in their past and current response to problems.

Unfortunately the responses of counselors often violate these norms. Stereotypes may cloud their perceptions of the client. Counselors who work with older clients may develop styles of interaction that are not helpful. On the contrary they can be seen as patronizing or condescending; overprotective, "anything goes," and insensitive.

Overprotective. Within this style is the classic statement, "Let me do that for you." The counselor does not know if the client is or is not able to perform a task, but simply jumps in. One cannot be sure of the motivation behind this behavior. It may be a "mothering" response to an adult client who is seen more as a child; stereotypic beliefs that the client, because of age, is not capable; a gesture of impatience because the care provider does not have the patience to allow the client the time to complete the task at hand; a response to what the counselor sees as his/her duty to provide help for the "old"; a need for control over the situation.

Anything Goes. This might be seen as a mirror image of the above style. There is at the core of this pattern a viewing of self-destructive antics as "cute," much the same as winking at the behavior of a mischievous child. This might include responses to excessive drinking or inappropriate sexual behavior. For example, the view that excessive drinking of a 40 year old is self-destructive but the same behavior in a 70 year old is benign or humorous is devaluing later years, and is ageism. This category might also include expecting family and others to accept surly, demanding behavior from an elder without comment because they are old. These alienating behaviors will ultimately be quite harmful to the elder as they erode support and companionship.

Insensitive. The counselor who is inexperienced in working with older clients may seriously misinterpret the meaning of behavior. This would include misreading the increasing need of an elder to maintain control over person and environment, when so much of their lives is in and out of their control; the desire to maintain familiar surroundings when vision fades or agility lessens. This insensitivity may result from an inadequate gerontological education background. In a study focusing on service providers, social workers in particular, working with older clients, Peterson (1990) found that they limited formal training specific to this client group.

The issues behind client apprehension of counseling or psycho-therapeutic intervention and counselor barriers to fuller appreciation and understanding of the client are the difficult part of the assessment process. By comparison the task of collecting basic client background information is fairly straightforward. In collecting basic client informa-tion it is particularly important to let the information flow, let the problem emerge in context. Historical data are important only as needed to understand current issues. Counseling skills are needed to balance the client's need of services in full context to the problem and the counselor's need to help maintain focus and realistic time limits. Al-though frail clients may become tired during an extended interview, for most clients it may be the counselor who tires more quickly. The coun-selor needs skills to adeptly maintain focus during the interview and bring it to a close.

Because older adults are more likely than younger age cohorts to experience medical problems (many of which may be associated with significant behavioral changes), a basic physical examination and health history should be required as prerequisite for counseling intervention. Even with this precaution, research demonstrates a strong possibility that some organic mental disorder may be missed. Neuropsychological testing is advised to help identify organic mental disorder (Sheline, 1990). The counselor must be sensitive to signs of organic involvement, e.g., lapses in cognitive awareness, word substitution, or more serious psychiatric disorder. He/she must be aware of the very high suicide rates among elderly males and become acquainted with clues to suicidal intent. If the client's suicidal intent results from chronic and perhaps terminal illness, discussion with the client is not easy or clear cut. The counselor must be quite mindful of professional ethics and legal obligation in pursuing this discussion with the client; it would be a disservice to the client to refuse to discuss the matter or to cut off the client's expression of such intent.

Nonetheless, professional responses to this level of personal crisis is no longer as clear as it was even 10 years ago. For example, the difference between opting against "heroic" medical interventions, withdrawing (or not wanting to employ) life support systems (e.g., feeding tubes), and suicide is becoming murky. The recent introduction and employment of machinery to assist suicide for some persons are even more philosophically difficult. If this issue is a central core of the client's problem, referral to other professionals more able to handle these questions may be appropriate.

Older clients often have reduced supportive resources. Retirement incomes are often limited, physical vigor may be in decline and sensory changes may make driving problematic. It becomes necessary to have broader social support to compensate. The knowledge of whether these additional support are available must be ascertained during the assessment phase to bring meaning to the discussion of client options.

Intervention

In general, for a mentally nonimpaired older client, a cognitive and problem-focused approach would appear to be most effective (Kent, 1990; Parker & Brown, 1982). In a review of research relating specific treatment modalities to nonpsychotic depressions (the functional mental disorder, most common among older adults) Beutler and Clarkin (1990) report successful results with individual brief behavioral, cognitive, and interpersonal therapies. These interventions include education about depression, decrease of environmental stressors, reinforcement of environmental reinforcers, decrease of interpersonal conflict, resolution of grief, and focus on positive coping self-statements. In general, research evaluating deferential responses of older persons to different treatment modalities is quite limited (Brammer, 1984; Smyer & Intrieri, 1990).

If mental health professional view many of the problems that emerge in later years as stressors associated with failing health or problematic response to losses experienced by older adults, then it makes good sense to choose those approaches found to be most useful for all adults when experiencing stress. With this in mind one might recommend a mix of the following:

1. Relaxation therapies: T'ai Chi Ch'uan, which is an exercise/relaxation regime geared to older adults, Yoga, Progressive Relaxation.
2. Life style changes: exercise, change of diet, cessation of smoking, and moderation of alcohol use.

3. Cognitive therapy, the treatment approaches espoused by Aaron Beck (1976) and Donald Meichenbaum (1985): Beck believed that one's problems result from distortions of reality. These distortions are evident in the client's understanding and evaluation of self and the problem. The therapy is directed at changing the client's faculty or self-damaging cognition. Meichenbuam (1985) developed Stress Inoculation Training (SIT). This training provides the client with an understanding of the response to stress, teaches a variety of coping skills, provides opportunity to practice skills in counseling sessions, and provides support as the client tries out his/her coping skills in real life.

4. Other more problem-specific approaches such as Assertiveness Training or Time Management (Cotton, 1990): Although time management may not seem relevant to older adults who for the most part are retired with too much time on their hands, this is not the case for those elders who are caretakers for disabled spouses or children. These caretakers are often pushed beyond their limits by caretaking responsibilities. In addition to helping a caretaker client access community support services, time management programs would help him/her to assign priority to the roles and responsibilities faced and focus on the highest priority needs.

Selecting a course of action. Understanding the client and developing a working relationship have purpose only when they result in candid discussion of the client's problem and selection of a course of action. The client is ultimately responsible for the selection, but the counselor must help the client develop options. The following parameters control choice of action:

1. *The client's choices as an outgrowth of his/her values and the personal resources that are needed to support that choice.* Is the value of independence worth the day to day struggle that might ensue in the face of medical disability? Each choice must be discussed in light of the resources needed and the possible consequences of taking that path.

2. *The desires and resources of family members.* To what extent are family members willing and/or able to support the client's choices? Living with family is not an option if they do not have space or the time to provide extensive support services. Sometimes the problem runs the other way. Family members may be quite willing to provide help, but the client may not want to ask for or accept that help. Including the desires of family as a parameter is not meant to imply that family have final control over choice. They have choice only over the extent to which they are involved. Family members need to be helped to understand that the older client must make the final choice even when it means some risk. Obvi-

ously this would not be true if the older client were significantly mentally impaired, although even then choices that they can make should be
left to them. All human beings make choices that involve risk, whether
that be sky diving, travel off the beaten track, smoking, or living in high
crime areas. As adults they expect the freedom to make those choices,
when the risks are their own.

When the family member of concern is a spouse, the influence on
decisions is much more complex. Broad divergence of values and needs
can and do exist unresolved within long standing marriages. Extensive
problems here suggest that a more meaningful therapeutic approach
would be joint rather than individual contacts, just as extensive family
disagreement can be better resolved through family therapy.

3. *Accessible Community Resources.* The greater the range of community resources, e.g., different levels of protective residences, social centers, support groups, good transportation service, the greater the range
of choices for the client.

Making changes.   Once the client has made a choice of direction it is
the counselor's role to support and assist the client. The counselor
discusses obstacles, provides practice of new behaviors, models new
behaviors, helps the client understand relationships between thinking
and behavior, provides homework assignments to help client focus on
behaviors needing change, helps the client maintain focus on their
choices for change, and is around to encourage and support the client.
Are these suggestions unique to older clients? No, and perhaps that is
worth noting.

Termination and Evaluation

This is a time to review and evaluate. The problem facing the older
client frequently decry neat solutions. Losses of close family or friends
cannot easily be compensated for, declining physical health cannot be
cured but only adapted to, and life choices cannot be reversed. The
client is often forced to accept a course of action that he/she does not
really want, but that limiting conditions of health or finances make
necessary. Yet, many elders live joyful lives learning to conserve vital
energies for what is most important, and adapting to their limited
realities. Termination also varies in that with older clients the possibilities are greater that help will be needed again. Future losses in
functioning are more possible with older client and new adaptations and
solutions are needed. (For further discussion on evaluation, see Chapter
11, Evaluating Programs for Older People.)

A Case Illustration

The case that follows illustrates some of the processes and principles that have been discussed as part of counseling intervention.

Ms. M. lives in a Section 8 apartment complex in a small town. The apartments are well situated in a pleasant neighborhood close to a grocery store, pharmacy, and two or three other small shops. The apartments are well kept, attractively landscaped, and have attracted residents that are well spoken, nicely dressed, involved in community and family affairs, and protective and caring of each other. Ms. M. is a bit outside this mold, however, particularly as reported by the apartment manager. The manager has asked the County Department of Aging to send someone to see Ms. M. because her behavior is causing concern for other residents and the manager.

After first moving into the apartments Ms.M. accepted the welcoming visits by residents, but after 2 or 3 weeks she became rather surly when they knocked at her door and told some of her neighbors, in no uncertain terms, to leave her alone. The manger reported that she had seen Ms. M. outside on cold days with only a sweater on and that the other day she called the manger on the special helpline twice because she could not find her keys. Ms. M. responded with anger to the manger's attempts to provide guidance. Her anger was expressed in ways the manger found unacceptable. The manger was having considerable regrets having accepted Ms. M. as a resident.

The worker assigned by the agency, Ms. G., called Ms. M. saying who she was and asked if they could set up a time for her to stop by and talk. It was arranged with surprisingly little difficulty.

Ms. M., 82 years old, neatly dressed and groomed, received Ms. G. at the time of the appointment. The apartment was neat and Ms. M.'s possession were neatly arranged. She did grumble a bit wishing that she could have had an apartment on the other side of the building because the view was better. But aside from this, she chatted about herself and some of her experiences; she was a remarkably good raconteur. She stiffened angrily when told that the manger expressed concern with her going outside not warmly dressed. Her fist came down on the tale to accompany her response that she was quite able to know how warmly she should dress and that she had added a lining to her sweater and it was quite warm indeed. She was not at all happy with the manger whom she considered a nosy busybody. Ms. M. did accept setting up another appointment. It seemed important to set up the time so as not to interfere with Ms. M.'s television game show and the bingo games she loved.

Ms. G. learned, during the course of the first two interviews, that Ms.
M. was a widow and had lived alone for the past 35 years. Moving to the
apartments was a second choice for her; she would have preferred a
small house but her current finances would not allow that. She had a
heart ailment that curtailed her activities and made the protectiveness of
this environment necessary. It even meant relocating to this small town
to be closer to family. Family members visited but chose to avoid the
apartment manager and her complaints. The choice of apartment, for
there were two available, had been rather rushed and she did not feel
that she had been allowed time to choose. She felt closed in by the too
active socializing at the apartments and responded in a less controlled
way than she might have in the past. To her these visits were often
intrusive. She wanted, needed, and was accustomed to much greater
privacy. When asked about the incident of the missing keys, she stated
that it was just a little joke. Ms. M. had suffered a recent health emergency and been hospitalized briefly; it was suspected that she had not
been taking her medicine properly. This only affirmed the feeling by
some that she was not able to properly care for herself.

Ms. G. had been more successful than other health care workers who
had called on Ms. M. in the past. First, she had been careful to consult
with Ms. M. in the timing of her visits. She quickly realized that this
client needed to feel in control in her dealings with others. She had lived
in a very independent, adventurous, self-directed life. Her failing physical health was imposing restrictions that she had difficulty accepting.
She feared dementia and continuing loss of health.

In some sense Ms. M. might be considered a rather typical client. It is
not simply that she faces the stressful events of relocation, failing health,
specters of increasing mental and physical disability, but also that these
challenges have overwhelmed her ability to cope and threatened her
basic and long standing life-style. Although the roots of that inability to
cope may lie in long past events or relationships that shaped her character into what it is, today is the issue.

The challenge of this case is to help the client to deal with a stressful
relocation, a new environment, deteriorating health, and a loss of the
level of control over her life she values. The counselor needs to find a
way to tap into the strength and will that enabled her to live independently and face past challenges and use that to face her changing
circumstances. This might best be done by helping her to look at her
neighbors' attention as concern for her and the desire to include her in
their social network and also to look at how her angry/rude responses,
as perceived by others, are not acceptable by them. To the extent that
the manager and other residents would allow greater privacy, some
problems might be avoided. Obviously another problem has been the

extent to which, in this small town, information spreads all too easily. This is something that will not change. Ms. G. can help her client understand it and help her devise ways to live with it. She can also help her client understand the need to work with the visiting nurse and understand the concern others have that she take her medicines regularly and that changes, perhaps, associated with the heart condition made it necessary for her to use "reminders" to make sure she took the medicines correctly.

This case illustrates the frequent lack of an "ideal" solution to the problems that confront older adults. There is not cure for Mrs. M.'s health problems. Options are more limited than ever in the past and dependency needs increase. There is certainty that her heart condition will grow worse. It is obvious she values her independence and privacy more than she has concern over possible health crises. The extent to which her heart problem has led to mental and behavioral changes further complicates the picture. It is also quite possible that Ms. M. may be suffering from a mild depression occasioned by the recent series of events. For Ms. M. the best defense has always been a good offense.

This case is typical also because the client did not seek assistance but rather was referred by others in the environment. The older adult who seeks psychotherapeutic services with relationship or adjustment problems is rather uncommon today.

Conclusion

Counseling the older adult has been discussed in this chapter within narrowed parameters. The focus has been on those older adults who are able to provide self-care but who are endangering those capabilities or existing supports by unhelpful responses to the changes that are occurring in their lives. To the extent that these interventions are successful, further unnecessary losses in life quality may be prevented.

References

Beck, A. T. (1976). *Cognitive therapy and the emotional disorders*. Madison, CT: International Universities Press.

Beutler, L. E., & Clarkin, J. F. (1990). *Systematic treatment selection: Toward targeted therapeutic interventions*. New York: Brunner/Mazel.

Brammer, L. M. (1984). Counseling theory and the older adult. *The Counseling Psychologist, 12*, 29–37.

Butler, R. N., & Lewis, M. I. (1982). *Aging and mental health: Positive psychosocial and biomedical approaches*. St. Louis: C.V. Mosby.

Campbell, R. J. (1989). *Psychiatric dictionary* 6th ed. New York: Oxford University Press.

Chodorkoff, B. (1990). Providing psychotherapy in private practice. *Generations, XIV,* 27–30.

Cotton, D. H. G. (1990). *Stress management: An integrated approach to therapy.* New York: Brunner/Mazel.

Dagon, E. M. (1982). Planning and development issues in implementing community-based mental health services for the elderly. *Hospital and Community Psychiatry, 13,* 137–141.

Ganote, S. (1990). A look at counseling in long term care settings. *Generations, XIV,* 31–34.

Grady, S. (1990). Senior centers: An environment for counseling. *Generations, XIV,* 15–18.

Gurian, B. (1982). Mental health outreach and consultation services for the elderly. *Hospital and Community Psychiatry, 33,* 142–147.

Kaufman, S. R. (1986). *The ageless self: Sources of meaning in late life.* Madison: University of Wisconsin Press. (Reprint by the New American Library, New York, New York.)

Kent, K. (1990). Elders and community mental health centers. *Generations, XIV,* 19–21.

Lazarus, R. S., & Folkman, S. (1984). *Stress, appraisal, and coping.* New York: Springer.

Lewin,T. (1990, March 28). Strategies to let elderly keep some control. (Second article in the series—Care of the elderly: Private burdens, public choices. *New York Times, 1,* 11.

Lustbader, W. (1990). Mental health services in a community health center. *Generations, XIV,* 22–23.

Matthews, S. H. (1979). *The social world of old women: Management of self-identity.* Beverly Hills, CA: Sage Publications.

Meichenbaum, D. (1985). *Stress inoculation training.* New York: Pergamon Press.

Mirowsky, J. & Ross, C. E. (1989). *Social causes of psychological distress.* New York:Aldine de Gruyter.

Myers, J. K., Weissman, M. M., Tischler, G. L., Holzer, C. E., Leaf, P. J., Orvaschel, H., Anthony, J. C., Boyd, J. H., Burke, J. D., Kramer, M., and Stolzman, R. (1984). Six-month prevalence of psychiatric disorders in three communities. *Archives of General Psychiatry, 41,* 959–967.

Neugarten, B. L. (1976). Adaptation and the life cycle. *The Counseling Psychologist, 6,* 16–20.

Neugarten, B. L. (1982). Older people: A profile. In B. L. Neugarten (Ed.), *Age or need?: Public policies for older people.* Beverly Hills, CA: Sage Publications.

Parker, G. B., & Brown, L. B. (1982). Coping behaviors that mediate between life events and depression. *Archives of General Psychiatry, 39,* 1386–1391.

Peterson, D. A. (1990). Personnel to serve the aging in the field of social work: Implications for educating professionals. *Social Work, 35,* 412–415.

Robins, L. N., Helzer, J. E., Weissman, M. M., Orvashcel, H., Bruenberg, E., Burke, J. D., & Regier, D. A. (1984). Lifetime prevalence of specific psychiatric disorders in three sites. *Archives of General Psychiatry, 41,* 949–958.

Schlossberg, N. K. (1990). Training counselors to work with older adults. *Generations, XIV*, 7–10.

Shapiro, S., Skinner, E. A., Kessler, L. G., Von Korff, M., Cottler, L. & Regier, D. A. (1984). Utilization of health and mental health services. *American General Psychiatry, 41*, 971–978.

Sheline, Y. (1990). Quantifying undiagnosed organic mental disorder in geriatric inpatients. *Hospital and Community Psychiatry, 41*, 1004–1008.

Smyer, M. A. & Intrieri, R. C. (1990). Research and practice issues: Evaluating counseling outcomes. *Generations, XIV*, 11–14.

Tobin, S. S., & Gustafson, J. D. (1987). What do we do differently with elderly clients? *Journal of Gerontological Social Work, 10*, 107–121.

Vaux, A., & Meddin, J. (1987). Positive and negative life changes and positive and negative affect among the rural elderly. *Journal of Community Psychology, 15*, 447–458.

2

Family Counseling: An Emerging Approach in Clinical Gerontology

ELOISE RATHBONE-McCUAN

Introduction

As the American population ages and the society begins to redefine itself as an intergenerational and multigenerational culture, it becomes inevitable that practitioners recognize the aging transformations of the family. In the field of gerontological social work one of the practice advances of the 1980s was the shift in focus from predominant attention to the aged individual to include more attention to the aging family.

This chapter presents a discussion of the later life family as a growing client group being served in the mental health and medical care delivery sectors. Its primary objective is to illustrate ways that family counseling can be integrated into the social health continuum that is being structured throughout society to meet the needs of elderly persons.

To understand the potential of family counseling to help solve the family-based dilemmas associated with the aging process, the clinician needs to have a perspective on the aging family. Several different counseling approaches, developed largely form the perspective of the two-generational family, have been adapted successfully. The chapter illustrates how clinical social workers can use the focus on the family to meet goals for the client and the larger family unit. The field of gerontological social work has made significant strides in the availability of family-oriented social work intervention provided to older clients, thereby, beginning to respond to the needs of aging families. Progress has been limited, however, because of public policies that operate in contradiction to family needs for direct support and economic supplements. The conclusion of the chapter looks at the future of family counseling in the context of broader social research issues that are part of the knowledge-building agenda for this decade.

Changing Social Relationships among the Aging Population

Butler and Lewis (1982) make the point that families will develop in ever increasing different forms. Their delineation of the most common types of social relationship groups encompasses family and family-like units, definitions that focus on understanding the client system as it applies to gerontological social work. Counseling is provided beyond the nuclear family as there is increasing need for the clinician to provide services to modified and extended families as well as to different people who, although not family members, fulfill family roles and perform important functions. Table 1 summarizes the definitions of family and family-like units that Butler and Lewis (1982) identify as central to the changing social world of elderly Americans.

An increasing number of multigenerational families now span four and five generations. More cases served by social workers will involve multigenerational influences that require adaptation in each generation. For example, providing daily care to an impaired greatgreatgrand-mother may be a necessity that requires caregiving responsibilities to be performed by a daughter who is of postretirement age. A 70-year-old woman may be caring for her 90-year old mother. At the same time she may also be called on to care for her greatgrandchild of age 2 because her daughter of age 45, grandmother of the child, and the child's mother are both employed.

This pattern of two-directional caregiving in which middle genera-tions of women are assuming care responsibilities for the oldest and youngest generations (Brody, 1981) has been recognized as a social dilemma only within the past decade. Elder care has also become an issue in the workplace as a source of family responsibility that may impact on productive work roles (Anastas, Gibeau, & Larson, 1990; Denton, Love, & Slate, 1990). Another changing relationship structure is the replacement of nonblood kin by other people who are responsible for care and maintaining the social contacts with the elderly person. The presence of nonkin family members in previously assigned family roles of elder care occurs for many different reasons including longevity and geography. The age of elderly persons may place them in a position of outliving younger generations of family members, or because of geo-graphic separation only close friends may remain in reasonable prox-imity. The friendship network substitutes for the lack of available fami-ly. In other circumstances, history of family estrangements and family conflicts may result in younger generations of family members avoiding contact and responsibility for the oldest generation.

These changing family forms require that social workers have a new framework for understanding the intimate social arrangements that

Table 1. Definitions of Families and Other Family Like Units

General definition of family: Those who consider themselves economically and emotionally related to each other by blood (consanguinity) or by marriage (conjugality).

Nuclear family: A married pair (conjugal) with dependent children and an independent household, bound to outside kin by voluntary ties of affection or duty.

Extended family: All of those related to one another by blood or marriage.

Modified and extended family: Separate households for all but the very old or sick, with a complex, viable supportive pattern of family relationships with kin. The nuclear family is part of the extended kin family. The latter is a highly integrated network of social relations and social mutual assistance—vertical over generations and bilateral to other kin.

Household: A number of persons who share a residence, exchange services, and give emotional support to each other.

Social network: Those individuals who share a residence, exchange services, and give emotional support to each other.

Support system: A group of individuals who join together to give support and assistance to each other sometimes for a specific purpose.

---

surround many elderly people. Such arrangements may become the focus of what was once considered to be family but no longer falls into the narrow construct. Of necessity, social workers must rethink the meaning of the concept of family system and give greater attention to the diverse intimate social units connected to the older person and linking them to other resources in the larger systems environment.

Family Systems as a General Practice Framework

Before discussing how family systems theory has guided the evolution of family therapy in social work and its utility for working with older families, the reader is encouraged to reflect on the profession's history with the family. Long before social workers were engaged with families in the role of therapist, the profession was attending to the family. The family took a secondary position only during the era when social work was diverted to concentration on the individual and personal pathology. Sherman (1981) states:

> however differently family processes were understood and approached clinically over the full history of social work, the family was a central consideration in theory and in practice, except during the psychological-psychiatric ingestive decades, when the interest in the family qua family made way for the concentration of the individual and his psychology and psychopathology, with the family more peripherally in evidence only as the developmental matrix for the individual. (p. 11)

Clinical social workers are devoted to enhancing the psychosocial health and economic well-being of clients and work with individuals, couples, families, and small groups. Family therapy focuses more exclusive attention on the family unit. As Sherman (1981) pointed out, "Seeing family members together is not sacrosanctly reserved for family therapists: Seeing some family members together is not necessarily family therapy" (p. 9). From another perspective clinical social work is a specialty and family therapy is one of its most rapidly expanding subspecialties. The majority of clinical services provided to aging families do not qualify as "prefamily therapy" even though there is an increasing interest in the application of family therapy to solve intergenerational problems associated with the aging process. Irrespective of whether the clinical intervention is labeled as therapy, most counseling offered to older families reflects a systems perspective because this is the general foundation for social work practice with families. Rhodes (1986) noted the importance to clinicians of understanding how the family functions as a system. "Each individual member of the family, and each subsystem of the family, must be seen as a component of the entire family system. Families are viewed as open systems in which members enter and exit over the course of the life cycles, thereby altering the boundaries of the family. Experience has shown that most families are best understood from a three-generational perspective of interlocking reciprocal and repetitive relationships" (p. 482).

Over the past four decades, the incremental development of family systems theory has produced general agreement among clinical social workers on basic concepts. The core areas of conceptual agreement have not received extensive empirical testing, but they remain as the foundation of family therapy theory. These areas of agreement are that behavior of family members is interlocking, family problems repeat from one generation to the next, and an individual's symptoms reflect wider problems in the way family members related to each other (Rhodes, 1986).

Rationale for Applying Family Intervention with the Aged

Edinburg (1985) identified three major advantages that frame a rationale for the viability of family work as a valuable mental health practice with the aged:

1. *Nonpathological Perspective.* The family systems view focuses on making the system as functional as possible rather than identifying and curing pathology. Whereas much of the emotional discomfort suffered by the elderly is adaptive, a natural fit exists between this type of approach and older persons' identified problems.

2. *Focus on the Support System.* Unlike any other treatment approach, family therapy approaches make the support system of the elderly the primary focus of assessment and intervention. Given the role the family plays in the care of the aged, such a focus is potentially quite useful.
   3. *Access to Issues Not Easily Accomplished in Other Treatment Modalities.* This area includes attention and power relationships, as well as relating behavior to a series of conceptual schemes designed to give the missing pieces on how (or why) the family behaves as it does with the older relative. Any practitioner who has worked with families of the elderly knows that there are communication patterns, specific power relationships, and undercurrents (dynamics) that are related to how family members interact on behalf of the older relative. The many family therapy approaches attempt to uncover and alter disharmonious patterns (pp. 226–227).

The Larger Systems Context of Aging Family Intervention

The problems facing the aging family can originate within the family, but it is more likely that dysfunction will emerge because of internal issues and from specific larger systems. Imbers-Black (1988) discusses the current interest among family therapists to better address the interplay between the family and larger systems: "The problem of families and larger systems have been highlighted in a small but growing literature that has concerned itself primarily with problems arising between families and specific kinds of larger systems such as hospitals, schools, probation, or with specific presenting problems in families and particular treatment (service delivery) systems designed to address these problems" (p. 7). Most of the contact social workers have with aging families is within the context of larger systems that control access to the resources needed by the aged family members.

For example, obtaining acute and/or long-term care for an aged family member places other family members in short- or long-term interaction with specific health care providers. These may include home-health workers or physicians in clinics, hospitals, or nursing homes. Increasingly these health settings employ professional social workers who connect with the family because they are receiving services from the organization.

The specific purpose of the social work contact might be to obtain medical care such as outpatient cataract surgery for the aged family member. The aged patient and family are expecting a routine surgical procedure that will require additional support with activities of daily living such as shopping, meal preparation, and transportation. The family has planned to provide this support, but neither they nor the patient is prepared to hear the surgeon say that there is massive retina deterioration and that rapid visual deterioration can be expected. Knowing that the aged person is likely to have a significant visual disability can create a major crisis for the family. The social worker's first contact with the family may have been directed toward arranging for some homemaker assistance and senior citizen transportation to lessen the amount of responsibility that family members would have to assume during the postoperative recovery. This new diagnosis required that the family receive not only the postsurgical services, but more clinical counseling to deal with the longer range consequences of potential blindness. With permanent disability comes a need for numerous adaptations for the elderly person and the family. These adaptations might come in the form of transitions that create greater amount of reliance on family support long before the individual and their family had anticipated. A change in residence may be required if visual disabilities prevent the elder from remaining in their current residential setting. There is also the likelihood that many more formal organizations might become involved in the life of the family. Social workers have a role to play with families who are adjusting to greater dependency on formal organizations. Some families have no experience with negotiating formal services provided from outside the family. Others may have a long history of negative experiences with the agencies and professionals that society has designated to provide help. In a very real sense, the social worker's primary responsibility to the family may take the form of advocacy and education to increase the possibility that the services received are accessible, appropriate, and sufficient to meet needs and resolve problems.

Social work intervention with older families should emphasize the worker's attention to the relationship between the family and larger systems. This is neither a new nor radical position. Family-oriented practice is increasing for aging families because society is being forced to support family functioning and caregivers into the latest stages of the family life cycle. This orientation to practice emerges from the general ecological perspective that has been applied in different models of practice. The Life Model (Germain & Gitterman, 1986) is derived from the ecological perspective. It places emphasis on the clients in the environment and on methods of practice that integrate work with individuals, families, and groups within an organizational, community, and cultural context. These are all components of professional service that can be helpful to clients and serve as the blueprint for counseling older families. Although the structure for the counseling can take many different forms other than the office-based model characteristic of family therapy, it is still an important psychosocial problem solving process.

Forms of Therapeutic Support for the Aging Family

One of the most exciting aspects of counseling with older families is the opportunity for the practitioner to design innovative programs to overcome some of the barriers limiting the availability of counseling services to older families through the mental health system. Some of the barriers include (1) clinicians individual orientation in psychopathology, (2) application of the medical care model to service to the elderly, (3) narrow parameters of reimbursement not extended to family care, (4) individual organic/disease bases of geriatric mental illness, (5) role of the older client in family and legal systems, (6) clinical orientations of the settings caring for the elderly, (7) logistics, and (8) clinicians bias against advanced age as a capacity for change that applies to both the individual and the family (Edinburgh, 1985).

Aronson (1983) identifies some of the most common forms of family involvement with elderly clients to be categorical disease self-help groups, special short-term groups, family role maintenance services, respite service, home care services, financial planning, and public policy formulation. These intervention formats focus on specific issues that confront older families. Because each forms of family involvement can be applied to enhance families coping with crises or long-term stress, all deserve consideration as legitimate approaches.

Illness Oriented Self-Help Groups

Among the first self-help groups that emerged for family members whose lives had been exposed to the traumas and stress of an illness was Alanon that emerged as part of the Alcoholics Anonymous movement. This has served as a model for helping elders with conditions such as strokes and Parkinson's disease. Since many chronic diseases may strike in old age and become more debilitating with age, older families have special needs to be able to cope with burdens and other dysfunctions associated with living with an ill family member. There are several ways that social workers may incorporate family self-help groups into their work with client families. The first may be to use this as an adjunct to the family counseling provided by a social worker to reduce the social isolation caused by the illness or as a means of helping families learn more about the disease and how other families cope with its impact. There are cases in which clinicians will recommend participation in self-help groups after the family is ready to terminate the therapy but need the ongoing support that can be offered from group participation. In other cases, families may not need professional clinical assistance and the social worker has assessed that active membership in a self-help group will be sufficient and that a self-help family group format is more suited to the type of informal help a family is willing to accept.

Short-Term Family Groups

This approach involves the interaction of different families working with a professional leader that is structured to meet the standard that all family members will meet together for a designated period of time as a group. Bell (1981) advanced this approach within the family therapy field and suggests that the group continues to meet until it has attained the goals of the therapy. Bell's clinical work emphasized the longer period of therapeutic involvement, but in working with this approach in a gerontological practice context the shorter term groups have more flexibility and a greater likelihood of client participation. An example of this approach, may be the family who needs therapeutic support to deal with the crisis of a nursing home placement. The length of the group sessions is usually adapted to the length of time required for realistic adaptation to the nursing home placement. As more nursing homes are becoming active in rehabilitation geared to return the patient to the community, the short-term group approach can also be helpful for families getting ready to receive the elderly person back in the community.

Family Role Maintenance Groups

Caregiver support groups can be applied as an approach for the spouse caregiver to learn better ways to manage stress and strain through the group experience. The crises that can arise in caregiving are not restricted to the caregiver. Different approaches are being developed to attend to the needs of different family members who may not assume the role of primary caregiver, but are affected by the events of maintaining a family member in the community. Maintaining family role connectedness can be an especially difficult emotional challenge for individuals who are trying to adapt to the decreasing physical abilities and cognition of someone in the middle stages of Alzheimer's disease. The isolating qualities of dementia can become a stimulus for family members to withdraw from the ill individual even though they want to maintain emotional ties and contact. This can be a common theme that each family member faces as they explore how they will frame their role in the family system, a system that is adapting to the progressive stages of dementia.

Respite Groups

As caregiver burden has become recognized as a major mental health stress in later life, diverse programs have been initiated to reduce the physical and psychic drain through respite care. There are times when attitudes within the family system block the effective use of respite services because families believe that all of the care must be delivered by the family. The expectancies exist that one or two members do the majority of unrelieved caregiving. Families need to be educated about how caregiving can be provided without creating breakdown. Part of this learning involves helping the family system to open its boundaries and allow assistance to be offered from external sources without negating family commitments. Social workers often encounter family opposition to use of outside assistance and find it necessary to work within the system to help members learn how to utilize external resources. A specific illustration of family barriers might be the resistance to the diverse services that can be provided through in-home services whereby basic housekeeping, cooking, and personal care duties can be lessened for the family through the use of nonfamily labor and skill.

Financial Planning

The complex economic issues associated with the transitions and costs of the aging process can have tremendous impact on and consequences for the family system. Social workers often find that economic resources become the single greatest source of conflict within families as they attempt either to plan for or manage costly medial expenses such as private payment for nursing home or in-home care. Intergenerational attitudes about the use of resources and the contribution of financial assistance may spur hostile family interactions. These issues can sometimes be resolved in family counseling or otherwise managed by the family's reliance on external consultation about estate planning or management. Whenever possible, the social worker should try to encourage money matters to become a consideration as part of retirement planning. Retiring persons should also be encouraged to weigh financial decisions in a way that will consider whatever concerns they have about how their personal finances might impact on the family. This could be consideration of provisions for supporting a surviving spouse left impoverished by the cost of long-term care or assessed protection and distribution at earlier stages of the aging process.

Public Policy Formulation

If the gerontological social worker applies a larger systems perspective to practice with the older family, attention to these issues may overlap into that of public policy. One area of increasing concern is that of protection of the elderly person who is functioning at a marginal level and may need assistance. Help may be available in the from of conservators or other alternatives may exist under the status of power of attorney or representative payee for the elderly person (McKay, 1984). Counseling may demand that the practitioner understand what options are open to families faced with the limitations to autonomous decisions that are applicable to the elder's state or residence. Social workers may need to know about the family's reliance on external consultation about estate planning or management.

Social workers may need to know about their mandated status to report incidents of abuse, neglect, or exploitation that may occur within the family system. The policies of adult protective services may place the social worker in the shifting tides of family assistance and family harm to the elderly individual. An increasing number of states have adult protective service laws that define the limits of family behavior if it endangers the elderly individual. The practitioner is remiss if the understanding of family behavior does not include recognition of the protector role of the legal and human services systems.

On the other hand, working with the issues faced by older families demands that the practitioner include some aspects of group work and advocacy and link the formal and informal helping resources together. A significant amount of the counseling that is provided to older families follows along the more traditional lines of clinical work with younger families. Even traditional nuclear family work with the older or younger generations of family members can maintain ongoing concern for how public policies impact on family functioning.

Engaging the Aging Family in the Counseling Process

Herr and Weakland (1979) were the first clinicians to delineate specific guidelines that offered direction for applying a family systems orientation to the aging family. One of the greatest contributions of their model was to introduce work with the older family into the larger family therapy movement. Later, Herr and Weakland (1984) addressed the possibilities of using family therapy in cases in which the elderly person, as the identified patient, suffered from cognitive disorientation. The stigma of dementia remains a major reason for the continued resistance to apply family therapy as a clinical intervention intended to provide mental health services to the elderly.

Florsheim and Herr (1990) describe the process of elder family counseling as an approach that attempts to solve problems associated with aging by viewing them in relation to the elder's social-support system. No consistent evidence exits to suggest that older families are more resistant to counseling than younger families. As an initial step in the counseling process, there are numerous ways to make contact.

Some families find that they have been mandated to participate in clinical counseling to resolve some problems impacting on the elder's welfare. The majority of family involvement, however, is completely voluntary. Clinician therefore have to find ways of contacting families that increase their willingness for engagement. Florsheim and Herr (1990) encourage practitioners to solicit family participation as part of a cooperative problem-solving process that the family collaboratively undertakes with the worker. The exhaustion and frustration of many families who have attempted to handle problems without professional support can increase willingness to participate. Effective outreach implies that the practitioner must be very concrete with the family from the very start to help them understand the goals of intervention.

Most therapeutic involvement with the aging family takes place outside the office setting. For example, the home-health agency social worker goes into the home to make an assessment of what services are required to meet medical and social needs. Counseling may also take place in hospitals and institutional settings that rarely offer an orderly private environment in which to talk with family members. These settings may not be ideal, however, they are where the worker is most likely to find family members and to have a legitimate entry into their lives as an advocate for the elderly patient. A benefit of the informal contract is that it removes some of the stigma that individuals feel when going to a mental health center or to the office of a psychotherapist.

Agreement about the utility and appropriateness of using a problem-solving approach prevails among those who work with older families. For the reader oriented in clinical social work theory the concept of "problem-solving approach" jogs the memory back to the work of Perlman (1986). About her theoretical problem-solving orientation to human change she says:

> Growing older and presumably wiser I became increasingly sensitive to what a multiplex situation every case worker (practitioner) faced every day as he entered into the lives of his clients. So I was both pushed and pulled into our efforts to understand how people live and love and work and need and want and cope or fail—and beyond that how to engage and perhaps teach our clients some more effective and satisfying ways of dealing with problems of everyday life. (p. 246)

As described by Florsheim and Herr (1990) a general outline of the steps to include in the problem-solving approach with older families would cover the following:

1. Establishing initial contact with the client(s).
2. Helping the family define the problem in concrete behavioral terms.

3. Inquiring into what each significantly concerned person is doing in attempting to contain, handle, or resolve the problem.
4. Determining limited treatment goals that would be judged as indicators of small yet significant improvement in the problem.
5. Reviewing and summarizing information gathered about the family. This step includes the counselor making an initial evaluation of appropriate goals, of persons most involved in the problem, or persons most open to change, or reinforcers of the problem, and of ways the therapist, especially, can avoid similar behavior.
6. Conducting further interviews, attempting interventions specific to defined treatment goals, and evaluating the effects of interventions.
7. Termination of counseling.

These steps are illustrated in the case presentation that follows, which involves loneliness as a family process. Large (1989) indicates that loneliness has been characterized most frequently as an individual experience with attention being given to the family context that is interconnected with much loneliness as it is experienced by a singly family member. In placing the lonely family member in the family structure, Large states:

> As with other behaviors, it is not the loneliness itself that is problematic in families. Rather, it is the lonely individual's failure to produce change, the stuckness, which converts loneliness from an adaptive signal into a "pathological" state. Individuals in a family may have different tolerances for loneliness, just as they have different tolerances for pain or different ranges for affective expression. But the experience of loneliness and those behaviors that accompany it are subject to variables common to all emotional systems. These include family size, multigenerational structure, stage of development, interchange with other systems, cultural heritage, family myths, and so on, as well as experience within the family. (p. 27)

Family Intervention for Intergenerational Issues: Case Example

Social workers in long-term care settings often find it necessary to provide in-depth support to family members who are experiencing loss from the placement of an elderly member. New challenges are being presented to these practitioners as they are helping families to adjust not only to the placement but to the additional changes experienced by cognitive and physical deterioration in the middle and later stages of Alzheimer's disease. In the process of providing support to family members, the social worker may not only engage in confronting issues related to the patient's placement, but also attend to other family needs for improved communication and decision making.

Placement of Milton Kaiser, 74, into a specialized inpatient treatment unit for dementia care was initiated by his wife and only surviving daughter, Gail, age 54. Mr. Kaiser was placed on a waiting list at a local nursing home. While awaiting an available bed for Mr. Kaiser, the social worker established a close professional relationship with his wife and daughter. Then, Gail's husband died. Gail was denying her father's level of cognitive loss while at the same time grieving actively over her husband's death. Gail hoped to rebuild a relationship with her estranged 27-year-old daughter, Kim. Following her father's death, Kim decided to return to the home community and take over the management of the family photography business. Assuming an overly dominating voice in the lives of her mother and grandmother, Kim was in conflict with them over whether her grandfather should remain in the facility or be cared for at home.

Mrs. Kaiser requested the social worker meet with Gail, Kim, and herself in hopes "that some sense could be talked into Kim" regarding her anger about Mr. Kaiser's institutional placement. They defined family problem was conflict over where and how to care for Mr. Kaiser and the disruption this was creating in the relationship among the three generations of women. It was also apparent that Kim had little understanding of how her grandmother and her mother had shared the caregiving responsibilities for her grandfather. Neither of them seemed willing to talk about the burdens they had experienced when Mr. Kaiser was at home. Mrs. Kaiser and Gail were satisfied with the care provided at the facility. They felt that Kim was burdening herself with guilt about not being available to her grandfather during the prior years, but also that she was interfering in their decisions.

The worker met with Kim, her mother, and her grandmother on several occasions to discuss what each of them felt was the appropriate decision to make for Mr. Kaiser's care. The worker encouraged Mrs. Kaiser and Gail to tell Kim what it had been like for both of them to try to care for Mr. Kaiser in the months prior to his placement in the nursing home. They shared how they had felt isolated and burdened in the caregiver roles. Before closing the session the worker asked Kim to spend the next week reflecting on what decisions Mr. Kaiser would want to make about the circumstances of his care in the final stages of his illness. The worker acknowledged Kim's grief and encouraged her to attend an ongoing Alzheimer's family support group at the facility. Gail and Mrs. Kaiser each talked about their feelings of shame that Kim had broken the teaching of the church by committing "sexual sin." They described to Kim how it felt for them to have lost her as a daughter. The worker also provided the three women with a referral to a local psychotherapist who she knew to be experienced in work with gay and lesbian family issues.

In this case the worker knew that her role should not extend into family dynamics beyond resolving conflict that interfered with the family's attachment to the patient. However, the worker had received enough information about the intergenerational conflicts of these women to know that additional focused family therapy was important in the bonds of caring were to be lifted from the burden of pain and anger.

Future Research Directions

The focus of this chapter has been on intergenerational family relationships as they are experienced within the family aging process. Important concepts of theoretical, empirical, and practice interest are intergenerational transmission, intergenerational support and solidarity, and perceptions of intergenerational relations. Whereas social workers have taken the leadership for developing many programs that can be of assistance to older families, they have yet to contribute substantially to the knowledge of intergenerational family therapy. Frameworks for conducting this form of therapy are being developed in systematic ways from the fields of sociology and social psychology (Fine & Norris, 1989).

Some of the ways that social work practitioners can contribute to the knowledge building process of intergenerational family practice frameworks include the following:

1. Develop empirical research to test the family therapy theories they apply in clinical work.
2. Engage in research that meets the highest standards of qualitative methods and contribute to the knowledge accumulation needed for clinical intervention.
3. Frame the clinical concerns of family counseling in the larger sociopolitical systems contexts that have significant impact on the lives of aging families.
4. Participate in the interdisciplinary family therapy movement to recognize work with aging families as a legitimate and needed service for minority families, nontraditional family units, and family constellations that do not represent the assumed patterns of normative family aging in the American culture.

Conclusion

Future opportunities are abundant for social work practitioner to take the lead in advocating for more family-based services for older Americans. Unfortunately, it has been difficult to attract new professionals into the field of aging and too few graduate students are taking advantage of the specialized training that is available. Peterson (1990) reported that surveyed members of the National Association of Social Workers felt that gerontology was a growing area of social work employment, but most learned that they knew relatively little about the field of aging after graduating with the MSW degree.

Many practitioners continue to view social gerontology as noble work with the sick and infirmed. The experience of this author, a trained gerontological social worker in practice and education for over 20 years, has been one of continued expansion of gerontology into new fields of domestic violence, alcoholism, rural social work, feminist practice, and now family treatment. The areas of new uncharted clinical work with the aging family are exciting and rewarding. Family counseling with older families deserves the attention of many more practitioners now entering the field with plans to be family therapists or family practitioners. Their training in family systems theory is relevant and timely. Both the fields of medical and psychiatric social work have need for the combined expertise of family and social gerontology. In addition, the opportunity to work with the strengths and challenges of the aging family is very rewarding.

References

Anastas, J. W., Gibeau, J. L., & Larson, P. J. (1990). Working families and eldercare: A national perspective on an aging America. *Social Work, 35*, 405–411.

Aronson, M. K. (1983). Mobilizing the family. In M. K. Aronson, R. Bennett, & B. J. Gurland, (Eds.), *The acting-out elderly* (pp. 117–121). New York: Haworth Press.

Bell, J. E. (1981). The small group perspective: Family group therapy. In E. R. Tolson & W. J. Reid (Eds.), *Models of family treatment* (pp. 33–51). New York: Columbia University Press.

Brody, E. (1981). Women in the middle and family help to older people. *The erontologist, 21*, 471–480.

Butler, R. N., & Lewis, M. I. (1982). *Aging and mental health*, 3rd ed. St. Louis: C.V. Mosby.

Denmton, K., Love, L. T., & Slate, R. (1990). Eldercare in the 90's: Responsibility, employer challenge. *Family in Society, 71*, 349–359.

Edinberg, M. A. (1985). *Mental health practice with the elderly.* Englewood Cliffs, NJ: Prentice-Hall.

Fine, M., & Norris, J. E. (1989). Intergenerational relations and family therapy research: What we can learn from other disciplines. *Family Process, 28*, 301–316.

Florsheim, M. J., & Herr, J. J. (1990). Family counseling with elders. *Generations,* *14,* 40–42.

Germain, C. B. & Gitterman, A. (1986). The life model approach to social work practice revisited. In F. J. Turner (Ed.), *Social work treatment: Interlocking theoretical approaches,* 3rd ed. (pp. 618–645). New York: Free Press.

Herr, J. J., & Weakland, J. H. (1979). *Counseling elders and their families: Practice techniques for applied gerontology.* New York: Springer.

Herr, J. J., & Weakland, J. H. (1984). Conducting family therapy with elder clients. In J. P. Abrams and V. Crooks (eds.), *Geriatric mental health* (pp. 123–132). Orlando, FL: Grune & Stratton.

Imbers-Black, E. (1988). *Families and larger systems: A family therapists guide through the labyrinth.* New York: Guildford Press.

Large, T. (1989). Some aspects of loneliness in families. *Family Process, 228,* 25–36.

McKay, J. B. (1984). Protective services. *Generations, 8,* 10–13.

Perlman, H. H. (1986). The problem-solving model. In F. J. Turner (Ed.), *Social work treatment: Interlocking theoretical approaches* 3rd ed. (pp. 245–266). New York: Free Press.

Peterson, D. A. (1990). Personnel to serve the aging in the field of social work: Implications for educating professionals. *Social Work, 35,* 412–415.

Rhodes, S. L. (1986). Family treatment. In F. J. Turner (Ed.), *Social work treatment: interlocking theoretical approaches,* 3rd ed. (pp. 432–454). New York: Free Press.

Sherman, S. N. (1981). A social work frame for family therapy. In E. R. Tolson and W. J. Reid (Eds.), *Models of family treatment* (pp. 22–32). New York: Columbia Press.

3

Life Review/Reminiscent Therapy

MARION L. BEAVER

Introduction

Life review is a process that is believed to occur universally in all people in the final years of their lives, although they may not be totally aware of it, and may in part defend themselves from realizing its presence. The process is spontaneous, unselective, and seen in other age groups (i.e., adolescents, young adults, the middle-aged) as well. However, it appears that the intensity and emphasis on putting one's life in order are most striking in old age.

Over the years, a number of investigators have identified the life review as a psychological issue in which older persons put their storehouse of memories in order, dramatizing some, striving for consistency in others—perhaps as a way of preparing an ending for one's life story (Butler, 1963). Life reviewers often exhibit a strong drive to take stock of their lives and to resolve troublesome conflicts. Some may feel that they have been given a "second chance," and derive satisfaction over the prospect of reviewing their lives.

As one's past marches in review it is surveyed, observed, and reflected on by the ego (Butler, 1968). This process enables older persons to better understand events of the past and to give new and significant meaning to their lives. It may also lessen older persons fears about death. This kind of review has positive, constructive effects.

The Eriksonian concept of ego integrity versus ego despair is similar to the life review concept postulated by Robert N. Butler (1968). Life review refers to the process during which older adults reminisce about the past. This *critical*, self-analytical quality of the life review process helps the individual work through unresolved conflicts and promotes a sense of integration and satisfaction with oneself during the remaining years of life (Butler, 1963; Butler & Lewis, 1977).

The fairly common activity of reminiscing among the elderly serves important intrapersonal and interpersonal functions beyond and in addition to the life review process. Reminiscence in general helps individuals cope with the aging process, maintain self-esteem, and reinforce a sense of social attachment, belongingness, and continuity. Cormican (1977) stresses the adaptational qualities of typical reminiscence. She sees reminiscence as a method for releasing and rekindling personal strengths and a positive self-image.

Older people who are not depressed and bitter about their lives like to share their memories of good times with others. This kind of conversational sharing especially through group interaction is found to be very enjoyable by many older clients. For instance, inclusion of the socially isolated client in a reminiscence group may enable this person to gradually develop a sense of belongingness with other older people and therefore facilitate that person's desire to develop meaningful, new friendships.

Although reminiscence is now believed to have positive effects on those older people who engage in this process, this was not always the case. Butler and Lewis (1977) stress that in previous years the tendency of older people toward self-reflection and reminiscence was thought of as indicating a loss of recent memory and therefore a sign of aging.

In late life, people have a particularly vivid imagination and memory for the past and can recall with sudden and apparently remarkable clarity early life events. There is renewed ability to free associate and bring up material from the unconscious. In addition, there is a tendency to bring up troubling feelings about one's inevitable and approaching mortality.

Some older life reviewers have resolved their personal feelings about death. Others have not and may need help, first in recognizing the source of their anxieties and fears (death) and then in coming to terms with the inevitable (Butler & Lewis, 1977). Coming to terms with death is an emotional process that tests the mettle of each person. Invulnerability and immortality can no longer be maintained.

Life review is not necessarily limited to one's death. At various times, individuals may take stock of where they have been and where they plan to go. Such a mental process allows them to relive past events, sift them over, and deal with persistent conflicts (Turner & Helms, 1989).

However, as was previously stated, reviewing one's life is especially important for the elderly since it enables them to integrate those events they have observed or lived through. In addition, older people's expressions of feelings and/or reactions to the events can be verbalized. Some memories will undoubtedly produce nostalgia, others mild regret, and still others despair (Turner & Helms, 1989).

Although older people may have difficulty remembering some past and nearly forgotten events, "those who can think clearly and have good memory skills can bring clear and accurate episodes of their past to the conscious level" (Turner & Helms, 1989). In that case some events may be recalled very graphically and very vividly.

Life review may also be evident in dreams and thoughts. Older people frequently report dreams and nightmares that focus on the past and on death. According to Turner and Helms (1989) images or mental pictures of past events and symbols of death appear frequently in waking life as well, indicating that the life review is a highly visual process.

Older people are frequently plagued with a variety of painful losses. Thus an escape into the past may be a relief for some, and a more painful experience for others. In these latter instances, the older person's preoccupation with the past may cause panic, terror, or even suicide (Turner & Helms, 1989).

Guilt feelings may also play an important role as older persons review their lives. In these instances, older life reviews attempt to consolidate a meaningful judgment as to the manner in which their lives have been lived, and to prepare for death and cope with any fears of death. Were there any sins of omission and/or commission? Are there any wrongs for which they need to make atonement? Are there any grudges they need to resolve and let go of? These feelings should be dealt with seriously and not simply treated as meaningless expressions.

The life review process provides older persons with an opportunity to talk to an interested (active) listener. Older people have lived a lifetime in which they have experienced profound crises, and major historical and psychological events. Many have never had the opportunity to sift through such life crises as widowhood, divorce, sexual problems, retirement, chronic and/or acute illnesses, hospitalization and surgery, death and dying, and determine the impact these events have had on their lives. By getting in touch with past experiences, older life reviewers often not only resolve difficulties, but also achieve personal growth in the process.

Adversity is an inherent part of the human condition, but human beings grow in strength through meeting adversities. Life crises therefore represent opportunities for growth and mastery as well as sources of strain.

Life reviewers take an historical perspective of past experiences and how these have influenced subsequent personality development, behavior, and interpersonal relationships. Older people who have and can develop this ability can call on coping strategies that have been most effective in the past and adapt them to changed circumstances (Hooyman & Kiyak, 1988).

The life review taps primarily the retrospective memory of the older life reviewer. Retrospective memory involves the retention of information from the past. Once the life review process has begun, older persons may be quite surprised to find themselves able to recall events they previously thought had been forgotten. For instance, some excellent subjects for remembering include the sights and sounds, the moods and music of the twenties, the veterans of the various wars and the home front, the Great Depression, life on the farm, country fairs, fashion, fun and games, school days, and summer vacations. Birthdays also offer an opportunity to reflect on the passing years. Older life reviewers can be transported by their thoughts to another time and place, spend time with good friends no longer near, and communicate that time and place to someone who was not there.

Life reviews can be used in a variety of ways. Generally, the therapist asks older clients to construct their own life stories (Schaie & Willis, 1986). They might use family albums, diaries, yearbooks, old letters, and other memorabilia—and even interviews with family members and significant others to gain information about their behavior and emotions at crucial points in their lives.

By elaborating (working out in great detail or working out carefully) and formalizing (giving it form or shape; orderly in arrangement) the life review process, the therapist can explore suppressed guilt, long-standing fears and anxieties, and unfulfilled goals and ambitions—many of which have never been discussed until now.

As is often the case, by simply having someone who is willing to listen to one's own life story allows older life reviewers to integrate the disparate (different) features of their lives (Schaie & Willis, 1986). In other cases, by allowing unresolved conflicts to surface, client and therapist have an opportunity to deal with them directly.

The recovery of memories is believed to be one of the basic ingredients of the curative process (Butler, 1968). Butler sees this as a positive, therapeutic, and functional process that allows individuals to accept both the successes and failures of the past (Goldberg & Deutsch, 1977). The older life reviewer realizes that death is inevitable and makes the decision to make the most of the remaining years rather than regretting what has transpired in life.

Helping professionals generally associate self-awareness with health and lack of awareness with sickness or disease. It is in the last stage of life that the potential for self-awareness is possibly at its peak. Thus, older people can change and they continue to grow.

Theoretical Assumptions/Basic Concepts

The way (manner) in which individuals view themselves in relationship to time, their experiences, and other persons has spawned a number of interview-derived measurement techniques for use with the elderly. For instance, Kastenbaum (1965) applied developmental field theory to determine where a person is located in his/her "temporal life space." Spence (1968) derived a morale (adjustment) scale via cluster analysis that identifies four types of persons: unsettled planners, composed planners, disgruntled, and complacent. Thurnher (1973) described use of a "Life Evaluation Chart," a phenomenological evaluation by rating yearly satisfaction/dissatisfaction over the past and projected life span. The "Life Review Form" was developed by Butler and Lewis (1973). The "Life Review Form" is a personal mental health data form for older people. Data elicited include personal and family status, basic background information, medical and psychiatric information, and the like.

A number of qualities have been associated with successful aging. Such qualities include attitude toward life, personal independence, social acceptance, resilience, and patience. Life review (reminiscence) has been identified as a critical activity in old age.

In 1963, Butler postulated that reminiscence in the elderly was a *part of* a normal life review process brought on by the realization of approaching dissolution and death. Life review through reminiscence is characterized by the progressive return to consciousness of past experiences, particularly those associated with unresolved conflicts and disappointments (Butler, 1963). Apparently, these unresolved conflicts and disappointments can be looked at again and reintegrated. If the reintegration is successful, it can give new significance and meaning to an older life reviewer's life and prepare that person for death by mitigating fear and anxiety (Butler, 1963).

Since the 1960s a number of articles have been written about the life review process and its potential for increasing life satisfaction, extending cognitive function, alleviating depression, and sustaining a positive self-image. Thus, it appears that the life review process has numerous clinical applications.

When life review as a process is discussed, it is frequently linked with reminiscence. However, Merriam (1989) states that "simple reminiscence is defined as the recall of past experiences and is differentiated from life review reminiscing, which involves analysis and evaluation" (p. 761). Life review reminiscing can perhaps best be defined as "a detailed self-evaluation of personal experiences throughout life" (Huyck & Hoyer, 1982, p. 152). Thus, life review is the larger process that encompasses reminiscence.

Butler (1968) contends that "the life review, as a looking back process, proceeds toward personality reorganization" (p. 488). The personality reorganization that is believed to take place through the life review may, according to Butler (1968), "help to account for the evolution of such qualities as wisdom and serenity" (p. 490). So, once again, life review is not synonymous with reminiscence. Instead, life review is *inclusive of* reminiscence.

Perhaps the writings of Erikson (1950) and Butler (1963, 1968) have had the most profound effect on work in the area of reminiscence and the life review. Erikson's last stage of the epigenetic life cycle—that of ego integrity versus ego despair—posits that with approaching death the older person feels the need to review and evaluate his/her life. "The possessor of ego integrity is ready to defend the dignity of his own life style against all physical and economic threats" (Erikson, 1950, p. 268). It is this last stage in which older individuals must deal with impending death and accept their own lives as they have lived it.

If the older individual achieves ego integrity, then death will no longer be feared (Goldberg & Deutsch, 1977). However, if ego integrity has not been achieved, death continues to remain an issue for the older person. According to Erikson (1950) "despair expresses the feeling that the time is now short, too short for the attempt to start another life and to try out alternate roads to integrity" (p. 269).

Ego integrity essentially refers to a basic acceptance of one's life as having been inevitable, appropriate, and meaningful versus a sense of despair (fear of death) (Neugarten, 1968).

Butler's conceptualization of the life review includes reminiscing about the past from an analytical and evaluative perspective (Merriam, 1989). Apparently, life review is the process by which older people achieve Erikson's notion of ego integrity.

Peck (1968) identified in a more specific way three different kinds of psychological learning and adjustments that confront the elderly including the following: ego differentiation versus work-role preoccupation, body transcendence versus body preoccupation, and ego transcendence versus ego preoccupation. It is this last crisis, ego transcendence versus ego preoccupation that is germane to this discussion.

One of the crucial facts of old age is the appearance of the certainty of personal death (Peck, 1968). Older people know death is inevitable. However, the elderly are challenged to live the later years in a constructive way and to put death into perspective. The contributions older persons have made through children, the culture, and through friendships tend to exceed the limit of their lives. Peck (1968) does not see this as passive resignation or ego denial. Instead this kind of adaptation requires deep, active effort to make life more secure or more meaningful especially for those who will go on after one dies.

Those who persist on clinging to their own private, separate identities are denied the opportunity to contribute to the betterment of others' lives.

Themes in the Life Review

Older people frequently express a wish to undo some of the patterns of their life, that is, to *unritualize* behavior and *give* some newness to their experiences (Butler & Lewis, 1977). These people are undoubtedly looking for novel ways of dealing with life. Thus, workers should make a concerted effort to help life reviewers build new interests and new possibilities.

Older people are extremely conscious about time and may be more concerned with the *present* than anything else. Younger workers may have difficulty coming to grips with the fact that older people are not as future oriented as are their younger counterparts. Thus, workers must bring the life reviewer back to the here and now, the presentness.

Loss of loved ones, grief, and dysfunctioning of one's body as well as one's body parts are also common themes that surface during therapy (Butler & Lewis, 1977). Workers cannot bring back to life a loved one who has died, or restore youth to one's physical body, or absolve the older life reviewer from guilt. But workers can listen and help older people express, sort out, and deal with their feelings about these experiences. They can also help them examine the pluses in their lives as well as their ability to change and grow and deal with the realities of life.

In terms of assessment, it is important that background materials or information be collected. The end result should be a broad and thorough review of the person's history and current life situation (Butler and Lewis, 1977). Data collection ideally serves as an organizing function for both the worker and the client. It is helpful for workers because it enables them to get a better understanding of older clients and the situations in which they find themselves. The life history is organizing for clients because they can use the opportunity to review their lives, take inventory, and evaluate the meaning of their lives. The life history, therefore, becomes both diagnostic and therapeutic.

Generally speaking, life review therapy includes the taking of an extensive autobiography from the older person, and also from other family members as indicated. Such memories can be preserved through a variety of audiovisual aids. The older person may be encouraged to put together family albums, scrapbooks and other memorabilia.

"For those (older persons) who have children, a summary of feelings of parenting is important" (Butler & Lewis, 1977, p. 269). Likewise, for those who were unable to realize a deeply desired goal, an opportunity to examine those deep-seated feelings is also very important. A mixture of feelings may be expressed about these matters. Such feelings may include anger, resentment or bitterness, guilt, sadness, and shame. However, getting in touch with these deeply embedded feelings helps older life reviewers come to terms with such long standing memories.

Workers must accept the fact that older people can change, and that they are open to improvement by therapeutic procedures such as the life review. Therefore, any evidence pointing to the elderly as untreatable must be quickly abandoned. It is this kind of therapeutic pessimism that must be regarded as inappropriate, invalid, and counterproductive.

Although all elderly patients or clients may not be able to effectively interact or share personal experiences with the worker, there is the prevailing belief that most will benefit from the individual attention and the close interaction the life review allows. Life review is supportive. It involves listening, giving reassurance, showing interest and concern, and providing older patients with an opportunity to vent their feelings. Workers may also offer assistance when clients express troubling psychological thoughts particularly around their fears of approaching death. However, just spending time and talking with an older patient may be the most important therapeutic weapon workers have to offer. [Goldfarb (1955) demonstrated that even the brain damaged can benefit from psychotherapy.]

Studies on the Subject

There appears to be some support for the idea that the life review or reminiscing is related to a person's satisfaction with life (Havighurst & Glaser, 1972; Oliveria, 1977; Merriam & Cross, 1982; Haight, 1988). But, a couple of studies (Tekavec, 1982; Parsons, 1983) found no relationship between life satisfaction and adjustment.

In addition to life satisfaction and adjustment, it has been hypothesized that encouraging older persons to reminisce might improve morale and/or alleviate depression. The only relationship found in that regard appeared in an early study by McMahon and Rhudick (1964). They found that nondepressed subjects reminisced more than those who were depressed.

Studies linking reminiscence to enhancing self-concept have generally had mixed results. Lewis (1971) found that reminiscence supports the self in times of stress, whereas Boylin, Gordon, and Nehrke (1976) discovered a positive relationship between amount of reminiscence and ego integrity. However, four other studies reported no relationship between reminiscence and self-concept enhancement (McCarthy, 1977; Parlade, 1982; Parsons, 1983; Perrotta & Meacham, 1981–82).

Finally, two studies relating reminiscing to cognitive functioning had contradictory results. Hughston and Merriam (1982) found that women, not men, improved in cognitive functioning after a structured reminiscing program. McMahon and Rhudick (1964), however, reported that the tendency to reminisce was unrelated to the level of or decline in intellectual competency.

On the whole, the preponderance of evidence seems to indicate that the life review process, including reminiscence, functions as an adaptive mechanism or facilitates personality reorganization in late adulthood.

Other Related Theories and Concepts

Krapf's (1953) "time panic" concept, which refers to the terror one feels about the notion that time is running out, may also be pertinent to the life review process. Krafp (1953) discussed the atrophy (i.e., absence of a process rather than the presence of another, active, substitutive process) of the capacity to project oneself into the future.

Freud and most of his followers viewed the elderly with therapeutic pessimism. Others like Abraham (1949) and Grotjahn (1940) described some limited psychotherapeutic progress with older people. Goldfarb (1955), Linden (1953), Weinberg (1955), Butler (1963), and others devoted substantial amounts of their time and efforts in behalf of elderly patients. Goldfarb's brief therapy (1956), which is oriented toward amelioration of disturbed behavior, and Linden's work (1953) with group therapy are perhaps the best known of these efforts in therapy.

The existential component, i.e., the tendency of older people to seek meaning in their lives and come to terms with death, is apparent in therapeutic work with them. Other ideas include Buber's (1957) notion of the importance of relationship with others. Skinner's (1953) ideas regarding conditioning and extinction of dysfunctional patterns of behavior, and Jung's stages (1933) of development all apply to the elderly condition.

Step-by-Step Methods

1. There is no set pattern as to how the process of life review exhibits itself. The life review may first be observed in stray and seemingly intermittent thoughts about one's life and one's past (Butler, 1968). For instance, these thoughts may emerge in brief intermittent spurts or may become continuous. In addition, some thought patterns may undergo constant reintegration and reorganization at various consciousness levels (Turner & Helms, 1989).

Other clues to its existence include dreams and thoughts. The imagery of past events makes the life review a highly visual process. For instance, older people report the revival of sounds, tastes, and smells of early life (Butler, 1968). "I can still hear my mother playing the piano on Sunday afternoons," or "I can still see my father and his buddies arguing about who would win the World Series," or "I can still taste those delicious blueberry muffins my grandmother used to make." It is these kind of recollections that are frequently associated with the life review process.

Mirror-gazing is another manifestation of the life review. That is, the mirror becomes the tool into which older life reviewers can look into intently and steadily as a way to search for their lost youth. Some older people stare in wonder at the reflection they see. Some hardly recognize the image they see especially if there have been considerable changes (i.e., numerous wrinkles, heavy bags under the eyes, blotches on the skin, receding hair lines) in their physical appearance. Nevertheless, older persons may gently touch their faces again and again, smile or even frown, and talk to the reflection as part of the search and examination.

Mirror-gazing stimulates memories of by-gone years—or how older life reviewers once were—and enables them to recall a number of pleasant (i.e., a first date or kiss, wedding day, children, a favorite teacher, school days, family picnics and holidays), and not so pleasant (i.e., deaths, funerals, stockmarket crash) memories or events in their lives.

2. The life review sometimes proceeds *covertly*. However, the process may occur *overtly* as in the telling of memories to whomever will listen (Goldberg & Deutsch, 1977). At other times, it is conducted in monologue without another person hearing it. It is in many ways similar to the psychotherapeutic situation in which a person is reviewing his/her life in order to understand the present circumstances. Although the life review process is active, the content of the older reviewer's life unfolds slowly. This is not to suggest that the process is necessarily orderly. Some older people may be more preoccupied with certain events that happened at particular times in their lives, rather than the whole of it.

In its mild form the life review is reflected in increased reminiscence, mild nostalgia, and/or mild regret. In severe form the life review is reflected in anxiety, guilt, despair, and depression (Butler, 1968). In the extreme, preoccupation of the older life reviewer with the past may result in suicide. "The most tragic life review is that in which a person decides life was a total waste" (Butler & Lewis, 1977, p. 50). So, although the life review is thought to be a normative process, practitioners should be aware that its varied manifestations may include psychopathological ones.

3. Prompted by a typical stimulus such as a family celebration or an exciting trip, the life reviewer selects particular past experiences to come to mind, anyone of which could be selected to reminisce about. However, the one selected seems to have special meaning to the older reminiscer.

4. Workers should listen attentively and thoughtfully to the reminiscences of older people. They should also listen for the feelings that

accompany the reviewer's remarks. For instance, when talking about his/her growing up as a child, the reviewer may be animated when revealing childhood pranks, only to change his/her remarks to one of sadness over the loss of a childhood friend or the death of a pet. Continued discussion may bring on periods of tears and joy. There may be silences between the reminiscer's reviews of the past, but the worker must listen to the silences.

The reminiscences of older people should not be construed by the worker either as their living in the past, or as a preoccupation with themselves. In the past, this attitude on the worker's part has resulted in negative comments about the process as boring, meaningless, and time-consuming (Butler & Lewis, 1977).

5. Some older reviewers may require several sessions to tell their stories; others may require only a few. The use of family albums, scrapbooks, autograph books, and other memorabilia, the searching out of genealogies and pilgrimages back to places of importance, all evoke crucial memories, responses, and understanding in clients (Butler & Lewis, 1977). Memories such as these can be preserved by means of tape recordings and videos.

The worker may be both active and passive. For example, the worker may need to *actively question*, reassure, and/or explain. The worker may be passive by *listening* as the older life reviewer is allowed to recapture some of the memorable events of the past.

6. The goals of the life review include the following: (1) to deal with the whole range of life cycle events, (2) to enable older clients to review, renew, and evaluate their own past experiences, and (3) to enable the life reviewer to come to terms with death.

Other Processes and Tasks Related to Life Review

1. Establishing rapport. If anything meaningful is to be accomplished during the life review, clients must gain trust, and feel that they can involve themselves in a relationship in which they are free to be themselves. In addition, the worker must be perceived by the older client as understanding and genuinely interested in their reminiscences. In extending this concept to groups, "the task for clients older life reviewers is twofold, for they must not only develop trust in the worker but in other group members as well" (Hepworth & Larsen, 1990, p. 219).

Workers must also manifest various values and attitudes including acceptance, nonjudgmental attitude, clients' right of self-determination, respect for clients' worth and dignity, confidentiality, uniqueness and individuality, and problem-solving capacities.

2. As older clients are encouraged to get in touch with past experiences, workers must be aware that these descriptions are not neutral or

emotionless. Clients frequently express strong feelings about the facts as they review them. Some older clients will manifest their feelings through expressions of anger, joy, and sadness quite openly. Other clients will be less overt in their expressions of emotion.

Workers, therefore, need to be alert throughout the life review process for unexpressed feelings and respond in a way that would be helpful if the feelings were expressed. This means that workers must encourage older life reviewers to ventilate feelings that have been previously restrained or suppressed. This expression, whether spontaneous or encouraged, can bring about a great deal of relief. Hollis (1972) points out that "verbalization is an important way of reducing feelings" (p. 104).

Verbalization of guilt feelings of a life reviewer is more complicated. "The worker's attitude toward the guilt is of primary importance," according to Hollis (1972, p. 104). For instance, ventilation in this case should be followed by sustainment (i.e., expressions of the worker's interest in and concern for the older reviewer, and of continued good will toward that person). In other words, the worker conveys an attitude of acceptance toward the older person. Acceptance in this context means that whether the worker approves or disapproves of what older life reviewers have revealed about themselves, the worker continues to feel and convey a positive, understanding attitude toward them (Hollis, 1972).

3. Workers may become aware that the more older people relive past experiences, one event recalls another. Elderly people may derive marked gratification from talking freely about themselves. In fact, this may be the only time in their lives they have been given permission to indulge themselves.

A Case Example: Mrs. Payne

Background Information

Mrs. Payne, age 79, has been living alone ever since the death of her husband 4 years ago. Although her adult children, two sons and two daughters, have expressed concern about her living alone, Mrs. Payne made it very clear that she did not want to move in with any of her children. From all indications, Mrs. Payne appeared to have made a smooth adjustment following her husband's death. She continued to prepare her own meals and to do light housework. She visited sick friends, played bridge at least once a week, and continued to attend church on a fairly regular basis.

This active life-style apparently suited Mrs. Payne because it helped her take her mind off of her husband's death. A few of Mrs. Payne's closest relatives and friends expressed delight that she was able to keep up such a lively pace. On the other hand, they cautioned her to try and slow down, especially since she "wasn't getting any younger."

However, Mrs. Payne insisted that she enjoyed the active pace she was able to maintain. After all, she quickly informed all of those concerned that she was in perfectly good health. She had no chronic health problems (only a mild arthritic condition in her left hand), and was recently given a clean bill of health by her doctor.

Mrs. Payne's children were also pleasantly surprised at their mother's obviously good adjustment. The two daughters, both married and with families of their own, live in the same city as their mother and take turns visiting her on a regular basis. The two sons, both of whom are married and live out of state, call their mother on a regular basis.

Mrs. Payne also has a few close friends with whom she is in frequent contact.

Presenting Problem

Two days after her 80th birthday, Mrs. Payne fell and broke her hip. She was hospitalized for about a month, and on release learned that she had also developed a severe case of arthritis. And even though she managed to move around the hospital with the aid of a walker, her movements were restricted and curtailed because of her painful arthritic condition. Any stress that Mrs. Payne experienced caused the arthritis to flare up.

The physician advised that Mrs. Payne be kept as comfortable as possible and that she engage only in essential activities. He informed the daughters that their mother was experiencing some degree of difficulty in bathing, dressing, and in eating, and that she was in no position to perform any of her usual household chores. The physician was also concerned about Mrs. Payne's living arrangements and recommended that she be placed in a nursing home where she would be provided with the skilled care needed on a 24-hour basis. He mentioned two other options if the first was unacceptable to them. The additional recommendations were private duty care in Mrs. Payne's own home, or moving in with one of her daughters.

Since Mrs. Payne was scheduled to be discharged in a couple of weeks, the doctor advised that a realistic plan be devised as soon as possible. As a start, a hospital social worker was assigned to the case.

Worker Contacts

Mrs. Payne was first interviewed by the worker the following day. The worker informed Mrs. Payne that her primary purpose in working with her was to assess her situation, to determine the impact of her physical condition on her psychosocial functioning, to answer any questions she might have about her situation, and to prepare her for discharge planning from the hospital.

The worker was quite impressed with Mrs. Payne's understanding of her condition, and of her willingness to examine the options available to her on her discharge from the hospital. However, Mrs. Payne made it clear to the worker that she would not entertain any thoughts of moving in with either of her daughters. The worker informed Mrs. Payne that she respected her decision and had no intention of forcing her into accepting an option that was not acceptable to her.

However, the worker advised Mrs. Payne that, in the best interest of everyone, she would like to arrange for a meeting with Mrs. Payne and her two daughters, if that was acceptable to her. The worker added that it was important to try and work out the best possible plan.

Mrs. Payne indicated a willingess to arrange for such a meeting because she believed that this would provide her with an opportunity to convince her daughters that with a little help, she could continue to remain in her own home.

The worker mentioned that she was pleased that Mrs. Payne was open to the idea of a family meeting, and informed Mrs. Payne that she (the worker) would take responsibility of contacting the daughters.

The worker contacted the two daughters who agreed to come to the hospital to meet with their mother and the worker 3 days later. Both daughters arrived promptly for the scheduled meeting, and seemed anxious to arrive at an amicable solution to the problem.

The worker broached the subject by pointing out that since Mrs. Payne would be discharged from the hospital in about 2 weeks, it was essential that the family try to work out the best possible plan regarding her living arrangements. The worker also stressed the importance of everyone's input including Mrs. Payne's. The worker reminded the family that even though their mother was making progress by walking with the aid of a walker, she was still in no position to live at home on her own without any other supports. The daughters agreed that they had no intention of letting their mother return to her home to be on her own. Mrs. Payne quickly replied, "I'm not going to live anywhere else except in my own home, I'll be okay. I won't move in with anybody else!"

The worker admired Mrs. Payne's tenacity to be on her own for as long as possible, but wondered how she could do that now given the reality of her situation. Mrs. Payne mentioned the possibility of having a 24-hour duty nurse for as long as that could be arranged based on her insurance policies. She also mentioned the possibility of having her daughters come over during the day to spend a few hours with her—as their schedules allowed. The daughters agreed that would be an acceptable plan to them, but were quick to point out that if her condition worsened, they would most definitely investigate some other possible options.

The worker informed Mrs. Payne that her medical insurance was such that it would allow for 6 weeks coverage of a live-in 24-hour private duty nurse following her discharge from the hospital. Mrs. Payne and her daughters were pleasantly surprised by the news. Mrs. Payne expressed relief at the thought of returning to her own home. She attributed the good news to the foresight of her husband who always had her best interest at heart.

The worker acknowledged the pride and joy Mrs. Payne exhibited as she talked about her husband.

The Life Review/Reminisce Process

The worker sensed the deep desire of Mrs. Payne to talk about her husband. She observed the album that Mrs. Payne had placed on the table next to her bed. Mrs. Payne identified each person in the family album, but it was the pictures of her husband that she kept staring at and fondly talking about. Mrs. Payne began to sob softly, and repeated several times how much she missed him. The worker encouraged Mrs. Payne to relate how she had met her husband. The rest of the family meeting was spent with Mrs. Payne reminiscing and sharing memories about her husband and what a good husband and father he was.

She indicated that when she first met her husband over 60 years ago, she was a young girl of 16 years and she really was not attracted to him right away. However, he must have been smitten with her, because he kept asking her for a date until she finally agreed. She was 17 years of age at the time, and in her last year of high school when she went out on her first date with her husband to be. He was 18 and employed as an apprentice with the town's only newspaper. Mrs. Payne was impressed with Mr. Payne's job, and felt that he could only advance in this position. The Paynes married 2 years later and began a family of their own. She related that when the Depression came his parents insisted that they and their two young children move in with them. Although Mrs. Payne was opposed to this, her husband convinced her it was the best solution in the interim especially since he had lost his job.

Mrs. Payne became sullen as she painfully recalled the poor treatment she received at the hands of her husband's mother. The young Mrs. Payne apparently did all of the housework, while the older Mrs. Payne took care of the children until her son came home from job hunting. She felt resentful that her mother-in-law had literally taken over the care of her children, and vented a great deal of anger at her husband for not taking sides with her. She recalled that this was the only time in her marriage that she felt her husband was not supportive of her. Mrs. Payne also remembered that this was perhaps the most stressful period in their marriage.

It was during the Depression, and even though her husband was able to find temporary employment from time to time, he did not want to risk moving out of his parents' home until he had secured a permanent job. Fourteen months later, Mrs. Payne recalled the wonderful sense of pleasure and relief she felt after learning that her husband had found a job. By this time, she was pregnant with their third child, but was very eager to go out immediately to apartment hunt with her husband.

The worker and Mrs. Payne's daughters listened with interest and enthusiasm at these recollections. The worker acknowledged the pleasure, the relief, and happiness that exuded from Mrs. Payne when she learned that her husband had located a job. Mrs. Payne began to cry softly as she said, "Oh, yes it was wonderful news. I remember feeling as if the world had just been lifted from my shoulders, and I solemnly vowed that no matter what happens to me I would never live with anybody other than my husband again." And, as if to substantiate this vow, she said, "Now you see why I feel so strongly about being on my own in my own home."

The daughters indicated their understanding of their mother's position and confirmed once again their willingess to respect her wishes, and to do all that they could to make Mrs. Payne's plan work. Mrs. Payne expressed delight and said she felt relieved that they were able to talk about these things. The worker commented that she was too, and that she hoped that Mrs. Payne would be able to share other recollections with her children.

After the interview, the daughters commented to the worker that they originally had no idea why their mother was so adamant about not moving in with them, but that now they understood. The worker stressed that the family meeting was beneficial to each of them. She mentioned that she would continue to meet with Mrs. Payne on a daily basis until her discharge from the hospital. She also stated that she would check with the physical therapist to determine the extent of her progress. The daughters were encouraged to solidify their plans with their mother in order that her transition from the hospital to home would be as smooth as possible. The worker made it clear that she would take responsibility for arranging for a 24-hour duty nurse to assist Mrs. Payne for the first 6 weeks, and of looking into the possibility of arranging for homemaker services and transportation services whenever Mrs. Payne needed to see her physician.

The daughters thanked the worker for her helpfulness and for the excellent care their mother received during her hospital stay.

During subsequent visits, the worker found Mrs. Payne ready to open up and reminisce about a number of events in her life. The worker's time was mostly spent listening and empathizing with her as she described each event in detail. She told of her joys, frustrations, fears, and sorrows. On the whole, it seemed, that Mrs. Payne was quite satisfied with the way her life had turned out.

On the day of discharge, the daughters and some of their children came to pick up Mrs. Payne. The worker pointed to the progress Mrs. Payne had made in physical therapy as well as that which they had made sharing their memories with each other.

By engaging in the life review process, Mrs. Payne was able to work through, integrate, and come to terms with a very stressful period in her life. It is obvious to the reader that the painful feelings associated with living in the home of her husband's parents were deeply embedded within her, and were directly related to Mrs. Payne's refusal to move in with either of her daughters. However, by relating this painful experience, Mrs. Payne gained insight into why she was so determined to remain in her own home. Thus, Mrs. Payne's ability to go back in time and recall a specific event was of primary importance to the crystallization of her own personal concerns and philosophy about living in someone else's home.

Both the worker and Mrs. Payne's daughters were able to get a better sense of how moving in with her husband's parents had affected her life, and how it shaped her thinking over time. This was, no doubt, probably a growth-fulfilling experience for Mrs. Payne as well.

Strengths and Weaknesses

The life review/reminiscence, like any other helping method, has its strengths and weaknesses (or positive and negative aspects). The positive aspects of the life review are as follows:

1. Life review can lead to an honest appraisal of self-worth and a realistic awareness of present vulnerabilities and mortality.
2. Life review is a method that enables one to come to grips with previously unresolved conflicts and leads to a more positive self-concept.
3. Life review may provide a real attempt to change one's thoughts and actions. For instance, the older life reviewer may wish to right old wrongs or make friends with previous enemies.

4. There are those who believe that life review/reminiscence usually increases the adults' feelings of youth, competence, attractiveness, and closeness to others (Fallot, 1977; Perschbacher, 1984).

Reviewing one's life experiences is considered by those in the field to be a constructive process that enables the reviewer to positively assess his or her contributions and accomplishments. To substantiate this, Butler and Lewis (1977) stress that the life review is a necessary and healthy process and should be recognized in daily life as well as used in the mental health care of older people.

Some of the positive results of reviewing one's life include making up with enemies, coming to acceptance of mortal life, a sense of serenity, pride in accomplishment, and a feeling of having done one's best. It gives older reviewers an opportunity to decide what to do with the time left to them and to work out emotional and material legacies.

Although negative experiences (see below) have been reported by workers whose clients or patients have undergone the life review process, the bulk of experiences seem to be positive. Patients themselves can attest to the growth-producing, constructive alterations in personality and behavior that were most likely the consequence of the life review.

The negative aspects of the life review/reminiscence are as follows:

1. The life review process can lead to a sense of bitterness, regret, and despair. It can, in some instances raise anxiety and feelings of depression over what may be perceived as a wasted life (Schaie & Willis, 1986). In such instances, the older individual does not accept what has happened, but regrets past happenings and is extremely uncomfortable about them now. It is these individuals who make their remaining years miserable, live in dread of death, and yearn for things to be different from what they presently are. Responses such as these can be handled skillfully by a trained professional. Because of the nature of the underlying feelings and emotions that might surface, it is of primary importance that a skilled clinician be involved. Schaie and Willis assert that "use of life review by non-professionals might be fraught with potential danger" (p. 441).

2. The life review process is often time-consuming and the life reviewer may have to review and repeat the same experiences over and over again. This may seem as if the older person is preoccupied with him/herself.

3. Younger workers or therapists who work with the elderly may devalue the content of the information given, especially if it involves things that happened in the past. Some may even regard the tendency to reminisce as dysfunctional. Even earlier psychotherapists such as

Rechtschaffen (1959) were concerned about the emotional price paid when a patient, especially an older patient, reviewed the failures of the past. Butler (1968) contends, "it is probably reflective of psychiatrists' own countertransference concerns that the dangers of reviewing one's life in psychotherapy should be emphasized: underlying is the implication that truth is dangerous" (p. 494).

The varied behavioral affective states resulting from the life review include severe depression, states of panic, intense guilt, and constant obsessional rumination. Life events that are particularly difficult to bear and hard to face are forced retirement, death of spouse, especially when the marriage was pleasant, death of an adult child, major physical health problems, and so on. Life reviewers who face these problems may try to retreat less to the past, avoid the present, and put great emphasis on the future. The future is frequently perceived by these people as being able to deliver all their unmet wishes. Unfortunately for them, time is running out.

Conclusion

Life review is a looking-back process set in motion by the realization of approaching death. However, life review is not necessarily limited to one's death. People of all ages review their lives. But the life review process is more commonly observed in older persons because they have more time for self-reflection. Reviewing one's life may be a response to various crises of which imminent death appears to be one instance (Butler, 1968).

Whereas the positive side of the life review is very much like Erikson's ego integrity, the negative side can result in despair. Some pain, manifesting itself in the form of depression or anxiety, is expected as a person begins to recall certain events of the past (Goldberg & Deutsch, 1977). However, the process also contributes to the evolution of such characteristics as candor, serenity, and wisdom among certain of the elderly (Butler, 1968).

A resolution of life conflicts undoubtedly lifts a heavy psychological weight off the minds of elderly reminiscers. It is the life review process that accounts for increased reminiscence in the elderly (Butler, 1968).

References

Abraham, K. (1949). The applicability of psycho-analytic treatment to patients at an advanced age. In *Selected papers of psychoanalysis*. London: Hougarth Press.

Beaver, M. L., & Miller, D. (1985). *Clinical social work practice with the elderly.* Homewood, IL: The Dorsey Press.

Boylin, W., Gordon, S. K., & Nehrke, M. F. (1976). Reminiscing and ego integrity in institutionalized elderly males. *Gerontologist, 16,* 118–124.

Buber, M. (1975). The William Alanson white memorial lectures (Fourth Series). *Psychiatry, 20,* 95–129.

Butler, R. N. (1963). The life review: An interpretation of reminiscence in the aged. *Psychiatry, 26,* 65–76. Also in B. L. Neugarten (Ed.), *Middle age and aging* (pp. 486–496). Chicago: The University of Chicago Press, 1968.

Butler, R. N. (1968). The life review: An interpretation of reminiscence in the aged. *Psychiatry, 20,* 95–129.

Butler, R. N., & Lewis, M. I. (1973). *Aging and mental health: Positive psychosocial approaches.* St. Louis: C. V. Mosby.

Butler, R. N., & Lewis, M. I. (1977). *Aging and mental health: Positive psychosocial approaches.* St. Louis: C. V. Mosby.

Cormican, E. (1977). Task centered model for work with the aged. *Social Casework, 58,* 490–493.

Erikson, E. (1950). *Childhood and society.* New York: Norton.

Fallot, R. D. (1977). *The impact on mood of verbal reminiscing in later adulthood.* Paper presented at the annual convention of the American Psychological Association, San Francisco, California.

Goldberg, S. R., & Deutsch, F. (1977). *Life span and individual and family development.* Monterey, CA: Brooks/Cole.

Goldfarb, A. L. (1955). Psychotherapy of aged persons. IV. One aspect of the therapeutic situation and aged patients. *Psychoanalytic Review, 42,* 100–187.

Goldfarb, A. (1956). The rationale for psychotherapy with older persons. *American Journal Medical Science, 232,* 181–185.

Grotjahn, M. (1940). Psychoanalytic investigation of a 71 year old man with senile dementia. *Psychoanalytic quarterly, 9,* 80–97.

Haight, B. K. (1988). The therapeutic role of a structured life review process in homebound elderly subjects. *Journal of Gerontology, 43,* 40–44.

Havighurst, R. J., & Glasser, R. (1972). An exploratory study of reminiscence. *Journal of Gerontology, 27,* 245–253.

Hepworth, D. H., & Larson, J. A. (1990). *Direct social work practice: Theory and skills,* 3rd ed. Belmont, CA: Wadsworth.

Hollis, F. (1972). *Casework: A psychosocial therapy.* New York: Random House.

Hooyman, N. R., & Kiyak, H. A. (1988). *Social gerontology: A multidisciplinary perspective.* Boston: Allyn and Bacon.

Hughston, G., & Merriam, S. (1982). Reminiscence: A nonformal technique for improving cognitive functioning in the aged. *International Journal of Aging and Human Development, 15,* 139–149.

Huyck, M. H., & Hoyer, W. J. (1982). *Adult development and aging.* Belmont, CA: Wadsworth.

Jung, C. G. (1933). *Modern man in search of a soul.* New York: Harcourt, Brace and World.

Kastenbaum, R. (1965). Engrossment and perspective in later life: A developmental field approach. In R. Kastenbaum (Ed.), *Contributions of psychobiology to aging* (pp. 3–18). New York: Springer.

Krapf, E. E. (1953). On Aging. *Proceedings of the Royal Society of Medicine (London),* 46, 957–964.

Lewis, C. N. (1971). Reminiscing and self-concept in old age. *Journal of Gerontology,* 26, 240–243.

Linden, M. E. (1953). Group psychotherapy with institutionalized senile women: Study in gerontology in human relations. *International Journal of Group Psychotherapy,* 3, 150–151.

McCarthy, H. (1977). Time perspective and aged persons' attributions of their life experiences. *Gerontologist,* 17, 97.

McMahon, A. W., & Rhudick, P. J. (1964). Reminiscing: Adaptational significance in the aged. *Archives of General Psychiatry,* 10, 292–298.

Merriam, S. B. (1989). The structure of simple reminiscence. *Gerontologist,* 29, 761–767.

Merriam, S. B., & Cross, L. H. (1982). Adulthood and reminiscence: A descriptive study. *Educational Gerontology,* 8, 275–290.

Neugarten, B. L. (1968). Adult personality: Toward a psychology of the life cycle. In B. L. Neugarten (Ed.). *Middle age and aging* (pp. 137–147). Chicago: University of Chicago Press.

Newman, B. M., & Newman, P. R. (1987). *Development through life psychosocial approach.* Chicago: Dorsey Press.

Oliveria, O. H. (1977). *Understanding old people: Patterns of reminiscing in elderly people and their relationship life satisfaction.* Unpublished Ph.D dissertation, University of Tennessee, Knoxville.

Parlade, R. J. (1982). *Reminiscence and problem-solving approaches: A comparison study with a geriatric population.* Unpublished Ph.D dissertation, University of Georgia, Athens.

Parson, W. A. (1983). *Reminiscence group therapy with older persons: A field experiment.* Unpublished doctoral dissertation, University of Florida, Gainesville.

Peck, R. C. (1968). Psychosocial developments in the second half of life. In B. L. Neugarten (Ed.), *Middle age and aging* (pp. 88–92). Chicago: University of Chicago Press.

Perrotta, P., & Meacham, J. A. (1981–82). Can reminiscing intervention alter depression and self-esteem? *International Journal of Aging and Human Development,* 14, 23–30.

Perschbacher, R. (1984). An application of reminiscence in an activity setting," *Gerontologist,* 24, 343–345.

Rechtschaffen, A. (1959). Psychotherapy with geriatric patients: A review of the literature. *Journal of Gerontology,* 14, 73–84.

Schaie, K. W., & Willis, S. L. (1986). *Adult development and aging,* 2nd ed. Boston: Little, Brown.

Skinner, B. F. (1953). *Science and human behavior.* New York: Macmillan.

Spence, D. L. (1968). The role of futurity in aging adaptation. *Gerontologist,* 8, 180–183.

Tekavec, C. M. R. (1982). *Self actualization, reminiscence and life satisfaction in retired and employed older adults.* Unpublished doctoral dissertation, California School of Professional Psychology, Fresno, California.

Thurnher, M. (1973). Adaptability of life review interview to study of adult development. In L. F. Jarvik, C. Eisdorfer, & J. E. Blum (Eds.), *Intellectual functioning in adults* (pp. 137–142). New York: Springer.

Turner, J. S., & Helms, D. B. (1989). *Contemporary adulthood*, 4th ed. Fort Worth: Holt, Rinehart & Winston.

Weinberg, S. K. (1955). A sociological analysis of a schizophrenic type. In A. M. Rose (Ed.), *Mental health and mental disorder* (p. 220). New York: W. W. Norton.

4

Validation Therapy

NAOMI FEIL

Introduction: Purpose

There is a new breed of very old people burgeoning. Pneumonia is no longer "the old person's cure." The person who used to die at age 75 now lives to age 90. The old have become the old–old. For the first time in history, people live so long that some, who have not achieved integrity, enter a new stage of life. They face a new challenge: The struggle to complete unfinished tasks that have been swept under the rug for a lifetime. The Validation worker empathizes with the struggle of the disoriented old person. "Treatment is based on the premise that there is some logic behind all behavior, even disoriented behavior. Awareness of [present] reality is not the goal; the goal is to understand the personal meaning underlying an individual's behavior. Through empathic listening, the therapist attempts to discover the patient's view of reality in order to make meaningful emotional contact" (Dietch, Hewett, & Jones, 1989). The Validation worker becomes a trusted, nurturing "other." The disoriented old person feels safe. Dormant speech returns, anxiety lessens, gait improves, eyes light, and people begin to interact with others to the maximum of their capacity. They do not withdraw inward to vegetation. They express (verbally or nonverbally) feelings of well-being. Validated, they die in peace (Godemont, 1989; Fritz, 1986).

Background/Basic Concepts

Disoriented old–olds restore the incomplete task in order to resolve it before they die. Nature's changes, due to aging and increasing destruction of brain tissue, help them retreat to past-time. When loss of eyesight, hearing, recent memory, mobility, and sensory acuity blot out present time, the very old person can substitute the mind's eye, past sounds, remote memories, and old sensations. The person can no longer tell chronological clock-time. They have lost the logical thinking ability to separate seconds, from minutes, from hours, and from days. They measure their lifetime: they track time by memories, rather than by seconds on a clock. The very old disoriented person has now entered the stage beyond Erikson's "Integrity versus Despair" (Erikson, 1950). For the Validation therapy, this final life stage is called, "Resolution versus Vegetation." The final task is to resolve unfinished business before death in order to die in peace.

Validation therapy includes three characteristics:

1. A developmental theory for late onset demented very old people, now often called, "Probable Alzheimer's Diseased or with related disordered" (Jones, 1985);
2. A way of categorizing the behaviors of disoriented old people into four discrete, progressive substages, i.e., Malorientation, Time Confused, Repetitive Motion, and Vegetation;
3. Specific methods for communicating (verbally and nonverbally) with person in each substage.

The author began to develop the Validation method of relating to very old disoriented residents in 1963, diagnosed by the psychiatrist as "senile psychotic" or "organically brain damaged, with circulatory insufficiency." At autopsy, the majority of these residents were found to have Alzheimer's plaques and neurofibrillary degeneration (Weil, 1966). Reviewing each resident's case history, and interviewing family members, it was found that most of these residents had led normal lives until they reached their late seventh or eighth decade. Increasing physical deterioration accompanied increasing role losses: loss of work, home, spouse, parent-role, friends, and/or social activities. They would not or could not respond to present day stimuli in external reality. The author tried remotivation, reality orientation, behavior modification, and confrontation therapy in small group meetings. They would withdraw, vegetate, and become increasingly hostile when confronted with present reality, or with attempts to help them gain insights into their behaviors (Feil, 1967).

Here are three typical case summaries.

Case One. Mrs. F., age 88 years, diagnosed "senile dementia," stared into space, shouting: "There's Mother. She's got my laundry. I have to help her carry it. She might trip and fall." The therapist tried to orient Mrs. F. to present reality. She told Mrs. F. in a quiet, calm voice: "You are 88 years old. Your mother is dead." Mrs. F. shook her head and walked away from the therapist, muttering: "Well, I know that. And you know that. But my mother doesn't know that. She's carrying too much laundry, and I have to help her, so get out of my way!"

About 2 months later, the therapist verbalized Mrs. F's need to help her mother: "Mrs. F., your mother worked so hard. You must have been a wonderful help to her. You love her very much, don't you?" Mrs. F. nodded, burst into tears, and sobbed: "She was a wonderful mother. I should have helped her more. She died when she was only 30 years old." Mrs. F. knew that her mother was dead. She had to restore her mother with her mind's eye in order to finally express her grief and guilt. After 4 weeks of Validation, Mrs. F's facial muscles relaxed, her voice became less frantic, she no longer stared into space. She began to interact with the therapist. When the therapist stopped arguing with her and listened to her, she stopped calling for her mother. When her feelings were validated and acknowledged, her grief lessened.

Case Two. Mr. T. worsened after each contact. He was abusive, uncontrolled, and refused to take his medications. He had to be restrained and tranquilized for his own protection. He untied his restraints like Houdini. His language was abusive. Reality orientation made him worse. When the therapist gently reminded him of present reality, that he could no longer walk and that he was now living in the nursing home, he shouted: "God damn S.O.B. get me outta here." Members of the Validation team tried behavior modification, walking away whenever Mr. T. began to swear, and rewarded him when he was quiet. His swearing increased and he began spitting at staff and residents. The therapist tried to understand and validate his anger: "Mr. T., you hate being in this home don't you?" He stopped swearing for a moment and looked at the therapist, nodding his head. She continued: "You were a traveling salesman, weren't you? You used to move around, and people liked you. Now, you're stuck in this wheelchair. You can't stand feeling useless. You want to move." Mr. T. nodded and he and the therapist began to reminisce about his life as a salesman. After 6 weeks of daily Validation, his abusive behaviors lessened, and the therapist's tension was reduced. Through validation, Mr. T. had lessened the therapist's burn-out.

Case Three. In honor of the birth of the therapist's son, Mrs. J., age 88, gave the therapist some play money. The therapist reality oriented her and told her that play money has no value. Mrs. J. began to cry, and would not look at the therapist or talk to her. Mrs. J. had been a well-known philanthropist. She was restoring her dignity by giving the money. She was using the money to survive feelings of uselessness. She wanted to be a "giver of money" until she died. In fact, the therapist rejected her need to be useful by orienting her to the therapist's reality.

Mrs. J's reality and the therapist's were different. The therapist could leave the nursing home to care for her new baby. She was useful and needed. Mrs. J. had lost her role as a philanthropist. She could never leave the nursing home. In her wisdom, Mrs. J. used the play money to survive despair.

Neither reality orientation nor remotivation techniques helped these very old disoriented residents face present reality. Nor could they relate to the objects that the therapist used to stimulate awareness of present time in a remotivation group. Their attention span was too short. They would examine a flower for a moment, then they would drop it on the floor. They could not see the poem or newspaper. They were not able to look outside the window to establish the season of the year. They could remember neither the present day nor the date, nor did they care about the President of the United States. They remembered Woodrow Wilson, who was the President when life held meaning. Nor could they achieve new insights into their behaviors. These demented very old people had suffered massive loss of logical, cognitive, analytical thinking capacity. They could not intellectually achieve an "Aha" in order to change their behaviors. They did not want to change. They had lost self-reflective awareness. They withdrew when the therapist tried to inject new insights.

This led the author to develop a new approach that did not insist on participation in present reality and did not result in withdrawal inward. When the therapist listened with empathy, without judgment, the anxiety of the very disoriented nursing home residents lessened. They cried less, they talked more, they sat up, they began to become less self-centered and listened to each other (Feil, 1972). When their feelings were ignored, with little stimulation from the outside, their negative behaviors worsened. Isolated and sedated, the very old person often began to withdraw inward to vegetation.

Theoretical Assumptions

Eight basic helping principles developed by behavioral, analytical, and humanistic psychologies underlie the theoretical assumptions in Validation:

1. Accept clients without judgment: To validate is to accept without interjecting an opinion; without judging whether the facts are true or false.
2. The therapist cannot give insight or change behaviors if the client is not ready or willing to change.
3. Know the client as a unique individual.

4. Feelings that are expressed, acknowledged, and validated by the therapist will lessen. When feelings are ignored or denied, they gain strength. According to von Franz-Hillman (1971), Carl Jung wrote: "The cat ignored, becomes the tiger."

5. Each stage of life has a unique task that individuals must face at a prescribed time in the human life span. One must struggle to accomplish the task before he/she can successfully move on to the next task.

6. An ignored task demands to be heard at a later stage and be put back into place.

7. Early, primary, well-established learning survives and often returns when recent memory fails (homeostasis).

8. The brain is not the exclusive regulator of behavior in very old age. Behavior is a combination of physical, social, and intrapsychic changes that happen during the life span.

Autopsies have shown that many very old persons survive significant brain damage and stay relatively oriented, whereas others become severely disoriented with the same amount of damage to brain tissue (Wells, 1977). Those who survive to a very old age, who have denied an important life task, often enter a final, Resolution versus Vegetation stage. These old-old restore unfinished issues from the past in their struggle to complete their tasks in order to give their life meaning and to die in peace.

Step-by-Step Methods

The Validation therapist must first assess the stage of disorientation in order to apply the correct Validation technique. There are four discrete, progressive substages that occur in the final resolution struggle:

1. Malorientation
2. Time Confusion
3. Repetitive Motion
4. Vegetation

To correctly assess the stage of disorientation, the Validation worker completes the Validation History and Baseline Behavior form (Figure 1) by following these steps:

1. Observe the verbal and nonverbal behaviors.
2. Explore to determine the following: orientation to time, place, person; speech; mobility; logical thinking capacities; sensory acuity; reflective self-awareness; social controls; interactions with peers, family, and staff.

Figure 1.   History and Baseline Behavior

Precautions _____

RESIDENT: Age, Sex, Race, Birthplace, Employment history.	FAMILY BACKGROUND: SOCIO-ECONOMIC STATUS. Religious status. Close family relationships. (Names)
HEALTH INFORMATION: MEDICAL DIAGNOSIS. Length of hospitalization. Medications given. Previous mental or physical illness. Speech. Degree of loss to: Eyes, Ears, Mobility, Sensory acuity, recent memory?	STAGE OF DISORIENTATION: Maloriented? Time confused? Repetitive motion? Psychotic behavior? Oriented? Fluctuate between which stages?
ACTION PATTERN: Customary response to crisis. What precipitated hospitalization? Typical relationships. Past traumas. Typical response to aging losses. Physical behavior: Muscles, movement in space, eye-contact, response to touch.	IN THIS HOME: Friends? Activities? Movement? Speech and interaction with others? Relationship to Staff? Placement in the institution. Nightime behaviors vs. day-time. Eating behavior.
PROGNOSIS and TREATMENT PLAN: Overall specific goal for this individual. Baseline behavior. Goal in six months after group intervention.	RECOMMENDED ROLE IN GROUP:

3. Review the medical and social histories.
4. Interview the family and staff who are familiar with the older person both during the day and at night.

The worker then applies the correct Validation techniques found in the Individual V/F Validation Treatment Plan (Figure 2). A Validation team of three or more workers apply individual or group Validation on a consistent basis at regular intervals, at least once each week. The goal is to decrease anxiety, prevent withdrawal to vegetation, and increase self-worth for the old person while reducing burn-out for the caregiver. The Validation team evaluates progress bimonthly, using the Evaluation of Progress form (Figure 3).

Stage One: Malorientation

A Case Example. Mrs. Ida Fox, age 89, points an accusing finger at the housekeeper who has come to clean out her cluttered room. Orange peels float in the toilet bowl. Kleenex is stuffed under each mattress spring. Buttons, bits of dried-up food, debris, old newspapers tied with frayed, yellow bits of hair-ribbon, safety pins, tin cans, paper cups, sugar, salt, and pepper packets litter each corner of her room. Mrs. Fox purses her lips in fury, her voice shakes with anger: "You keep out of my drawers, you thief! You stole my oranges last week too. I keep those oranges in the toilet to refrigerate them. Leave My Things Alone!"

The housekeeper is a trained Validation therapist. She does not argue with Ida Fox, knowing that this 89-year-old woman is maloriented. There is a reason behind her behavior. Mrs. Fox has led a relatively normal life until recently: now she becomes a blamer. Her blaming increases with her physical deterioration. Her eyesight worsens. She cannot hear out of her left ear. Her recent memory is fading due to small strokes. Her daughter has suddenly moved 300 miles away to Nova Scotia. Never have so many losses hit her at one time. Ida Fox has always blamed others when things went wrong. Blaming has always been her way of surviving hard times. Her sister told the social worker that Ida Fox never blamed as much as she does now, because she never had so many things go wrong at one time. She blamed her husband for dying and leaving her without money; she blamed her daughter for leaving the oven gas on when it was Ida Fox, herself, who forgot that she had lit the flame. Ida Fox has never learned to trust that she can survive hard times and be responsible for her own mistakes. Her typical way of coping has been to displace her fears onto others. At age 89, when one catastrophe follows another, her blaming increases. Her accusations grow with her losses. Her present day losses trigger memories of earlier fear. Anger and frustration in present time, like a magnet, attract

Figure 2. Individual Validation® Treatment Plan. Validation: The Feil Method © 1988.

DATE: _____
V/WORKER: _____

Resident's Name: _____

Stage: (Maloriented) (Time Confused) (Repetitive Motion) (Combination)

Contact Time:
_____ Minutes Per Day _____ Minutes per Week

SELECT AND APPLY APPROPRIATE VALIDATION TECHNIQUE FROM COLUMN TWO:
(Write in letter or Validation Technique)
VERBAL VALIDATION: _____

Topic to Discuss: _____

Unfinished Life Task: _____

Preferred Sense: _____

Validation Technique: _____

NON-VERBAL VALIDATION:
Task-Oriented Movements: (baking, folding, mixing, writing, counting, pounding, serving, napkin stacking, etc.)
_____

COLUMN TWO
VALIDATION® TECHNIQUES:

I. VERBAL VALIDATION

A. Observe their Physical Characteristics (eyes, skin tone, muscles, hands, breathing, etc.)
B. Listen to the words the person uses
C. Match their preferred sense*
D. Ask: Who? What? Where? When? How? (avoid Why)
E. Repeat their key words. Paraphrase. Summarize.
F. Ask the extreme. (How bad? Worse? Best? etc.)
G. Reminisce: (How did it used to be before . . .)
H. Imagine The Opposite: (When are things better? Is there a time when your clothes are NOT STOLEN . . . etc.)
I. Can we find a creative solution together? What did you do when this happened before? Tap an earlier coping method that worked.

II. NON-VERBAL VALIDATION

A. Center. Put your Own feelings in the closet.
B. Observe their gut emotion.
C. Say the emotion out loud with emotion. Match the emotion.
D. Mirror their movement. Pick up their breathing. Match rhythms.
E. Link their behavior with the unmet need: love, safety, to be useful, to express gut emotions and to be validated.
F. Touch: (their cheek with the palm of your hand; the back of the head, the jaw line, the shoulder, the upper arm, etc.)

G. Maintain genuine eye contact.
H. Ambiguity. Use a vague pronoun (he, it, someone, that, etc.) when you cannot understand the word-doodles.
I. Sing familiar songs that match their feelings.

*Preferred Sense Words:

Visual: Look, picture, see, notice, watch, clear, bright, etc.

Hearing: Sounds like, loud, scratchy, noisy, clear, still, etc.

Feeling: Feel, hits, strikes, hurts, scary, touches, hard, heavy, etc.

(Repetitive Movements to Match and Mirror: Pacing, patting, clucking, swaying, dancing, praying, rhyming, painting, humming, playing musical instrument, ball throwing, singing, chanting, poetry, etc.)

Song Titles to Sing: _____

Appropriate Touch: _____

Validation Technique: _____

Sit Resident next to: _____
Encourage them to (sing, talk about, move, touch, etc.)

Equipment Needed: Bean bag, ball, rhythm instrument, food to serve neighbor, paper, pencil, poem, paints, dough, pots to wash, linen to fold, yarn, purse, elastic or parachute, other work materials of music tapes _____

Figure 3.   Therapy Evaluation Form.

KEY: 0-NEVER DOES		1-RARELY DOES	2-OCCASIONALLY DOES		3-FREQUENTLY DOES		4-ALWAYS DOES
NAME	TALKS IN GROUP	MAKES EYE CONTACT	TOUCHES	SMILES	SHOWS LEADERSHIP	PARTICIPATES (PHYSICAL)	*GENERAL COMMENTS ON GROUP MEETINGS*
							UNUSUAL RESPONSES INVITATION TO JOB
							MAIN RECURRING THEME
							PLANS FOR NEXT WEEK
							MAIN CONFLICTS
							RECOMMENDATIONS

similar feelings from the past. Loss of hearing in present time attracts the memory of when she lost her job during the depression. To keep in control, she begins to hoard, afraid of losing money, food, her identity. Her parents taught her as a child to "always keep in control; to keep her possessions in one place; never to make a mistake." Fearful of messing up, she holds on to objects that represent security. Food represents the nurturing love of her mother; the tissues folded in triangles represent her babies whom she lovingly diapered long ago; newspapers show her ability to read, her hair ribbons represent her youth. Her purse mirrors her personality. She clutches it to her, terrified if it should become lost, stuffing it with objects that represent her youth. She will not face her recent memory loss. She confabulates and uses filler words when she forgets the day or the date or someone's name. She stays far away from "the crazy people who don't know what day it is." Ida Fox is usually oriented to present time, but she is loaded with unfinished life tasks. She has never learned basic trust; learned that she can survive hard times. She is not happily oriented. She is maloriented. She carries a backpack of buried fear and anger, which she struggles to unload, at last, in her old age, before she dies. Often, she blames someone in present time to express her feelings about someone from the past. To express buried jealousy at a younger sister, she blames her roommate for stealing her clothes. The facts are not accurate, but her feelings are true.

The Validation therapist does not judge her to be "paranoid" at age 89. Ida Fox has never been mentally ill. The Validation worker understands that Mrs. Fox has entered the final resolution stage of life. She struggles to express anger, fear, and jealousy in her old age in order to resolve unfinished issues from the past. The Validation worker will not argue the truth of the facts. Nor does the Validation worker try to "fix up" the maloriented. They deny feelings and do not want insight into their behaviors. They want a trusted authority to believe their feelings. Listening to their feelings does not "feed the fantasy" or "buy into the delusion." Their behavior is not a fantasy or a delusion. It happened long ago. They bring past time to the present in order to wrap up loose threads before death. If no one listens, the maloriented blame even more. Ignored, they holler. Finally, medicated and isolated, they will often withdraw to time confusion and then to vegetation. The Validation worker listens exquisitely.

These are the nonverbal, physical characteristics of a maloriented old person:

1. Eyes narrow
2. Tight facial muscles
3. Pursed lips
4. Shallow breathing
5. Chin often juts out
6. Fingers point or arms are folded
7. Body movements are direct and purposeful
8. Constantly holds on to an object such as a purse, cane, or coat
9. Makes direct eye contact
10. Voice tone is harsh or whiny.

These are the verbal behaviors of a maloriented old person:

1. Speech clear
2. Uses blaming or accusing words such as "it's their fault . . . they stole my clothes . . . my bed is wet because there is a hole in the ceiling . . . my dentures don't fit, so the meat is too tough . . . the cook poisons the food."

These are the psychological behaviors of a maloriented old person:

1. Maintains tight control: Does not want to be touched
2. Does not face feelings
3. Does not want insight into their behaviors
4. Confabulates when confused or forgetful
5. Shuns disoriented peers
6. Resists change
7. Holds onto present reality
8. Projects fears onto others
9. Hoards, afraid of losing control
10. Is usually aware of present time and place
11. Without conscious awareness, expresses an unresolved life task from an earlier stage by using people or objects in present time to represent the past
12. Becomes the victim or the martyr.

The Validation worker builds trust by listening and genuinely exploring. The maloriented will not trust the worker who (1) confronts them with the truth, (2) patronizes them by pretending to agree with facts that are not true, or (3) attempts to reassure them that all will be well and "not to worry." The Validation worker knows that blaming is the only coping method of the maloriented. The more they lose, the more they accuse. Blaming others when losses hit has become a way to survive the loss. The worker respects their defenses and does not try to puncture their invisible protective bubble.

How to Validate the Maloriented

1. Acknowledge the therapist's own frustration. Center. Closet feelings.

2. Use nonthreatening factual words to help them express feelings and to build trust: Who? What? Where? When? How? Avoid "Why"! "Why" triggers an intellectual response and raises defenses. Intellectually, the maloriented person does not know "Why." They are aware on a deep level of awareness, but are afraid to become conscious of the reasons that underlie their behaviors. Like a sleeper who unconsciously swats a mosquito, their behavior is purposeful. Without awareness, they express buried fears to get rid of them.

3. Rephrase or paraphrase the maloriented person's key words.

4. Use their preferred sense (visual, auditory, kinesthetic). For example: If the maloriented person says, "I see a man under my bed," the worker uses visual words to explore: "What does the man look like? What is he wearing? Who does he remind you of? Is he tall?" If the

maloriented person says, "I hear noises at night," the Validation worker builds trust by using hearing words: "What does it sound like? Are the noises loud? Scratchy?" (If the maloriented person says, "I feel terrible all over," the worker uses kinesthetic words: "Where does it hurt? Is it a pressure? Is the pain sharp? Dull?" The Validation therapist builds trust by speaking the maloriented person's language.)

5. Polarity. Help the person express themselves fully by asking: "When was it the worst? How bad was it? How often?" (The maloriented couch feelings with facts. Telling the extreme of the situation relieves the maloriented of negative emotions.)

6. Reminisce. Example: "What was it like before? When you were younger?" Maloriented are aware of clock-time. They can consciously return to the past. Disoriented blend present and past time. They are tense-confused. They cannot tell clock-time. They cannot reminisce. The past has become the present for the disoriented.

7. Imagine the opposite to find a coping method. When the Validation worker has built sufficient trust, the maloriented old person may feel safe enough to give up some of the blaming behavior. For example, after 12 weeks of 5 minute Validation sessions given three times per week, the Validation worker asks: "Is there a time when there is *no* man under your bed?" The maloriented person may answer: "When you are with me, he never comes. Maybe I don't want to be alone." The Validation worker uses reminiscence to tap an earlier method of coping with loneliness: "How did you survive when your husband died? Were you alone then?" The maloriented person may answer: "I played his favorite tunes on the piano and I got out all of his pictures. That's how I lived through it." The Validation worker can bring the maloriented person records with the music she loves and find her husband's pictures to help this old woman cope with her loneliness.

The worker or family member has accomplished these Validation goals: (1) eased anxiety, (2) kept the maloriented communicating, (3) prevented their withdrawal inward, (4) helped the maloriented tie up loose threads from the past to resolve life, and (5) reduced burn-out for the worker and family.

A Case Example:

Ida Fox:	You stole my oranges. Give them back!
V/T (Validation therapist):	Where did you keep them?

The housekeeper knows that Mrs. Fox lived through the depression. The loss of her eyesight in present time triggers the memory of the losses she suffered during the depression, when she saw little food and had no ice-box. The facts are different, but the feelings of loss are identical. The V/T has empathy. Her voice-tone is genuine and respectful.

V/T: How many oranges did you have? Were they the big, eating oranges? (V/T uses visual words to help Mrs. Fox respond.)

The oranges represent safety and nurturing. Oranges were a delicacy when Mrs. Fox was a child.

Ida Fox: I had six big oranges. The kind my mother gave us for our birthday.
V/T: (Reminiscing) Were the oranges a big surprise?
Ida Fox: Oh, yes! We were poor, and mother worked hard for that orange. It's my 90th birthday next week. I wonder if the children will remember.

The Validation therapist spends 5 minutes three times each week with Ida Fox. In charting the changes over a 6-week period, the Validation team finds that Mrs. Fox blamed only once. Moreover, Mrs. Fox no longer accuses friends or family. Her children visit more often. She saves her blaming for the Validation team. She knows that the Validation therapists will believe her feelings and will listen with genuine respect. The Validation team gives quality time.

Mrs. Fox stopped accusing others for 2 years. When her daughter moved 3000 miles away, Mrs. Fox's blaming returned. The loss of her daughter in present time attracted her earlier losses. The Validation team had to renew their work. Mrs. Fox was resolving unfinished feelings. Without insight, her life tasks can never be completely resolved. She may continue to blame until she dies. However, her blaming will lessen and she will remain more or less oriented, interacting with others. She will not vegetate.

Stage Two: Time Confusion

A Case Example.   Joe Lake: "Mazie, Mazie!" Mr. Lake, age 88, calls his wife who died 10 years ago. He is tall, shoulders stooped, shaking with Parkinson's disease. He shuffles past the nursing station, slipping by the nurse, busy sorting medications after shift-change. A light breeze ruffles the curtains.

Like Houdini, Joe Lake carefully opens the door of the locked ward and slips out. He shuffles from the Alzheimer's ward, turns a few corners, opens doors, and finally gets into Jenny Ward's bed, smiling: "Mazie, here you are!" Mrs. Ward, an oriented 83-year-old resident, pushes him out of her bed, yelling: "Nurse! Get this crazy man out of my room!" The nurse on the Alzheimer wing is a Validation therapist. She follows the Validation steps.

These are the nonverbal, physical characteristics of the time confused old person:

1. Eyes blurry, unfocused
2. Facial muscles relaxed
3. Movements in space are vague, indirect
4. Breathing deep rather than shallow
5. Incontinent of bladder
6. Increasing damage to sight and (or) hearing
7. Some loss of mobility.

These are the verbal behaviors of the time confused old person:

1. Speech is often unclear. Loss of dictionary words.
2. "Word-doodles." Similar sounds blend. Forms unique words.
3. Often cries, shouts, laughs without control.
4. Returns to well-remembered early linguistic patterns: songs, poems, nursery rhymes.

These are the psychological characteristics of the time confused:

1. Raw emotions spill.
2. Loss of chronological clock time. Person no longer can distinguish minutes, hours, days, weeks. They measure time by memories. Instead of the clock, they keep track of their lifetime.
3. Loss of logical, metaphoric thinking capacity: They cannot put people or objects into categories. They can no longer compare similar things. They have lost the "as-if" thinking ability. A hand that feels as if it were like a baby, becomes a baby.
4. Loss of motivation to control emotions and conform to society's rules.
5. Movement back and forth in time. A person in present time can become someone from the past.
6. Uses the mind's eye with vivid eidetic images to restore the past. The earlier an event or image has been imprinted on memory, the longer it is retained (Shettler & Boyd, 1969). "The patient, himself, can activate the memory from within, stimulating the

same pattern of cortical nerve cell connections without the use of the sense organs" (Penfield, 1950).
7. Has no repertoire for coping with social and role losses, sensory losses and recent memory loss.
8. Denies losses and retreats to the past to survive an unbearable present reality.
9. Restores the past to resolve it.
10. Has intuitive wisdom. Can distinguish a genuine caregiver from a caregiver who does not care.
11. Struggles to fulfill basic human needs: (1) love, (2) identity, (3) to express their emotions and to be heard by a trusted "other."

The time confused will not trust a caregiver who (1) tries to orient them to present time and place, (2) patronizes them by pretending to agree with them, (3) restrains them, (4) prematurely reassures them, wanting to calm them down, (5) tries to modify their behavior with negative reinforcement, or (6) tries to use logic to give them insight into their behaviors. The time confused are no longer motivated to conform to present day social norms. Unlike the maloriented, they no longer strive to please authority figures. They are egocentric. The Validation therapist must use empathy to step into their world. Accepting their physical deficits—memory loss, loss of eyesight, hearing, speech, and logical thinking—the Validation therapist respects their intuitive wisdom.

How to Validate the Time Confused

1. If the time confused are verbal, use Steps 1–5 for the maloriented. Time confused blend present and past time, therefore they cannot deliberately reminisce. The past has become the present. Time confused can no longer think logically, therefore, they cannot imagine the opposite.
2. Touch. The time confused have lost their controls. The protective invisible bubble of the maloriented is gone. Feelings are incontinent.
3. Unlike the maloriented, the time confused respond positively to touch. Where you touch and how much pressure you apply are important. Different areas trigger different memories, and "Each person responds differently, depending upon their unique familial ways of touching" (Feil, 1989). "Previous stimulation of a group of nerve cells which has led to a state of satisfaction, increase its sensitivity to further stimulation of a like kind" (Zuckerman, 1950). For example, gentle pressure on the cheek with the palm of the hand triggers a well-remembered mother relationship. Touch the back of the head with cupped fingers to

elicit a father relationship. Massage the back of the neck to trigger a child relationship. Touch the ear lobe to the chin with the outer side of your hand to trigger a spouse relationship. The Validation therapist becomes a significant trusted "other" through touch.

4. Genuine, close eye contact. Without direct, close eye contact, the visually impaired time confused cannot see the worker.

5. Match their emotion. Time confused will respond by opening their eyes if the Validation therapist's voice mirrors the emotion of the time confused old person. Therapists find a time in their lives when they felt the same way as the time confused, i.e., anger, love, fear, sorrow.

6. Say their emotion out-loud. Use short, gut-level words. Time confused are not in their second childhood, but they have lost intellectual, verbal behaviors. They retain early, primary speech that survives brain damage.

7. Link their behavior to the unmet human need, i.e., love, identity, to express emotions. The Validation therapist accepts all feelings that are openly expressed. The therapist never inserts feelings or pushes the person to express hidden emotions.

8. Ambiguity. When the time confused use unique "word-doodles" and cannot explain their meaning, the Validation therapist uses a vague pronoun such as "he," "it," "something," "someone," "they," to keep the communication going. The Validation therapist is able to remain ambiguous; the meaning of the word is unknown. The time confused freely express the feeling underlying their speech. For example, a time confused man in an angry voice-tone shouts: "The fitzmathing went flop!"

V/T: *"That* made you very angry! *Something* bad happened?"

9. Music. Culturally significant, well-remembered, early-learned melodies are associated with family relationships and feelings of love, anger, grief, and fear. Music often excites dormant speech, stimulates awareness of clock-time, and improves gait. Music triggers energy and heightens attention span.

The goal of the Validation therapist is to (1) ease anxiety, (2) tap dormant speech, (3) motivate the use of social controls, (4) stimulate verbal and nonverbal interactions, (5) improve gait, (6) prevent withdrawal to repetitive motion, (7) give feelings of well-being and happiness, (8) stimulate self-awareness and awareness of others, (9) reduce the need for medication and physical restraints, and (10) lessen caregivers' burn-out.

A Case Example.   Validation therapist moves towards 88-year-old Joe
Lake directly, so that he can see her approach, since his peripheral
vision is damaged. The therapist bends close to make genuine eye
contact. Mr. Lake is somewhat deaf, and can lip-read if he can see the
therapist's lips. The therapist's voice is nurturing, soft, and caring. She
has taken a moment to center when she sees Joe Lake lying in Mrs.
Ward's bed. The Validation therapist knows that Mr. Lake has mixed up
present and past time in his desperate need for his wife, whom he loved
very much. Mr. Lake never fully grieved when his wife died suddenly.
He denied the enormity of his loss. To survive loneliness, he uses a
woman who looks like his wife in present time to restore his love. His
vision is poor. Looking at Mrs. Ward, he sees his wife clearly with his
mind's eye. The therapist thinks of a dear friend that she misses very
much. Her tone of voice reflects the sadness and the love that Joe Lake
feels.

V/T: (Gently touching Mr. Lake's upper arm) Mr. Lake, you miss
              Mazie very much.

Mr. Lake opens his eyes to make direct, meaningful eye contact with the
therapist. He recognizes her genuine emotion, which matches his feelings. He feels her empathy. The worker has linked Mr. Lake's behavior
to his unmet need. By matching his feelings and verbalizing them with
empathy, she has helped him become more aware.

Joe Lake: She is a fine woman. Where did she go? Mazie, where are
              you? I have to follow up the roots so she won't filla full.
              (Mr. Lake moves from the bed toward Mrs. Ward, his voice
              full of fear and worry.)
V/T: (Touching Mr. Lake's jaw-line with the palm of her hand to
              build instant trust. Touching fingers, hands, or wrists rarely
              elicits responses due to poor circulation in the extremities.)
              You're worried that she might fall? Is she moving too fast?

The therapist does not understand Mr. Lake's unique word-doodles.
He has combined sounds to form his personal speech. The Validation
therapist uses "ambiguity" to keep communicating with Mr. Lake, ex-
pressing his feelings, not worrying about the dictionary meaning of his
words.

Joe Lake: She can't see the trees in the dark. She'll fall in the fillmill.
V/T: Is it dark now? Does she go out alone in the dark on your
              farm?

The therapist uses visual words to build trust and help Mr. Lake express his fear about his wife's death. She knows that on a deep level of awareness, Joe Lake knows that his wife is dead. He must restore her in order to grieve so that he can die in peace. He is resolving unfinished feelings.

Joe Lake:	She is a fine woman. She works so hard. All alone in the dark.

The Lake's lived on a farm.

V/T:	Did she go out alone to the well?

Joe Lake nods, as he and the therapist walk, arm in arm, back to the Alzheimer ward. They talk as they walk. The therapist uses exploring techniques: "Who? What? Where? When?" (See techniques 1–5 for the maloriented.) As they talk, Mr. Lake's anxiety decreases, his gait improves, his word-doodles lessen, and he does not need medication. The worker gently guides Joe Lake toward Sally Smith, a nurturing time confused 85-year-old woman on the Alzheimer wing. The Validation therapist sits with them for 2 minutes.

V/T:	Mrs. Smith, this is Joe Lake. He misses his wife, Mazie very much. When you miss your husband, what do you do?
Ms. S:	I cry. Then I say The Lord's Prayer.
V/T:	Do you think praying would help Mr. Lake?
Ms. S:	We can try.

Together, they pray, holding hands.

V/T:	Mazie was a sweetheart. Did you ever sing together "Let me call you sweetheart?"

The Validation therapist begins to sing the familiar love song. Mrs. Smith and Joe Lake continue to sing together as the therapist says goodby.

This Validation intervention has taken 7 quality minutes. Within 30 minutes, the nursing assistant, a member of the Validation team, will sing with Mrs. Smith and Joe Lake to keep them communicating. Old time confused rarely initiate interactions. The Validation team must facilitate the nonverbal communication, on a regular basis throughout the day. (See Validation Treatment Plan, Figure 2.) Both Mr. Lake and Mrs. Smith become members of the Validation group, which meets once each week. They sit next to each other in the group, hold hands, and dance together. Mrs. Smith is the hostess, and serves Mr. Lake. Within 6 weeks, Mr. Lake does not leave the floor to search for his wife. He expresses his grief in the Validation group and gets comfort. A Validation group can keep time confused interacting so that they will not withdraw to repetitive motion.

Stage Three: Repetitive Motion

Case Example One.   Jennie Folk strokes her hand lovingly, crooning: "Schh, m'love. Schh. Don't cry. Momma's gonna sing you a lullaby. Ma. Ma. Ma. Ma." Mrs. Folk cannot see her hand. Her brain no longer informs her of its position. She has damage to her kinesthetic nervous system. She is no longer aware of her body's whereabouts in space. Her hand feels soft as if it were her baby. Her vivid mind's eye sees her infant in the cradle. She strokes her baby-hand, loving it.

Case Example Two.   Larry Rose, a former lawyer, pounds his left knee in fury, shouting: "Damn judge. Son of a bitch!" He moves his right hand up and down the arm of his wheelchair. His fingers make walking motions. He mutters: "Buckeye and 105th. Fix it up! Do it right!"

The Validation team applies individual Validation interventions for 3 minutes, six times per day with very disoriented old–old people who are in repetitive motion.

These are the nonverbal, physical characteristics of Stage Three:

1. Eyes, ears, and mobility deteriorate
2. Severe damage to control centers; complete incontinence
3. Increasing damage to brain tissue (little strokes often with Alzheimer-type plaques and neurofibrillary tangles)
4. Body movements are repetitive.

These are the verbal behaviors of the old–old person in repetitive motion:

1. Movements replace speech
2. Word-sounds are monosyllabic and primary
3. Paces, clucks, pats, hums, word-doodles in repetitive rhythms.

Piaget (1952) wrote that movements precede speech. Body movements and sensations are "the sensorimotor forerunners of verbal behaviors. When the object is no longer present, the movements in abbreviated form are the same movements involved in the initial perception" (as quoted in Ginsberg & Opper, 1969). When a mother leaves, the infant wails. Hours pass. Longing for the mother, the infant gets an idea! The mother rocked the infant. The infant mimics the rocking motion. The motion becomes the mother. The infant stops wailing and feels nurtured by the rocking movement. Later, when the cognitive structures are in place, the child learns the objective, dictionary word, "mother," which becomes classified and stored in the left brain. When the speech centers become damaged in old age, the disoriented old person returns to early, primary, well-established preverbal behaviors. Immobilized and alone in the nursing home, the old person rocks back and forth to restore the mother in order to feel safe and nurtured. Body movements are the tickets to the past. Motion triggers emotion. This is not a second childhood. The old disoriented survive loneliness and uselessness by using what they still possess: kinesthetic memories, the mind's eye, and sounds from the past.

These are the psychological characteristics of Stage Three, repetitive motion:

1. Loss of all social controls
2. Movements express human needs: love, identity, usefulness, expression of raw anger, fear, or grief and pleasure
3. Loss of all logical connections. Can no longer tell the difference between similar things, i.e., a hand feels like a baby; the hand becomes the baby
4. Uses objects and body parts to substitute for people or activities from the past
5. Loss of chronological clock-time
6. Loss of self-reflective, self-awareness
7. Loss of body-awareness and identity.

Those in repetitive motion become more anxious, and their pounding, crying, and pacing increase if they are ignored, negatively behavior modified, punished, prematurely reassured, or ridiculed. They will quickly vegetate if they are physically and/or chemically restrained.

The Validation therapist must (1) respect their intuitive wisdom to restore the past to survive isolation, and (2) accept their physical and mental deterioration. The Validation therapist cannot retrieve damaged brain cells, but he/she can stimulate nonverbal interactions to prevent vegetation.

How to Validate the Repetitive Mover

1. Observe the physical characteristics to assess the emotion
2. Center and tap a similar emotion
3. Link their behavior to the unmet human need
4. Touch to stimulate trust and well-established relationships

5. Use close, direct eye contact
6. Match their emotions
7. Say their emotions, using simple gut-level words
8. Use music that is culturally meaningful and well-established
9. Mirror their movements. Move with the person, pick up their breathing, match their arm movements, their body rhythms, genuinely match their repetitive motions, their gait, dance to their tempo. Genuine mirroring establishes eye contact and often results in some verbal behaviors.
10. Use ambiguity to trigger some verbal communication.

The Validation therapist must match the movements with empathy. The blind old person in repetitive motion will "see" that a therapist is not genuine; the deaf old person will "hear" ridicule in a tone of voice. The goal is to prevent vegetation, restore communication, lessen the need for restraints and medication, reduce anxiety, and stimulate whatever dormant speech still exists. Use one-to-one Validation at specified intervals throughout the day. The person in repetitive motion will usually not benefit from a Validation group, unless the therapist can stop their repetitive movements through touch. The repetitive motions raise anxiety for the other group members, and can destroy the group.

Case Example One. The Validation therapist observes Jennie Folk rocking and crooning to her hand. The Validation therapist does not know that the hand has become a baby, but she does know that Mrs. Folk's only role in life was motherhood. The therapist knows her social history and has communicated with her children. The Validation therapist bends close to Mrs. Folk, mirroring her hand movements, using "ambiguity":

V/T: (In a soft, low, loving voice) Mrs. Folk, you are a good mother. You take good care of your babies. You love them very much.

Mrs. Folk looks into the therapist's eyes and smiles. The therapist sings a well-known lullaby. Mrs. Folk joins the therapist. They sing three songs for 3 minutes. Mrs. Folk no longer strokes her hand. Her dignity as a mother is restored. The Validation team reinforces this interaction for 3 minutes six times each day. After 6 weeks, Mrs. Folk began to look at others, became less egocentric, and no longer stroked her hand. Her gait improved. She moved outward toward others and did not vegetate.

Case Example Two. The Validation therapist observes Larry Rose smacking his left knee in fury.

V/T: (In a voice that reflects anger) You are so angry, Mr. Rose.
                 Did that hurt you? Did it give you pain?

Larry Rose becomes aware of his anger and nods.

Mr. Rose: God Damn, S.O.B. Judge. Buckeye and 105th. (The fingers
                 of his right hand move rapidly back and forth on the arm of
                 his chair.)
V/T: Did the judge rule against you on Buckeye and 10th? You
                 hate him!
Mr. Rose: That's right. I do!

Mr. Rose begins to cry. His feelings have been validated. His pounding
stops. He is resolving his life, restoring his law practice so that he can
vindicate himself. He wants to die in peace, feeling that his life has been
worthwhile. The arm of his chair had become the street where he
practiced law. His finger movements had restored his daily walk to his
law office on Buckeye and 105th Street. His knee, inflicted with Paget's
disease, had become the judge who hurt him many years ago. Using his
mind's eye and muscle memory, he returned to the past to wrap up his
life. The Validation therapist helped him justify having lived.

Stage Four: Vegetation

A Case Study. George Judson, age 91, sits slumped in his geriatric
chair. His chin rests on his chest, his breathing is slow, his hands limp,
sway without purpose, sometimes banging the wheel. He does not
hear. He does not look up when the therapist approaches his chair. His
eyes remain closed. His speech is gone. Occasionally, he mutters a
monosyllable. His lower lip dangles. He is fed, toileted, bathed, and
medicated. He is a living dead person.

Two years ago, when George Judson walked with his cane, he demanded to leave the nursing home. He was time confused and wanted
to go to work. He was told:

George, you are 89 years old. You live in the nursing home. You cannot
work anymore. Today is Tuesday, September 23rd.

George Judson was outraged:

Damn It! I know I'm in a nursing home. That's why I have to get out of
here. Right now! I have to milk my cows! Now get out of my way!

George Judson pushed the nurse. He was restrained and medicated. No
one validated George Judson by walking beside him, matching his

movements, and acknowledging his need to be working on his farm. Today, the Validation team massages George Judson's shoulders and back, for 90 seconds, three times a day, bending close, saying with empathy: "You miss your farm. You milked those cows every day, rain or shine. You worked hard!" George Judson barely opens his eyes. Occasionally, his head moves toward the worker and his arms stop flailing.

In vegetation, movements lose their purpose. Repetitive touch can evoke some response, but there is rarely any communication. In this stage, withdrawal is complete. The old–old no longer stimulate themselves through repetitive movements. When old disoriented people have been isolated in a geriatric chair for months, they progress quickly to the vegetation stage. It is usually too late to tap dormant speech or communicate with music and movements.

Forming the Validation Group

The maloriented are threatened by disorientation, and usually do not benefit from a Validation group. Those in repetitive motion raise anxiety in group members, and should receive individual, not group, Validation.

Time confused (Stage Two) benefit from a Validation group. A group provides (1) heightened energy, (2) increased attention span, (3) improved gait, (4) stimulation of memories of former social and familial groups, (5) social roles, (6) increased speech, (7) incentive to become less egocentric—they listen to each other and help each other solve common universal human needs, (8) improvement in activities of daily living, such as eating skills, and (9) reduced anxiety and increased feelings of well-being.

How to Form a Validation Group

1. Select group members who will benefit
2. Assign familiar roles that will not raise anxiety
3. Sit group members close to people they like, to stimulate relationships
4. Select topics (subjective human needs and unfinished issues) based on knowledge of the social history and interviews with family
5. Select well-remembered, familiar songs
6. Select appropriate movements based on the medical history.

The video, *The More We Get Together* (Feil, 1978), illustrates the three stages and documents the Validation group with actual nursing home residents. The Validation therapist must work with staff and families in order to successfully continue the Validation group. Privacy, equipment, toileting before the meeting, transport to the meeting, and evaluation of progress are dependent on the cooperation of all levels of institutional staff.

Weaknesses of Validation

Not everyone can practice Validation. A nursing assistant who can accept the deviant, sometimes bizarre behaviors of disoriented old people without judging them can be highly effective. A caregiver cannot do Validation who is judgmental, who expects immediate progress, and who has difficulty relating to the following: (1) people who freely express feelings (the disoriented), (2) people who act out unfinished issues without cognitive awareness (the maloriented), (3) people with severe cognitive deficits, i.e., damage to logical thinking, speech, social controls, (4) people who need to be touched in order to respond, (5) people who can no longer see, hear, or walk, (6) people who do not want to be reminded of present time and place, (7) people who struggle to return to the past to feel safe or to resolve unfinished issues, and (8) old people who have regressed to primary speech, but who have retained intuitive wisdom.

Validation does not help everyone. Old people with severe physical deficits who have integrity, who do not have to restore the past, and who have been validating themselves throughout their lives do not need Validation. Validation can improve the quality of life during the Validation time period, but cannot stop the progressive deterioration of those diagnosed *early onset* Alzheimer's disease.

The elderly who become disoriented in their 40s or 50s, have severe organic damage. Cognition may be totally destroyed. They do not retreat because of damage to eyes or ears or mobility. Touch, eye contact, music, and rhythms may help for a moment, or not at all. The therapist or family member cannot predict the behavior of the *early onset* Alzheimer patient.

Mentally handicapped and mentally ill older people can benefit from the basic helping techniques for the maloriented, but the therapist cannot predict that their behavior will improve. Chronically ill older people who do not retreat to the past do not benefit from Validation.

The administration must support the Validation therapist in order to ensure the success of the Validation group. Therapists can practice individual Validation without the support of administration, but all levels of staff must work with the Validation therapist in order to effectively conduct a Validation group.

Strengths of Validation

Family members who use Validation with maloriented old relatives can usually keep them functioning independently, in their own homes. Validation, applied on a consistent basis, can prevent the maloriented from withdrawing further into time confusion, unless they suffer a tremendous stroke or other physical trauma. The time confused will usually not retreat to repetitive motion if they participate in a weekly Validation group, and receive daily individual Validation. Individual Validation can stave off vegetation for those who are in repetitive motion.

Validation can considerably lessen burn-out for the family member and staff worker. The Validation therapist does not argue, simply listens exquisitely. As the disoriented old person improves, the caregiver feels tremendous relief. Validation techniques are simple, and can be taught to all levels of staff, to volunteers, and to families.

If the Validation therapist leaves the facility, the disoriented old person can easily transfer to another Validation worker who has the same quality of touch, the same nurturing voice tone and the same respect and empathy.

Individual validation for the maloriented takes no more than 5 quality minutes three times each day, split by a Validation team. Individual Validation for the disoriented takes only 60 seconds six times a day by the Validation team. The Validation group takes 40 to 60 minutes once each week. Preparation time is minimal, since the same topics, songs, movements, roles, and goals are continued at each meeting. Evaluation of progress after the meeting takes no more than 15–20 minutes, using the Evaluation of Progress Form (Figure 3).

There is no formula for working with human beings. Maloriented old people can become disoriented within 5 minutes. The Validation therapist does not get "hardening of the categories!" The Validation therapist respects the uniqueness of each maloriented or disoriented old–old person who has survived a lifetime and who continues to struggle for integrity.

References

Dietch, J., Hewett, L., & Jones, S. (1989). Adverse effects of reality orientation. *Journal of American Geriatrics Society, 37*, 10.

Edward Feil Productions. (1978b). *The more we get together* (Videotape). Cleveland, OH: Author.

Erikson, E. (1950). *Childhood and society*. New York: W. W. Norton.

Feil, N. (1967). Group therapy in a home for the aged. *The Gerontologist, 7,* 192–195.

Feil, N. (1972). *A new approach to group therapy: Research findings.* Unpublished paper presented at the Gerontological Society of America Annual Scientific Meeting, Puerto Rico.

Feil, N. (1989). Validation: An empathic approach to the care of dementia. *Clinical Gerontologist, 8,* 89–94.

Fritz, Paul A. (1986). *The language of resolution among the old–old: The effect of Validation therapy on two levels of cognitive confusion.* Paper presented at the Speech Communication Association Meeting. Chicago: November, 1986.

Ginsberg, H., & Opper, S. (1969). *Piaget's theory of intellectual development.* Englewood Cliffs, NJ: Prentice-Hall.

Godemont, M. (1989). *Psycho-geriatirsch woonproject* (Unpublished report). Huis Perrekes, Zammelseweg, Belgium.

Jones, G. M. M. (1985). Validation therapy: A companion to reality orientation. *The Canadian Nurse,* March, 20–23.

Penfield, W. (1950). The cerebral cortex and the mind of man. In Peter Laslets (Ed.), *The physical basis of mind.* New York: Macmillan.

Piaget, J. (1952). *The origins of intelligence in children.* New York: W. W. Norton.

Shettler, F. G., & Boyd, G. S. (1969). *Atherosclerosis.* Netherland: Elsevier/North Holland Biomedical Press.

von Franz-Hillman. (1971). *Jung's typology.* Zurich: Spring Publications.

Weil, J. (1966). Special program for the senile in a home for the aged. *Geriatrics, 21,* 197–202.

Wells, C. (1977). *Dementia.* Philadelphia, PA: F. A. Davis.

Zuckerman, M. D. (1950). In P. Laslett, (Ed.), New York: Macmillan Co.

5

Behavioral Analysis and Therapy in the Field of Gerontology

BRUCE A. THYER, KIM THYER, and SUSAN MASSA

The service provider active in the field of gerontology will find it extremely useful to become familiar with the fundamental concepts of learning theory and the practice methods that comprise the field of behavior analysis and therapy. The discipline known as behavior analysis is exerting a significant impact within the field of gerontology in terms of theoretical conceptualizations of the aging process, etiological hypotheses regarding a number of the problematic behaviors associated with old age, and developing empirically supported interventions to improve the quality of life for elderly citizens. Health and human service workers have made major contributions to the emerging interdisciplinary field of behavioral gerontology, and this chapter will review some of these contributions and describe several practice applications of the behavioral approach.

Basic Concepts

The contemporary field of behavior analysis is comprised of three major but conceptually distinct areas. The first of these is the philosophy of science called *behaviorism*. Behaviorism is an amalgam of a number of philosophical perspectives which the reader may have encountered elsewhere (see Table 1).

The fundamental precept of behaviorism is that it is useful and scientifically justifiable to undertake the study of behavior as a valuable subject matter in its own right, and not simply as the reflection of unobservable processes. In particular, the behaviorist attempts to fully explore a person's behavior prior to developing causal explanations

Table 1.   Some of the Components of the Philosophy of Behaviorism

Determinism—the assumption that all behavior has (potentially) identifiable causes that are amenable to scientific analysis.

Parsimony—the preference to explore the simpler of the available, but adequate explanations of a phenomenon prior to assuming that more complicated explanations are operative.

Operationism—the practice of developing specific descriptions of a given behavioral phenomena of interest, in such detail as to permit other interested practitioner-researchers to similarly reliably and validly measure that phenomena.

Empiricism—the preference to rely on data obtained from appropriately conducted scientific investigations to develop explanations for a behavior or interventive techniques.

Avoidance of Reification—reluctance to attribute reality status to hypothetical constructs in the absence of adequate empirical evidence of the existence of those constructs.

Avoidance of Circular Reasoning—the recognition that in developing explanations for a given behavioral phenomena, causes and effects must be clearly distinguished from one another. It is not permissible, for example, to claim that an inner state *causes* a particular behavior, if the only evidence for the existence of that state is the very behavior it is presumed to cause.

based on inner mental states or nonspecific physiological processes. This view is not tantamount to a rejection of the existence of private events (e.g., wishes, feelings, consciousness) or of the salience of various processes within the brain or body as a whole, but is rather an area of emphasis. Just as the geneticist attempts to develop accounts of behavior almost exclusively derived from chromosomal theory and the principles of natural selection, or the psychoanalyst focuses on the person's purported mental apparatus to the exclusion of social or reinforcement variables, the behaviorist's attention is to the relevance of the person's past and present learning history and of contingencies of reinforcement and punishment in an effort to explain why a person behaves the way he or she does. The roles of heredity and physiological variables have always been recognized by behaviorists as important (Skinner, 1966), but these processes form the primary subject matter of different disciplines (genetics, neuroscience, physiology, etc.). The behaviorist's focus on the consequences that have followed a person's actions and how these consequences affect subsequent behavior is highly congruent with health and human service professionals' traditional emphasis on the person-in-situation context and on the transactional relationship between the individual and his/her environment. With respect to the field of gerontology this view has been stated by Skinner and Vaughn (1983) as follows: "Enlightened developmental psychologists go beyond mere growth. They recognize that what develops is the world in which people live. People do things in different ways as they grow older because different things happen to them" (p. 32), and "An essential point is the role played by consequences. We do what we do because of what follows when we have done it. Some things 'have to be done' in the sense that if we do not do them, unpleasant consequences will follow. . . . We learn about the consequences either from experience or from the reports of others who have in turn experienced them or been told about them" (p. 33).

In contemporary formulations, the term "behavior" is used to refer to whatever a person *does*, regardless of the public nature of these processes. Barker (1987) provides such a definition: "Any reaction or response by an individual, including observable activity, measurable physiological changes, cognitive images, fantasies and emotions. Some scientists even consider subjective experiences to be behaviors" (p. 14). Thus, inner physiological states are held to be a form of behavior, as are feelings, the functioning of the brain, what has been called consciousness, hopes, wishes, aspirations, etc., in fact the entire realm of human functioning. Although Watson (1913) originally held that behavior referred only to one's observable actions, over 50 years ago Skinner (1938) expanded the scope of behaviorism to encompass *all* human activity, overt and covert, as the subject matter of this discipline.

The field of behavior analysis attempts to account for as much of human comportment as possible without recourse to nonphysical causal agents (e.g., the mind, cognition), through a thorough examination of the role of learning theory principles in potentially explaining such phenomena. No one can reasonably deny the relevance of the variables emphasized by behavior analysts. However, dignified scientific and philosophical discourse is likely to continue as to the extent to which contingencies of reinforcement, punishment, and related factors (e.g., shaping, modeling, extinction) are influential relative to other, non-behavioral, factors. It is not the contention of behaviorists that an analysis of human behavior *only* in terms of learning theory variables is liable to lead to a complete account of the phenomenology of being human. Theirs is the humbler attempt to see to what extent such factors are operative, prior to entertaining physiological, genetic, and related variables.

The second major component of behavior analysis is a highly developed research methodology known as *the experimental analysis of behavior* (TEAB). TEAB is characterized by the intensive study of one or a very few numbers of persons and repeatedly measuring a client's problem over a period of time, as opposed to traditional or nomothetic research, which studies larger numbers of people but most often obtains just a few observations of them. Within health and human services, TEAB is reflected in the approach to practice research called single system research designs (reviewed in Thyer, 1991a) and has proven to be an extremely valuable methodology for answering questions such as "Did my client get better during treatment?" or the more difficult question such as "Was my intervention the cause of my client's improvements?" Within gerontology, Jackson and Patterson (1982) provide an excellent review of this research methodology as applied to practice-research with elderly clients.

The third major domain of behavior analysis has been variously labeled "behavior therapy," "behavior modification," or the term used in this chapter, "applied behavior analysis." At present there are over 35 journals that are explicitly devoted to publishing behavior analytic research, two major international applied behavioral associations, and dozens of national or regional ones. The behavioral approach is now a major model of practice in all of the human services (social work, psychology, psychiatry, education, etc.), and its traditional focus upon well-grounded empirical research studies warrants the close attention of all practitioners active in the field of gerontology.

The conceptual foundation of behavioral analysis and therapy falls under the rubric of contemporary social learning theory, an umbrella term referring to the processes of respondent (Pavlovian) conditioning, operant (reinforcement and punishment) conditioning, and observational learning (imitation). Unlike most accounts of behavior among the elderly, social learning theory is not a "stage theory" in the sense of Freud, Piaget, Erikson, etc. The human life span is not divided up by behavior analysts into discrete (or even overlapping) stages characterized by certain behavioral features, skills, or deficits. Rather, the human being is seen as possessing the capacity to learn (i.e., alter one's behavior) from birth via the above three mechanisms (respondent conditioning, operant conditioning, imitation), with such capacities remaining until death. The fallaciousness of traditional stage theories is now widely recognized by developmentalists and more recently by social work educators (Germain, 1987). No such stage theory has been adequately supported by empirical evidence; at best such models have served heuristic purposes. As newer, more accurate knowledge of human development accrues, the need for speculative stage theories diminishes as factual data fill the void previously occupied by these earlier conceptualizations.

The role that social learning theory plays in the development (and sometimes the disappearance) of new behavioral repertoires among the elderly is described in a number of other sources (Cautela, 1969, 1972; Baltes & Zerbe, 1976; Schonfield, 1980; Thyer, 1991b) and will not be reviewed here. Suffice it to say that strong research evidence exists that clearly demonstrates that the comportment of elderly persons, even those with severe organic impairments, is influenced by the antecedent stimuli that precede their actions (via respondent conditioning) (Collins & Plaska, 1975; Halbertsam et al., 1971), by the consequences that follow their behavior (via operant conditioning) (Ankus & Quarrington, 1972), and through observing others (Corby, 1975). Behavioral analysis and therapy in the field of gerontology attempt to utilize this basic science knowledge regarding human comportment to address selected problems experienced by elderly persons and, in some cases, their caregivers. Guided by the empirically supported principles of learning theory, the behavioral health and human service worker assisting elderly clients may develop etiological hypotheses regarding certain problematic areas of functioning, and from such hypotheses (and the existing empirical practice-research literature) formulate one or more intervention strategies aimed at assisting the aged. Three such examples, drawn from the principles of respondent (i.e., Pavlovian or classical) conditioning, are described in the next section.

Practice Drawing on Respondent Conditioning Principles

Most health and human service workers have heard of the bell and pad device as a method of helping persons achieve nighttime urinary continence and are aware that this device's operation is based on respondent learning principles. By repeatedly pairing the act of enuresis and the accompanying distended bladder (a neutral stimulus) with the sound of a loud bell (an unconditioned stimulus) that wakes one up (an unconditioned response), the sensations of having a distended bladder will eventually wake one up (the conditioned response) in the absence of the noise of the alarm. Although most human service practice with this device has been conducted with children and adolescents (Sluckin, 1989), it has been shown to be helpful with elderly nursing home residents as well (Collins & Plaska, 1975). Since urinary incontinence is a serious problem for many elderly persons and is a major cause of nursing home placements (Ouslander, 1983), it is clear that the simple but effective bell and pad technology illustrates one benefit of service provider's familiarity with the principles of respondent conditioning.

Another behavior therapy technique based on respondent conditioning principles is the procedure known as *guided mourning*, useful in the treatment of clients who suffer from morbid grief following the death of a spouse or other loved one. A client for whom this technique is appropriate was described by Sireling, Cohen, and Marks (1988):

122 Bruce A. Thyer et al.

A woman of 69 visited her GP (general practitioner) regularly for three years after her mother died. A year after her last visit her husband died too, while away from home. She became severely anxious and took an antidepressant and a minor tranquilizer. A year after her husband's death she had tremor, palpitations, churning abdomen, insomnia, and guilty ruminations. She thought she heard him cough or bringing her morning tea, avoided baking pastry (her husband's favorite food), kept his spectacles and other belongings, and repeatedly checked that the clock that had stopped the night he died was ticking. Anxiety worsened on the 7th and 17th of each month, her husband's birthday and date of death, respectively. She and her husband had been very close. They had courted from age 14. She never made friends, rarely went out, and had never worked outside the home. (p. 125)

Obviously, grief reactions of this severity are quite incapacitating. Fortunately, a number of controlled studies have demonstrated that guided mourning is highly effective in helping such persons overcome morbid grief.

The technique involves encouraging the grieving client to expose him/herself to situations (conditioned stimuli) that evoke inappropriate grief, instead of avoiding these circumstances, as is the "natural" reaction. Sireling et al. (1988) describe a series of such tasks one female client (whose mother had died) was asked to undertake, activities representative of the treatment activities involved in guided mourning therapy:

(1) visiting the crematorium to look at smoke emerging from the chimney; (2) asking her grandmother to describe the body's appearance in the hospital chapel; (3) talking about mother's final illness; (4) bringing mother's photograph to several sessions and looking at it for prolonged periods; (5) listing mother's positive and negative attributes (to elicit avoided anger with her); (6) writing a letter to mother complaining about not being told the diagnosis, and reading this aloud to mother's photograph; (7) spending fixed period in mother's bedroom; (8) wearing shoes and jewelry given by her mother. (p. 124)

The theory is that prolonged and consistent exposure to (as opposed to avoidance of) these anxiety-evoking stimuli will elicit weaker and weaker grief responses, similar to repeatedly exposing a person to a conditioned stimulus without ever again pairing this conditioned stimulus with an unconditioned response. Such experiences lead to what is called, in respondent theory, extinction of conditioned responses.

The experimental evidence of the efficacy of guided mourning as a method of helping persons in overcoming morbid grief is now quite extensive (as reviewed in Sireling, Cohen, & Marks, 1988), to the point where this therapy may now be viewed as the treatment of choice for such individuals. Since the death of loved ones is an increasingly common occurrence as one ages, the clinical significance of guided mourning to the care of elderly clients is obvious.

A third instance of utilizing respondent conditioning theory was described in the behavioral treatment of an elderly woman who suffered from a severe phobia, described below.

Description of the Client

The client was a 70-year-old widow, Mrs. Weber (a pseudonym), who was referred to the University of Michigan Medical Center Phobia Clinic, following 3 years of unsuccessful verbal psychotherapy and gradual real life desensitization treatment for a severe fear of dogs. Mrs. Weber reported that while on a walk 4 years earlier, she was unexpectedly attacked by a large Saint Bernard dog, whereby she was knocked down from behind and repeatedly bitten on the head, stomach, and buttocks. A passer-by pulled the dog off her and took the client for emergency room treatment. Subsequently she experienced stark terror on seeing or hearing any dog. As time passed Mrs. Weber began to curtail her outdoor activities, such as walks or shopping, for fear of meeting dogs. Four months after the attack she entered into verbal psychotherapy, which did not result in symptom alleviation. During the last year of her 3 years of dynamic psychotherapy she was instructed to begin a program of self-conducted gradual real life desensitization that produced some improvements. However, while on another walk 9 months before her referral to the Phobia Clinic, Mrs. Weber observed a Doberman Pinscher dog approaching her from about 150 yards away. While anxiously attending to the oncoming animal, she slipped on a patch of ice, fell, and broke her hip, resulting in a 4-month convalescence and a marked resurgence of her fear of dogs. At the time of her subsequent referral by her psychotherapist, Mrs. Weber was experiencing severe functional limitations in her daily activities, which were beginning to assume agoraphobic-like proportions, as well as ongoing nightmares and insomnia related to her anxiety about dogs.

Apart from this disabling fear Mrs. Weber appeared to lead a satisfying life, was active with friends and outside interests, and had close family ties. She held a doctorate degree and had been retired for 7 years.

Treatment Program

Since there were no medical contraindications precluding the use of anxiety-eliciting procedures, prolonged real life exposure therapy was selected as the treatment method after the technique was explained to Mrs. Weber and her consent obtained. She was told that less discomforting methods were available, should she desire them, such as systematic desensitization or very gradual, therapist-assisted real life desensitization, but that rapid real life exposure was generally more efficient for the treatment of small animal phobias (see Thyer, 1987, for a review). She was assured that she would determine the pace of treatment and that she could terminate a session at any time, should she choose to do so.

The first and second treatment sessions used a 10-pound and a 50-pound dog, respectively, as the anxiety-evoking stimulus. Mrs. Weber was brought into the room where the dog was secured on a leash, and she was then induced through verbal persuasion and support to approach the dog as closely as possible. After she was comfortable with the dog in close proximity to her and having him lick her hands, she was left alone in the room with the animal for several minutes. Mrs. Weber then took the dog outside for a walk, in the presence of the therapist. In both sessions she habituated to the proximity of the dog within half an hour.

The third session consisted of an hour long visit to the local humane society. Here, following several minutes of exposure to the barking of dozens of dogs simultaneously, Mrs. Weber quickly lost her pronounced startle reflex previously elicited whenever she heard a dog bark. By the time the session was concluded she was calmly reaching into cages, petting a variety of dogs, including a Doberman Pinscher, and letting them lick her.

In the fourth session, Mrs. Weber entered a room where an 80-pound Afghan hound was secured. The dog was brought close to her as rapidly as she would permit. After 15 minutes she was comfortably feeding the animal dog biscuits, and another dog, a 95-pound Great Dane, was announced and brought into the room. At the sight of the larger animal Mrs. Weber became very anxious and burst into tears. After 2 minutes she calmed down and gradually allowed the therapist to bring the dog closer and closer. Proceeding as rapidly as Mrs. Weber would permit, the therapist induced her to pet both dogs and to feed them in response to a variety of tricks they performed. She soon became adept at firmly commanding the animals to sit, lie down, play dead, speak, etc., and was able to do this comfortably while the therapist left the room for 5 minutes. Before the end of the session Mrs. Weber was feeding both animals dog biscuits, while the Afghan, seated by her feet, and the Great Dane, placed on the couch along side of her, barked loudly and repeatedly. Throughout the latter portion of this 1½ hour session, Mrs. Weber repeatedly exclaimed to the therapist that she could not believe that she was actually engaged in these activities, yet remaining calm. The fifth session was similar to the fourth, except that only the Great Dane was used, and the client did not experience any significant anxiety at any point.

Between all therapist-conducted exposure sessions Mrs. Weber completed a series of mutually agreed-on behavioral homework tasks consisting of going on walks and visits for gradually longer periods of time in unfamiliar neighborhoods where it was possible she would unexpectedly encounter free-running dogs, an activity in which she had previously been unable to engage. Mrs. Weber reported success in accomplishing these tasks, and treatment was terminated at the end of the fifth session, since she was no longer experiencing any phobic symptoms either within the treatment sessions or during her daily routines.

Telephone contacts at 3 and 6 months after termination indicated a maintenance of therapeutic gains and continued satisfaction on the part of the client about her improvements. Mrs. Weber was readily able to go out and perform her daily tasks, and the sight and sound of dogs no longer filled her with dread. Ruminations about dogs as well as nightmares of them and related insomnia were also absent throughout the follow-up period.

In the above case, the client was a full and active participant in the design and conduct of treatment. There was no coercion employed, of course, and although such a treatment was at times stressful for Mrs. Weber, with therapist support she persevered and ultimately overcame her disabling phobia. Her avoidance behavior related to dogs and her subjective distress when exposed to them were conceptualized as learned (conditioned) responses acquired through the processes of respondent learning, in this case associated with two severely traumatic experiences. This etiological formulation is supported by well-controlled laboratory-based studies with humans (Malloy & Levis, 1988) as well as practice wisdom. Drawing on this etiological hypothesis based on respondent conditioning theory, a treatment program exploiting the principles of respondent extinction was employed and proven successful. This case provides a simple illustration of the heuristic value of theory in guiding health and human service practice. (Much of the above section was originally published in Thyer, 1981.)

Practice Drawing on Operant Learning Principles

The service provider in the field of gerontology and geriatrics knowledgeable of the principles of social learning theory and of the research methods of the experimental analysis of behavior can usefully apply such knowledge and abilities to a wide variety of problem areas relevant to the field of gerontology. The book by Pinkston and Linsk (1984a) is a superlative exposition on applying the operant behavioral analytic model to social work practice with the elderly and is highly recommended. Included are detailed descriptions of work with families and nursing home caregivers, the conduct of pretreatment assessments, including reliably observing behavior, and environmental modification procedures. Among the detailed case examples and problem areas addressed are increasing independence and promoting social contacts among elderly clients, improving self-care skills, reducing urinary incontinence, promoting rational speech among dementia patients, and reducing hallucinations and depression. The Pinkston and Linsk (1984a) text relies almost exclusively on the operant model of human comportment, and the above review indicates the diversity of problem areas in which this approach has been successfully employed. The following section describes another example of behavioral analysis and therapy in the field of gerontology that draws on the operant model of practice.

This study was a community-based investigation of the effectiveness of one operant procedure, known as prompting, as a strategy to help promote safety belt use by elderly drivers. To date, no safety belt promotion study specifically targeting elderly drivers has been published, despite the social significance of motor vehicle accident-related injuries and fatalities to America's aged. According to the National Safety Council (1987), in 1986, 6500 (14%) of the 47,900 motor vehicle fatalities occurred among drivers and passengers aged 65 years or older. Of the 1,800,000 recorded injuries, approximately 120,000 (7%) were inflicted on elderly vehicle occupants. Accidents (of all types) are the sixth and eighth most common cause of death among males and females, respectively, aged 65 or older (Verbrugge, 1987), and motor vehicle accidents undoubtedly form a large proportion of such studies. Clearly there is a need to develop practical means of promoting consistent safety belt use by elderly drivers and motor vehicle passengers. The study described below is basically a replication of an earlier community-based behavioral experiment employing a sample of university faculty and staff personnel (Thyer, Geller, Williams, & Purcell, 1987), this time targeting a group of elderly drivers.

Project Site and Clients

This study was undertaken at a local senior citizens' center in Tallahassee, Florida, during the summer of 1987. As a part of the center's community services, a free hot meal was served to area senior citizens at noon, Monday through Friday. No means test was necessary to qualify for this program. The Senior Citizens' Center parking lot was located immediately adjacent to the entrance, and a number of elderly drivers drove to and from the noon meal program, using the center's parking lot. Permission to conduct this study was granted by the center's Director.

Observational Procedures

Graduate students served as observers for each day of the study and sat in an automobile parked down the street from the center's parking lot exit where a clear view of exiting drivers was available. A second observer was scheduled to be present every other day for the purpose of documenting the reliability of these safety belt observations. Each observer independently recorded the over-the-shoulder safety belt use of each exiting driver, along with the driver's race and gender. No individual identifications were made of these exiting drivers (e.g., names or license plate numbers). Observations were made between the hours of noon and 1:00 PM, Monday through Friday, corresponding to the time period when virtually all exiting drivers were senior citizens who had attended the noon meal program.

Experimental Design and Intervention

Driver safety belt use was unobtrusively recorded by the observers for a 7-day period. On the eighth through twenty-first consecutive observation days, a female graduate student stood to the side of the parking lot's exit and displayed a placard to the drivers exiting between noon and 1:00 PM. The placard, more fully described in Geller et al. (1985) and Thyer et al. (1987), is an 11 × 14 inch sign that reads on side one, "Please Buckle Up—I Care," and on side two, "Thank you for Buckling Up." The sign was held chest high, and side one was displayed to each driver. If the driver was observed to buckle-up, or was already buckled, the prompter reversed the sign to display the message on side two. No other manipulations were employed to stimulate compliance (e.g., verbal instructions, gestures). Observers continued to record safety belt use during this 14-day intervention phase in a manner identical to that during the preceding 7-day baseline period. After day 21, the prompting intervention was discontinued, and observations continued as before, for a further 6 days. The end of the semester (and access to student observers and prompters) precluded a restoration of the prompting strategy. Thus, this study conformed to an A–B–A single-system (or time-series) research design (Thyer, 1991a). These observational and intervention procedures were identical to those employed by Thyer et al. (1987).

128   Bruce A. Thyer et al.

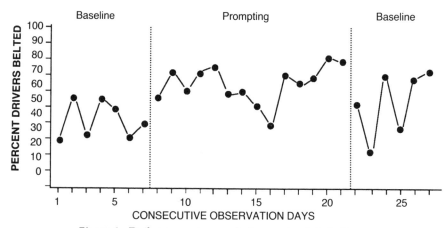

Figure 1. Daily percentages of observed safety belt use.

Results

A reliability observer was present on 48% of the observation days. Daily interrater agreements for driver safety belt use ranged from 67 to 100%, with a mean agreement of 84%. A total of 110 drivers were observed during the first baseline phase, 295 during the prompting phase, and 97 during the return to baseline condition. Observations indicated that 123 of the exiting drivers were black, 379 were white, 217 were male, and 285 were female. A total of 502 drivers were observed during the course of this study.

Daily percentages of observed safety belt use for the exiting drivers are depicted in Figure 1. During the first baseline phase, safety belt use averaged 42%. During the prompting phase, safety belt use increased to a mean of 60%, and it declined to a mean of 48% during the second baseline condition.

Discussion

The data in Figure 1 show a modest functional relationship between the prompting strategy and safety belt use, comparable to that observed in earlier studies employing a more general sample of drivers of all ages. The senior citizen drivers' baseline use of safety belts was comparable to that observed in the local community's population (Thyer & Landis, 1988), and their positive response to the prompting intervention is approximately equivalent to that of other local drivers (Thyer et al., 1987). Researchers did not assess passenger use of safety belts, whether or not the drivers began using their belts in other settings, or the long-term impact of the program. These are all obvious limitations of the study, but not necessarily questions needed to be answered in preliminary investigations of this nature.

Safety belt use is a form of discriminated operant response. People buckle their safety belts only under highly specific circumstances (e.g., about to travel in an automobile), and do not buckle up if they are not in a car (while seated at the dining room table, for example), or if seated in the car and not about to travel (e.g., while cleaning the car's interior). Current operant theory (Hayes, 1989; Thyer, 1991b) distinguishes between contingency-shaped and rule-governed behavior. The former is acquired when a person directly experiences the consequences of her/his own action (is reinforced, for example). Rule-governed behavior is behavior that is initially acquired via instructional methods (spoken directions, written explanation, gestures provided by another, prompts, signs, etc.). Most complex adult operant behavior is not contingency-shaped but is rule-governed, and prompting safety belt use among motor vehicle occupants using the signs described in the above study has been so conceptualized in previous community-based interventions designed and conducted by social workers (Williams, Thyer, Bailey, & Montgomery, 1989). Studies such as the above are best viewed as beginning efforts on a continuum of scientific investigations intended to develop reliable methods of safety belt use promotion among the elderly, efforts whose effects are more durable than the temporary increases obtained through prompting with placards.

Practice Drawing on the Principles of Observational Learning

The capacity to acquire new behavior through observing others is found in a large number of nonprimate and primate species, including humans. From the perspective of the behavior analyst, persistent imitative behavior is a complex form of operant activity. One's efforts at imitating others produces consequences for oneself, and to the extent that an imitated behavior is reinforced, two processes simultaneously occur: the imitated behavior is strengthened, and the generic operant called "imitation" is strengthened as well. Over the course of one's lifetime, one learns that reproducing behaviors modeled by others, behavior that appears to generate reinforcing consequences for the model, is likely to yield reinforcement for oneself as well. Over time, some modeled behaviors will be imitated by an observer in the absence of immediate reinforcement, probably because the observer has experienced a history of intermittent reinforcement for imitation, a schedule of reinforcement likely to generate persistent modeling. Behavior analysts employ the principles of observational learning in helping elderly clients either to reacquire or develop for the first time adaptive interpersonal skills (see, for example, Corby, 1975).

One such study conducted by social workers was reported by Berger and Rose (1977). Institutionalized elderly patients (mean age of 79 years) were randomly assigned to receive either behaviorally oriented interpersonal skills training or to one of two control treatments. Those in the training program received intensive individually conducted therapy sessions conducted by graduate social work students and involved role-playing, guided practice, and rehearsal of selected interpersonal skills, coaching, and modeling. Clients were selected on the basis of their expressed difficulties in certain interpersonal situations (e.g., making a reasonable request, refusing an inappropriate request, making conversation, responding to an unfair action or statement). Treatment involved only three 1-hour training sessions, but nevertheless produced significant improvements in the elderly residents' interpersonal skills, with respect to the situations they had rehearsed and practiced with their therapists. Such improvements were not noted among clients in the control conditions.

Toseland and Rose (1978) were able to employ similar social skills training procedures, in large part derived from observational learning principles, with therapy provided in group settings to elderly clients. Clients ($n = 53$; mean age $= 69$ years) were recruited from community agencies serving senior citizens. Behaviorally oriented interpersonal skills training provided in a group context was found very helpful in improving the social skills of older adults, while modeling was a component of the social group work program offered by Toseland (1977) to older persons requesting help in learning problem-solving skills. Pinkston and Linsk (1984b) extended the application of modeling as a therapeutic tool by training the family caregivers of impaired elderly persons to use the principles of imitative learning to help their older family members. Examples of problems addressed through this project included general self-care, incontinence, eating difficulties, hygiene, and ambulation.

Summary

Much has been left untouched in this review of the current applications of behavioral analysis and therapy within the field of gerontology. The intentional design of living environments, structured in such a way as to reduce the social isolation of nursing home residents (Blackman, Howe, & Pinkston, 1976; Jenkins, Felice, Lund, & Powell, 1977; Peterson, Knapp, Rosen, & Pither, 1977; Quattrochi-Tubin, & Jason, 1980;

Goldstein & Baer, 1976; McClannahan & Risley, 1974, 1975; Lawton, 1980; Carstensen & Erickson, 1986) or to promote reality orientation (Greene, Nicol, & Jamieson, 1979; Hanley, 1981) has not been addressed. Neither has the use of positive reinforcement techniques to promote adherence to medical regimens by older adults (Dapcich, & Hovell, 1979; Engel, 1983), to restore mobility (Libb & Clements, 1969; MacDonald & Butler, 1974; Wiswell, 1980; Burgio et al., 1986), or to help the elderly regain lost social or interpersonal skills (Blackman, Gehle, & Pinkston, 1979; Geiger & Johnson, 1974; Hoyer et al., 1974; Mueller & Atlas, 1976; Praderas & MacDonald, 1986; Linsk, Howe, & Pinkston, 1975). Particularly exciting is the use of behavioral methods to augment memory, to facilitate so-called cognitive functioning, and to promote the older person's functional autonomy (Lindsey, 1964; Bellucci & Hoyer, 1975; Rinke et al., 1978; Robin, 1983; Skinner, 1983; Skinner & Vaughn, 1983; Meichenbaum, 1974; Haley, 1983; Bourgeosis, 1990).

Behavioral methods may be taught to the family members and other caregivers of impaired elderly persons with considerable success, permitting a stretching of scarce professional resources, as has been demonstrated by Green, Linsk, and Pinkston (1986), Linsk, Pinkston, and Green (1982), Pinkston and Linsk (1984b), and Haley (1983). The utility of applied behavior analysis in work with older adults is not limited to individual therapy or group work, however. The safety belt study described above was an example of community-based human service practice. Similarly, Bunck and Iwata's (1978) experimental study on promoting senior citizens' participation in a nutritious meals program took place in a community-based context and not in a consulting room, private home, or nursing facility.

Two final areas worthy of mention are the use of contingency management procedures to improve the caregiving skills of the *staff* of nursing homes and other facilities providing services to the elderly (e.g., Burgio et al., 1990; Fabry & Reid, 1978), and the use of operant techniques to improve the lives of elderly persons who are developmentally disabled (Foxx et al., 1986; Kleitsch, Whitman, & Santos, 1983).

The behavioral approach has obviously been applied across the spectrum of practice in work with elderly clients. As a model of psychosocial intervention it is unique in having an extremely strong foundation of empirical research support. Health and human service workers have been at the forefront of this emerging field of behavioral gerontology and it seems ethically incumbent on those practitioners providing services to geriatric clients, their families, institutional caregivers, and agency staff to be familiar with both the conceptual foundations of behavior analysis and the interventive techniques derived from such theory.

References

Ankus, M., & Quarrington, B. (1972). Operant behavior in the memory disordered. *Journal of Gerontology, 27,* 500–510.

Baltes, M. M., & Zerbe, M. B. (1976). New approaches towards aging: A case for the operant model. *Education Gerontology, 2,* 383–405.

Barker, R. L. (1987). *The social work dictionary.* Silver Spring, MD: National Association of Social Workers.

Bellucci, G., & Hoyer, W. J. (1975). Feedback effects on the performance and self-reinforcing behavior of elderly and young adult women. *Journal of Gerontology, 30,* 456–460.

Berger, R. M., & Rose, S. D. (1977). Interpersonal skills training with institutionalized elderly patients. *Journal of Gerontology, 32,* 346–353.

Blackman, D. K., Gehle, C., & Pinkston, E. M. (1979). Modifying eating habits of the institutionalized elderly. *Social Work Research and Abstracts, 15*(3), 18–24.

Blackman, D. K., Howe, M., & Pinkston, E. M. (1976). Increasing participation in social interaction of the institutionalized elderly. *The Gerontologist, 16,* 69–76.

Bourgeois, M. S. (1990). Enhancing conversation skills in patients with Alzheimer's disease using a prosthetic memory aid. *Journal of Applied Behavior Analysis, 23,* 29–42.

Bunck, T. J., & Iwata, B. A. (1978). Increasing senior citizen participation in a community-based nutritious meal program. *Journal of Applied Behavior Analysis, 11,* 75–86.

Burgio, L. D., Burgio, K. L., Engel, B. T., & Tice, L. M. (1986). Increasing distance and independence of ambulation in elderly nursing home residents. *Journal of Applied Behavior Analysis, 19,* 321–328.

Burgio, L. D., Engel, B. T., Hawkins, A., McCormick, K., Scheve, A., & Jones, L. T. (1990). A staff management system for maintaining improvements in continence with elderly nursing home residents. *Journal of Applied Behavior Analysis, 23,* 111–118.

Carstensen, L. L., & Erickson, R. J. (1986). Enhancing the social environments of elderly nursing home residents: Are high rates of interaction enough? *Journal of Applied Behavior Analysis, 19,* 349–355.

Cautela, J. R. (1969). A classical conditioning approach to the development and modification of behavior in the aged. *The Gerontologist, 9,* 109–113.

Cautela, J. R. (1972). The Pavlovian basis of old age. In D. P. Kent, R. Kastenbaum, & S. Sherwood (Eds.), *Research planning and action for the elderly.* New York: Behavioral Publications.

Collins, R., & Plaska, T. (1975). Mowrer's conditioning treatment for enuresis applied to residents of a nursing home. *Behavior Therapy, 6,* 632–638.

Corby, M. (1975). Assertion training with aged populations. *The Counseling Psychologist, 5,* 69–74.

Dapcich-Miura, E., & Hovell, M. E. (1979). Contingency management of adherence to a complex medical regimen in an elderly heart patient. *Behavior Therapy, 10,* 193–201.

Engel, B. T. (1983). Behavioral medicine. In R. F. Walker & R. L. Cooper (Eds.). *Experimental and clinical interventions in aging* (pp. 335–342). New York: Marcel Dekker.

Fabry, P. L., & Reid, D. H. (1978). Teaching foster grandparents to train severely handicapped person. *Journal of Applied Behavior Analysis, 11,* 111–123.

Foxx, R. M., McMorrow, M. J., Bittle, R. G., & Ness, J. (1986). An analysis of social skills generalization in two natural settings. *Journal of Applied Behavior Analysis, 19,* 299–305.

Geiger, O. G., & Johnson, L. A. (1974). Positive education for elderly persons: Correct eating through reinforcement. *The Gerontologist, 14,* 432–436.

Geller, E. S., & Bruff, C. D., & Nimmer, J. G. (1985). "Flash-for-life": Community-based prompting for safety belt promotion. *Journal of Applied Behavior Analysis, 18,* 309–314.

Germain, C. B. (1987). Human behavior in contemporary environments. *Social Service Review, 61,* 566–580.

Goldstein, R. S., & Baer, D. M. (1976). A procedure to increase the personal mail and number of correspondents for nursing home residents. *Behavior Therapy, 7,* 348–354.

Green, G. R., Linsk, N. L., & Pinkston, E. M. (1986). Modification of verbal behavior of the mentally impaired elderly by their spouses. *Journal of Applied Behavior Analysis, 19,* 329–336.

Greene, J. G., Nicol, R., & Jamieson, H. (1979). Reality orientation with psychogeriatric patients. *Behavior Research and Therapy, 17,* 615–617.

Halbertsam, J. L., Zaretsky, H., Brucker, B. S., & Guttman, A. R. (1971). Avoidance conditioning of motor responses in elderly brain-damaged patients. *Archives of Physical Medicine and Rehabilitation, 52,* 318–327.

Haley, W. E. (1983). A family-behavioral approach to the treatment of the cognitively impaired elderly. *The Gerontologist, 23,* 18–20.

Hanley, I. G. (1981). The use of signposts and active training to modify ward disorientation in elderly patients. *Journal of Behavior Therapy and Experimental Psychiatry, 12,* 241–247.

Hayes, S. C. (Ed.) (1989). *Rule-governed behavior: Cognition, contingencies, and instructional control.* New York: Plenum.

Hoyer, W. J., Kafer, R. A., Simpson, S. C., & Hoyer, F. W. (1974). Reinstatement of verbal behavior in elderly patients using operant procedures. *The Gerontologist, 14,* 149–152.

Jackson, G. M., & Patterson, R. L. (1982). Single case behavioral treatment. In R. L. Patterson (Ed.). *Overcoming Deficits of Aging: A Behavioral Approach* (pp. 89–110). New York: Plenum.

Jenkins, J., Felice, D., Lund, B., & Powell, L. (1977). Increasing engagement in activity of residents in older people's homes by providing recreational materials. *Behaviour Research and Therapy, 15,* 429–434.

Kleitsch, E. C., Whitman, T. L., & Santos, J. (1983). Increasing verbal interaction among elderly socially isolated mentally retarded adults. *Journal of Applied Behavior Analysis, 16,* 217–223.

134 Bruce A. Thyer et al.

Lawton, M. P. (1980). Psychosocial and environmental approaches to the care of senile dementia patients. In J. O. Cole & J. E. Barrett (Eds.). *Psychopathology in the aged* (pp. 265–278). New York: Raven Press.

Libb, J. W., & Clements, C. (1969). Token reinforcement in an exercise program for hospitalized geriatric patients. *Perceptual and Motor Skills, 28*, 957–958.

Lindsey, O. R. (1964). Geriatric behavioral prosthetics. In R. Kastenbaum (Ed.), *New thought on old age.* New York: Springer.

Linsk, N. L., Howe, M. W., & Pinkston, E. (1975). Behavioral group in a home for the aged. *Social Work, 20*, 454–463.

Linsk, N. L., Pinkston, E. M., & Green, G. R. (1982). Home-based behavioral social work with the elderly. In E. M. Pinkston, J. L. Levitt, G. R. Green, N. L. Linsk, & T. L. Rzepnicki (Eds.), *Effective social work practice: Advanced techniques for behavioral interventions with individuals, families, and institutional staff.* San Francisco, CA: Jossey-Bass.

MacDonald, M. L., & Butler, A. K. (1974). Reversal of helplessness: Producing walking behavior in nursing home wheelchair residents using behavior modification procedures. *Journal of Gerontology, 29*, 97–101.

Malloy, P., & Levis, D. J. (1988). A laboratory demonstration of persistent human avoidance. *Behavior Therapy, 19*, 229–241.

McClannahan, L. E., & Risley, T. R. (1974). Designs of living environments for nursing home residents: Recruiting attendance in activities. *The Gerontologist, 14*, 236–240.

McClannahan, L. E., & Risley, T. R. (1975). Design of living environments for nursing home residents: Increasing participation in recreation activities. *Journal of Applied Behavior Analysis, 8*, 261–268.

Meichenbaum, D. (1974). Self-instructional strategy training: A cognitive prosthesis for the aged. *Human Development, 17*, 273–280.

Mueller, D. J., & Atlas, L. (1976). Resocialization of regressed elderly patients: A behavioral management approach. *Journal of Gerontology, 27*, 390–392.

Ouslander, J. G. (1983). Incontinence and nursing homes: Epidemiology and management. *The Gerontologist, 23*, 257.

Peterson, R. F., Knapp, T. J., Rosen, J. C., & Pither, B. F. (1977). The effects of furniture rearrangement on the behavior of geriatric patients. *Behavior Therapy, 8*, 464–467.

Pinkston, E. M., & Linsk, N. L. (1984a). *Case of the elderly: A family approach.* New York: Pergamon.

Pinkston, E. M., & Linsk, N. L. (1984b). Behavioral family intervention with the impaired elderly. *The Gerontologist 24*, 576–583.

Praderas, K., & MacDonald, M. L. (1986). Telephone conversation skills training with socially isolated, impaired nursing home residents. *Journal of Applied Behavior Analysis, 19*, 337–348.

Quattrochi-Tubin, S., & Jason, L. A. (1980). Enhancing social interactions and activity among the elderly through stimulus control. *Journal of Applied Behavior Analysis, 13*, 159–163.

Rinke, C. L., Williams, J. J., Lloyd, K. E., & Smith-Scott, W. (1978). The effects of prompting and reinforcement on self-bathing by elderly residents of a nursing home. *Behavior Therapy, 9*, 873–881.

Robin, J. (1983). Behavioral medicine: Beneficial effects of self-control training in aging. *International Review of Applied Psychology, 33,* 153–180.

Schonfield, A. E. D. (1980). Learning, memory, and aging. In J. E. Birren & R. B. Sloane (Eds.), *Handbook of mental health and aging* (pp. 214–244). Englewood Cliffs, NJ: Prentice Hall.

Sireling, L., Cohen, D., & Marks, I. M. (1988). Guided mourning for morbid grief: A controlled replication. *Behavior Therapy, 19,* 121–132.

Skinner, B. F. (1938). *The behavior of organisms.* Englewood Cliffs, NJ: Prentice-Hall.

Skinner, B. F. (1966). The phylogeny and ontogeny of behavior. *Science, 153,* 1205–1213.

Skinner, B. F. (1983). Intellectual self-management in old age. *American Psychologist, 38,* 239–244.

Skinner, B. F., & Vaughn, M. E. (1983). *Enjoy old age: A program of self-management.* New York: Norton.

Sluckin, A. (1989). Behavioral social work treatment of childhood nocturnal enuresis. *Behavior Modification, 13,* 482–497.

Thyer, B. A. (1981). Prolonged *in-vivo* exposure therapy in the treatment of a 70-year-old woman. *Journal of Experimental Psychiatry, 12,* 69–71.

Thyer, B. A. (1987). *Treating anxiety disorders: A guide for human service professionals.* Newberry Parks, CA: Sage.

Thyer, B. A. (1991a). Single system designs. In R. M. Grinnell (Ed.). *Social Work Research and Abstracts,* 4th ed. Itasca, IL: F. E. Peacock. In press.

Thyer, B. A. (1991b). Behavior analysis and human development: A person-in-environment perspective. In M. Bloom (Ed.), *Human development: Context, continuity, and change.* Columbia, SC: University of South Carolina Press. In press.

Thyer, B. A., Geller, E. S., Williams, M., & Purcell, E. (1987). Community-Based flashing to promote safety belt use. *Journal of Experimental Education, 55,* 155–159.

Thyer, B. A., & Landis, J. (1988). Is the Florida safety belt law effective? *American Journal of Public Health, 78,* 323.

Toseland, R. (1977). A problem-solving group workshop for older persons. *Social Work, 22,* 325–326.

Toseland, R., & Rose, S. D. (1978). Evaluating social skills training for older adults in groups. *Social Work Research and Abstracts, 14*(1), 25–33.

Verbrugge, L. M. (1987). From sneezes to adieux: Stages of health for American men and women. In S. S. Tobin (Ed.), *Health in aging: Sociological issues and policy directions* (pp. 17–57). New York: Springer.

Watson, J. B. (1913). Psychology as the behaviorist views it. *Psychological Review, 20,* 158–177.

Williams, M., Thyer, B. A., Bailer, J. S., & Montgomery, D. F. (1989). Promoting safety belt use with traffic signs and Prompters. *Journal of Applied Behavior Analysis, 22,* 71–76.

Wiswell, R. A. (1980). Relaxation, exercise, and aging. In J. E. Birren & R. B. Sloane (Eds.), *Handbook of mental health and aging* (pp. 943–958). Englewood Cliffs, NJ: Prentice-Hall.

6

Prescribed Therapeutic Self-Help for the Elderly: The Rational Behavioral Approach

MAXIE C. MAULTSBY, JR.

Introduction

The elderly population has replaced thrill seeking adolescents and young adults as people most likely to have a prescription or non-prescription drug-induced illness. The drugs most often abused are prescription and nonprescription drugs, believed to decrease or eliminate emotional distress. So, the four main reasons why many elderly people find the freedom of retirement emotionally distressing are: first, America is failing to adequately prepare its elderly for personally meaningful lives in retirement. Retirement means no paying job. A paying job is the average American's most valuable and objective basis for maintaining a sense of personally satisfying self-worth. Second, in a highly mobile society retirement means advanced age plus the ever-present emotional distress of probable and actual abandonment. Children, relatives, and friends are constantly forming new family ties and/or moving away. Third, retirement means reduced income, that most often causes a regretted change from preferred single family to "less" desirable apartment or more communally based living. Those changes elicit the stress of making new friends; for most older people making new friends is more of an unwanted burden than a pleasure.

Finally, there is the anticipation of one's own death. In the elderly community, death is usually life's most frequent and significant event. Though everyone knows that death is unavoidable, death still is considered the worst of all human tragedies, especially if it occurs in relative social isolation. Rare is the physician who has not heard at least once: "Doctor the thing that I fear most is dying alone or among strangers."

Understandably, therefore, the longer people live the greater the emotional stress of just living.

To some degree, adults in general and elderly people in particular usually believe that people should be able to analyze and solve their own emotional problems. That is probably why each year at least one best seller is an emotional self-help book. Self-help books describe the possibilities and joys of helping oneself. But, self-help books rarely give people an easy-to-use, instantly helpful, yet medically sound ways of emotional self-help without the pseudohelp of legal or illegal drugs.

This chapter describes one of those rare, easy-to-use, instantly helpful and medically sound way of emotional self-help. This self-help routine was taken from the rational self-help method called Rational Self-Counseling (Maultsby, 1975, 1984, 1986) or RSC for short.

To the extent that emotionally distressed elderly people (or anyone else) can learn anything at all, they can learn how to instantly start counseling themselves in a personally satisfying as well as healthier way. This result is especially likely when health professionals prescribe and monitor the self-help concepts and techniques used in RSC. And best of all, the energy and intellectual ability required to learn basket weaving or any other common recreational therapy activity are all that is required to learn RSC.

When most people first hear of teaching people to counsel themselves, their first question is: "Is it safe to let people counsel themselves, especially emotionally distressed, elderly, lay-people?"

Yes, it is safe. But no one could stop elderly people (or anyone else) from counseling themselves, even if it were not safe. Here is why. Self-counseling is thinking ideas that one believes, then reacting logically to those ideas.

It is irrelevant where people get an idea, from a friend, a relative, the newspaper, T.V., or divine revelation. Before that idea can have any influence on those people's emotional or physical behavior, those people have to think, believe, and react logically to that idea. But merely by thinking, believing, and reacting together to an idea, people instantly make that idea their idea. That is why self-counseling is the only effective kind there is. That fact makes self-counseling the only basis for self-control.

So, whether or not to allow people to counsel themselves is never a legitimate question. The only legitimate questions are whether or not to teach emotionally distressed people a mental and emotionally healthy way of counseling themselves, or—as is now usual—just ignore the unhealthy and problem creating way those people are now counseling themselves. Rational Self-Counseling will be a method of choice, for health professionals who are interested in helping people learn an easy-to-learn, instantly helpful, yet medically sound way of counseling themselves.

Rational Self-Counseling (RSC)

Rational Self-Counseling is the emotional self-help method, routinely included in Rational Behavior Therapy (Maultsby, 1984). RSC is what makes Rational Behavior Therapy a short-term psychotherapy that produces long-term results.

Both Rational Behavior Therapy and RSC are based on the same psychosomatic learning history. This medically sound theoretical way of understanding human emotional and physical behavior has this unique and attractive feature. It gives health professionals the most clinically useful explanation of how and why emotionally distressed people can quickly improve their emotional and behavioral self-management without alcohol or other drugs.

Five Main Theoretical Assumptions in RSC

First, people's undrugged, undiseased brain is their main organ of survival, comfort, and self-control. Second, people create and control both their desirable and undesirable reactions via the direct influence their minds have on their brains. Third, the most clinically useful way to think of the mind is that it consists mainly of people's beliefs and attitudes. Fourth, the main way personal beliefs and attitudes influence people's brains is via the sincere words they choose to use to think. Fifth, the sincere words people use to think are entirely real symbolic stimuli that substitute for the corresponding, objective stimuli and elicit the same or similar mental, emotional, and physical reactions that the real stimuli elicit. For example, the word "steak" for the average hungry American will trigger the same mental and emotional preeating reactions that a real steak would trigger (Figure 1). Or, the written or vocal message: "Your mother just died" would trigger essentially the same grief reaction as would actually seeing one's mother's demise.

Main Therapeutic RSC Concepts

The five main RSC concepts discussed here are (1) the healthy concept of rational, (2) the A,B,C model of healthy human emotions, (3) the concept of cognitive-emotive dissonance, (4) the concept of prescribed rational bibliotherapy, and (5) the rational versus the irrational concept of "should."

Figure 1: Class lecture.

The Healthy Concept of Rational

Most people think "rational" means what they believe; they also believe that what is irrational is what someone else believes that differs from what they believe. To verify that fact, think of the last time someone accused you of thinking or behaving irrationally or vice versa. Were the two of you in agreement either time? Of course not!

So, who was really thinking or behaving rationally? With only that datum, no one can say for sure. All one can say is that both of you disagreed. But for a concept of rational to be healthy for anyone, at any time, in any place, the concept must go beyond people's personal agreements or disagreements to the level of optimum emotional and physical health for everyone. That prerequisite distinguishes the healthy concept of rational used in RSC from the common, everyday concept of rational that most people use.

The healthy concept of rational describes mental, emotional, and physical behavior that simultaneously obeys at least three of the five rules for optimally healthy self-control. Thoughts, emotional feelings, or physical reaction that do not simultaneously obey at least three of those five rules cannot be either optimally healthy or rational for those people at that time. Therefore, it is usually best for those people to immediately replace such thoughts, feelings, or physical reactions with ones that have these three features: (1) they are personally acceptable to those people, (2) these thoughts and reactions simultaneously obey three or more of the five rules for optimally healthy self-control, and (3) these people are willing to think and act out those more rational thoughts, feelings, and physical reactions every time they now think and act out their objectively irrational thoughts, feelings, or physical reactions.

Next are those rules for optimally healthy and therefore rational self-control:

1. It is based on obvious facts.
2. It best helps one protect his/her life and health.
3. It best helps one achieve his/her short- and long-term goals.
4. It best helps one avoid his/her most dreaded or undesirable conflict with other people.
5. It best helps one feel emotionally the way one wants to feel without alcohol, other drugs, or brain damage.

A Typical Case History

Mrs. McCoy was a 76-year-old widow who had been depressed for 2 years. But because of her religious beliefs she had not sought professional help. Instead, she only counselled with her minister and suffered alone. Mrs. McCoy received temporary relief for several hours after most of those consultations. But 2 years later she was still daily depressed more than she wanted to be. After hearing about his work in helping elderly patients help themselves emotionally, her minister referred her to the author.

At age 50 (26 years prior to this consultation) Mrs. McCoy's husband had died suddenly, of a heart attack. Her eldest daughter was then having marital difficulties that quickly led to separation and divorce. It was mutually convenient and generally helpful for that daughter and her three children to begin living together with Mrs. McCoy, in her house. They all got along so well that Mrs. McCoy and that daughter continued to live together for the next 23 years.

After 23 years of mutually satisfactory, family living, Mrs. McCoy understandably concluded that she and her daughter would live together for the rest of her life. Cupid, however, is indefatigable. That year Mrs. McCoy's daughter met an eligible bachelor and began courting. The next year they married and the daughter moved into her new husband's house.

From the beginning of that courtship, Mrs. McCoy's depression began and continued until her first professional consultation with the author a year after the daughter's marriage.

Behavioral Groupings for Therapeutic Self-Help

In both Rational Behavior Therapy and Rational Self-Counseling, behavioral problems are viewed as being mainly not-learned or learned behavioral problems. Not-learned behavioral problems are inappropriate for Rational Self-Counseling. These people have a psychiatric disease. Their treatment needs to be given or supervised by a psychiatrist or other medical doctor. Next are the main distinguishing features of learned behavioral problems. They are the problems for which Rational Self-Counseling is ideal.

Learned behavioral problems have at least three of the following four behavioral signs:

1. These people will not show any significant signs of having a psychiatric disease. They will not have delusions or hallucinations; they will know who they are, where they are, and why they are there. In addition, they are still able to function acceptably in most of their life areas. Only with reference to their designated problem areas will these people have significant difficulties.

2. These people will give a credible history for their problem that is consistent with their cultural and/or subcultural experiences. In addition, mild forms of their problems will be common in the everyday lives of other people in that culture and subculture. For example, milder forms of Mrs. McCoy's depressive reactions to their daughter's courtship and marriage are common among most loving male and female parents. But those depressive reactions do not usually last 2 years.

3. These people's main emotional problems usually are intense, self-defeating anger, fear, and depression, or some combination of those three emotions. But these emotions will have plausible, easily recognizable precipitating events associated with their onset.

4. The history of people with learned behavioral problems shows objective evidence that these people sometimes voluntarily influence the onset, intensity, or duration of the emotional distress associated with their problem. Next is an example of that event.

McCoy's Common Sense Self-Help Maneuver

Dr. M: Give an example of what a typical day is like when you are having the most problems with your depression.

Mrs. M: I guess the last time was probably her birthday.

Dr. M: O.K. Now tell me about that day.

Mrs. M: Well, I called her to wish her a happy birthday and I told her I loved her; which I do. And she said: Thank you mother, I love you too. And when she said that I couldn't talk anymore, I hung the phone up.

Dr. M: And how did you feel the rest of the day?

Mrs. M: Just like I said, I felt like my heart was broken. That it just absolutely was broken.

Dr. M: How did you get yourself over that feeling?

Mrs. M: I employed my mind with something else, to get that off of me.

Early in their lives, most people discover that they cannot have miserable emotional feelings without first having miserable thoughts. So, when people decide "I've suffered enough about this thing" they usually try to distract themselves from it. To the extent that they are successful, they immediately feel better. But only until something again reminds them of the old event. Then they repeat that cycle of pain, distraction, and temporary relief.

For most of life's disappointments, that "common sense" self-help maneuver is sufficient. But Mrs. McCoy obviously needed some "*un-common sense*" self-help. When such self-help is Rational and is taught, the teaching/learning process usually starts with the distressed people learning their emotional A,B,Cs.

A,B,C's of Healthy Human Emotions

The A,B,C model of healthy human emotions was formulated by Dr. Albert Ellis (1963). This emotional model describes basic principles of healthy self-control that operate in all normal people from birth to death. Consequently, people usually have a significant amount of unnoticed but helpful knowledge about their emotional A,B,Cs. Consequently, people often can learn their emotional A,B,Cs as quickly by doing prescribed reading about them [i.e., *You and Your Emotions* (Maultsby & Hendricks, 1974)] as they can by having their emotional A,B,Cs personally explained to them. A combination of both maneuvers usually produces the most rapid therapeutic progress.

When people think objectively about their emotions they see the next fact clearly. Before people have an emotional feeling, they first notice something. What they notice is called A, or the activating event in their emotional A,B,Cs. To react in a personally meaningful way to an A-activating event, people must first evaluate it, using their current beliefs and attitudes about its seeming implications for their survival, comfort, and self-control. Those evaluating beliefs and attitudes are the B in their emotional A,B,Cs.

There are only three major types of evaluative beliefs and attitudes. They are either relatively positive, relatively negative, or relatively neutral. Those evaluative thoughts trigger and maintain the relatively positive, negative, or neutral emotional feelings that people have about their A-perceptions. Therefore, no matter how many different types of emotional labels or names people can think of, they will fit into one of those three emotional groups. Consequently, people's B-beliefs and attitudes force their brains to trigger real, logical, and correct positive, negative, or neutral emotional feelings about their A-perceptions. Those emotional feelings are the C in the A,B,Cs.

A.   An *activating* event or people's perception.
B.   People's *belief* (i.e., sincere thoughts and attitudes about their perception at A).
C.   People's *consequent* emotional feelings about A, which are *always* triggered by B, their beliefs and attitudes about A.

A common question: "Are human emotions really that simple?" Yes, they are. But initially many people refuse to believe it. Why? Because A,B,C type emotions are not the most common types in everyday life experience. In everyday life, people seldom first perceive, then noticeably think and only then feel. Instead they usually react as Evelyn did (Figure 2).

First, Evelyn saw (or more precisely, perceived) the alligator in her lap. That was A, her activating event. Then Evelyn instantly jumped up in panic at C, without taking time to think anything at B. So it could not have been her conscious beliefs at B that frightened her; she did not take the time to consciously think them.

The key concept here is *habit*. People most often react the way they are in the habit of reacting. But no one is born with habits. And like all habits, emotional habits have to be learned. In addition, they are learned according to the same neuropsychological mechanisms of repeated practice that control all habit learning. Those facts become clear when people carefully study the A,B,C Model of New Life Experiences.

The A,B,C Model of New Life Experiences:

A.   People's perception of task to be understood and learned.
B.   People's beliefs (i.e., sincere, correct thoughts and attitudes about their A-perceptions). "Sincere thoughts" usually refers to people's most transient beliefs. Those ideas have not yet been

Figure 2: Evelyn.

repeatedly thought enough in that situation for them to have become those people's *habitual* way of thinking about the A-event.

C-1. People's most logical emotional feelings for their B-beliefs and attitudes about A.

C-2. People's most logical physical reactions for their B-beliefs and attitudes about A.

This model summarizes the normal sequence of the essential neuro-psychophysiological mechanisms involved in learning any habit. One way of getting people to see that fact most quickly is to help them analyze the correct car-driving habit (Figure 3).

First, student drivers perceive the car with its driving instruments; that is A. Second, they sincerely think correct-driving thoughts at B (i.e., "The first thing I do is put the gear in park; then I put my foot on the brake and turn on the ignition; next I put the gear in drive, but I keep my foot on the brake until no traffic is coming," etc.) That is B. Third, those sincere thoughts at B trigger the most logical emotional feeling and correct physical reactions for those sincere thoughts. Those emotional feelings and physical reactions are the C-1 and C-2 in the A,B,Cs of new life experiences.

Figure 3: Student driver.

At first, the student's emotional feeling will probably be mild apprehension or anxiety. That is the logical, healthy, emotional reaction for a new learning experience, especially one that is potentially dangerous. But with enough correct practice, the student would quickly learn the safe, correct beliefs and attitudes plus the secondary, correct driving habits they produce. During that same time, the student's brain will automatically replace his initial anxiety with the calm, emotional feelings that are logical for rational confidence of success. From that point, he will be able to drive correctly without consciously thinking his initial, correct-driving thoughts. Yet he will be a better driver than he ever was before.

Now let us look at what that student will have had to do to arrive at that stage in the correct, car-driving habit. He would have had to repeat the same perceptions, sincere thoughts, emotional feelings, and physical actions enough times for his brain to convert those repeatedly paired perceptions and sincere thoughts into semipermanent neuropsychological units called beliefs and attitudes.

Habitual Beliefs. In everyday language, people use the word "belief" to refer to both their sincere thoughts and habitual beliefs. However, habitual beliefs are the spoken from of the semipermanent a–B type neuropsychological unit that, after enough practice, the brain creates and stores in its memory for all such A-events. Beliefs make it possible for people to practice having instant but correct emotional and/or physical reactions at C-1 and C-2, in response to just their memory or imagination of old repeated As and Bs, even though the old As (i.e., the external stimuli) are not or never have been present. For example, after people learn the correct driving beliefs they can sit in their homes and practice driving by merely closing their eyes and imagining themselves driving a car. Their mental picture and emotional feelings they trigger will quickly increase those people's driving skills. (Those are the main mental and behavioral mechanisms involved in learning phobias, as well as in practicing desired new emotional habits in RSC.)

The Belief Model of Habits

a–B.   Only habitual B-beliefs and attitudes about a remembered A-perception.

C-1 and 2.   Most logical as well as usual emotional feelings and physical reactions for those B-beliefs and attitudes.

Attitudes. At the same time human brains form beliefs, they also form *attitudes.* In fact, attitudes are the unspoken forms of beliefs. More accurately, attitudes are the unspoken forms of the semipermanent A–b type of neuropsychological unit that, after enough practice, the brain creates and stores in its memory for all such A-events. Attitudes make it possible for people to have instant but correct emotional and/or physical reactions at C, in response to the perception of old real or imagined A-events, without the necessity of first thinking the old sincere thoughts at B. For example imagine the scene shown in Figure 4. The driver immediately slammed on the brakes and felt afraid all without taking time to think anything. His unspoken attitude was: "I'm about to have a terrible accident; I'd better stop immediately," or words of equivalent meaning.

Why is that the most valid explanation of that driver's reactions? Behavior "speaks louder" than words. The driver reacted as if he had thought those beliefs. Attitudes are revealed by correctly answering this question—"If the person had needed to think sincere, reaction-triggering thoughts before having the reactions he/she has, what would those sincere thoughts have been?" With the auto driver, most probably they would have been the same, or quite similar to the beliefs suggested above. That analysis is based on the following universal law of learned human behavior.

All learned behaviors make logical sense, based on the people's beliefs about their perceptions of the moment. Therefore, unless people are in the process of learning new reactions to old A-perceptions, their reactions reflect their habitual beliefs about those perceptions.

Figure 4: Near accident.

Now, suppose the driver above had seen the same child running down the sidewalk, parallel to the street. Then he probably would have continued to maintain his speed and feel calm about doing it; again, all without consciously thinking anything. Why? Because his controlling attitudes then would have been the unspoken form of beliefs such as these: "There is no danger; I have no reason to slow down or feel afraid."

The Attitude Model of Habits

A–b.   Only the usual A-perceptions without the old B-sincere thoughts about those perceptions.

C-1 and 2.   Most logical as well as usual emotional feelings and physical reactions for those A–b-perceptions.

Attitude-triggered emotional feelings are the ones most people incorrectly accuse "It," or "he," "she" or "they" (i.e., the external world) of making them feel. The ubiquitous "He hurt my feelings," "She made me mad," "It upsets me," are common everyday examples of the popular "It-Monster" myth of emotional control that confuses emotionally distressed people. Still, as the last illustration showed, attitude formation is an essential brain function for healthy living. Without attitudes people could not protect themselves or others in the emergency situations of daily life.

Eliminating the Confusing "It-Monster" Myth. The A,B,C model of human emotions makes the next fact obvious. Statements such as "It upsets me, makes me mad, makes me feel good, depresses me, etc." are just socially acceptable magical thinking. There is no "it monster" outside people's minds that can force them to have emotional feelings that are contrary to their personal beliefs and attitudes. Therefore, each individual (with his/her beliefs and attitudes) is the only "It" that makes them feel the emotions they feel.

It is fortunate that nature programmed human brains to react that way. That fact frees people to feel any positive, negative, or neutral emotions they want to feel, about any life situation, even though that situation does not change one iota. That is why helping people take the "It-Monster" out of their self-understanding immediately empowers them. They instantly become free to exercise whatever personally desirable emotional control over the emotional ship of fate that they desire. The next excerpt shows Mrs. McCoy's learning her emotional A,B,Cs.

Dr. M: To get over your depression most quickly, the first thing you need to learn is what your emotions are made up of. Once you understand how your emotions work, you can immediately start controlling them more to your satisfaction. But, I want to emphasize one thing about that. You can immediately start changing your emotions. *But,* you can't permanently change them immediately. You have the emotional feelings you now have, only because they are now your habits. But they follow the same principles that any habits follow; if you understand that, then you understand all you need to know to start changing them to your satisfaction. It doesn't matter which emotions we're talking about—the deep sincere hurt, depressive feelings that you have now, or whether we're talking about happiness or love, anger, fear, or what have you. So, let's talk about something that's totally unrelated to your problem, so that you can be free to pay the most attention; because as I said, if you understand any emotion completely, you understand all you need to know to understand all of your emotions.

(Note: Why use an example that is unrelated to depressed people's problem to teach them their emotional A,B,Cs? That maneuver decreases the possibility that depressed people will get undesirably distressed while reviewing the A,B,Cs of their problem. The less avoidable emotional distress people have in learning their emotional A,B,Cs, the faster they usually learn them.)

Dr. M: O.K., let's assume that you are walking across your lawn and
            you look down and you see that you are about to step on a
            coiled rattlesnake. How do you think you'd immediately feel?
Mrs. M: A snake? Afraid and get out of the way.
Dr. M: Fine; that's a normal, natural response. But suppose you saw
            the same object before you got close to it, while you were
            calm, but curious about it and you said: "I wonder what that
            is?" and then as you get closer to it you say: "My God, that
            look's like a dangerous black snake." Then how do you think
            you'd feel?
Mrs. M: Why, I'd be more frightened.
Dr. M: Right, you'd be more frightened. But before you run away,
            suppose you take a second look and you see that it really is a
            harmless little garden snake; then you would quickly calm
            down again. Right?
Mrs. M: Right! I'd just get my hoe and kill it.
Dr. M: You'd get a hoe and kill it because even though it's harmless
            you wouldn't want to be bothered with it. O.K., I can under-
            stand that. But let's take a closer look at what would have
            happened to you emotionally.
               Before you can have an emotion, about anything, you have
            to first be aware of that thing. So, you would have seen the
            snake; that's "A" in the A,B,Cs of your emotional reaction.
            Next you would have thought something about the snake. At
            first you thought it looked like a black snake; black snakes are
            dangerous; so you would have felt afraid. But on second look
            you would have seen that it was a harmless snake; so you
            would stop feeling afraid; but you would have still gotten a
            hoe and tried to kill it, right? O.K. Now, your evaluative
            thoughts about "A" would have been "B," your beliefs in
            your emotional A,B,Cs. Then, the emotional feelings and
            actions you would have had would have been "C" in your
            emotional A,B,Cs.

The therapist cannot review too much. Once have given people an easily
understandable example of the A,B,Cs of their emotions, it is a good
idea to immediately review those A,B,Cs; that gets them firmly fixed in
their minds.

Dr. M: So, now we had the snake out there at "A" and then the
            things you would have thought about it at "B" and the
            feelings you would have felt at "C." And "C" also could
            include your physical actions; in the case of fear, you'd run
            away; but in this case you would have calmly tried to get rid
            of the snake; O.K. Now you see, most people would have the
            mistaken idea that your fear would have been caused by the
            snake. And you probably would have thought that too; you'd
            probably say "The snake frightened me," right?

Mrs. M: Yes.

Dr. M: But you see, that's a mistake. In reality, you would have frightened you about the snake. That's why people need to know their emotional A,B,Cs. If you know your A,B,Cs you can see not only that you create, maintain, and eliminate all of your emotional feelings, you see exactly how you do it. Now let's go back through the A,B,Cs again. First, you see something; that is "A," your perception of what was outside of you. Now, most people have the mistaken idea that it is "A" the external event that causes them to feel their emotions at "C." And if you believe that, and if you don't like the way you're feeling at "C," the solution is to change "A," or get rid of "A," right?

Mrs. M: Yes.

Dr. M: Right! But you may not be able to get rid of "A." That's why it's so important to know your A,B,Cs. For example, you are now feeling crushed, depressed, and lonely because . . .

Mrs. M: Because of "A."

Dr. M: Right, because of "A." Your daughter is married, and you can't do anything about that.

Mrs. M: No.

Dr. M: So, if you believed that "A" is what is controlling your depression at "C," then the only thing you can do is suffer. But, fortunately it's not that way. It's not "A" that controls your depressive feeling at "C": you do it with your beliefs and attitudes at "B".

Cognitive-Emotive Dissonance

As used in Rational Behavior (and here), cognitive-emotive dissonance has this specific meaning: It is the experience of thinking in a new way about something and having the emotional reaction that people normally describe as "That feels wrong to me." or "That doesn't feel right." Now let us see why cognitive-emotive dissonance occurs.

Like most people, these people usually will have achieved their successes in life by immediately accepting and acting on ideas that feel right to them and ignoring or rejecting ideas that feel wrong to them. But when people are trying to improve their emotional control the ideas that at first feel wrong to them are usually the new facts they need to instantly accept and immediately start acting on continually in their daily lives. At those times, their brain and their new, more rational thoughts will be telling them the correct way to behave. But, their "gut" (i.e., their emotional feelings) will be telling them: "Oh, no! That doesn't feel right! Reject it and do what feels right." *That unavoidable stage in all emotional reeducation is called cognitive-emotive dissonance.* Unless people

Figure 5: Flat world.

are taught how to correctly interpret it, they tend to resolve it by ignoring their new, more rational ideas and resume counseling themselves with their old, irrational, problem-creating beliefs.

Here is a maneuver to help people most quickly understand and rationally handle that potential barrier to improved emotional control. The therapist gently, but instructively describes this fact. In the dark ages, the fact that the world is round felt so wrong to even the most well-educated people that they just laughed at it, ignored it, and sometimes put to death the people who insisted on repeating it (Figure 5).

But the world was just as round in the dark ages as it is today. Obviously then, the only thing that has happened is this: At some point the misinformed people of the dark ages became willing to ignore their misleading "gut" feelings and started to use their brain's rational thinking to direct their behaviors. That's also what nature seemed to have intended them to do in the first place.

Why then do so many people ignore that scientific fact and make decisions with their "guts?" Mainly because of emotional confusion. They either do not know or they misinterpret the next law of healthy human nature.

New facts always feel wrong at first, especially when they conflict with old beliefs. They are three reasons for this. First, people do *not* hold beliefs that they sincerely think are wrong. Second, the ideas that people say feel right to them are the ones they *already* believe. Therefore, those ideas trigger the same familiar emotional feelings those people normally get when their reactions are objectively correct. Third, when an idea is associated with feelings that these people say "feels right," they assume their feelings prove that idea is a fact, or is good and should be acted on without question. But the next, instructive, personal example usually helps people see clearly when ideas that "feel right" are the most unhealthy ideas on which to act.

Imagine that you are a two-pack-a-day cigarette smoker. If you are, every 10 to 15 minutes, the most natural, normal, and right feeling idea for you to think is: "I need a cigarette." The most natural, normal, and right feeling action for you then is to immediately smoke a cigarette. But would your idea be a fact or your actions be healthy for you? Of course not.

For you to improve the health of your thinking and actions, what would you have to do first? You would first have to be willing to think the initially "wrong feelings" idea—"I don't need or want a cigarette"— *not* once or twice, *but* every time you used to think—"I need a cigarette." In addition, you would have to also do the very abnormal and "wrong feeling" act of refusing to smoke a cigarette. How many times? *Every* time that you get the "then" normal and natural, but unhealthy urge to smoke.

But, just as soon as you practice thinking and acting in that "wrong feeling," abnormal and unnatural, but healthy way enough times, what would happen? Your rational new, nonsmoking, but healthy way of thinking, feeling, and acting will start feeling so *right, natural,* and *normal* that you will simply refuse to think and act in your old way, which incidentally would then feel wrong, abnormal, and unnatural.

Four instantly useful insights:

1. People's feelings of rightness tell them *only* that what they are thinking or doing at the moment is what they are in the habit of thinking or doing.
2. A "right feeling" does not mean that people's thinking or action is good or healthy for them.
3. The previous true story shows that in new learning situations, "feeling wrong" tells people *only* that what they are thinking and doing at the moment is something that they have *not* yet practiced enough to make it their habitual reaction.
4. A right feeling often means that what people are doing is bad or unhealthy for them.

Now the important question! How can people quickly yet reliably know when to pay attention to their "right feelings" and when to ignore them? Remember! When people are being exposed to facts that can improve their thinking, emotional feelings, or physical self-control, those ideas feel wrong to them at first. But they are usually the new facts and reactions that they need to practice to most quickly improve their self-control. The ideas and reactions that instantly feel right to them will usually be their old ideas and reactions, which they then need to permanently ignore and stop acting out.

The therapist wanted Mrs. McCoy to see that emotional self-improvement is really emotional reeducation. The basic principles of emotional reeducation are the same as they are for learning any new habit. To emphasize that fact, the therapist used the example of Mrs. McCoy's bell ringing class at church to get her to discover all she needed to know and remember about emotional reeducation and to most quickly improve her emotional control.

Dr. M: What we've accomplished so far is helpful self-understanding, called intellectual insight. But, that doesn't solve the problem; it just tells you what you have to practice to solve it. It's like playing the piano; do you know how to play the piano?

Mrs. M: I used to and I am now in a bell-ringing class at the church.

Dr. M: O.K., bell-ringing class. When you went to the first bell-ringing class and they explained to you what each bell did and how to hit it and you took notes and got a little book. Right? Do you have a little book?

Mrs. M: Yes, we have a little book.

Dr. M: Well, after that first class, even though you understood everything perfectly, were you able to ring the bell perfectly, or even as well as you wanted to?

Mrs. M: No.

Dr. M: Well, I assure you that your emotions are more complex than ringing those bells. So, if you couldn't ring those bells perfectly, just because you understood how it's done, don't expect to control your emotions the way you want to control them instantly. But, you certainly started learning how to ring those bells, right in the first session, right? Well, that's what you've done here. You have started learning what you need to practice to start controlling your emotions better. But I predict that the next time you call your daughter, even at work, you're still going to feel some of that hurt. So expect it and don't be surprised or disappointed; you haven't learned enough yet about improved emotional control to start controlling your emotions perfectly. Just like with your bell ringing, you have to first learn what you need to think and practice before you can learn to react the way you want to react. It's the same with all of your emotions.

	Today, all I want you to remember is that the hurt feeling you have, that depression you have, you create it. It's not "it," your situation, or the fact that your daughter lived with you all these years, then moved out. It's you who have been incorrectly believing that it was that fact that has been making you feel lonely, depressed, and so forth. But that's a mistake. It was your evaluations of that fact that hurt and depress you. One of your evaluations was: "I can't help but be hurt." Right? But we know that was a mistaken idea because you don't get as hurt now as you did three months ago. Right?
Mrs. M:	Right.
Dr. M:	Three months ago you couldn't talk about it without crying. Today you've talked about it almost an hour, and I haven't seen a single tear. Now we're just going to take that fact one step further. Just like you have stopped hurting yourself about it a little bit, I'm going to teach you how to stop hurting yourself about it at all. But it's not going to happen instantly. I want you to remember that fact, because I don't want you to get false hopes and dash out and try to do what's impossible and fail, be disappointed, then jump to the incorrect conclusion that you can't do it and give up.

Prescribed Rational Bibliotherapy

Any worthwhile self-help idea is worth being exposed to at least three times; that is why the therapist reminds people that hearing about their emotional A,B,Cs in their RSC session is *only* that—just hearing about them. They do not start learning and benefiting from having heard about their emotional A,B,Cs until they involve themselves in applying them in everyday life. Prescribed rational bibliotherapy is a pleasant, yet highly effective way to ensure that people quickly start making that daily-life application.

Rational Bibliotherapy means frequently reading easy-to-understand self-help books and articles that are based on Rational Behavior Therapy (Maultsby, 1984).

Clinical research (Maultsby & Graham, 1974; Maultsby, Knipping, & Carpenter, 1974) indicates that the most effective bibliotherapeutic assignments are short (8–12 pages) chapters and articles, that are well illustrated with Sunday comics type characters. For the best patient/client compliance with prescribed bibliotherapy the assignments need to be accompanied by easy-to-understand, goal-directed reading instructions. Equally as important, the readers must be able to readily identify with the comic characters.

The standard, prescribed Rational Bibliotherapy booklet—*You and*

Figure 6: Examples of emotional A, B, C's.

Your Emotions (Maultsby & Hendricks, 1974)—has all of those characteristics. Next are examples of how the emotional A,B,Cs are illustrated
in Chapter One of *You and Your Emotions* (Figure 6).

How therapists introduce patients/clients to Prescribed, Rational Bibliography greatly influences how cooperative they will be. Here is a
common, yet highly effective routine. First, the therapist tells patient/
clients:

> All of the self-help concepts and techniques that you need to learn are
> described and illustrated with pictures in the booklet titled *You and Your
> Emotions*. It's not usually available in bookstores but the interested can get
> it by return mail for $8.75 from: I'ACT, 3939 West Spencer Street, Ap-
> pleton, WI 54914. In the meantime I shall lend you one of my office copies
> to read until your copy arrives. You are to read ONLY one short chapter
> per week. But you are to read it exactly as prescribed on this instruction
> sheet.

Next is that sheet of instructions. (Readers of this chapter have the
author's permission to reproduce that instruction sheet as well for the
free use by their patients/clients.)

YOUR PRESCRIBED READING INSTRUCTIONS

Following these directions will help you help yourself feel and act the
way you want to in the shortest time possible. Unless otherwise instructed, repeatedly read ONLY the one assigned chapter per week.

Set aside 10 minutes a day for your self-improvement time. If possible
set aside the same time each day; that is the best way to make your self-
improvement reading quickly become a habit for you.

The human mind is most open to new learning when people first wake up in the morning and just before they fall asleep at night. Why not wake up 10 minutes earlier than usual and immediately do your self-improvement reading before you get up, then read another 10 minutes before you go to sleep at night.

DAY ONE   Read your assignment once, just to see what it's about.

DAY TWO   Read your assignment again and while you're reading it, look for ideas that you disagree with. Write them down so that you can discuss them in your next session.

DAY THREE Read the assignment again and look for ideas you agree with. Write these ideas down and bring them with you to your next session.

DAY FOUR   Today as you do your prescribed reading, look for events that are similar to events you've seen in the lives of relatives, friends, or even enemies, if you have any. Again, write-up these events and bring the write-ups to your next session.

DAY FIVE   As you read today, look for events similar to events in your life in which you've already applied some of the self-help ideas discussed in the reading. Bring your notes about them to your next session.

DAY SIX   While reading the assignment today, think about what you have learned that you could have but didn't apply to make your life happier or more productive or more satisfying. Write down why you didn't use your new knowledge. The most common reason is: "I didn't know about it then" or "I didn't think about it."

DAY SEVEN Read your assignment again, and *review* your notes to prepare for their discussion in your next RBT session.

Immediate Results with Rational Bibliotherapy

Mrs. McCoy did her prescribed, rational bibliotherapy, 10–20 minutes each day. That was all the prescribed self-help she needed to immediately start eliminating her 2-year-old depression without drugs or electric shock. Next is Mrs. McCoy in her second RSC session.

Mrs. M: I feel that since I was here last week that I have overcome one thing. My daughter and her husband stopped by on business yesterday and I just absolutely acted civilized. People might say, oh, well, I wouldn't give in to all that kind of thing; but if you do it once, or you keep doing it, you don't know how good it makes you feel. You feel so much better . . .

Dr. M: Right . . .

Mrs. M: And so I feel like I've progressed a little.

Dr. M: Well, I would say that's a big step forward.

In those few seconds Mrs. McCoy described much more eloquently than the therapist could have the tremendous joy and pleasure people instantly feel once they prove this fact to themselves: They can improve their emotional control, even though they have been depressed because they have been incorrectly believing that they could not do it.

Instant Self-Analysis

There is a relatively small group of *irrational* but so called "common sense" beliefs that most people in Western society hold to some degree. Because virtually everyone holds these beliefs, most people accept them without question. Understandably therefore people rarely think of these beliefs as possible causes of their emotional distress. Yet, two or more of these irrational beliefs are usually at the core of most emotional distress in everyday life.

In RSC irrational common sense beliefs are called psychoemotional pollutants. (The author has put the 15 most common psychoemotional pollutants in a short Unhappiness Potential Inventory, which he will share with the readers on request.) The main irrational "common sense" beliefs that were keeping Mrs. McCoy depressed were as follows:

1. I believe that some people as well as some life events are just plain terrible or awful. There are just no other words for them, and I can't stand either those people or those events.
2. I believe that people (including me) are the same as their behavior (i.e., stupid acts mean that person is stupid).
3. Some things or events are so undesirable that they should never exist or happen, and I get very upset when they do exist or happen. But other things or events are so desirable that they should always exist or happen, and I get very upset when they don't.
4. I've tried to change myself, but I just can't do it.

The Camera Check of Facts

The first rule for rational self-counseling is to base your beliefs on the obvious facts of the activating event. Usually, emotionally distressed people confidently believe they are most consistently applying that rational will. Yet, emotionally distressed people violate the First Rational Rule the most. To correct that flaw, RSC requires people to do the camera check of facts.

In the A,B,C model of life events, the As are supposed to describe facts that a video camera would have recorded. Why? Because the brain works like a camera. The healthiest self-control occurs when people describe their A-events the way a video camera would have recorded them. When the therapist asks: "Would your statement pass the camera check?" that means: "Are you stating only obvious facts without mixing in personal beliefs about them?"

For example, the statement "My daughter got married and moved out of my house after we had lived together for twenty years" would pass the camera check. But the statement "By getting married and moving out of my house, my daughter made me look like an old, worn out shoe that she just threw in the garbage" would *not* pass the camera check for an obvious fact. On a video tape, Mrs. McCoy would not look like a shoe; she would still look like the human being that she was.

Why would it be better for healthy emotional control for people to replace the second statement with the first one? Because factual statements do not upset or depress people; only people's upsetting or depressive but nonfactual beliefs and attitudes about facts do that. For the healthiest emotional control, therefore, people's mental pictures of their A-activating events must be able to pass the camera check. Just observing the rule significantly reduces most people's daily emotional distress.

Often it is as important to separate relevant facts from irrelevant facts as it is to separate personal beliefs from relevant facts. That first maneuver immediately enabled Mrs. McCoy to quickly understand and start coping better with her conflicting emotions about her daughter's marriage.

Mrs. McCoy wanted to feel good about her daughter's happy marriage. So the marriage itself was an irrelevant fact in Mrs. McCoy's depression. But Mrs. McCoy had believed in the "It-Monster" myth about the cause of her emotions and that belief kept her from seeing that her daughter's marriage was not a relevant fact in her depression. Next is how the therapist helped Mrs. McCoy make that insight.

Dr. M: There are two sets of conflicting As or activating events in your situation. But you mistakenly see them as one set of depressing events. That's the main reason you feel guilty and depressed, even though you want to feel good about your daughter's happy marriage. The main activating event for your depression is not your daughter's happy marriage; instead, it's your depressive beliefs about these facts: Your daughter lived with you for 22 years; you worked very hard to help make both of your lives together as happy as possible; you understandably expected that you two would continue that living arrangement as long as you lived. Right?

Mrs. M: Well yes, but I really am glad that she found a nice man and
           got married. I raised her and all of my daughters to believe in
           Christian marriage. But instead of me feeling good like I
           know I should, I feel just awful, like it's a terrible thing. That
           sounds crazy I know, but that's the way I feel.
Dr. M: I understand exactly what you are saying, and the first thing I
           want to do is to reassure you; you are not crazy. It is perfectly
           normal, logical, and understandable for you to be depressed.
           And it's fortunate that your reactions are normal, logical, and
           understandable; if they weren't, I would not be able to help
           you get yourself get over them.

(Note: It is very important to repeatedly reassure people that their
emotional problems are normal, logical, and understandable. Otherwise, depressed people are likely to decide that they are either crazy or
about to go crazy. But, sane, intelligent, depressed people often feel so
ashamed about their suspicion that they might be going crazy, that out
of fear of having that event discovered they stop trying to help themselves. In their minds, abnormal, illogical, and unnatural behavior
means the person is crazy. That is another reason why learning the
emotional A,B,Cs is so immediately reassuring and empowering to
people. In their minds, because the A,B,Cs make their emotional conflict
logical and understandable, they do not have to worry about going
crazy.)

Dr. M: The first rule for rational and therefore healthy self-
           management is obvious fact. I think that both of the events in
           your depression would pass the camera check for obvious
           facts. So, let's look at your beliefs and attitudes about those
           facts. Your beliefs and attitudes about the fact that your
           daughter married a nice man are positive; therefore it's logical
           for you to want to feel happy about that.
Mrs. M: That's right; but I just can't seem to do it.
Dr. M: I understand that; but fortunately that appearance is incor-
           rect. You see, for every perception or conscious, sincere
           thought people have, they also have an accompanying un-
           spoken but equally powerful positive, negative, or neutral
           attitude about the thought. But because attitudes are un-
           spoken, people frequently ignore them and, therefore, don't
           realize that their own attitudes are triggering the intense
           emotions, which they normally blame on it, their external
           situation. So for now, let's put aside the irrelevant fact that
           your daughter has a happy marriage to a nice man, whom
           you would like to enjoy as a son-in-law. Instead, let's focus
           objectively on a situation where an elderly man had worked
           very hard for twenty years to build a mutually helpful rela-

	tionship with someone; then after twenty years the other person leaves that relationship for another one with a different person. Do you think that man would feel good about that fact?
Mrs. M:	No, I don't see how any man could feel good about it.
Dr. M:	How would he feel?
Mrs. M:	Sad, disappointed.
Dr. M:	Maybe even depressed and a little upset with himself for being depressed about it?
Mrs. M:	Why yes. But I don't see how he could help it.
Dr. M:	That's right; under those circumstances, it would be perfectly natural and normal for anyone to feel upset and depressed. So isn't it fair to say that could also be true of even you?
Mrs. M:	But I shouldn't feel that way; I should be happy for my daughter; but I can't seem to do it.

Mrs. McCoy was reacting emotionally as if she had these two core depressive attitudes: First, that the undesirable event of being left to live alone should not happen to anyone, least of all to her. The second core attitude seemed to be that it was awful for her to be depressed, when this daughter, like her other daughters, was happily married.

To quickly handle that type of painful emotional bind, therapists and counselors need to know the following facts about the word and concept "should."

Rational versus Irrational Shoulds

Almost all unhealthy anger, guilt, and depression is caused in large part by the irrational belief or attitude that "Some things or events are so undesirable that they just should not ever exist or happen, and it makes me very upset when they do exist or happen. But some other things or events are so desirable that they should always exists or happen, and it makes me very upset when they don't."

Why are those attitudes irrational? Because they break the universal law of specific cause and effect, which is that emotions (and all other desirable and undesirable events) occur *only* when what is essential for them to occur has been done. Conversely, when what is essential for emotions (and all other desirable or undesirable events) to occur has been done, those emotions or events have to and therefore should occur. Therefore, for the following two reasons, Mrs. McCoy and her daughter had reacted and were still reacting exactly as they should have been reacting.

Table 1.   Irrational and Rational Should

Irrational Should	Rational Should
1. Refers to what *isn't* fact.	1. Refers to what *is* fact.

2. The irrational should is judgmental and subjective.
  a. Refers only to what the speaker demands or wants, even though the speaker has not done what's necessary to get it.
  b. Assumes that what the speaker wants or doesn't want is right, and/or wrong for everyone.
	2. The rational should is nonjudgmental and objective.
	  a. Refers only to what had to be or will have to be, given the specific preceding circumstances.
	  b. Recognizes that what is right or wrong differs with people, times, and place.

3. The irrational should is magical thinking; it implies that things can and ought to exist merely because the speaker wants or demands that they exist, without doing what's necessary to make them exist.	3. The rational should is conditional or scientific thinking. It recognizes that things cannot exist unless what's necessary to make them exist is done first.
4. The irrational should triggers unproductive anger toward others and/or guilt feelings toward oneself. Therefore the speaker wastes valuable emotional energy that could be used to improve the situation.	4. The rational should triggers rational emotions toward others as well as toward oneself. It leads to calm study of the existing facts and a rational decision of what's best to do.
5. The irrational should leads to self-defeating motivation to "get back" or "get even" or "avoid."	5. The rational should leads to rational motivation to work toward changing what the speaker doesn't like.
6. With irrational "shoulds," the speaker tries to get other people to do something without the speaker first doing what's necessary to get them to do it.	6. The speaker recognizes that to get people to do something, he or she must first do what's necessary to influence them to do what the speaker wants.

1. People have *no other* choice than to do the things that their healthy brains, under the direction of their minds, force them to do. Because of the way the minds of Mrs. McCoy's daughter and husband were directing their brains, their marriage and separate living condition had to occur. Since they had to occur, they most certainly should have occurred.

2. As the emotional A,B,Cs clearly showed her, Mrs. McCoy was upsetting and depressing herself with these two upsetting and depressing attitudes: (a) it is terrible to be unexpectedly left to

live alone; therefore, anyone (including her) would have to feel terrible about it having happened to them. (b) It is awful, even sinful, to feel bad about deserving people's good fortune, least of all one's own children's good fortune.

As long as Mrs. McCoy stayed under the influence of such attitudes, she had to continue being upset and depressed. *Therefore*, she should have been just as upset and depressed as she was. But all she had to do to immediately improve her situation was to replace her irrational "should" attitudes about it with this rational "should" statement: "Everything is exactly as it now should be, even though it's not what I wanted for me. So, until I can change it to the way I want it to be for me, I shall keep myself pleasantly calm rationally."

To confidently prescribe those rational "should" ideas, the therapist or counselor must first know and believe in the objective validity of the following characteristics of irrational versus rational "shoulds." [Space limitations do not allow for a discussion of them here, but interested readers will find detailed discussions of those two "shoulds" concepts in *Rational Behavior Therapy* (Maultsby, 1984) and *Coping Better . . . Anytime, Anywhere* (Maultsby, 1986). Table 1 indicates some characteristics of irrational and rational should.]

Therapeutic insight here is that people almost never get or stay upset when they clearly see that everything about their situation is as it *should* be. Why? Because that would be crazy behavior. Sane, intelligent people are not willing to seriously engage in crazy behavior.

Case History Outcome. Mrs. McCoy required just 10 half-hour sessions using prescribed therapeutic self-help to overcome her 2-year depression. At her 2 year follow-up she was still living alone, but she was enjoying a personally satisfying relationship with all of her daughters and their husbands.

Four Parting Caveats

First, unless the readers have been trained in Rational Behavioral Therapy, some may be a little reluctant to believe that Mrs. McCoy did so well so rapidly. The fact that a 76-year-old lady can eliminate a 2-year-old depression that rapidly and completely without drugs may not feel right to them at first. (Should the reader like to obtain audio or video tapes of Mrs. McCoy's sessions, write to Dr. Maxie Maultsby at Department of Psychiatry, Howard University Hospital, 2041 Georgia Avenue, N.W., Washington, DC 20060.) Second, prescribing therapeutic self-help is *not* arbitrarily telling people what they should and should not do.

Rather it is getting them to sincerely ask and answer this question: "Does my description of this event fit the obvious facts?" or "Will my perceptions of this event pass the camera check?" Next get them to check their current B-beliefs and reactions to their A-event with all five of the rational questions.

For the reader's convenience, the five questions are repeated below:

1. Is my idea based on obvious facts?
2. Will my idea or reaction best help me protect my life and health?
3. Will my idea or reaction best help me achieve my short- and long-term goals?
4. Will my idea or reaction best help me avoid my most dreaded conflicts with other people?
5. Will my idea or reaction best help me feel emotionally the way I want to feel without alcohol or other drugs or brain damage?

To be ideally rational and therefore healthy, an idea, emotion, or action must deserve three or more honest "yes" answers to the five rational questions. Otherwise, it is best for the person to replace that idea, emotion, or action with one that does deserve at least three honest "yes" answers for those questions about that situation.

Third, there is a bit more to the rational approach to prescribed therapeutic self-help than space allows to be presented in this chapter. But interested psychotherapists and counselors can immediately start helping people help themselves by correctly applying the contents of this chapter.

Fourth, prescribed therapeutic self-help can be included in any technique of psychotherapy or counseling. How one includes it is more a matter of personal style than a specific method. [Interested therapists and counselors can quickly develop their own personal style by reading the self-instructional case histories found in *You and Your Emotions* (Maultsby, 1974), *Help Yourself to Happiness* (Maultsby, 1975), *Rational Behavior Therapy* (Maultsby, 1984), and *Coping Better . . . Anytime, Anywhere* (Maultsby, 1986)].

Summary

The rational approach to prescribing therapeutic self-help for the elderly is a quick, yet safe way to help older persons help themselves emotionally with little or no mind-altering drugs. The three main steps are (1) teach emotionally distressed elderly people their emotional A,B,Cs and the healthy concept of rational self-help, (2) prescribe daily rational bibliotherapeutic reading, and (3) give those people weekly individual or group sessions in which the therapist monitors their attempts to apply the prescribed rational self-help concepts and techniques as described in their sessions and their Prescribed Rational Bibliotherapy.

Any practicing psychotherapist or counselor can quickly learn to use this method of helping people help themselves. The minimum continuing professional education effort is a careful reading of the self-instructional case histories found in the Maultsby references. Ideally the therapist or counselor will supplement that continuing professional education with one or more training workshops in Rational Behavior Therapy. Information about those workshops is available from the author.

References

Ellis, A. (1963). *Reason and emotion in psychotherapy*. New York: Lyle Stuart.

Maultsby, M. C. (1975). *Help yourself to happiness through rational self counseling*. New York: Institute for Rational Living.

Maultsby, M. C. (1984). *Rational behavior therapy*. Englewood Cliffs, NJ: Prentice-Hall.

Maultsby, M. C. (1986). *Coping better . . . anytime, anywhere*. New York: Simon & Schuster.

Maultsby, M. C., & Graham, D. T. (1974). Controlled study of effects of psychotherapy on self-reported maladaptive traits, anxiety scores, and psychosomatic disease attitudes. *Journal of Psychiatric Research, 10,* 121–132.

Maultsby, M. C., & Hendricks, A. (1974). *You and your emotions*. Lexington, KY: Rational Self-Help Aids, Inc.

Maultsby, M. C., Knipping, P. J., & Carpenter, L. L. (1974). Teaching self-help in the classroom with rational self-counseling. *The Journal of School Health, 44,* 445–448.

7

Small Group Processes and Interventions with the Elderly

STEVEN R. ROSE

In recent years an increasing interest in group interventions with the elderly has surfaced related to the increasing number of elderly persons in the population, changing attitudes to the elderly, and the greater interest in psychotherapy and private practice among mental health and social service professionals. The purpose of this chapter is to describe the theoretical bases, intervention methods, and comparative strengths and weaknesses of small group interventions with the elderly.

Changing societal and professional attitudes toward the elderly influence group services. Attitudes to the elderly tend to be negative and reflect stereotyped beliefs about impending diminution of physical and mental capacities, personality attributes, and financial dependence (Hansson, 1989; Hopkins, 1980; Monk, 1981). Indeed, ageism, low income, and poor health affect the elderly much more than age-related changes per se (Lawton, 1990). Such thinking biases observations and leads workers to overlook meaningful motivations and emotional reactions in the elderly (Kubie & Landau, 1953). Many elderly persons possess considerable life satisfaction, characterized by zest, fortitude and resolution, goal congruence, positive self-concept, and positive mood (Neugarten, Havighurst, & Tobin, 1961, 1968). Professionals are coming to realize the positive attributes, including planning, productivity, and potential for change possessed by many elderly persons (Klein, LeShan & Furman, 1965; Schloss, 1988; Sorensen, 1986). Workshops have been conducted to increase the empathy of professionals toward old people (Coffman & Coffman, 1986). Also, video programs have been used to alter the attitudes of the elderly to increase their likeliness to use mental health services (Woodruff, Donnan, & Halpin, 1988). Preparation for group work and group therapy with the elderly entails creation of new skills and attitudes toward old age through practicum and other educational methods (Malnati & Pastushak, 1980; Moerman, 1988). The personal element, even if addressed indirectly, is often important to elderly group members who wish to know the leader.

Theoretical Assumptions and Context

Small group interventions, including group work and group therapy, with the elderly are understandable within the context of group therapy and group dynamics. One important aspect is group development, which often involves a process beginning with sharing and trust building, then consideration of power, control, and decision-making issues, followed by feelings of intimacy, and finally closure (Beaulieu & Karpinski, 1981). A central aspect of small group intervention with the elderly involves the group as a place in which, from an existential viewpoint, members needs for acceptance are met (Krill, 1986). The small group is also a place in which psychosocial difficulties relating to interpersonal interaction have the potential to be resolved. The special problems of the aged represent, in part, a variety of changes they experience in group memberships and participation in various groups. Such views are consistent with the membership perspective of social work (Falck, 1988).

Multiple theories are used to explain and guide group work and group therapy with the elderly, including role, psychoanalytic, behavioral, and stress theories. Role theory provides a useful perspective for understanding the transitions in social positions experienced by the elderly (Lowy, 1963; Scharlach, 1989). Loss of occupational and family roles by the elderly suggests the use of group work as the medium for role replacement. Socialization groups, which have been used with a wide range of clients, lend themselves to group work with the elderly and their families (Cox & Ephross, 1989; Hartford, 1980; Matorin & Zoubok, 1988; Silverstone & Burack-Weiss, 1983). Such groups fulfill important resocialization and activity needs of many elderly persons.

Psychoanalytic theory provides a good basis for comprehending the psychodynamics, conflicts, and emotions of elderly clients (Levine & Poston, 1980; Sorensen, 1986). A psychoanalytic viewpoint includes attention to the expression of sexual and aggressive instincts in group processes (Fisher, 1988; Kubie & Landau, 1953). Psychoanalytic theory provides an essential base for conducting group psychotherapy with the elderly.

Behavioral theories are useful in understanding and changing the habits, actions, and skills of the individual elderly client in the group setting. Behavioral group interventions with the elderly are procedurally explicit and readily lend themselves to evaluation. Behavioral group therapy has been shown to improve patterns of in-group verbal interaction and members have reported satisfaction with the therapy as well as improvement in their overall functioning (Gallagher, 1981). A psycho-educational approach to behavioral group therapy has been applied to helping elderly persons improve their life satisfaction, and cope with depression, care giving, and bereavement (Breckenridge, Thompson, Breckenridge, & Gallagher, 1985). Cognitive-behavioral theories have been used to help treat depressed geriatric outpatients in groups (Steuer & Hammen, 1983). Multimodal behavior group therapy has been shown to be effective in reducing the number of problems and improving the morale of elderly persons (Zgliczynski, 1982).

Stress theory is important in understanding elderly group members who frequently experience multiple psychosocial stressors, including mental and physical illness, loneliness and isolation, caretaking of an aged spouse, loss of family members, and housing and relocation problems (Hainer, 1988; Matorin & Zoubok, 1988; Petty, Moeller, & Campbell, 1976). Group work often directly focuses on positive coping with stress, promotion of health, and greater competence and self-esteem (Beaulieu & Karpinski, 1981; Klein et al., 1965).

The tyes of group work offered to the elderly vary extensively, according to theoretical base and purpose. Many types of groups for helping the elderly exist, including, yet not limited to, remotivation and reality orientation; music, art, and dance; women's consciousness-raising; psychodrama; movement, exercise, and yoga; discussion; traditional psychotherapy; disability-specific treatment; life skills; special interest; leisure time; and neighborhood groups (Lowy, 1985). Group psychotherapy with the elderly consists of insight-oriented group therapy, including analytic group therapy and life-review group therapy, and supportive group therapy, including verbal/social group therapies, rehabilitation/activity therapies, and cognitive-behavioral group therapies (Tross & Blum, 1988). The emphasis in the practice of group psychotherapy with the elderly has been in supportive group therapy (Lothstein, 1988).

The purposes of group work with the elderly include the following: emotional support, rehabilitation and restoration of roles and functions, prevention of deterioration, increase mental agility, support intellectual capacities, education, enhance interpersonal competence and social integration, provide a sense of importance and affirm identity, afford opportunities for life-review, sharing, self-expression, and leadership, reduce mental health problems, and enhance life quality (Bienenfeld, 1988; Grotjahn, 1978; Monk, 1981; Samberg, 1988; Shura, Saul, 1988a;

Sidney, Saul, 1988; Stern, 1988). Among many goals of mental health discussion groups for the elderly are the following: to encourage self-acceptance and self-esteem, to broaden members' perspectives about their changing roles and related behavior, to accept individual, gender, and cultural differences, to improve communication skills, to understand that behavior is motivated and meaningful, and to understand the relatedness of thinking and feeling (Klein et al., 1965). Purposes for people, including staff, who take care of confused and disoriented elderly persons include demonstrating good communication, sharing knowledge of illness, treatment techniques, and of nursing home placement, and providing support and respite for families (Saul, 1988).

The auspices of group work and group therapy with the elderly vary virtually to the same degree that living arrangements and service provision for the elderly vary (Lowy, 1963). Many settings, including multiservice, community, senior, adult day health, and rehabilitation centers, veterans and religious facilities, family service associations, settlement houses, homes for the aged, nursing homes, and hospitals offer group work as a helping modality (Lowy, 1985). The particular setting and its characteristics significantly influence the type of group available as well as its functioning. Ideally, group work with the elderly addresses the challenges, demands, and adjustments of group living in the institutional setting or the changes in social and physical functioning that occur while living in the community setting.

The focus on group psychotherapy with the elderly and most group work with the frail elderly has been in the institution (Lothstein, 1988; Silverstone & Burack-Weiss, 1983). Group work with the elderly also addresses the challenges, demands, and adjustments of group living in the institutional setting for the elderly person. Group work with the elderly in institutions often involves practice with members who are impaired, dependent, and in poor health. Members in such settings may seek improvement in their quality of life and in the conditions of the institution. In institutional settings it is important to allow the elderly freedom of choice in regard to joining groups (Morrin, 1988). Several types of groups are most appropriate in institutions. Where institutions for the elderly are suppressive the poetry group offers the opportunity to set a free and creative atmosphere (Shura, Saul, 1988b). The healing effects of movement are obtainable in dance therapy groups in residential facilities for the elderly (Samberg, 1988). Reality orientation and reminiscence groups are particularly useful in nursing homes (Hancock, 1987).

Group work with the elderly in the community is a fairly recent phenomenon, with the first reference to such groups appearing in the mid-twentieth century (Weiner & White, 1988). For the socially isolated elderly the social influence of the group is often great (Silverstone & Burack-Weiss, 1983). The group's status in the community influences its security as well as impact on the members (Kubie & Landau, 1953). Those elderly living in the community often function independently and many are in relatively good health although they sometimes live with chronically ill spouses. Elderly persons in public and private housing complexes often are isolated and need the camaraderie and support that the small group provides (Beaulieu & Karpinski, 1981; Petty, Moeller, & Campbell, 1976).

Elders helping elders in groups provides benefits, including those that accrue to the leader, according to the principle whereby the helper often gains at least as much gain as the person being helped. Elderly persons who need to be needed by others are likely to find satisfaction in helping other aged individuals. Historically, self-government has been important in group work with the elderly and continues so today, as in residential groups for the frail elderly (Kubie & Landau, 1953; Silverstone & Burack-Weiss, 1983). Furthermore, the elderly individual is likely to find support by being a member of a cohesive group that provides socialization and self-help where attitudes of caring and concern are readily expressed (Fisher, 1988; Hainer, 1988; Hancock, 1987; Lakin, 1988; Matorin & Zoubok, 1988; Stern, 1988; Weiner, 1988). Support groups are often available for old persons with very ill spouses, widows, and widowers, as well as for members of particular ethnic or racial groups (Beaulieu & Karpinski, 1981; Lowy, 1985).

Composition, Membership, and Leadership

Cultural and ethnic factors are important in group work and group therapy with the elderly and, along with age factors, influence the extent to which elderly persons comfortably engage in self-disclosure in the group setting (Goodman, 1988). Both psychotherapy and self-help groups offer considerable help to elderly Hispanic persons (Franklin & Kaufman, 1982; Sanchez, 1986). When group work with the elderly involves members of diverse backgrounds, dealing with, acknowledging, and valuing cultural differences, and mutual acceptance, which at times is a challenge in forming a cohesive group, becomes an important issue (Foster & Foster, 1983; Klein et al., 1965; Kubie & Landau, 1953; Steuer & Hammen, 1983).

The composition of groups for the elderly varies. All groups strive for a balance of homogeneity in member characteristics to provide a common base for solidarity and heterogeneity in member characteristics, as in personality, to promote lively interaction, and modeling possibilities.

The elderly, as an age cohort, are highly heterogeneous in health status, sensory functioning, intellectual and social competence, problem-solving skills, and involvement, which leads to a lively dynamic process within many groups (Hansson, 1989; Kubie & Landau, 1953; Shura, Saul, 1988a). In group psychotherapy with the institutionalized mentally ill elderly, inclusion of persons with heterogeneity of diagnoses is often advisable (Bienenfeld, 1988). However, to balance the heterogeneity in the composition of groups the worker seeks homogeneity factors that provide a shared basis for group unity (Foster & Foster, 1983). A general guideline is that homogeneous groups are better for frail elderly, including those with severe hearing loss, whereas heterogeneous (multi-generational age, and gender) groups are better for the active elderly (Benitez-Bloch, 1988; Silverstone & Burack-Weiss, 1983). Although a controversy exists whether the appropriate age composition of group work with the elderly ought to be homogeneous or heterogeneous (Bienenfeld, 1988) many elderly enjoy being in groups with those of other ages, partly because many, though not all, share the stereotypes of old people held by many other members of society (Kubie & Landau, 1953; Lakin, 1988). Although group psychotherapy of psychotic and neurologically impaired elderly has received much emphasis (Lothstein, 1988), including such persons in groups with well-functioning individuals can be distressing to the latter who may be concerned with developing such problems themselves (Lakin, 1988).

Extant knowledge permits one to indicate who is appropriate for group work and for group therapy. The frail elderly, when included in the group, need the protection of the leader, which also points to the need for careful composition of elderly groups. In addition to the careful selection of members for groups an initial orientation to and preparation for the group to set members expectations is usually very useful for the members and promotes the effectiveness of the group (Goodman, 1988; Weiner, 1988).

Inclusion refers to admission of aged persons to as well as engagement and participation in the group, despite sensory and cerebral dysfunction (Sorensen, 1986). The inclusion criteria for group membership for the elderly include the person's age and their need of continued treatment, as well as their ability to function constructively in small groups, to tolerate the dynamics and demands of groups, to have needs that are fulfilled by the group, and to have the capacity and motivation to participate (Matorin & Zoubok, 1988). Positive factors for member selection and group composition include adequate language, memory, and social skills, nonvoluntary social isolation and fair mental health, and a history of personal losses and good prior psychotherapy experience (Cooper, 1983; Foster & Foster, 1983). According to Lakin (1988), group therapy for elderly persons is useful for clients who do not need more personal support than the group and leader can provide, who are not overly fearful, and whose communication patterns are not markedly impaired.

Exclusion criteria for group membership are related to limited tolerance of and accommodation to the deficits and handicaps of the elderly person that impede their ability to interact in the small group setting. For elderly persons to whom the sharing of private thoughts and feelings in a group setting is unacceptable, activity groups are more appropriate than verbal, interactional group psychotherapy (Goodman, 1988). Elderly persons who are unable to tolerate the demands and dynamics of small groups or who have severe mental health disorders, including severe anxiety, depression, paranoia, psychoses, and organic brain syndromes, frequently benefit more from help provided on an individual rather than a group basis (Foster & Foster, 1983). Elderly individuals who are highly withdrawn or highly aggressive in group settings are often experienced as too disturbed or too disturbing by others in many groups for the elderly.

Related to composition in group theory and practice with the elderly is membership and leadership (Burnside, 1978a,b). Evidence exists that professionally led groups have a greater impact in improving the mental health of the elderly than peer-led groups (Lieberman & Bliwise, 1985). Typically, sociodemographic differences exist between worker and elderly client, and large gaps in age can be problematic in group work (Lakin, 1988). Frequently, the leader is younger and therefore has a different existential life perspective than most of the members, who are likely to have diverse backgrounds, including persons with little formal education, knowledge, and acceptance of psychological theories. Without proper orientation by the leader, many elderly members tend to be unaware of the group's purposes during early meetings and initially are not always likely to see the group as a problem-solving medium and are resistant to participate in group activities. Furthermore, after becoming more aware of the purpose of the groups many elderly members often are very concerned about practical problems in daily living and have considerable difficulty in listening to others, which can impede group interaction (Klein et al., 1965; Monk, 1981; Silverstone & Burack-Weiss, 1983). Group interaction varies according to the ages of group members, with research findings showing that elderly persons show more boundaries and self-disclosure, and less support and boredom, when compared with young adults (Lakin, Bremer, & Oppenheimer, 1983).

In regard to leadership style for active elders a correspondingly active approach is appropriate and useful (Lothstein, 1988). As the group develops elderly members often lessen their dependence on the group leader, and leadership emerges within the group, a change that is to be welcomed and encouraged by the practitioner (Kubie & Landau, 1953). A moderately directive leadership style, with the use of warmth, acceptance, flexibility, and humor, encouraging feasible member independence is often recommended (Goodman, 1988; Klein et al., 1965). Important functions of the group leader include enhancing coping skills, anxiety reduction, and emphasizing a positive viewpoint (Weiner, 1988) as well as coaching, motivation building, conflict resolution, group decision-making, and role creation (Kubie & Landau, 1953). Working with the sensory impaired frail elderly requires communicating to make use of relatively unimpaired senses (Silverstone & Burack-Weiss, 1983). Training in group leadership for working with the elderly is highly recommended (Klein et al., 1965).

Characteristics of the Elderly Member

Common needs of the elderly, which are differentially met as groups develop, include love and affirmation, usefulness, growth through learning, status and identity, ego integration and gratification, and life review, and expressive, contributory, influence, and transcendence needs (Lowy, 1982, 1985). Group work with the elderly is designed to meet their needs, with groups composed of members whose background and personality characteristics form an interactive and effective group to help the elderly members solve common problems that they experience and engage in social action in living in a difficult social environment (Lowy, 1985). The needs of the elderly are met internal and external to the group. The group atmosphere is one in which respect for one another is encouraged, and where members support one another. The group should be a safe environment where elderly members are protected from physical and verbal aggression, assault, and abuse from others, and where plans of action are formulated to maximize their safety outside of the group itself.

Most elderly persons are concerned with maintaining their physical and mental health. Health promotion is an important area for group work with the elderly (Schloss, 1988). The group engages in activities to promote well-being of body and soul within its meetings and beyond. Such activities tend to be preventive, interventive, and rehabilitative. Examples include blood pressure screening, exercise programs, and discussions about health and food (Silverstone & Burack-Weiss, 1983). Group work with the elderly at times includes the preparation, serving, and cleanup of hot, nutritious meals, thereby providing social and physiological benefits (Fisher, 1988; Lowy, 1985). Group activities with a focus on diet and nutrition, exercise and fitness, and cognitive alertness and mental functioning are feasible for many elderly persons. Group work also involves the educational method of discussing sound, healthy, and economical patterns of food buying, preparation, and consumption. Some groups are devoted to helping the elderly and their families cope with illness, and there is potential for further development of groups devoted to caring for persons with physical and mental disorders.

Frequently, transportation is an important aspect of group work with the elderly. For groups that are composed of members who live in the community transportation needs should be arranged to bring the members to a central meeting place (Silverstone & Burack-Weiss, 1983). For institutional groups the issue of transportation often involves the facilitation of ease of mobility. Transportation is also provided as an inherent aspect and activity of the group, as in travel and touring, or to meeting places in the community where other activities take place.

The elderly commonly suffer from multiple losses of loved ones, as well as of physical health, financial security, employment, and other time-structured activities, leading to decreased self-esteem, and grief, bereavement, and narcissism (Hainer, 1988; Hansson, 1989; Schloss, 1988; Sorensen, 1986). Multiple losses resulting in depression (Fisher, 1988) often provide the motivation for the elderly person to enter group psychotherapy (Lothstein, 1988). In such instances, the group fulfills the functions of sharing the widespread experience of losses, providing social support and interpersonal relationships, and providing structured and regular use of time. Groups are useful for those elderly persons who have suffered from losses of peers and roles (Toseland & Rivas, 1984). The group further serves to help elderly persons make adjustments in those areas of their lives outside of the meetings.

In the group setting the elderly, many of whom desire autonomy, are likely to report struggling with their ambivalent, angry, and guilty feelings about becoming more dependent, particularly on their grown children who act as if they were their parents (Klein et al., 1965; Lothstein, 1988; Matorin & Zoubok, 1988; Monk, 1981; Weiner, 1988). Indeed, the group is designed to help the elderly person meet the normative demands and changes that occur at that particular point in the life cycle where attachment and dependency become paramount (Rathbone-McCuan, 1988).

The group also helps the elderly overcome their feelings of isolation by allowing them to interact with peers with whom they share similarities of personality, experiences, needs, and interests. The group provides a social network for the aged and provides links to other persons and organizations, further decreasing the isolation experienced by the elderly, particularly those without significant others. Further-more, the group sometimes functions to enhance the social competence of its aged members through social skills training or social problem-solving methods.

Themes and Methods of Practice

Many groups for the elderly are thematic, dealing with topics such as accepting and coping with retirement, finances, quality of health and other services, aging, endings and beginnings, growth, intergeneration-al gaps and changes in family relationships, nostalgia and remembering past good experiences, hope versus despair, dependency, depression, loneliness, alienation, and isolation, losses of family, friends, health, and functioning, grief and bereavement, fears of illness, dying, and death, power versus weakness, passivity versus activity, decline and physical disability, and love, intimacy, touching, and sexuality (Bienen-feld, 1988; Dreyer, 1989; Foster & Foster, 1983; Goodman, 1988; Hainer, 1988; Kubie & Landau, 1953; Matorin & Zoubok, 1988; Mayadas & Hink, 1974; Michaels, 1977; Morrin, 1988; Weiner, 1988). Mental health discus-sion groups, which are preventive, educational, and promote strength, typically consider a wide range of subjects that have been classified as follows: practical problems, such as housing, personal relationships, such as the role of grandparent, abstract concepts, such as conformity, and social organization, such as the meaning and use of clubs and centers (Klein et al., 1965).

A balance between addressing positive and negative themes is useful in many groups with aged members. In working with the frail elderly one addresses issues of dependency as well as uses activities to promote reciprocity and perceived competence (Silverstone & Burack-Weiss, 1983). Different types of groups vary in their emphasis on positive and negative feelings. For instance, dance therapy groups permit expression of both positive and negative feelings (Samberg, 1988) whereas art therapy groups allow for the safe expression and release of negative feelings (Morrin, 1988). In some groups disabilities and pathologies are deemphasized (Shura, Saul, 1988b). Highly charged issues, such as inpatient hospitalization and electroconvulsive treatment for the treat-ment of severe mental illness, are sometimes dealt with indirectly (Goodman, 1988). Whereas some groups are devoted entirely to one theme, other groups are devoted to multiple themes (Schloss, 1988). Groups provide members with the opportunity to share similar social and emotional difficulties (Fisher, 1988).

Group work with the elderly includes related methods that reflect a diversity of theories and intervention approaches. One example involves the active use of reminiscences, oral history, and life review, fulfilling a common, important need of the elderly (Lowy, 1985; Morrin, 1988). Often, reminiscence groups rapidly promote group cohesiveness and interaction (Lesser, Lazarus, Frankel, & Havasy, 1981). Group work with the elderly often involves talking about concrete issues rather than here-and-now process issues (Lakin, 1988). Occasionally, one sees a collectivity of older persons develop into a true group (Kubie & Landau, 1953).

At times, group work practice with the aged is combined with discussion, psychodrama and sociodrama, activity therapy, the arts and art therapy, creative writing, autobiography, and oral history, poetry, dance and movement therapy, drama, and music (Fisher, 1988; Getzel, 1983; Hartford, 1989; Johnson, 1985; Kubie & Landau, 1953; Morrin, 1988; Nordin, 1987; Samberg, 1988; Schloss, 1988; Shura, Saul, 1988a,b; Silverstone & Burack-Weiss, 1983; Stern, 1988). Group therapy techniques include sensory retraining for regressed elderly persons with motoric and cognitive deficits, reality orientation for the confused elderly, and remotivation therapy for the institutionalized elderly with good verbal and cognitive skills (Foster & Foster, 1983). Also, individual counseling is often made available to those elderly persons who can make use of it in addition to the group work (Kubie & Landau, 1953).

Group work approaches that benefit the elderly either directly or indirectly include work with the relatives of the elderly (Rathbone-McCuan, 1988). When sufficient numbers of elderly persons are available and sufficient motivation exists, group work for family and couples helps members cope with financial and mental health problems relating to changes in family structure and roles (Lowy, 1985). Often, educational, therapeutic, supportive, and self-help groups for spouses and other family caregivers of disabled or elderly persons ill with Alzheimer's and other diseases help the caregivers deal with crises, delayed help-seeking, and issues related to denial, anger, and grief (Aronson, 1988; Aronson, Levin, & Lipkowitz, 1984; Beaulieu & Karpinski, 1981; Brubaker & Schiefer, 1987; Cohen, 1983; Davis, 1983; Hartford & Parsons, 1982; Hausman, 1979; Schmidt & Keyes, 1985; Shibbal-Champagne & Lipinska-Stachow, 1986).

A Case Example

A socialization group was conducted under the auspices of a community mental health center (McBroom, 1976; Weinstein, 1969). The members were elderly women who had once been institutionalized for severe, chronic mental illness and who were now living in their own homes in the community. The members experienced loneliness and social isolation, and needed social interaction and support to maintain their adjustment and capacity for independent living.

The group was a long-standing one with a stable membership. Members were referred to the program through the staff at the community mental health center. As staff turned over at the center, the leadership of the group changed several times over many years, yet the membership remained stable. Attendance was expected and was regular. The group was long-term and continual in nature, consistent with contemporary knowledge of the needs of the chronically mentally ill for long-term care to maintain community functioning. The small group provided social activities, including frequenting a local restaurant and sightseeing in a van. The group met regularly, one morning every few weeks. The practitioner, accompanied by a driver, transported the women to the community mental health center where they were seen for an informal, unobtrusive social and mental health evaluation by a psychiatric nurse, who regularly monitored their psychotropic medications, and, as needed, by a psychiatrist.

Statements by the leader focused on conscious and observable material (Klein et al., 1965; Rathbone-McCuan, 1988). Verbal interaction by members at the meetings of the group, held in community locations, tended to be quiet, dyadic, and intermittent. The members continued to reside in the community and maintain their level of functioning. The group was successful in maintaining the elderly women in community living and minimizing deterioration.

Effectiveness

The empirical literature on group work and group therapy with older persons is diverse in its findings. Some evidence exists showing the greater effectiveness for cathartic grief group work than social and topical discussion group work in lowering the depression of grieving geriatric outpatients (Michaels, 1977).

Some authors claim that group therapy with the elderly shows some benefits without one form of treatment showing greater effectiveness than another (Tross & Blum, 1988). Another study showed the effectiveness of behavioral role-play, problem-solving, and social group work methods in increasing the interpersonal competence of elderly persons (Toseland & Rose, 1978). One research study showed no benefits for group work with the elderly (Cetingok & Hirayama, 1983). Yet another study indicated greater improvement for insight-oriented group psychotherapy when compared to behavior-oriented group therapy for the elderly (Ingersoll & Silverman, 1978). In contrast, findings from another study suggest somewhat greater effectiveness for a cognitive-behavioral approach than a psychodynamic one (Steuer et al., 1984). Problem-solving groups have been reported to be effective in increasing the social skills of elderly persons (Toseland, 1977).

Support groups for moderately and normatively stressed elderly persons living in the community have shown reductions in anxiety regarding aging, more effective problem-solving, and more use of community resources (Petty, Moeller, & Campbell, 1976). For urban widows, self-help, confidant, and women's consciousness-raising groups have been shown to improve self-esteem, increase grief intensity, and increase negative attitudes to remarriage, with the consciousness raising group yielding more significant positive life changes and higher group evaluations than the other types (Barrett, 1978).

Reminiscence group therapy has been shown to be better than supportive group therapy in reducing depression among demented elderly nursing home residents (Goldwasser, Auerbach, & Harkins, 1987). Also, although both conventional reminiscence groups, involving the recall of memories from stages in the life cycle, and experiential reminiscence groups, emphasizing focusing on feelings and thoughts, have been shown to yield favorable improvements in member satisfaction and self-concept, the conventional reminiscent groups yielded more inclusive types of reminiscing and the experiential reminiscent groups yielded the most use of feelings and thoughts in remembering the past (Sherman, 1987).

Although little research has been done on the process and outcome of group self psychology in regard to work with the elderly, some anecdotal reports exist suggesting its usefulness (Weiner & White, 1988). It has been claimed that activity group psychotherapy is cost-effective in reducing institutionalization and use of expensive health care (Fisher, 1988). It has been reported that the outcomes of group therapy with confused and disoriented elderly persons include changes in behavior and improved socialization among the members, improved caregiving methods, the provision of support to members and their families, and significant existential experiences (Sidney, Saul, 1988).

Immediate and subsequent outcomes of group work with the elderly are not identical (Toseland & Rose, 1978). For instance, structured group counseling has been demonstrated to have an immediate yet not persistent effect in reducing the state anxiety of primary caretakers of elderly patients in nursing homes (Hendrix, 1982).

A number of gaps exist in the literature, including the relative sparsity of rigorous evaluations of the effectiveness of group interventions with the elderly. Also, although many group interventions with the elderly are oriented to prevention and are classifiable as secondary and tertiary prevention, more prevention activity using small groups with the elderly needs to be reported in the literature (Klein et al., 1965). Furthermore, relatively little is known about how group composition and interaction vary according to the stage of the life cycle in the overall aging category (ranging from the youngest to the very oldest, frail elders).

Conclusions

The small group has a number of features that potentially make it a good experience for the elderly person. For the isolated elderly living alone in the community and for the institutionalized elderly living with many other persons in a highly dependent status, the small group offers the potential for solace, companionship, and support. Ideally the small group is a place that offers safety for members while fulfilling many psychosocial needs. The group fosters human development, adds knowledge, insight, and understanding, changes attitudes, and helps members acquire skills and competencies for living. Verbal psychotherapy groups and activity group psychotherapy provide the elderly with opportunities for interpersonal learning, development of trust, emotional expression, and conflict resolution (Fisher, 1988). Discussion and psychotherapy groups instill hope and offer the universality factor, which is useful for many elderly persons (Klein et al., 1965; Kubie & Landau, 1953; Shura, Saul, 1988a; Weiner, 1988; Yalom, 1985; Zgliczynski, 1982). Specific types of groups vary in what they offer the elderly person. For instance, poetry groups have numerous advantages, including evoking humanness, appealing to high levels of cognitive and emotional functioning, and enhancing self-esteem (Shura, Saul, 1988b).

Group work has the potential to do harm as well as good, and is not suited for all elderly persons (Hartford, 1980). Although the small group poses potential disadvantages for the elderly person, the professional literature has tended not to emphasize these. The small group possesses fewer hazards to the sturdy members and greater hazards to the physically, socially, and emotionally weak and fragile members who are more vulnerable to the effects of stress.

A number of results and rewards may be expected by those who conduct group interventions with the elderly. Chief among these include the pleasures in providing for one's elders and promoting the development of social services that will be used by many persons. Group work with the elderly is challenging, and the activity is often enjoyable to the practitioner (Klein et al., 1965). With proper consideration of the setting, type of group, needs of the elderly, knowledge of gerontology, respectful attitudes to the elderly, and group work and therapy skills, the likelihood of providing a humane, satisfying experience for elderly persons is enhanced.

References

Aronson, M. K. (1988). Selecting family caregivers of Alzheimer patients for group psychotherapy. In B. W. MacLennan, S. Saul, & M. B. Weiner (Eds.), *Group psychotherapies for the elderly* (pp. 189–196). Madison, CT: International Universities Press.

Aronson, M. K., Levin, G., & Lipkowitz, R. (1984). A community-based family/patient group program for Alzheimer's disease. *The Gerontologist, 24,* 339–342.

Barrett, C. J. (1978). Effectiveness of widows' groups in facilitating change. *Journal of Consulting and Clinical Psychology, 46,* 20–31.

Beaulieu, E. M., & Karpinski, J. (1981). Group treatment of elderly with ill spouses. *Social Casework, 62,* 551–557.

Benitez-Bloch, R. (1988). Including the active elderly in group psychotherapy. In B. W. MacLennan, S. Saul, & M. B. Weiner (Eds.), *Group psychotherapies for the elderly* (pp. 33–41). Madison, CT: International Universities Press.

Bienenfeld, D. (1988). Group psychotherapy with the elderly in the state hospital. In B. W. MacLennan, S. Saul, & M. B. Weiner (Eds.), *Group psychotherapies for the elderly* (pp. 177–187). Madison, CT: International Univerisities Press.

Breckenridge, J. S., Thompson, L. W., Breckenridge, J. N., & Gallagher, D. E. (1985). In D. Upper & S. M. Ross (Eds.), *Handbook of behavioral group therapy* (pp. 275–299). New York: Plenum.

Brubaker, E., & Schiefer, A. W. (1987). Groups with families of elderly long-term care residents: Building social support networks. *Journal of Gerontological Social Work, 10,* 167–175.

Burnside, I. M. (1978a). Group membership. In I. M. Burnside (Ed.), *Working with the elderly: Group process and techniques* (pp. 55–68). North Scituate, MA: Duxbury.

Burnside, I. M. (1978b). Problems in leadership and maintenance. In I. M. Burnside (Ed.), *Working with the elderly: Group process and techniques* (pp. 69–87). North Scituate, MA: Duxbury.

Cetingok, M., & Hirayama, H. (1983). Evaluating the effects of group work with the elderly: An experiment using a single-subject design. *Small Group Behavior, 14,* 327–335.

Coffman, S. L., & Coffman, V. T. (1986). Aging awareness training for professionals who work with the elderly. *Small Group Behavior, 17,* 95–103.

Cohen, P. M. (1983). A group approach for working with families of the elderly. *The Gerontologist, 23,* 248–250.

Cooper, F. W. (1983). The effects of two group approaches on self-esteem among the elderly. (Doctoral dissertation, Kent State University, 1982.) *Dissertation Abstracts International, 43,* 3406B.

Cox, C., & Ephross, P. H. (1989). Group work with families of nursing home residents: Its socialization and therapeutic functions. *Journal of Gerontological Social Work, 13,* 61–73.

Davis, J. L. (1983). Support groups: A clinical intervention for families of the mentally impaired elderly. *Journal of Gerontological Social Work, 5,* 27–35.

Dreyer, P. H. (1989). Postretirement life satisfaction. In S. Spacapan & S. Oskamp (Eds.), *The social psychology of aging* (pp. 109–133). Newbury Park, CA: Sage.

Falck, H. S. (1988). *Social work: The membership perspective.* New York: Springer.

Fisher, D. B. (1988). Activity group psychotherapy for the inner-city elderly. In B. W. MacLennan, S. Saul, & M. B. Weiner (Eds.), *Group psychotherapies for the elderly* (pp. 121–130). Madison, CT: International Universities Press.

Foster, J. R., & Foster, R. P. (1983). Group psychotherapy with the old and aged. In H. I. Kaplan & B. J. Sadock (Eds.), *Comprehensive group psychotherapy* (pp. 269–278). Baltimore: Williams & Wilkins.

Franklin, G. S., & Kaufman, K. S. (1982). Group psychotherapy for elderly female Hispanic outpatients. *Hospital and Community Psychiatry, 33,* 385–387.

Gallagher, D. (1981). Behavioral group therapy with elderly depressives: An experimental study. In D. Upper & S. M. Ross (Eds.), *Behavioral group therapy, 1981: An annual review* (pp. 187–224). Champaign, IL: Research Press.

Getzel, G. S. (1983). Poetry writing groups and the elderly: A reconsideration of art and social group work. *Social work with Groups, 6,* 65–76.

Goldwasser, A. N., Auerbach, S. M., & Harkins, S. W. (1987). Cognitive, affective, and behavioral effects of reminiscence group therapy on demented elderly. *International Journal of Aging and Human Development, 25,* 209–222.

Goodman, R. K. (1988). A geriatric group in an acute care psychiatric teaching hospital: Pride or prejudice? In B. W. MacLennan, S. Saul, & M. B. Weiner (Eds.), *Group psychotherapies for the elderly* (pp. 151–164). Madison, CT: International Universities Press.

Grotjahn, M. (1978). Group communication and group therapy with the aged: A promising project. In L. F. Jarvik (Ed.), *Aging into the 21st century: Middle-agers today* (pp. 113–121). New York: Gardner.

Hainer, J. (1988). Groups for widowed and lonely older persons. In B. W. MacLennan, S. Saul, & M. B. Weiner (Eds.), *Group psychotherapies for the elderly* (pp. 131–138). Madison, CT: International Universities Press.

Hancock, B. L. (1987). *Social work with older people.* Englewood Cliffs, NJ: Prentice-Hall.

Hansson, R. O. (1989). Old age: Testing the parameters of social psychological assumptions. In S. Spacapan & S. Oskamp (Eds.), *The social psychology of aging* (pp. 25–51). Newbury Park, CA: Sage.

Hartford, M. E. (1980). The use of group methods for work with the aged. In J. E. Birren & R. B. Sloane (Eds.), *Handbook of mental health and aging* (pp. 806–826). Englewood Cliffs, NJ: Prentice Hall.

Hartford, M. E., & Parsons, R. (1982). Use of groups with relatives of dependent older adults. *Social Work with Groups, 5,* 77–89.

Hausman, C. P. (1979). Short-term counseling groups for people with elderly parents. *The Gerontologist, 19*, 102–107.

Hendrix, F. G. (1982). The effect of structured group counseling on the anxiety level of primary caretakers of geriatric patients. (Doctoral dissertation, University of Georgia, 1981.) *Dissertation Abstracts International, 42*, 4300A.

Hopkins, T. J. (1980). A conceptual framework for understanding the three "isms"—racism, ageism, sexism. *Journal of Education for Social Work, 16*, 63–70.

Ingersoll, B., & Silverman, A. (1978). Comparative group psychotherapy for the aged. *The Gerontologist, 18*, 201–206.

Johnson, D. R. (1985). Expressive group psychotherapy with the elderly: A drama therapy approach. *International Journal of Group Psychotherapy, 35*, 109–127.

Klein, W. H.; LeShan, E. J.; & Furman, S. S. (1965). *Promoting mental health of older people through group methods: A practical guide.* New York: Manhattan Society for Mental Health.

Krill, D. F. (1986). Existential social work. In F. J. Turner (Ed.), *Social work treatment: Interlocking theoretical approaches*, 3rd ed. (pp. 181–218). New York: Free Press.

Kubie, S. H., & Landau, G. (1953). *Group work with the aged.* New York: International Universities Press.

Lakin, M. (1988). Group therapies with the elderly: Issues and prospects. In B. W. MacLennan, S. Saul, & M. B. Weiner (Eds.), *Group psychotherapies for the elderly* (pp. 43–55). Madison, CT: International Universities Press.

Lakin, M., Bremer, J., & Oppenheimer, B. (1983). Group processes in helping groups: Toward a developmental perspective. *International Journal of Aging and Human Development, 18*, 13–24.

Lawton, M. P. (1990). Residential environment and self-directedness among older people. *American Psychologist, 45*, 638–640.

Lesser, J., Lazarus, L. W., Frankel, R., & Havasy, S. (1981). Reminiscence group therapy with psychotic geriatric outpatients. *The Gerontologist, 21*, 291–296.

Levine, B. E., & Poston, M. (1980). A modified group treatment for elderly narcissistic patients. *International Journal of Group Psychotherapy, 30*, 153–167.

Lieberman, M. A., & Bliwise, N. G. (1985). Comparisons among peer and professionally directed groups for the elderly: Implications for the development of self-help groups. *International Journal of Group Psychotherapy, 35*, 155–175.

Lothstein, L. M. (1988). Psychodynamic group therapy with the active elderly: A preliminary investigation. In B. W. MacLennan, S. Saul, & M. B. Weiner (Eds.), *Group psychotherapies for the elderly* (pp. 67–87). Madison, CT: International Universities Press.

Lowy, L. (1963). Meeting the needs of older people on a differential basis. In National Association of Social Workers (Ed.), *Social group work with older people* (pp. 43–67). New York, NY: NASW.

Lowy, L. (1982). Social group work with vulnerable older persons: A theoretical perspective. *Social Work with Groups, 5*, 21–32.

184   Steven R. Rose

Lowy, L. (1985). *Social work with the aging: The challenge and promise of the later years*, 2nd ed. New York: Longman.
Malnati, R. J., & Pastushak, R. (1980). Conducting group practica with the aged. *Psychotherapy: Theory, Research, and Practice, 17,* 352–360.
Matorin, S., & Zoubok, B. (1988). Group psychotherapy with geriatric out patients: A model for treatment and training. In B. W. MacLennan, S. Saul, & M. B. Weiner (Eds.), *Group psychotherapies for the elderly* (pp. 107–120). Madison, CT: International Universities Press.
Mayadas, N. S., & Hink, D. L. (1974). Group work with the aging: An issue for social work education. *The Gerontologist, 14,* 440–445.
McBroom, E. (1976). Socialization through small groups. In R. W. Roberts & H. Northen, (Eds.), *Theories of social work with groups* (pp. 268–303). New York: Columbia University Press.
Michaels, F. (1977). The effects of discussing grief, loss, death, and dying on depression levels in a geriatric outpatient therapy group. (Doctoral dissertation, Auburn University, 1977.) *Dissertation Abstracts International, 38,* 910B.
Moerman, C. (1988). Using group training methods to prepare students for group work with older adults. In B. W. MacLennan, S. Saul, & M. B. Weiner (Eds.), *Group psychotherapies for the elderly* (pp. 269–279). Madison, CT: International Universities Press.
Monk, A. (1981). Social work with the aged: Principles of practice. *Social Work, 26,* 61–68.
Morrin, J. (1988). Art therapy groups in a geriatric institutional setting. In B. W. MacLennan, S. Saul, & M. B. Weiner (Eds.), *Group psychotherapies for the elderly* (pp. 245–256). Madison, CT: International Universities Press.
Neugarten, B. L., Havighurst, R. J., & Tobin, S. S. (1961). The measurement of Life satisfaction. *Journal of Gerontology, 16,* 134–143.
Neugarten, B. L., Havighurst, R. J., & Tobin, S. S. (1968). Personality and patterns of aging. In B. L. Neugarten (Ed.), *Middle age and aging* (pp. 173–177). Chicago: University of Chicago Press.
Nordin, S. R. (1987). Psycodrama with the elderly. *Journal of Group Psychotherapy, Psychodrama, and Sociometry, 40,* 51–61.
Petty, B. J., Moeller, T. P., & Campbell, R. Z. (1976). Support groups for elderly persons in the community. *The Gerontologist, 15,* 522–528.
Rathbone-McCuan, E. (1988). Group intervention for alcohol-related problems among the elderly and their families. In B. W. MacLennan, S. Saul, & M. B. Weiner (Eds.), *Group psychotherapies for the elderly* (pp. 139–148). Madison, CT: International Universities Press.
Samberg, S. (1988). Dance therapy groups for the elderly. In B. W. MacLennan, S. Saul, & M. B. Weiner (Eds.), *Group psychotherapies for the elderly* (pp. 233–243). Madison, CT: International Universities Press.
Sanchez, C. D. (1986). Self-help: Model for strengthening the informal social support of the Hispanic elderly. *Journal of Gerontological Social Work, 9,* 117–131.
Saul, Shura (1988a). The arts as psychotherapeutic modalities with groups of older people. In B. W. MacLennan, S. Saul, & M. B. Weiner (Eds.), *Group psychotherapies for the elderly* (pp. 211–221). Madison, CT: International Universities Press.

Saul, Shura (1988b). The poetry group. In B. W. MacLennan, S. Saul, & M. B. Weiner (Eds.), *Group psychotherapies for the elderly* (pp. 223–231). Madison, CT: International Universities Press.

Saul, Sidney. (1988). Group therapy with confused and disoriented elderly people. In B. W. MacLennan, S. Saul, & M.B. Weiner (Eds.), *Group psychotherapies for the elderly* (pp. 197–208). Madison, CT: International Universities Press.

Scharlach, A. E. (1989). Social group work with the elderly: A role theory perspective. *Social Work with Groups, 12,* 33–46.

Schloss, G. A. (1988). Growing old and growing: Psychodrama with the elderly. In B. W. MacLennan, S. Saul, & M. B. Weiner (Eds.), *Group psychotherapies for the elderly* (pp. 89–104). Madison, CT: International Universities Press.

Schmidt, G. L., & Keyes, B. (1985). Group psychotherapy with family caregivers of demented patients. *The Gerontologist, 25,* 347–350.

Sherman, E. (1987). Reminiscence groups for community elderly. *The Gerontologist, 27,* 569–572.

Shibbal-Champagne, S., & Lipinska-Stachow, D. M. (1986). Alzheimer's educational/support group: Considerations for success—awareness of family tasks, pre-planning, and active professional facilitation. *Journal of Gerontological Social Work, 9,* 41–58.

Silverstone, B., & Burack-Weiss, A. (1983). *Social work practice with the frail elderly and their families.* Springfield, IL: Charles C. Thomas.

Sorensen, M. H. (1986). Narcissism and loss in the elderly: Strategies for an inpatient older adults group. *International Journal of Group Psychotherapy, 36,* 533–547.

Stern, R. (1988). Drama gerontology: Group therapy through counseling and drama techniques. In B. W. MacLennan, S. Saul, & M. B. Weiner (Eds.), *Group psychotherapies for the elderly* (pp. 257–265). Madison, CT: International Universities Press.

Steuer, J. L., & Hammen, C. L. (1983). Cognitive-behavioral group therapy for the depressed elderly: Issues and adaptations. *Cognitive Therapy and Research, 7,* 285–296.

Steuer, J. L., Mintz, J., Hammen, C. L., Hill, M. A., Jarvik, L. F., McCarley, T., Motoike, P., & Rosen, R. (1984). Cognitive-behavioral and psychodynamic group psychotherapy in treatment of geriatric depression. *Journal of Consulting and Clinical Psychology, 52,* 180–189.

Toseland, R. (1977). A problem-solving group workshop for older persons. *Social Work, 22,* 325–326.

Toseland, R. W., & Rivas, R. F. (1984). *An introduction to group work practice.* New York: Macmillan.

Toseland, R., & Rose, S. D. (1978). Evaluating social skills training for older adults in groups. *Social Work Research & Abstracts, 14,* 25–33.

Tross, S., & Blum, J. E. (1988). A review of group therapy with the older adult: Practice and research. In B. W. MacLennan, S. Saul, & M. B. Weiner (Eds.), *Group psychotherapies for the elderly* (pp. 3–29). Madison, CT: International Universities Press.

Weiner, M. B., & White, M. T. (1988). The third chance: Self psychology as an
effective group approach for older adults. In B. W. MacLennan, S. Saul, &
M. B. Weiner (Eds.), *Group psychotherapies for the elderly* (pp. 57–66). Madison, CT: International Universities Press.

Weiner, W. (1988). Groups for the terminally ill cardiac patient. In B. W.
MacLennan, S. Saul, & M. B. Weiner (Eds.), *Group psychotherapies for the
elderly* (pp. 165–175). Madison, CT: International Universities Press.

Weinstein, E. A. (1969). The development of interpersonal competence. In D. A.
Goslin (Ed.), *Handbook of socialization theory and research* (pp. 753–775). Chicago: Rand McNally.

Woodruff, J. C., Donnan, H., & Halpin, G. (1988). Changing elderly persons'
attitudes toward mental health professionals. *The Gerontologist, 28,* 800–802.

Yalom, I. D. (1985). *The theory and practice of group psychotherapy,* 3rd ed. New
York: Basic Books.

Zgliczynski, S. M. (1982). Multimodal behavior therapy with groups of aged.
Small Group Behavior, 13, 53–62.

II

MACRO PRACTICE IN GERONTOLOGICAL HUMAN SERVICES

Introduction

PAUL K. H. KIM

Macro practice, which is interchangeably used with terms such as indirect or nonclinical practice, focuses on a broader scope of services impacting on small communities such as service agencies, organizations, and neighborhoods. This concept extends not only to a larger number of people and a variety of social institutions such as social, health, education, and religious institutions, but goes beyond, to levels of state, region, nation, and even to the world. Macro practice approaches, therefore, primarily include program planning, development and evaluation; administration, management, and supervision; formulation and implementation of service policies; community organization, development, and social action; consultation, etc. Unlike clinical intervention strategies in the field of gerontological human services, macro techniques are most effective when/if the target problem is essentially related to larger systems beyond the client's immediate dominion, and/or when/if the issue is rather pervasive or pandemic. Moreover, one of the functional objectives of macro practice is to facilitate efficacy and effectiveness of clinical practice.

Chapters in this section emphasize critical theory and skills aspects of macro practice in social planning, administration, and management, program evaluation, consultation, and fund raising techniques. Ginsberg (Chapter 8) provides a precise introduction to macro practice by denoting (1) political wisdom and the imperativeness of empirical facts in the organization of macro practice, (2) knowledge and value bases of social planning, (3) funding sources for programming, and (4) the importance of mobilization, organization, and sustenance of community volunteers.

Social planning as a problem-solving approach on a larger scale is expressly defined by Lohmann (Chapter 9) as "a prelude to strategic or structural decision-making" toward goals specified by the organization

189

and as program monitoring in terms of any impeding factors that under-
mine the program's success. This chapter reviews a genealogy of social
planning during the last eight decades and characterizes developmental
techniques of social planning by ordering and forbidding, regulatory,
and bureaucratic modes that have evolved into constituency development, goal displacement, and cooptation. A procedural stage of social
planning augments the needs assessment to facilitation, i.e., resource
analysis, alternatives and priority setting, implementation, and evaluation.

Based on the reality of professional social work education, Raymond
(Chapter 10) presents contingency or situational, as well as operational,
approaches to management, which are simultaneously applied in the
administrative process. Whereas the former is related to management
principles "within the context of the environment," the latter focuses on
the functional responsibilities of the administrator or manager of the
program and/or service agency. Accordingly, the central crux of organizational administration and management (i.e., planning, organizing,
staffing, directing and leading, and controlling) is discussed from theoretical and practical perspectives.

Program evaluation is an important tool for the accountable implementation of service programs in the field of gerontological human
services. It addresses not only the "how much" issue (quantitative
"bean count") but also the "how well" matter (qualitative "valuing")
implicated in the service program, and thus it is the guiding principle for
service professionals to effectively and efficiently perform their duties.
Nancy Lohmann (Chapter 11) clearly points to factors that need to be
considered in program evaluation, i.e., framing the research question in
accordance with the kind of evaluative research (either formative or
summative); the purpose, utility, and the audience of such evaluation
reports; etc. A number of practical quasiexperimental designs (including
sampling and data collection and analysis methods) appropriate for
evaluating service programs are discussed. The important issue associated with program evaluation is articulated as well in terms of reliability
and validity.

Human service professionals with respective advanced degrees and/
or postacademic experiences in both fields of clinical and macro gerontology are normally and frequently invited to be consultants for specific
service activity. The major reason for having consultants is for "new and
inexperienced" professionals and/or programs not to repeat what "old
and experienced" colleagues and/or service activities have already
achieved and practiced, so that the former becomes capable of establishing the knowledge and service footing equivalent to those of the latter.
Washington (Chapter 12) explains practical phases of consultation, i.e.,

entry, assessment, response, disengagement, and closure. In addition to functions of consultation, i.e., prevention, intervention, and evaluation, Washington contends that consultation should be directed to problem-solving orientation based on the consultant's expert knowledge and experience.

The amount of program funding is the essential ingredient for quantity and quality human services, irrespective of fields of practice, namely, child welfare, aging, mental health, correction, industrial services, etc. It is the most powerful key to the success of human services, particularly when those services are to be provided within the political and economic structures of capitalism. And thus, without exception, professionals in the field of gerontological human services must be competitive and imaginative—much more than those in other fields, since the capitalistic ethos may harbor and breed prejudice against the aging and aged.

Kim (Chapter 13) asserts that American private and public funds for human services and relevant research are readily available, though the successful securement of such funds is through a rather "keen" competition. In his chapter, sources and effective means to locate such funds for gerontological human services are explained. In addition, organizational structure and subsequent contents that possibly "good" competitive grant and contract applications should contain are exemplified.

8

Principles of Macro Practice with and on Behalf of Older Adults

LEON H. GINSBERG

Although most of the attention given to work with older adults focuses on direct "micro" services such as counseling with them and their families, helping them secure and effectively use human services, and managing their use of services and programs through processes such as case management, some of the most critical work with and on behalf of older people is performed at the "macro" or larger system level. It is likely that most of the progress made on behalf of older adults in recent decades has resulted from those larger scale activities. In fact, it is typically the macro services that lead to the establishment of micro or direct services and it is macro activity that typically makes it possible for resources to be allocated by public and private bodies for services to client groups, including the aged.

Macro services have historically been a crucial part of the human services professions (Meenaghan, 1987). They grew out of a variety of early activities, particularly those of the settlement houses, the coordinating roles of the Charity Organization Societies, and the planning and allocating functions of social welfare planning agencies and community fund-raising programs (Dinitto & McNeece, 1990; Kadushin, 1985).

Concepts of Macro Practice

Macro practice is a generic term that is used for many kinds of processes that are used in the human services professions. Included in macro practice are a variety of similar and dissimilar activities such as community organization, social planning, grassroots organizing, balancing needs and resources, fund-raising, and many others (Dinitto &

McNeece, 1990; Meenaghan, 1987). Essentially, however, all of these activities have some common features. For example, all are based on some kind of problem-solving or at least problem-addressing approach. The macro processes provide means for identifying problems, determining their rank order of importance in the community or social system in which they are found, identifying ways to overcome them, locating the means for overcoming those problems, and actually dealing with the problems. One author says macro work includes planning, administration, evaluation, and community organizing (Meenaghan, 1987).

Of course, the problems addressed through the macro practice process are of a larger scale and more general than the problems of an individual, family, or other small social unit. Usually, macro practice applies to something at least as large as a neighborhood or a special interest or special needs group, a community, or even a state or nation. The focus is not so much on the specific means for dealing with the problems faced by the individuals who share the need but on developing mechanisms for making it possible for other individuals or groups to address those needs (Paget, 1990).

Social Problems of the Aging and Preparation for Macro Practice

This text refers to the social problems of older people including their needs for economic assistance, housing, health care, social activities, transportation, and many other practical and economic necessities. It is within this range of social problems that macro practice on behalf of the aging is carried out.

A social problem is generally defined as one that has an impact on a relatively large number of people, that has potentially negative consequences for a large segment or several segments of a society or community, and that deals with serious matters of health, life and death, as well as economic security (Dobelstein, 1990; Etzioni, 1964, 1968).

Social workers who study at the baccalaureate or master's level for the profession of social work all learn something about macro practice and develop some skills in carrying it out (Council on Social Work Education, 1984). In some master's program, there are opportunities for specialized studies and the development of specialized competence in the use of macro methods in the social welfare system.

Types of Macro Practice Used with the Aging

A variety of human services agencies have macro practice components that are organized and operated for services to the aging—to help older people overcome and deal with their social problems. These agencies include United Ways, social planning councils, area agencies on aging, senior centers, state commissions on aging, and, in various forms, local special interest programs for helping the aged overcome some of their social problems.

Any form of macro practice may be useful for service to older adults, depending on the nature of the problem. Some of the more important types of macro practice are discussed in this chapter along with the application of those methods to helping older adults overcome problems.

Political Action and Lobbying

Older adults constitute the single most active age group in American politics. Because the number of older adults is growing (U.S. Bureau of the Census, 1990), older adults are becoming an increasingly important part of the American electorate. The state legislatures, the U.S. Congress, and both the President of the United States and the governors of the 50 states in addition to those who govern the territories are highly responsive to and concerned about the needs and wishes of the aged.

Clearly, political action as a part of that overall process called political lobbying has been one of the most important activities on behalf of older adults during the second half of the twentieth century. It was through political action that the most fundamental and severe problem facing older people through much of American history and through the 1960s was, in part, solved. That problem was a lack of economic sufficiency. Many older people simply did not have enough money to meet their basic food, clothing, health care, and shelter needs. Retirement often did not bring a sufficiently large pension or Social Security payments to make a decent life possible (Jansson, 1990). Mandatory retirement for older adults further complicated the process because even those adults who had not planned to retire and, therefore, did not have large retirement resources, often found themselves forced out of jobs because of their ages (Harbert & Ginsberg, 1990).

Organized political action through various contacts between aged people, advocates and lobbyists for them, and decision makers in the U.S. Congress, in particular, led to a variety of programs beginning in the 1960s that have turned the older members of the U.S. population from an economically deprived group to a generally better supported group who can, by and large, meet their own financial needs through their own retirement and other programs. Health programs, such as Medicaid and Medicare, have made a vast difference in the ability of elderly people of all ages and income levels to obtain adequate hospital and physician care. Social Security (OASDI) is now "indexed" (Ozawa, 1987), which means that older people receive Social Security payments that rise with inflation so that there are never long periods of time during which Social Security payments do not better represent the cost of living for older adults (Dobelstein, 1990).

In addition, federal and state laws have been passed that protect the pensions of workers so that they can count on retiring adequately in their later years, outlawed discrimination in employment on the basis of age alone, reduced mandatory retirement so that those who prefer to work may be able to do so, and created a number of programs for work placement and training that can help the elderly obtain jobs so that many can be self-supporting (Hurwitz, 1987). Housing for the aged also falls in this category as do special educational programs for adult learners. All of these efforts, which dramatically and effectively serve older people, resulted from political action (Dear & Patti, 1987).

Political action or lobbying requires that older people be brought together for the identification of their problems and to discuss potential solutions to those social problems. Obviously, the political action has to be about problems that are real and of real concern to older clients. Political action, like all politics, requires organization. People must organize in fairly large numbers to identify problems, develop plans for dealing with them, and carry out strategies for overcoming those problems (Mahaffey & Hanks, 1982; Ginsberg, 1988).

Perhaps the most important step in the political action or lobbying process is that of engaging a "lobbyist" or a specialist with another kind of title who can help the older adults convince their city councils, county governments, state legislatures, or the U.S. Congress to develop a new program or make some changes in an old one that will benefit the older people of the specific jurisdiction or of the whole nation (Haynes & Mickelson, 1986).

Typically, the actual lobbying, action, or influence generating is done by the older people, themselves, with the guidance and professional help of the lobbyist, who is often a human services worker whose special area of practice is "macro." Older people who want to bring about political change must learn about the public policy-making process and must learn how to reach and influence individual legislators or executive branch agents, whose legislative proposals are often the basis for political action, in ways that will help them help other people (Dear & Patti, 1987).

Older people speak with a strong voice in the lobbying process because, as was mentioned, older people constitute a large and growing portion of the American population. Furthermore, older people also vote in elections. Some 69% of people over 65 voted in the 1988 election (U.S. Bureau of the Census, 1990). Political figures know that and for those kinds of reasons, alone, many support the wishes of their older constituents. A growing population group that votes is a formidable instrument for lobbying. The issues about which lobbying or political action are directed for older people are numerous. They may be as specific as providing or maintaining a supplement to Supplemental Security Income clients, an option not exercised by all states but that, when exercised, makes a great deal of difference to the incomes of older people. The other issues that are often seen as crucial are the overall budget, senior citizen programs, taxes, and homestead exemptions for older people, hospital costs, and employment legislation dealing with older workers.

Many times the lobbying on senior citizen issues is done through organizations such as the National Council on Aging, the American Association of Retired Persons (AARP), or state chapters of AARP that may well be involved in local activities (Minahan et al., 1987). However, Area Agencies on Aging, State Units on Aging, and individual senior centers are also often important actors in the political action or lobbying processes.

Perhaps the most dramatic recent example of the power of older people to effect legislation was the passage in 1988 of the Catastrophic Coverage Act program, which was designed to help older people make use of federal programs when they had long-term disabling illnesses that would otherwise pauperize them. However, many older people apparently believed that the legislation would provide for their support in nursing homes, a fear that many older people experience about their futures (Boise, 1990).

However, when the Catastrophic Coverage Act was implemented, it was discovered that it did not pay for extensive quantities of new nursing home care. The financing of the program was also largely based on additional tax payments by relatively affluent older citizens. Angered by the higher taxes and the lack of a guaranteed nursing home program, older people began to question their wisdom in supporting the statute. In 1989 they lobbied Congress and Congress, under the leadership of some of the strongest advocates for the older population, repealed the Catastrophic Coverage Act because it did not appear to meet the needs of or desires of the aged. The federal government returned many of the premiums that older people had paid for the program.

The aged also realized that a relatively small proportion of older people would actually benefit from the legislation because many— especially the relatively affluent—already had major medical and other kinds of insurance to help them deal with the possibilities of a catastrophe. Thus, the mobilization and use of political power by older people on issues affecting older people have been among the most important phenomena in recent American life and have been among the most critical factors in the development of American social policy since World War II.

However, the political action of older people has not been done only with and by the elderly. In many cases, the elderly operate in coalition with groups such as the National Association of Social Workers, medical associations, nursing groups, hospital and nursing home organizations, and others to mutually address legislative and public policy issues that are of special concern to the elderly.

Human services workers who carry out macro activities are involved in the political process in several ways. They help organize older adults as a means of identifying their needs or concerns, they help train older adults on working with legislatures and the executive branch of government, and, at times, they work directly as lobbyists on behalf of the aging to effect change in public policy dealing with aging (Dear & Patti, 1987).

Organizing the Aging for Activities and Needs Assessment

The operation of senior centers, groups for older people, and various activities programs of cultural, recreational, and educational varieties requires the organization of older people to identify their program preferences and to manage those programs (Harbert & Ginsberg, 1990; Wenocur, 1987). Not the least of the concerns about the program activities is that of securing attendance at activities, which often requires some kind of organization. Human service workers with macro responsibilities often find it important to identify the older people in a community. Sometimes that requires little more than searching lists of members of existing senior citizen organizations, finding church rosters that include large numbers of older members, and compiling master lists of those who might be interested in participating in programs. Some workers spend a good part of their time canvassing neighborhoods and running advertisements in newspapers and on radio and television to find older adults who are interested in programs (Brawley, 1983).

Very often, effective work with older people in this kind of area of responsibility requires organizing activities such as bringing all the people together to identify, either in writing or through oral interviews, their interests or needs. A subsequent activity is often that of selecting, preferably through election by the older citizens themselves, planning committees and officers to direct or at least assist in the direction of the aging programs. These kinds of activities may initially be termed "needs assessments," a process whereby the requirements of a group are identified and refined through direct communication with those who have needs of services (Moroney, 1987; Wireman, 1987). Subsequent to identifying the needs and planning the programs in ways that express the interest of those to be served, the macro-oriented worker often spends a major portion of his or her time consulting with the planning body and the officers chosen by that body. Participants for the activities are often recruited by the officers through the efforts of the staff.

To be more specific, a typical kind of activity of this sort is that of working with, for example, a group of Hispanic older adults in a city to organize some kind of Hispanic program for older adults. A macro worker would identify Hispanic people above a certain age, communicate with them, try to solicit their participation in a planning and organizing meeting, and then attempt to organize some permanent program. That program may be a senior center or an older Hispanic persons' club. The participants might be helpful in defining the kinds of sociocultural, recreational, and educational activities that might help meet their needs. The worker would help them define their objectives, clarify their program, and carry it out.

The program might be as straightforward as education on the use of the English language. It might be one of organizing and operating a carpool or transportation system for older citizens. It might be as simple as developing a health education and health monitoring program to help the members monitor and deal with problems of blood pressure or diet. The program might become one of flexibility exercises or other physical exercise activities. The program might deal with opportunities to maintain current information on life in the Hispanic nation of origin of the participants. The macro worker's task is to help the participants identify those needs or concerns and to help them translate those needs or concerns into programs that will assist them in meeting their needs.

Social Planning for the Aging

A macro activity of growing importance in today's context is social planning. The general idea of social planning is to ensure that as many needs are met as is possible and that there is a minimum of duplication of effort on behalf of populations of clients. With the growing number of older adults in the United States, social planning for the aged has become a matter of major importance. Older people have many needs and there are, as always in the human services, limited resources for meeting them. Therefore, careful planning is required to make sure that the most important needs are met and that there is little or no duplication of activities so that the funds can be spread over the most crucial activities.

For the macro worker, social planning requires both technical and sociopolitical kinds of activities. That is, effective planning requires research on a variety of subjects and also requires meeting with and working with people politically so that the needs of people might most effectively be met (Gilbert & Specht, 1974).

With regard to technical activities, workers need to know about the numbers and location of older citizens. Data of that kind are developed through the study of census materials for the locality in which the work is being done or, in the case of nationwide social planning, through studies of complete census materials for the nation. In addition, workers may conduct research to determine the size and nature of the aging population through carefully studying a selected sample of the older population. One is able to learn, through such activities, about the ages, health status, living arrangements, transportation needs, and other characteristics of older people. The information gathered, in turn, provides the basis for planning programs and activities for the older people.

Planners also need to know about a variety of other elements in order to effectively serve the aging. One of the most important areas of knowledge is the range of programs and services available for the older adults in a community. The planner needs to know the organizations that provide services, the kinds of services that are provided, eligibility requirements, and, for the planner, the most important element—the extent and use of the services by the older population. The planner will want to know about ways in which transportation problems are resolved, health care is handled, housing provided, and economic needs met for older people (Kramer & Specht, 1983).

Macro workers who carry out social planning activities may be employed by and reponsible to a variety of different kinds of organizations. They may be staff members of committees of the state legislature that are charged with appropriating money and developing legislation for the benefit of older people. They may work for social planning or community councils that identify community needs and make recommendations about resolving them. They may work for United Ways in recommending the allocation of funds, a subject that is discussed later in this chapter. In general, macro workers are part of organizations that are the context for human service delivery (Holland & Petchers, 1987).

Social planning requires the kinds of specific, detailed information suggested here. The technical information developed in the social planning process is critical to determining, for example, how many clinics are needed to help meet the health needs of older adults, how many senior centers are reasonably required for meeting the social and recreational needs of older people, and how transportation problems are being addressed and can best be addressed for older people. Planning programs without collecting and using such information can lead to the development and operation of programs that are not needed and that will not be used. It can also lead to the possibility of organizing programs to meet needs that are relatively minor compared to some strikingly severe problems faced by older adults. However, by the time that is understood, the community may have already obligated all of the available funds with little possibility of obtaining more funds to meet some of the more fundamental needs of the older citizens.

However, as is suggested at the beginning of this chapter, social planning requires more than the collection and use of technical information. In addition, workers with the aging need to base their planning decisions not only on facts and figures but also on the social and emotional needs of older people. That means social planners must meet with, talk to, or otherwise solicit the attitudes and opinions of older people themselves, if their planning is to be correct and effective. For example, one may discover that although the statistics show a large number of older people live in a community and, therefore, significant quantities of senior housing may be needed, the older people, themselves, may, by and large, be home owners or may have satisfactory living arrangements with relatives. The community may have an excellent home visitation program for helping older people meet their household maintenance and health needs in their own homes, which may further suggest that shelter needs are not critical in the community, despite the data that might indicate otherwise in other communities. Such information is often available only through more targeted and specific research and through meetings and other kinds of direct encounters with older people. Therefore, the effective social planner connects with senior citizens, themselves, in analyzing their needs and concerns as well as dealing with research data and statistical information.

Planners may also find that community values, as expressed by powerful community leaders, are also critical in the planning process. The top contributors, for example, to the United Way or the most powerful legislators from the area, or some other highly influential individuals and groups may have strong feelings about the best programs for the community's older citizens. The effective social planner must be aware of and must take into account the convictions of such "power structure" groups because their attitudes will clearly have an impact on any final decisions about human services for older people in the community (Rothman, 1987).

For example, the community's top decision-makers may believe that health and housing services are the most crucial kinds of activities for older people and they may press for the majority of the available funds to be used for such services. Older people, on the other hand, may clearly indicate that their top concern is transportation. They may identify their most serious problem as the fact that they cannot travel to church, to the homes of friends, to visit their families, or even to health services because they lack adequate public transportation. They may also lack the means, either financial or physical, to own and operate personal automobiles, and may not have family or friends who can transport them. Therefore, given a choice, they may place a higher priority on transportation than anything else. Older people frequently do. In such circumstances, it often becomes the job of a macro worker to persuade community decision-makers that their concerns and priorities ought to better match those of the older citizens (Brody & Brody, 1987).

Nutrition services are another example of occasionally divergent opinions in the community. There is a long and well-financed tradition of providing at least one hot meal a day at many senior centers. The meal is, for some lower income senior citizens, the only full meal they have on any given day. However, some may think that transportation to the senior center to obtain the meal is a more pressing need than the provision of the meal itself. Still others may be too physically ill to make use of a centralized meal function. Those individuals may think that the highest priority should be placed on home-delivered meals. Still others may have enough money to buy their own food and may have strong preferences about what they would like to eat but lack the ability, for a variety of reasons, to prepare their own meals at home. Their top priority in the area of nutrition might be having homemaker staff members of a senior center come to their homes to help them prepare a series of meals that they might freeze and consume between visits from that staff.

Even something as concrete as meeting nutritional needs, as can be seen from the above discussion, requires sensitive work on the part of the social planner for other people's services.

Obtaining Financial Resources for Services to the Elderly

Clearly one of the most important activities implied so far in this chapter has been obtaining funds and using them to meet the needs of older adults. Finding and effectively using funds is a classic responsibility of the macro worker. It is a truism that programs cannot be developed or carried out without resources. Therefore, one of the major macro preoccupations is the development of those resources (Demone & Gibelman, 1984).

When resources are discussed, the usual assumption is that one is discussing money. Of course, money is the main resource used in developing and operating programs. After all, staff members must be employed and paid, as well as provided with the fringe benefits that are associated with employment. Facilities have to be rented. Transportation has to be developed or purchased. Materials such as arts and crafts supplies, food, and books are needed for most senior citizen activities. Therefore, many programs start with resources. Those that start with needs or program desires often break down when they reach the resource development stage.

Sources of Funds.   Funds are available from a variety of sources for the operation of senior citizen programs. Macro workers must be aware of those sources and the ways in which they can be obtained in the fund developing process.

Local, state, and federal government funds.   Extensive amounts of money are appropriated every year for senior citizens programs through the Older Americans Act. The funds are given in the forms of direct grants to state and local senior citizen programs to help them mount activities such as the operation of senior programs, the provision of meals, and the construction and operation of senior citizen housing, and in many other direct ways for the benefit of senior adults. Other programs provide financial assistance such as Social Security benefits, Supplemental Security Income, and Food Stamps, which are available to low income older people (Bell, 1983).

Much of the money allocated by the federal government for senior citizen programs is provided for organizing and planning senior citizens services more than for the provision of direct services, which often are treated as the responsibility of state and local governments rather than the federal system. Federal funds for the agency pass through the State Commission or Unit on Aging for ultimate reallocation to individual programs and localities. The assumption is that the central state planning body knows the needs and requirements of older people throughout the state better than the federal government. State agencies, in turn, operate through Area Agencies on Aging, which are regional bodies that coordinate and operate multicounty programs. The eventual allocation of the money to local programs is done directly to senior centers and other kinds of local activities.

State governments allocate extensive amounts of money for senior programs and state funds are allocated throughout the United States for senior citizen activities. Again, these are often provided directly to state agencies on aging, which, in turn, allocate them with guidelines to area agencies, which, in turn, provide them to local programs where the services are provided. Some county and city governments also provide funds for older people's programs (Harbert & Ginsberg, 1990).

Overall, the largest single source of funds for programs to serve the aged is government. Government is often first and most important place to turn for senior citizen programs and services. For that reason, most workers with the aging who perform macro tasks are very knowledgeable about, and closely tied to agencies that appropriate and allocate funds for serving older people.

Community-donated funds.   The United Way is a national organization that plans for, trains personnel for, and otherwise supports local United Ways. Most communities have local counterparts, some that serve single cities, others that serve counties, and still others that serve multicity or multicounty areas. The overall program objectives are always the same—to efficiently raise funds through private contributions that can be reallocated for the provision of services to people who need them. There is a large emphasis in United Way programs on services to children, family counseling, and programs that provide other kinds of help to individuals and families such as the Salvation Army (Moroney, 1987).

Often a portion of the money raised by the United Way goes for the provision of services to older adults through either free standing special programs or as part of the services of existing United Way beneficiary agencies such as Family Service Associations, YMCAs and YWCAs, and other organizations that serve people of various ages.

The money raised by United Ways is collected through voluntary contributions, usually by volunteer solicitors whose work is supported by professional staff members, most of whom would be defined as macro human services workers. The decisions about where the money will go are made on the basis of budget requests by the individual agencies to whom the funds are provided. Committees on allocation and the United Way board study those written and oral requests from the agencies and make their decisions on the basis of their other obligations and the amounts of funds available.

United Way programs are an important source of money for senior citizen services. They are a source of funding to which macro human services workers often turn in their quest for support of programs.

Foundations. Some of the money for work on behalf of and in service to senior citizens is provided by private foundations. These organizations are set up by individuals and corporations that allow some of their wealth to be exempted from taxes. They allocate money for services based on their own special purposes or on the requests for funds from various kinds of agencies and programs. Many times, foundation monies are used to purchase or construct senior citizen facilities. In other cases, foundations pay for needs assessments such as some of those described earlier in this chapter. Some foundations provide ongoing financing or programs for senior citizens including meals programs, transportation, social and cultural activities, and health services (Kilbride & Andrews, 1987).

Many macro workers with the aging, who attempt to obtain help for their clients, are knowledgeable about working with foundations. They maintain contact with such organizations and request funds from them for the benefit of their older people. Foundations are often an important source of funds, usually for getting programs started but, often, also for sustaining programs.

Other voluntary contributions. Some senior citizen programs find that funds are available from individuals and organizations on a voluntary basis that are different than the United Way contributions that those same organizations and individuals might make. People may contribute money spontaneously and voluntarily. In other cases, people may be periodically solicited for financial assistance by the macro workers with the organization. In still other cases, macro workers find that they can obtain buildings, equipment, furniture, and the like through the voluntary contributions of individuals and organizations. Many senior center buildings are donated either rent free or with the complete title and ownership given over to the senior center by former owners, who might include individuals, school systems, or churches. Computers, craft materials, and other kinds of resources may be provided on similar donated bases. Retail appliance dealers, construction companies, and virtually every other kind of business may be involved in the provision of help to a senior center program.

Sectarian contributions. A variety of religious or ethnic organizations also contribute funds and other resources for senior programs. Planning and allocating bodies such as Jewish Federations, and Catholic Social Services, Lutheran Social Services, and the Church of Jesus Christ of Latter-Day Saints, or Mormons provide extensive help to senior programs. Some churches and synagogues, themselves, donate or operate, as part of their overall activities, senior center programs. There is a high correlation between church membership and attendance and aging. That is, many of the most active members of churches are older people. Therefore, the churches are an important source of aid for their own senior center programs or for older adult programs in the larger community.

Organization of Volunteers

Volunteers are a basic resource in social welfare (Schwartz, 1984). Much of what is done with and for senior citizens is done by volunteers. The resources they represent are often worth a great deal—sometimes as much as the cash budget of the senior center or senior adult organization. Volunteer physicians, social workers, recreation workers, nurses, attorneys, and educators are among those who help with the operation of the senior program and, at times, with the maintenance of senior adult facilities.

Voluntary activities of that kind do not happen spontaneously. They often require the services of the macro worker to identify volunteers, solicit their help, and coordinate their activities so that the volunteer help is spaced out properly and available to those who need it when they need it most. Effective macro workers seek volunteers in organizations such as churches, governments, professional organizations, and corporations. Many times they are able to obtain the services of people who are not employed on a full-time basis or who are retired, themselves, to help older people. Much of the volunteer help for older people in aging programs is provided by high school and college age youngsters who are willing to help senior citizens and who are capable of doing so. Many volunteers, in all phases of the human service system, are elderly people (Manser, 1987).

Macro workers who organize and work with voluntary resources such as these also know the importance of maintaining a complete roster of volunteer workers, being in touch with the volunteers so that their services are used when they have agreed to help, training the volunteers on the needs of senior citizens and on the ways in which the program operates, and recognizing the volunteers with certificates as well as recognition functions such as lunches, dinners, and other awards ceremonies.

Conclusion

As has been discussed, macro services are an important part of the operation of human services for senior citizens. The processes of outreach, planning, coordinating, financing, and social change activities on behalf of older adults are critical parts of the provision of services to older people.

It is likely that these kinds of larger system activities are a more central part of senior citizen programs than they are of programs for people in other age groups such as families and children. The senior citizen movement and programs for senior citizens grew out of political and community organizing activities such as those that have been described in this chapter. Many programs that are familiar to human services workers came from the political and social change activities of older people and their advocates. The importance of coordinating and organizing services for older people cannot be overemphasized. Macro activities lay a basis for all of the direct service and administrative efforts that are performed on behalf of older people. For these reasons, macro services for the elderly are of great importance.

It is also likely that programs serving older people require workers who understand not only the provision of direct services but also the provision of indirect or macro services on their behalf. In programs for older people, employed workers need to understand not only the direct provision of services but must also have the ability to plan for, organize, and carry out services in some of the ways described in this chapter. Workers with the aging are often required to be generalists—both organizing and delivering services on behalf of their elderly clients and serving them directly.

References

Bell, W. (1983). *Contemporary social welfare*. New York: Macmillan.

Boise, L. (1990). The demise of the catastrophic coverage act: A reflection of the inability of congress to respond to changing needs of the elderly and their families. *Journal of Sociology and Social Work, 17*, 107–123.

Brawley, E. A. (1983). *Mass media and human services*. Beverly Hills, CA: Sage.

Brody, E. M., & Brody, S. J. (1987). Aged: Services. In A. Minahan et al. (Eds.), *Encyclopedia of social work*, 18th ed. (pp. 106–126). Silver Spring, MD: National Association of Social Workers.

Council on Social Work Education. (1984). *Curriculum policy of the master's degree and baccalaureate degree programs in social work education*. Washington, DC: Author.

Dear, R. B., & Patti, R. J. (1987). Legislative advocacy. In A. Minahan et al. (Eds.), *Encyclopedia of social work*, 18th ed. (pp. 34–42). Silver Spring, MD: National Association of Social Workers.

Demone, H. W., Jr., & Gibelman, M. (1984). Reaganomics: Its impact on the voluntary not-for-profit sector. *Social Work, 29*, 421–427.

Dinitto, D. M., & McNeece, C. A. (1990). *Social work: Issues and opportunities in a challenging profession*. Englewood Cliffs, NJ: Prentice-Hall.

Dobelstein, A. W. (1990). *Social welfare policy and analysis*. Chicago, IL: Nelson-Hall.

Etzioni, A. (1964). *Modern organizations*. Englewood Cliffs, NJ: Prentice-Hall.

Etzioni, A. (1968). *The active society*. New York: Free Press.

Gilbert, N., & Specht, H. (1974). *Damnations of social welfare policy*. Englewood Cliffs, NJ: Prentice-Hall.

Ginsberg, L. H. (1988). Social workers and politics: lessons from practice. *Social Work, 33*, 245–247.

Harbert, A., & Ginsberg, L. (1990). *Human services for older adults: Concepts and skills*, 2nd ed. Columbia, SC: USC Press.

Haynes, K. S., & Mickelson, J. S. (1986). *Affecting change: Social workers in the political arena*. New York: Longman.

Holland, T. P., & Petchers, M. K. (1987). Organizations: Context for social service delivery. In A. Minahan et al. (Eds.), *Encyclopedia of social work*, 18th ed. (pp. 204–217). Silver Spring, MD: National Association of Social Workers.

Hurwitz, D. S. (1987). Retirement and pension programs. In A. Minahan et al. (Eds.), *Encyclopedia of social work*, 18th ed. (pp. 507–512). Silver Spring, MD: National Association of Social Workers.

Jansson, B. (1990). *The Reluctant welfare state*. Belmont, CA: Wadsworth.

Kadushin, A. (1985). *Supervision in social work*, 2nd ed. New York: Columbia University Press.

Kilbride, Z., & Andrews, F. E. (1987). Foundations and social welfare. In A. Minahan et al. (Eds.), *Encyclopedia of social work*, 18th ed. (pp. 650–655). Silver Spring, MD: National Association of Social Workers.

Kramer, H., & Specht, H. (Eds.). (1983). *Readings in Community Organization Practice*, 3rd ed. Englewood Cliffs, NJ: Prentice-Hall.

Mahaffey, M., & Hanks, J. W. (Eds.). (1982). *Practice politics: Social work and political responsibility*. Silver Spring, MD: National Association of Social Workers.

Manser, G. (1987). Volunteers. In A. Minahan et al. (Eds.), *Encyclopedia of social work*, 18th ed. (pp. 842–851). Silver Spring, MD: National Association of Social Workers.

Meenaghan, T. M. (1987). Macro practice: Current trends and issues. In A. Minahan et al. (Eds.), *Encyclopedia of social work*, 18th ed. (pp. 82–89). Silver Spring, MD: National Association of Social Workers.

Minahan, A. et al. (Eds.). (1987). *Encyclopedia of social work*, 18th ed. Silver Spring, MD: National Association of Social Workers.

Moroney, R. M. (1987). Social planning. In Minahan et al. (Eds.), *Encyclopedia of social work*, 18th ed. (pp. 593–602). Silver Spring, MD: National Association of Social Workers.

Ozawa, M. N. (1987). Social security. In A. Minahan et al. (Eds.), *Encyclopedia of social work* 18th ed. (pp. 644–654). Silver Spring, MD: National Association of Social Workers.

Paget, K. 1990. Citizen organizing: Many movements, no majority. *The American Prospect*, 2, 115–128.

Schwartz, F. S. (1984). *Voluntarism and social work practice: A growing collaboration*. Lanham, MD: University Press of America.

U. S. Bureau of the Census. (1990). *Statistical abstract of the United States: 1990*, 110th ed. Washington, DC: U.S. Government Printing Office.

Wenocur, S. (1987). Social planning in the voluntary sector. In A. Minahan et al. (Eds.), *Encyclopedia of social work*, 18th ed. (pp. 625–631). Silver Spring, MD: National Association of Social Workers.

Wireman, P. (1987). Citizen participation. In A. Minahan et al. (Eds.), *Encyclopedia of social work*, 18th ed. (pp. 275–280). Silver Spring, MD: National Association of Social Workers.

Rothman, J. C. (1987). Community theory and research. In A. Minahan et al. (Eds.), *Encyclopedia of social work*, 18th ed. (pp. 308–316). Silver Springs, MD: National Association of Social Workers.

9

Social Planning and the Problems of Old Age

ROGER A. LOHMANN

Introduction

Social planning is very much a part of the development of the social work profession. An important segment of social workers continue to practice in this area, even though it has been an area of relative neglect in the professional literatures of both aging and social work in recent years. In this chapter, some basic approaches to social planning are examined with particular attention to the issue of community planning of services for the aged.

Planning in general can be defined as a process of preparing a set of decisions for action in the future to achieve a set of goals by optimal means (Dror, 1963). As such, the planning process is an elective one, often associated with the administration of a program or agency, and which usually occurs in the early stages of a large undertaking or enterprise (such as the creation of the original Aging Network in the 1960s), or at the beginning of a new phase of development (such as the introduction of Area Agencies on Aging in the 1970s). In the first instance, planning is usually a prelude to strategic or structural decision-making on "critical decisions," through which the basic direction and domain of the enterprise are established, and programs are opera-tionalized (Selznick, 1953). In the second instance, a planning process is frequently engaged to deal with specific problems—shortcomings, gaps in service, programmatic failures, or the need for reform.

Both types of planning are evident in the field of aging services. American society has been struggling with the tremendous task of developing entirely new social institutions and practices to respond to the unprecedented growth of the elderly population that has occurred in recent decades. And social planning is one of the arenas in which that struggle has been carried forward.

There are many excellent discussions of social planning theory available. (See, for example, Morris & Binstock, 1966; Kahn, 1969; Friedmann, 1973; Mayer, 1972; Lauffer, 1978.) Most social planning theory is built, implicitly or explicitly, on problem-solving models with which social work students should be familiar. In this chapter, therefore, theory is not discussed in-depth. Instead, selected issues with implications for the planning of aging services will be examined.

One of the most widely known aspects of contemporary social planning theory is the tripartite distinction of community practice into three approaches: Locality development, social action and social planning (Rothman, 1979). This set of distinctions, which appears to have made its way into many introductory social work texts, is somewhat misleading in fashioning social planning as the abstract, intellectual, and rationalistic alternative to direct political action and the remote, detached, or elitist alternative to hands-on neighborhood or client involvement. Effective social planning necessarily incorporates both effective political action and widespread involvement.

Social welfare planning is a term that is sometimes used to distinguish social planning in which the outcomes are presumed to be social agencies, programs, or services. (Innovations in housing for the elderly, retirement communities, tax exemptions and adjustments, and support groups are among the many nonprogram or service outcomes of aging-related planning.) Program planning is another term for such efforts. Program planning is the assessment of social needs in a population, efforts to meet those needs through coordinated deployment of resources and on-going evaluation of the results of planned intervention.

One of the most fundamental distinctions in contemporary planning theory is John Friedmann's distinction of allocative and innovative planning (Friedmann, 1973). Allocative planning is concerned with allocation of money, resources, or other scarce values among alternatives, whereas the latter is most concerned with expanding the range of alternatives. Both have been factors in recent social planning efforts in the area of aging services. Routine budget decision-making, for example, associated with grant awards and renewals ordinarily involves allocative planning, whereas periodic initiatives expanding the range of community services (such as the implementation of the Older Americans Act Title III-C nutrition program or the gradual shift of III-B programs toward community-based services) constitute innovative planning enterprises.

Social planning is problem-solving on a large scale, or to use a popular cliche, "macro" problem solving. In the case of social welfare planning, this is most likely to involve changes in organizational goals, legal or functional reforms, or alteration of attitudes and values in a population

(Morris & Binstock, 1966). Social planning oriented toward social struc-tural changes may involve changing the membership of a group or class, changing its roles, or redefining its statuses (Mayer, 1972). Social plan-ning may also involve planned replacement of the population in a territory or development of a regional socioeconomic infrastructure. Both of these approaches came into play, for example, in the planning of the Appalachian Regional Commission (Hansen, 1969). Unfortunately, as the cases of Appalachia and rural America generally demonstrate, large-scale population shifts can have the effect of concentrating and exacerbating the problems of the least mobile population groups such as the old, who may be left behind when caregivers and support groups move away (U.S. Commission on Rural Poverty, 1965).

Why engage in social planning? The reasons can be many and varied. Alfred Kahn (1969) identified 10 major social planning tasks including (1) translating social goals into effective programs, (2) coping with major social problems, (3) introducing social (nonmarket) considerations, (4) responding to gaps, fragmentation, and other failures in service pro-grams, (5) redesigning services to meet the intended "target popula-tion," (6) reviewing the viability of selected fields, (7) responding to inconsistencies and diffuseness in service strategies, (8) allocating scarce resources, (9) promoting the migration of concepts form one field of social welfare to another, and (10) absorbing new technology (pp. 1–11).

Planning Is Not a Method

Social planning is sometimes characterized as one of a repertory of social work methods. Although it is certainly possible to discuss social planning as a methodology, to do so misses some very fundamental points. When one speaks of "social work methods" what usually comes to mind is a set of unique and integrated skills and techniques of intervention whose use is unique to social work and guided by practice principles and values of the profession. The "methods" of community practice are by no means exclusive to the social work profession, but are instead the general methods of group and public problems—solving through discussion, debate, and decision-making utilized generally in democratic communities.

Community practice in general and social planning in particular do not fit easily into the type of methods approaches popular in social work education. Education for community practice is much more amenable to historical and comparative approaches emphasizing the complex inter-play of actual organizational, political, and economic forces in real situa-tions. Social planning is, as the definition above suggests, most fundamentally a process of preparing for decision-making (i.e. action). It is the planning situation (just prior to decision making) and not unique planning methods (i.e., problem-solving) that distinguishes the planning enterprise.

There is (or should be) an element of planning preceding decision-making at all levels of social work practice. Recently, for example, there has been recognition of planning in the case management process. The ubiquity of planning at various levels of social work activity, however, should not be confused with the distinctive phenomenon of social planning. What is called "social planning" is best understood as the problem-solving that precedes recognizably "big" (or critical) decisions and "Big" (supraindividual) client units. (For a classic exposition of "critical decisions," see Selznick, 1953.)

Because of this characteristic, social planning is what might be termed an extraordinary rather than an everyday approach, and that fact explains its relative decline in recent years, as well as the shifts in emphasis noted below.

The process of social planning is also generally dialectical and recursive: planning ordinarily involves a phase of "planning the planning" in which the problems to be solved are prioritized, and the elements of planning to be emphasized are identified. In some cases, for example, defining the problem virtually consumes the entire task. In other cases, definition is virtually ignored, and much attention is devoted to prioritizing alternatives.

Community, State, and Organization: A Brief History of Social Planning

Social work interest in planned change and the deliberate, planful modification of social relations and institutions is relatively recent. It has its origins in the Progressive idea of social reform and progress (Commager, 1967). The intellectual and practical origins of social planning ideas and practices in social welfare can be traced directly to three distinct groups of "reform darwinists" operating during the Progressive Era in the United States and England. In each case, social planning was no mere abstraction or academic parlor game, but an integral component of an approach that mixed theoretical speculation and actual practice. Each was also what would today be called a "generalist" approach in which "micro" interventions with individuals and families were mixed with community development, social action, and basic social research as circumstances dictated.

There was a Chicago group included Jane Addams, George Herbert Mead, John Dewey, and W. I. Thomas and other social workers and sociologists (Deegan, 1988; Dewey, 1933; Janowitz, 1966). (W. I. Thomas, for example, wrote that "the problem of social reconstruction is to create new schemes of behavior—new rules of personal conduct and new institutions—which will supplant or modify the old schemes and correspond better to the changed attitudes, that is, which will permit the latter to express themselves in action and at the same time will regulate their active manifestations so as not only to prevent the social group from becoming disorganized but to increase its cohesion by opening new fields for social cooperation.")

This group operated principally out of the Hull House settlement and the Department of Sociology at the University of Chicago. To them, professional social workers owe some key concepts including a dynamic, processual view of society as a changing set of relationships and the model of general problem-solving, which links together planning, decision-making, and evaluation. (Although Dewey is most frequently cited as the source of the problem-solving model, this view was widely shared among the Chicago pragmatists, and is ultimately traceable to the original founder of American pragmatism, Charles Sanders Pierce. The dynamism discussed in Dewey's article on the "Reflex Arc" concept, published in 1898, is at the heart of the planning–decision-making evaluation cycle as well as the contemporary model of a "feedback loop" in so-called "systems" theory.)

At the core of the London group were Beatrice and Sidney Webb, leaders of the Fabian Socialists and relentless campaigners for municipal reform and industrial democracy (MacKenzie & MacKenzie, 1977). The Fabian emphasis on local reform is the basis of both the community emphasis in social planning and the concept of social planning as a component of comprehensive community planning. (The role of social elements in comprehensive planning is most extensively developed by Mayer, 1985.)

Important in the New York group was Robert deForest, John Glenn, Homer Folks, Mary Richmond, and others at the intersection of the Charity Organization Society movement and the activist-oriented Russell Sage Foundation. [No adequate account of the community practice contributions of the Russell Sage group currently exists, although the two-volume history of the Foundation (Glenn, Brandt, & Andrews, 1947) contains much information that is still useful.]

Each of these groups had a well-developed conception of planned change and was aware of the full range of intervention possibilities even as they distinguished between "wholesale" reform efforts such as social planning and the "retail" reform of relief and casework. For them, the difference was a strategic choice. The polarization of method specialization in social work was left for others. Interestingly, each of these three groups was open to valuable, even critical, contributions by both male and female participants, and the Chicago group centered around Hull House was open to the possibilities of racial and ethnic diversity as well.

Aging planning, of course, was not a specialized concern of any of the early reform darwinists or Progressives. The aged were still a small proportion of the total population (only 4.6% in 1900); epidemics of communicable diseases were still rampant and there were few effective treatments or cures for any of the chronic diseases, so intervention beyond comfort and caring was largely futile; and family responsibility was still the official policy of the Poor Law inspired local relief system that put major emphasis on public caring for the aged only as a last resort.

The first evidence of a changing position of the aged, and of major social planning activity for the aged, comes in the 1920s. Lubove (1968) traced the growth of state level concerns with the growing problems of income maintenance of the aged through the 1920s that led up to the national social security program in the 1930s. Although the states lacked the financial resources to deal effectively with the income maintenance issue on their own, this period marked the beginnings of an important historical transition of planning from the voluntary sector of the community to the government.

The Depression, Public Planning, and the Totalitarian Planning Model

The depression of the 1930s was a period of dashed hopes and unrecognized achievements for social planning. Domestically, the Tennessee Valley Authority was the broad-scale attempt at regional economic planning (Streib, 1984). Internationally, Communism and Fascism introduced broad new connotations of economic planning as state control, and in reaction the notion grew up in some circles that all forms of planning were antithetical to freedom.

There were at least two national social planning efforts affecting the aged during the 1930s that have gone largely unnoticed in the social planning literature. Planning of the Social Security system was of a very sophisticated type, in which the detailed implications of the social insurance concept were operationalized. Realizing the commitment to the social insurance principle meant planning and implementing a self-financing system based on a perpetual network of intergenerational transfers. Planners of this system had to work out an actuarially sound employer/employee tax system as well as a system of national registration of workers and adequate control of payouts. All of this had to be accomplished within a set of rigorous constitutional, legal, and political constraints, while resisting efforts of some Congressmen to turn the program into a vehicle of political patronage.

At the same time, planned implementation of Old Age Assistance and other programs of the state–federal public assistance system, which largely replaced the local relief system during the depression, is another major undocumented planning activity. In this case, state and federal planners has to work out a myriad of administrative details and build an entirely new state and local assistance bureaucracy.

Community Planning and the Postwar Takeoff

In the two decades after the second world war, social work interest in social planning was closely linked to the expanding voluntary "community chest" (later, United Way) or health and welfare council movement (Harper & Dunham, 1959). In its most common form as a federation of associations aspiring to represent entire communities, these United Way-type entities typically embrace two distinct components with planning implications: a fund-raising organization ("the campaign committee") and an allocative planning organization (sometimes called "the admissions and allocations process"). Needs assessment, resource analysis, review of alternative, priority determination, program development, and a range of other social planning techniques are frequently employed in this context.

Well before there was an Administration on Aging (AoA), a variety of prototypical aging programs, in particular senior citizens' clubs or membership associations and senior activity centers, were planned and implemented through such voluntary sector means. An associated practice innovation that evolved during this period was the "demonstration grant" in which a foundation would fund a community association or agency to work out and implement a program or service with particular promise. This model of planning was later incorporated into the original Older Americans Act.

The postwar era also saw the decline of the European colonial empires and the emergence of social planning in the entirely new guise of guiding the social structural changes of the emerging new nations. Interest in national social and economic "community development" emerged in the United Nations and the international agriculture community in this period. Closely associated with national transitions away from colonialism in Asia and Africa, the international community development movement drew little attention among domestically oriented social workers in the United States. Also in the postwar period two other types of social planning evolved that have had important consequences for contemporary social planning efforts in social work. Both are very distant from what many social workers associate with social planning.

In the late 1940s, Congress created the Council of Economic Advisors, and set in motion a limited form of national economic planning for a capitalist economy directed at changes in new economic indicators rather than empirical changes in social and economic institutions. Such planning is, by its every nature, "conservative," foregoing an interest in structural change and seeking to measure fluctuation only in an intact set of economic institutions. Several important social indicators emerged from this planning effort, including the unemployment rate and more recently the poverty rate and the Retired Couple's Budget, which may be the most important age-related economic indicator of this type.

The postwar housing boom in the United States also set in motion the need for a second set of local planning institutions with implications for aging. So-called "physical planning" or land-use planning directed at regulating new suburban growth and urban redevelopment gradually evolved into "comprehensive urban planning" (Frieden & Morris, 1968; Mayer, 1985). The existing U.S. system of housing for the elderly was one of several major products of this particular comprehensive planning effort.

Planned Social Change

A generalized resurgence of interest in social planning arose in the social sciences during the 1960s around the concept of "planned change" (Bennis, Benne, Chin, & Corey, 1976). The planned change orientation is heavily grounded in a behavioral science perspective that places great emphasis on distinguishing between "basic" social sciences such as sociology and psychology and "applied" social sciences like social work. The role of practice (including planning) in this perspective is to apply the basic scientific insights developed and tested by the basic sciences. This is a dramatically different concept of social science from that shared by the reform darwinists. To its adherents, the planned change orientation suggested an entirely new relationship between government and the social sciences, patterned after the "research and development" orientation of scientists and engineers in the defense and space industries.

One such application was the development of "opportunity theory" of poverty from the Ford Foundation financed Grey Areas Project directed at prevention of juvenile delinquency in the early 1960s, and its subsequent application in the war on poverty through the Economic Opportunity Act of 1964 (Marris & Rein, 1967). The planned change movement was predicated on an underlying political triangle of action-oriented social scientists in universities, their colleagues in control of a range of social programs (including portions of the AoA) in the federal bureaucracy, and an informal caucus of liberal Congressmen, supportive of funding for these "new welfare" programs. It has had little genuine appeal outside these rather narrow boundaries.

The New Laissez-Faire

The years since 1972 have not been kind to American social planning. Many of the federal programs supporting social planning practice have been eliminated or drastically scaled back, and individual organizations have had to rely increasingly on their own resources to plan. As a result, social planning practice today resembles social planning practice in 1950, in that it is largely restricted to the initiatives of individual organizations and local communities. At the same time, the rising popularity of "strategic planning" with its implicit organizational focus is also a clear indicator of a major shift in the locus of social planning efforts. The trend is distinctly away from the community as a locus of planning attention, in favor of planning directed at enhancing the position and resources of individual organizations.

Contemporary Social Planning Practice and Aging

Community Planning Councils

Probably the oldest intact social planning systems for aging in most American communities today are the networks of community planning that grew up in the voluntary sector in the period after World War II. Usually a federation of member social agencies and community leaders, with fund-raising and planning components, such entities go by a variety of names including "Community Councils" and "Community Chests." In some cases, these local planning systems have established subcommittees on aging, long-term care, or community care to deal particularly with aging issues.

During the 1960s and 1970s, at least six additional identifiable planning systems grew up. Although little is left of most of them today, they are worth noting anyway.

Aging Network

With the creation of Area Agencies on Aging (AAA) amendment in the 1970s, an entire national planning network was created for the planning of aging services. Up to that point, funding decisions for AoA funds had been largely centralized in state offices of aging. The AAA amendment introduced a new level of processing in the substate regions as well as a somewhat standardized process of initiation, review, and approval of project proposals. The resulting system was often cumbersome, redundant, and never involved very large sums of money, but it did result in creating at least the vestiges of a standardized service delivery system for the aged in local communities across the country.

Some of the other objectives of the early system were not quite so durable. For example, in the early 1970s, the Senior Centers were to become a "focal point" for aging services in local communities. Although they may be that in some small and rural communities, in larger urban communities where most of the elderly live, the focal point strategy has been decidedly unsuccessful in dealing with the problems of service coordination and control. In general, the larger and more complex the service delivery system, the more likely it is that the "focal point" strategy has been ineffective.

The Aging Network, complete with what has to be one of the most arcane bureaucracies imaginable, remains largely in place today. However, its role is almost entirely limited to delivering existing services. Its planning phases are almost entirely a thing of the past.

Title XX of the Social Security Act

Approximately at the same time as the initiation of the AoA regionalization strategy, Congress also enacted an amendment to the Social Security Act adding the twentieth title (or chapter). (Medicare was Title XVIII and Medicaid Title XIX). Title XX (now the Community Services Block Grants Program) is noteworthy from a planning standpoint for three reasons:

1. It took advantage of the open-ended nature of Congressional allocations to the states through the public assistance process, in which state-matching funds were the only practical limitation on program spending.
2. It established "deinstitutionalization" of children, the mentally ill, retarded, and old as a national policy objective. (This was part of a network of related policy changes that occurred at the time.)

At the same time, the Older Americans Act was amended to increase the emphasis on community and in-home services as alternatives to nursing homes, the Developmental Disabilities Act to encompass the concept of "Normalization," and the Community Mental Health Reconstruction Act to embrace the concept of "Community Support Systems" for the mentally ill. Together, they add up to a planned movement away from a "relief" strategy dating from the 1830s and a return to "outdoor relief"— or in more contemporary terms, community and in-home services.

3. Title XX also consolidated broad ranging financial support for children's services and aging services into a single title, thereby setting up, at least locally for agencies supported by Title XX funds, the spectre of age politics and competition between needy children and the old for services. The creation of the Social Service Block Grant program out of Title XX in the mid-1980s shifted the locus of planning and the politics of generational conflict to the state agency level.

Health Planning Act

Unlike most other social planning occurring in the 1960s and 1970s, state health planning made explicit (and effective, even if controversial) provision for implementation. The "Certificate of Need" was an approval issued by state health planners to new programs and services that fell within the largely statistical guidelines established for the state. Thus, new home health services or nursing homes could be developed only after a state level review in which it was determined that the number of such services had not already exceeded allowable limits and a "Certificate of Need" has been issued.

This gave state administrators who were in a position to make use of it (and not all were) a strong weapon to encourage development of community-based services. In at least one state, for example, a ban on new nursing home construction has been in effect for nearly a decade, but states and local community attempts to beef up community and in-home services have been hamstrung by limited funding availability.

Service Reorganization Initiative

Some of the planned changes of the 1970s were largely symbolic, although they were frequently presented in the name of enhancing effectiveness and efficiency. For example, many states changed the names of their "public welfare" agencies to the more neutral euphemism of "human services," and the social work literature largely followed suit. The term "social work administration" virtually disappeared from professional vocabulary, for example, and was replaced by "human services administration." Such shifts, however superficial they may appear, are a stable and long-established aspect of symbolic policy in the profession of social work. In the same way that "public welfare" was abandoned, it had replaced the earlier term "public assistance," which, in turn, had replaced "public relief."

The more substantive part of the service reorganization initiatives of the 1970s, however, were the pattern of bringing aging, health and social services, and income assistance programs of various sorts together under a single umbrella agency with titles such as "Department of Health and Human Services." This was, perhaps, a set of belated state legislative responses to the creation of the umbrella department of Health, Education and Welfare (HEW) in the 1950s, and mirrored directly by the federal devolution of the Department of Education out of HEW in 1980s.

Policy Institutes

Since the mid-1960s, a portion of the burden of gerontological social policy planning in the United States has been borne by independent or free-standing policy institutes engaged in applied research and policy analysis activity. Such work is typically conducted under contract for federal or state agencies.

The "policy institute" is a kind of merger of the demonstration grant strategy with the university-based or free-standing research and development group. The Brookings Institution (perhaps the grandmother of this model), the Urban Institute and the Institute for Research on Poverty at the University of Wisconsin; the Institute for Interdisciplinary Studies (now Interstudy) in Minneapolis, which planned the HMO (Health Maintenance Organization) Amendment to Medicare; and at the Heller School, Brandeis University, which developed the SHMO (Social HMO); and the Duke Medical Center work on the OARS (Older Adult Resources and Services) are among many examples of such effort.

The policy institute approach to social planning offers a number of advantages for public officials. One of the advantages that this approach offers is the use of trained, technical specialists not burdened with daily administrative responsibilities and distractions to examine policy options and alternatives on a sustained basis. Another indisputable advantage for public officials is that independent contracted policy planning is easily ignored or discounted when that is politically convenient or necessary. On the down side, the emphasis on expertise in such policy-making also contributes to corresponding decreases in community and client participation in decision-making.

Long-Term Care Policy Initiatives

Beginning in the mid-1980s, there were signs of state level movement in the direction of states attempting long-term care policies on their own. In the inflationary cycle of the later 1970s, many state governments were in severe financial jeopardy because of the burden of matching federal Medicaid expenditures, and several states were rumored to be on the verge of bankruptcy at the time.

Federal research and policy in the 1980s became increasingly preoccupied with issues of cost containment and less interested in substantive policy issues. A proposal for a "Title XXI" to provide federal support for personal care was stillborn, and the wave of tax-cutting and program elimination that accompanied the first Reagan administration made it clear that little in the way of leadership on aging issues would be forthcoming from the federal government in the 1980s.

Federal inattention, however, did not value the tremendous pressures of a growing aging population, and the fiscal pressures of exploding health care costs of the aged were compounded by double digit inflation in the late 1970s. In the decade of the 1980s, a number of states began to independently plan community-based and comprehensive "long-term care" reforms designed to meet future needs within the increasingly restrictive federal fiscal environment.

The long-term impact of this on state aging services networks may turn out to be substantial. Alter (1988) suggests that integration of Medicaid programs with the Aging Network funded by AoA is already changing the structure of community-based elderly services. The resulting second generation system serves a larger volume of clients because it is more centralized, differentiated, and formalized and smaller in size.

Housing Policy

One of the interesting planning systems that arose in the 1960s only to virtually disappear by the early 1980s was the network of urban planners working on the design and construction of special housing for the elderly. By the late 1970s, public housing projects for the elderly, which were popular with urban residents and big city political forces, had virtually replaced less popular and controversial public housing for AFDC families. When a large number of Housing and Urban Development (HUD)-funded programs were consolidated in the early 1980s, public housing for the elderly was effectively erased from the HUD agenda along with the rest of the federal housing effort.

Planning Technology

As noted above, social planning is not a method. This does not mean, however, there are not specific techniques that are frequently employed by the social planner. It would appear that there is such a technology at least in the sense of a more or less ad hoc, experience-tested accumulation of techniques that can be usefully applied in various social planning contexts (Morris,1970; Zweig & Morris, 1966).

In an early essay on "Rational Control in Social Life," W. I. Thomas spoke of "ordering and forbidding" techniques as the oldest forms of social intervention (Janowitz, 1966). The application of such "regulatory" techniques to problems of public health, child labor, and other fields may be the signature of the Progressive era legacy of social planning by the reform darwinists. At the same time, one of the legacies of New Deal planning would certainly be the development of large-scale, bureaucratic organizations, such as state departments of public welfare, which incorporated individual problem-solving into their rules and routines. With this trend came the gradual discovery of the repertory of organizational techniques and strategies such as constituency development, goal displacement, and cooptation (Selznick, 1949).

Contemporary planning technologies can be divided into two broad categories, which Perlman and Gurin (1972) labeled "analytic techniques" (e.g., needs assessment) and "interactional techniques" (e.g., cooptation). In the first category are various techniques used in analyzing situations, client groups, and problems. In the second category would be various strategies for facilitating the planning process. The analytic techniques of social planning can also be further categorized by the stages of the planning process in which they are most likely to be used. For this purpose below, Hyman's six-state model is utilized, and the planning process divided into needs assessment, resource analysis, alternatives, priorities, implementation, and evaluation (Hyman, 1976). Only the first two of these will be examined here, because of space limitations and also because planning techniques for generating alternatives and determining priorities are much less standardized and in general use. Finally, evaluation techniques are the topic of Chapter 11 in this book.

Needs Assessment

Needs assessment is a generic term used to describe a range of problem-solving activities used when the principal practice problem is defining, assessing, or estimating the characteristics of a social problem experienced by a given population. Such efforts are ordinarily seen as the initial stage of most problem-solving, decision-making, and planning models. Needs assessment may involve either encyclopedic attempts to identify the full scope of age-related needs through use of an instrument like OARS, or they may involve highly selective and targeted investigations. Iutcovich and Iutcovich (1988), for example, examined the transportation needs of the elderly. Following Hyman (1978) further, one can divide analytical needs assessment techniques into five basic types: key informant, commission study panel, rates under treatment (unmet needs measurement), census data/social indicators, and survey.

Among the interactional needs assessment techniques, Nominal Group Process (Delbecq, Van de Ven, & Gustafson, 1975) might be employed with either key informants or commission/study panels. Such panels might also be constituted as small, informal study groups, large public forums, or even formal public hearings. The process for the White House Conferences on Aging in 1950, 1960, and 1970 incorporated a commission/study panel approach. When the key informants are recognized as experts on the need or issue in question, the Delphi technique may be especially suitable.

Analytically, rates-under-treatment information is most likely to be generated from synthesis of agency case records. Annual reports, planning studies, and research data are also somewhat less likely sources of information.

Census type information may come from institutional census reports (e.g., the kind of tables published regularly on higher education in the Chronicle of Higher Education). Comparable institutional census data on human services activity is relatively rare in human services, although it may sometimes be available (as in the case of state human services program data in such categories as AFDC and Food Stamps). The most likely source of census data are the various censuses conducted by the U. S. Bureau of the Census. The census of population is conducted every 10 years. Interesting data on nonprofit agencies may be available through the U. S. Census of Services, conducted every 5 years, in years ending in 2 and 7.

In addition to needs assessment, per se, there are a number of alternative analytical protocols available that cover much of the same territory. Reiner, Reimer, and Reiner (1968) for example, make an interesting and useful distinction between client groups and client populations in their proposal for "Client Analysis." At the level of policy planning and analysis, Rivlin (1971) has outlined a fairly complete model she terms simply "Systematic Thinking." Where areas and geographic factors are a major consideration, Social Area Analysis (Shevky & Bell, 1955) may be an appropriate model. Trend Analysis has also been shown to be useful approach in cases where time-related changes are of central importance (Meehan, Locke, & Lohmann, 1984). When the issues involve interorganizational relations, input–output models may be useful (Lohmann,

1976). Detailed examination of organizational dynamics may be approached from a number of perspectives, including goals analysis (Perrow, 1974) and simulation or modeling activities.

A popular computer game for the Apple Macintosh called SIMCITY, for example, provides a fascinating medium for simulating aspects of city and/or neighborhood dynamics that might be applied to some aspects of neighborhood relocation questions in aging planning. General simulation models, such as the one-line and multiline cafeteria models, might be usefully applied to many aspects of aging service problems.

Social planners have, in some instances, tended to slight the use of qualitative methods. However, narrative descriptions of the actual operation of service delivery systems, case studies, policy reviews, and legislative histories all have potential applications in social planning for the aged. Maldonado (1985), for example, places the public policy treatment of the Hispanic elderly in an explicitly historical context.

In conducting needs assessments, social planners often tend to avoid legal documents and research strategies. (For an exception, see Lammers & Klingman, 1986.) In cases in which there has been extensive litigation, depositions, and friend-of-the-court briefs, trial transcripts, rulings, and court orders can be fascinating and useful sources of planning information.

All other approaches to needs assessment pale, however, in comparison with the popularity of the survey as an instrument for conducting a needs study. Garcia (1985) illustrates the use of such a survey with the Hispanic elderly of Tampa Bay Florida. John (1988) details the use of statistical cluster analysis techniques with survey results.

Insufficient attention is also paid at times to the effective presentation of needs assessment information. A broad range of desktop publishing and presentation software is available for all types of professional computers and workstations today to facilitate the preparation of data tables, maps, charts, diagrams, flow charts, and assorted other types of presentations.

Resource Analysis

Interactional techniques of resource analysis generally revolve around telephone and face-to-face interviews of professionals, public officials, board members, and others for purposes of generating timely and accurate information on available resources and gaps in existing services. Questionnaire surveys, inventories, and fill-in-the-blank interview schedules are often useful analytical supplements to such information-gathering techniques. Constructing questionnaire surveys, however, that capture the appropriate level of detail regarding the actual dovetailing of services as they actually operate (and not just the way they are supposed to function) can be a daunting task.

Students of social planning may be accustomed to thinking of resource analysis only in terms of gaps in service. Resource analysis may also be used to identify significant developments in the organization's environment that may affect the feasibility of the planning endeavor (Morris & Binstock, 1966).

Techniques borrowed from strategic planning in business called the "environmental scan" can be readily and usefully applied to resource analysis in aging planning. Such scans may involve reviews of professional literature, summaries of items appearing in newspaper or periodical literature, summary tables listing brief abstracts of actual programs operating in a given area, and a broad range of other similar devices.

Such scans may also involve close examination of the interactional environment of the organization. Advocates of strategic planning, in particular, have given a good deal of attention to identifying and categorizing the constituencies or "publics" to which a program or service must respond. In an earlier discussion of this question, Dahl (1960) constructs the issue in explicitly political terms as "Community Influence Analysis." More recently, the importance of the community has been gradually minimized and the strategic position of the organization emphasized (Hudson, 1974). Lauffer (1986), for example, terms a similar process "marketing" and identifies six key publics of an organization: consumers, legitimators, resource suppliers, partners in service delivery, staff, and policy makers. The community planning perspective has not been entirely abandoned, however. Preston and Guseman (1979) examined the reasons for overlap between different measures of community leadership. Brilliant (1986) traces the decline of community-wide planning councils during the past two decades and examines five current models of community planning and problem-solving and argues for more social work involvement in each.

One of the standard forms of resource analysis in social planning is the program or service inventory, often presented in the form of a service directory or resource listing. Such inventories, built on a myriad of discrete facts such as names and phone numbers, are expensive to compile and extremely difficult to keep updated. Although they may be highly useful for service workers, they seldom provide much useful planning information and are often a kind of by-product of social planning efforts.

A major issue in the performance of social resource analysis involves the classification of programs and services. The UWASIS classification system created by Russy Sumariwalla and his associates for United Way of America is a useful scheme for classifying human services by goal (United Way of America, 1976). More recently, Sumariwalla and other members of a planning group for Independent Sector have devised an ingenious alphanumeric classification system for the nonprofit/voluntary/independent sector (National Center, 1987). This system has been adopted for use by the IRS in gathering data on nonprofit organizations. McCaslin and Golant (1990) recently suggested a typology of aging-specific services.

Alternatives

Interactional and analytic techniques for generating alternatives tend to fall into at least two broad classes: Change-oriented techniques are directed at generating new, novel, or unprecedented and innovative alternatives, whereas tradition-oriented techniques are directed at identifying tested, workable alternatives already in use elsewhere. Despite the rhetorical patina of change surrounding social planning, much actual work on identification of alternatives is relatively traditional, oriented to examining solutions to problems already in place in other, comparable communities.

A major issue in the identification of alternatives in all forms of planning is the question of when to stop. In general, what Braybrooke and Lindblom (1963) call the "synoptic" approach of economists and others suggests that full rationality demands identification of all possible alternatives. In contrast, Lindblom's approach, labeled variously "incrementalism," disjointed incrementalism," and more recently "strategic analysis" places planning and policy analysis in its explicit historical context and provides guidelines for limited—partial, remedial, and serial—consideration of alternatives (Lindblom 1959, 1979; Braybrooke & Lindblom, 1963).

A related line of analysis is Simon's suggestion (1976) that the actual behavior of planners and decision-makers might be characterized as involving what he termed "satisficing"—serial review of alternatives that is terminated when the first fully acceptable solution is arrived at (Simons, 1976). A number of social planners have sought to refine and improve on Lindblom and Simons without generating much of any lasting interest. In general, consideration of alternatives in contemporary social planning tends to be characterized by relatively limited attention to the deliberate generation of alternatives and behavior approximating that described by Lindblom and Simons. In particular, the use of field tests, simulations, pilot projects, demonstration projects, and scenario writing—all of which are used to generate alternatives in various other fields—are used only infrequently in the social planning context at the agency and community level.

Priority Determination

Even more neglected is the systematic attention to interactional and analytic techniques in the area of priority determination in social planning. Quite frequently today, calls for "needs assessment" in the context of community concern for age-related and other social problems are actually pointing to the need for priority determination. When funding is cut, when decisions over allocating limited funds must be made, and in other circumstances, simply adding to the already-overwhelming stock of known needs will do little to solve this problem.

The most critical question in contemporary social welfare decision-making at all levels is how to "prioritize" or rank in priority order existing needs and feasible alternatives. In the brief interlude of relatively abundant federal funding in the late 1960s through the mid-1970s, such decisions were made on a highly centralized basis and community and state decision-makers became comfortable merely responding to federal mandates and guidelines. Although circumstances today are dramatically different, social planning and decision-making rhetoric has not fully adjusted to the changes that have occurred.

One aspect of the priority determination question involves the criteria to use in making such determinations. Lohmann (1989) suggests the use of Life Satisfaction Scales as a policy-relevant criterion in aging planning. The OARS (Older Adult Resources and Services) Model can also be applied to the priority problem in planning as a unidimensional scale for ranking problem cases or individuals. In focusing the issue on individuals, however, the difficult problem of which problems are greater is downplayed: Are mental health needs greater or lesser than social needs?

A critical issue in priority determination is who should decide what priorities will be: agency administrators, supervisors, workers, legislators, clients, community residents, or others? A characteristic approach, which does more to disguise this issue than to answer it, is to seek refuge in a distribution formula. This is the approach of Congress in the Graham–Rudman–Latta approach to the federal budget deficit, and it is also commonly employed by aging network agencies. This does not resolve the question; it merely routinizes it.

An important related issue is the response of the minority whose priorities were not adopted. In a fully functional priority-setting system, one could expect that all (or at least most) of those involved would recognize the legitimacy of the result and adopt the resultant priorities as their own. In the current climate of agency, program, and client advocacy and interest group activity, however, this seldom (if ever) occurs, and adoption of any set of social priorities at any level is most likely to signal the beginning of a new round of overt and covert efforts to modify them.

Implementation

Implementation is a topic in which social planning shades over into social administration. In fact, much of the best of the contemporary literature on implementation, or as it is often termed by social workers "program development," is to be found in the social administration literature. (This is not particularly surprising, since social planning and social administration tend to be lumped together as "macro methods" in many of the schools of social work and agencies where the producers of this literature practice.)

In the implementation of social planning outcomes through interactional techniques, one might reasonably expect the skills of social workers to really shine. Regrettably, this is often not the case. A broad range of practical, commonsense techniques for personal consultation with key actors, staff, client, and public information meetings, public education campaigns, press conferences, and briefings are all-too-often ignored and badly handled.

Surprisingly, the record is often considerably better in the area of analytical techniques of implementation. In particular, the current literature documents the use of organization charts, work programs, policy and procedure manuals, information systems, task analyses and job descriptions, scheduling procedures (including PERT and GANTT charts), staff training plans, and many other analytical techniques to be applied to the problems of implementing a planned decision.

Taietz (1975) take a novel approach to the issue of implementation by suggesting a community development approach to aging service development, in which more fundamental services are expected to precede others that are partially dependent on them. Empirical tests in one state suggested that the development of aging services corresponded with this approach (Lohmann & Wu, 1980).

Evaluation

There are three quite distinct approaches to evaluation of flow in and out of the planning literature. On the one hand, there are the applications of social and behavorial research methodology to the task of program evaluation. In an era of rather severe limits on the availability of public funds, it is perhaps not surprising that the social-behavorial model of evaluation—which can be quite expensive to implement—has had less impact on social planning than other models.

A second, quite distinct (and limited) approach involves the examination of goals and policy of an organization (Perrow, 1974; McCaslin & Golant, 1990). The third approach involves the application of some variant of cost–benefit or cost-effectiveness methodology, around which an enormous literature far too vast to cite here has been built up.

Conclusion

Social planning has gone from an early emphasis on community as the modal point to an emphasis on public policy planning at the state and federal level and recently to an emphasis on organizational issues and initiatives. Social planning has been a primary tool in the long-term development of new institutions and practices brought about by the unprecedented increases in the size of the aged population. There is every reason to believe that these trends will continue, and that some social work practitioners will be involved in this complex and exciting process.

References

Alter, C. F. (1988). The changing structure of elderly service delivery systems. *Gerontologist, 28,* 91–98.

Bennis, W. G., Benne, K. D., Chin, R., & Corey, K. E. (Eds.) (1976). *The planning of change,* 3rd ed. New York: Holt, Rinehart & Winston.

Braybrooke, D., & Lindblom, C. (1963). *A strategies of community organization,* 3rd ed. Itasca, IL: F. E. Peacock.

Commager, H. S. Ed. (1967). *Lester ward and the welfare state.* Indianapolis, IN: Bobbs Merrill.

Brilliant, E. L. (1986). Community planning and community problem-solving: Past, present and future. *Social Service Review, 60,* 568–589.

Dahl, R. A. (1960). The analysis of influence in local communities. In C. R. Adrian (Ed.), *Social science and community action.* East Lansing, MI: Michigan State University Institute for Community Development and Services.

Deegan, M. J. (1988). *Jane Addams and the men of the Chicago school.* New Brunswick, NJ: Transaction Books.

Delbecq, A. L., Van de Ven, A. H., & Gustafson, D. H. (1975). *Group techniques for program planning: A guide to nominal group and delphi processes.* Glenview, IL: Scott, Foresman.

Dewey, J. (1933). *How we think.* New York: Plenum Books.

Dror, Y. (1963). The planning process: A facet design. *International Review of Administrative Sciences, 29,* 44–58.

Frieden, B., & Morris, R. Eds. (1968). *Urban planning and social policy.* New York: Basic Books.

Friedmann, J. (1973). *Retracking America: A transactive theory of planning.* New York: Anchor Doubleday.

Garcia J. L. (1985). A needs assessment of elderly hispanics in an inner city senior citizen complex: Implications for practice. *Journal of Applied Gerontology, 4,* 72–85.

Glenn, J., Brandt, L. E., & Andrews, F. E. (1947). *Russell sage foundation 1907–1946.* New York: Russell Sage Foundation.

Hansen, N. M. (1969). *A review of the Appalachian regional commission program.* Austin: University of Texas Press.

Harper, E. B., & Dunham, A. (1959). *Community organization in action: Basic literature & critical comments.* New York: Association Press.

Hudson, R. B. (1974). Rational planning and organizational imperatives: Prospects for area agencies on aging. *Annuals of the American academy of political and social science, 415,* 41–54.

Hyman, H. H. (1976). *Health planning: A systematic approach.* Germantown, MD: Aspen Systems Corp.

Hyman, H. H. (1978). *Health planning methods.* Germantown, MD: Aspen Systems Corp.

Iutcovich, J. M., & Iutcovich, M. (1988). Assessing the transportation needs of Pennsylvania's elderly population. *Journal of Applied Gerontology, 7,* 514–529.

Janowitz, M. Ed. (1966). *Rational control of social life.* Chicago: University of Chicago Press.

John, R. (1988). Use of cluster analysis in social service planning: A case study of Laguna Pueblo elders. *Journal of Applied Gerontology, 7,* 21–36.

Kahn, A. (1969). *Theory and practice of social planning.* New York: Russell Sage Foundation.

Lammers, W. W., & Klingman, D. (1986). Family responsibility laws and state politics: Empirical patterns and policy implications. *Journal of Applied Gerontology, 5,* 5–25.

Lauffer, A. (1978). *Social planning at the community level.* Englewood Cliffs, NJ: Prentice Hall.

Lauffer, A. (1986). To market, to market: A nuts and bolts approach to strategic planning. *Administration in Social Work, 10,* 31–40.

Lindblom, C. (1959). The science of muddling through. *Public Administration Review, 19,* 79–88.

Lindblom, C. (1979). Still muddling, not yet through. *Public Administration Review, 39,* 517-526.

Lohmann, N. (1989). Service providers and life satisfaction. *Journal of Applied Gerontology, 8,* 8–17.

Lohmann, R. A. (1976). *Matrix analysis and social planning.* (mimeo).

Lohmann, R. A., & Wu, P. (1980). *The hierarchy of aging services: A replication study.* Paper presented at the Fifth Annual National Conference on Social Work in Rural Areas.

Lubove, R. (1968). *The struggle for social security, 1900–1935.* Cambridge, MA: Harvard University Press.

MacKenzie, N., & MacKenzie, J. (1977). *The fabians.* New York: Simon & Schuster.

Maldonado, D., Jr. (1985). The hispanic elderly: A Socio historical framework for public policy. *Journal of Applied Gerontology, 4,* 18–27.

Marris, P., & Rein, M. (1967) *Dilemmas of social change: Poverty and community action in the U. S.* New York: Atherton Press.

Mayer, R. (1972). *Social planning and social change.* Englewood Cliffs, NJ: Prentice Hall.

Mayer, R. (1985). *Policy and program planning: A developmental perspective.* Englewood Cliffs, NJ: Prentice Hall.

McCaslin, R., & Golant, S. M. (1990). Assessing social welfare programs for the elderly: The specification of functional goals. *Journal of Applied Gerontology, 9,* 4–19.

Meehan, K.; Locke, B.; & Lohmann, R. (1984). A model for human service planning. *Proceedings of the 10th national rural social work institute.* Columbia, MO: University of Missouri School of Social Work.

Morris, R. (1970). *Is there a technology of social planning?* (Mimeo)

Morris, R., & Binstock, R. (1966). *Feasible planning for social change.* New York: Columbia Univ. Press.

National Center for Charitable Statistics. (1987). *National taxonomy of exempt entities.* Washington, DC: Independent Sector.

Perlman, R., & Gurin, A. (1972). *Community organization and social planning.* New York: John Wiley and Council on Social Work Education.

Perrow, C. (1974). The analysis of goals in complex organizations: Human device organizations. In Y. Hasenfeld and R. English (Eds.), *Human service organizations: A book of reading* (pp. 214–229). Ann Arbor, MI: University of Michigan Press.

Preston, J. D., & Guseman, P. B. (1979). A comparison of the findings of different methods of identifying community leaders. *Journal of the Community Development Society, 10,* 51–62.

Reiner, J., Reimer, E., & Reiner, T. A. (1968). Client analysis and the planning of public programs. In B. Frieden and R. Morris (Eds.), *Urban planning and social society* (pp. 377–395). New York: Basic Books.

Rivlin, A. (1971). *Strategic thinking for social action.* Washington, DC: Brookings Institution.

Ross, P. J., Bluestone, H., & Hines, F. K. (1979b). *Indexes and rankings for indicators of social well-being for U. S. counties.* Springfield, VA: U. S. Dept. of Agriculture, Economics, Statistics and Cooperative Services.

Rothman, J. (1979). Three models of community organization practice: Their mixing and phasing. In F. M. Cox, J. L. Erlich, J. Rothman, & J. E. Tropman (Eds.), *Tactics and techniques of community practice.* Itasca, IL: F. E. Peacock.

Selznick, P. (1953). *Leadership in administration.* Evanston, IL: Row and Peterson.

Selznick, P. (1949). *TVA and the grassroots: A study in the sociology of organizations.* Berkeley, CA: University of California Press.

Shevky, E., & Bell, W. (1955). Social area analysis. Stanford CA: Stanford University Press. Reviewed by O. D. Duncan, *American Journal of Sociology, 61,* 84–85.

Simon, H. (1976). *Administration: A study of administrative processes in administrative organizations,* 3rd ed. New York: Free Press.

Streib, G. (1984). TVA: A model project for these times. *Journal of Applied Gerontology, 3,* 117–124.

Taietz, P. (1975). Community facilities and social services. In R. C. Atchley and T. O. Byerts (Eds.), *Rural environment and aging* (pp. 145–156). Washington, DC: Gerontological Society of America.

232   Roger A. Lohmann

U. S. Commission on Rural Poverty. (1965). *The people left behind.* Washington, DC: U. S. Government Printing Office.
United Way of America. (1976). *UWASIS II.* Alexandria, VA: United Way of America.
Zweig, F., & Morris, R. (1966). The social planning design guide. *Social Work, 11,* 13–21.

10

Management of Services for the Elderly

FRANK B. RAYMOND, III

Introduction

The administrators of programs that serve the elderly come from a variety of backgrounds. They differ significantly in the type and extent of their educational preparation, and their previous practice experiences cover a wide range. During recent years, however, increasing emphasis has been placed on the recruitment of administrators who have an educational background combining graduate training in the social sciences and management. Social work has proven to be one of the best equipped disciplines to provide this kind of educational experience.

There are several reasons why social work education is especially appropriate in preparing people to become managers of services for the elderly. First, graduate study of social work provides one with a broad understanding of the field of human services rather than a focus on one narrow component. Such a broad-based perspective is essential for the administrator of a program serving the aging. There is a plethora of services for the elderly and those who administer these programs must understand the larger system of services and be able to relate the agency he/she manages to the broader array of programs.

Second, graduate social work education is suitable to prepare administrators of organizations for the elderly because of both the extensiveness and intensiveness of this type of education. Master's degree programs in social work are longer than most other graduate degree programs in human services, usually requiring 2 years of study beyond the baccalaureate degree. Moreover, this long period of training normally includes four semesters of field work, whereas other types of degree programs may require little or no field work. This field experience, a hallmark of social work education, is particularly important in enabling students to go beyond the acquisition of knowledge and to develop skills in applying this knowledge in real life situations. Managers of programs serving the elderly need more than a textbook or classroom orientation in order to be able to function successfully in this complex field of practice. The practical experience gained through field placement is of crucial importance.

Finally, graduate study in social work is appropriate for the preparation of administrators of elderly services programs because of its humanistic orientation. Although there is no question that other disciplines, such as business administration and public administration, teach many of the same management theories as social work, they do so from a different philosophic orientation. Social work education stresses client-centered values and emphasizes that services should be planned, organized, and delivered with a humanitarian objective. Thus, for example, while the administrator with a social work background and the administrator with a business administration background may be equally trained in applying techniques of cost–benefit analysis in an organization serving the aging, philosophic differences may influence the ways they would define benefits and, consequently, make programmatic decisions affecting the elderly client.

As graduate education programs in social work have increasingly offered specializations and concentrations, opportunities have expanded for students to acquire specialized knowledge and skills in the administration of services for the elderly. With the tremendous growth of baccalaureate degree programs in social work that prepare students for beginning level generic practice, graduate programs have increasingly developed concentrations in terms of methods of practice, population groups served, fields of practice, social problems, etc. In fact, the social work education accrediting body, the Council on Social Work Education, requires that graduate degree programs offer some type of concentration during the second year of study. With these developments in graduate education, opportunities to specialize in administration and/or to concentrate in gerontology have become widely available. More than ever, MSW programs are equipped to educate students specifically for practice as administrators of programs serving the elderly.

Even though social work education is appropriate for preparing managers of programs serving the aged and some schools have begun to develop concentrations in gerontology, it should be noted that neither social work nor any other academic discipline that prepares such administrators utilizes a distinct body of knowledge concerned with management of programs for the elderly. Such a body of knowledge does not exist. Historically, in fact, relatively little discussion has appeared in the professional literature regarding administrative practices in agencies serving the aged. Although certain aspects of the administrator's role have been addressed, such as program planning and the fiscal management of health care programs, a thorough body of knowledge has not yet been developed in this field. It is interesting that so little has been written on this subject, given the importance of the administrator's job.

There are several possible reasons why so little discussion has appeared in the literature regarding management techniques in services for the elderly. First, the wide variation of agencies serving the elderly makes it particularly difficult to develop managerial principles that would have universal applicability. A number of writers (Rogers, 1980; McQuillan, 1974; Miller, 1969) have described the management of specific types of programs, such as extended care facilities. The information contained in this literature, however, is not related to the management of other types of programs serving the elderly.

At the opposite extreme from such specialized management literature one finds writings that deal with the management of human services agencies in general (Weiner, 1982; Meenaghan, Washington, & Ryan, 1982; Austin, 1981; Abels & Murphy, 1981; Bresnick, 1983; Weinbach, 1990). This literature often serves as the base for management courses in schools of social work and other disciplines that prepare human service workers. Such material provides the student with an introduction to the general field of management in human services. Although these texts are an improvement over literature that describes the administration of *any* organization, human service or otherwise, the reader is still left with the responsibility of applying the content to a specific field of practice, such as programs serving the elderly.

A systematic body of knowledge regarding the management of programs for the aging is needed. Programs serving the elderly, like other components of the human services field, have been criticized increasingly during recent years for being unable to demonstrate the impact of their services. Administrators of such programs are now more responsible than ever for demonstrating accountability. They must be able to plan, develop, manage, and modify their programs successfully in order to achieve greater effectiveness and efficiency, and this requires a thorough understanding of managerial principles. Certainly there are factors related to an agency's success that may be beyond the control of administrators, such as federal or state regulations, funding levels, or expanding case loads. However, there are many aspects of agency operation for which administrators have considerable responsibility and authority and they are accountable for the agency's performance relative to these areas. To make appropriate decisions in these areas where they have managerial discretion and thus enhance agency performance, administrators of programs serving the elderly need to be knowledgeable of organizational management and theory as it applies to their agencies.

Although a systematic body of knowledge concerning the administration of organizations serving the elderly is needed, this does not mean that there should be a specialized theory of management unique to these organizations. Rather, existing management theory should be applied as appropriate to agencies serving the elderly. Furthermore, the application of management theory to the operation of these types of organizations should not be done in a prescriptive manner. Whereas in earlier years some organizational theorists have sought to develop management theories that prescribed *the best* ways of managing organizations (Taylor, 1947), during recent years there has been a trend among organizational theorists toward "contingency," or situational, approaches to management (Carlisle, 1973). That is, rather than advocating the one best way of managing an organization, these writers contend that management theory should develop knowledge of fundamental relationships and basic techniques that can be applied to a given practical problem for the purpose of achieving the best possible results for *that* situation (Koontz, O'Donnell, & Weihrich, 1986). This chapter will reflect a contingency perspective on management theory in organizations for the aging. Given this perspective, the social worker's role as administrator of an agency serving the elderly will be discussed in terms of the application of management principles within the context of the environment, the organization, and the particular parties involved.

Management theory as applied to agencies serving the elderly will also be presented within the framework of the "operational" approach. This is an approach that attempts to analyze management in terms of what managers actually do. This is an eclectic approach that brings together from all approaches to management those elements of each that relate to actual managing and that can be most useful to practitioners in understanding their job. The central core of knowledge about managing is organized, or classified, in the operational approach according to the major functions that all managers perform: planning, organizing, staffing, directing and leading, and controlling (Koontz, O'Donnell, & Weihrich, 1986). Theoretical content relative to each of these managerial functions will be presented in the remainder of the chapter as it applies to organizations serving the elderly.

Planning

For administrators of programs serving the elderly to ensure optimal agency effectiveness and efficiency it is essential that the agency's purposes and objectives and methods of obtaining these be clearly articulated. Furthermore, all program staff should know exactly what they are expected to accomplish and should understand how their work relates to the overall goals of the agency. Creating this framework of under-standing is the function of planning, which is the most basic of all managerial functions. Simply stated, planning is deciding in advance what to do, how to do it, when to do it, and who is to do it.

The other managerial functions performed by the administrator of a program serving the elderly—organizing, staffing, directing and lead-ing, and controlling—are designed to support the accomplishment of the agency's objectives. Hence, planning logically precedes the execu-tion of all other managerial functions. In other words, adequate plan-ning must occur for the administrator of a program serving the elderly to be able to establish the objectives of the program, create the kind of organization that can best attain these objectives, decide the type of personnel that are needed, determine how these personnel are to be directed, and define the kinds of control to be applied to ensure that objectives will be achieved.

Those persons who manage services for older adults often feel that their potential for planning is severely restricted, given the constraints within which they must operate. These constraints include factors such as the legal structure of the organization, federal regulations regarding services to the elderly, case loads whose sizes cannot be predetermined or controlled, budgetary limitations, staff size, and so on. However, the manager of *any* organization is faced with constraints, although they must be of a different nature, and these constraints do not preclude successful planning.

Given the constraints that may affect planning, the administrator of an agency serving the elderly can still exercise a wide range of choices in developing plans. For example, Koff (1988) describes a variety of service needs of the chronically impaired elderly. He makes the point that each of these may be funded by one or more federal sources. Reductions in funding from one source may constitute a constraint on the administra-tor requiring him/her to develop plans for acquiring funding from other sources. Or an Area Agency on Aging may experience a rapid growth of older individuals in the area it serves, coupled with insufficient commu-nity services to serve these potential clients. Faced with these con-straints, the administrator of the Agency on Aging may, in addition to promoting the development of new services, develop plans for enhanc-ing the integration of existing services through care coordination and case management (Evashwick, Ney, & Siemon, 1985).

The administrator of an agency serving the elderly must recognize that there are many types of plans that may be appropriate for use by the particular agency. Since plans, by definition, encompass future courses of action, plans are varied. Koontz et al. (1986) classify plans as purposes or missions, objectives, strategies, policies, rules, procedures, programs, and budgets. Although these different types of plans vary in scope and purpose, they are interrelated. In a given agency each type plan should be seen as one component of a larger gestalt. That is not to say, however, that each administrator in an agency will be involved in the development and implementation of each type of plan. Rather, the administrator's role will vary relative to the agency's structure and one's position within the organizational chain of command.

For planning to be successful in a program serving older adults, the chief administrator should involve other persons throughout the organization, including other administrators and lower level staff, in the planning process. As a result of this involvement the other members of the agency's staff will have a clearer understanding of what is expected of them and will have a stronger commitment to carrying out activities to achieve objectives that they helped establish. For example, if the staff of an adult day care program participate in developing a statement of philosophy that expresses the values of the program (Koff, 1988), they should strongly believe in the mission statement that is based on this statement of philosophy. Or the staff of a multipurpose senior center might participate in developing an outreach plan. By helping determine the target population and methods of locating the older persons to be served, the staff will likely have a greater commitment to carrying out the other steps of this plan—contacting the potential client and making him/her aware of available services, providing assistance to ensure the individual has access to services, and making a follow-up contact to ensure that the older person has received the service (Harbert & Ginsberg, 1990). As these examples illustrate, although responsibility for agency planning must rest with the administrator of the program serving the elderly, many benefits can be realized from including staff in the decision-making process.

All planning is ultimately aimed toward the attainment of the agency's goals and objectives. Indeed, unless goals and objectives are clearly established during the planning process there will be no way the administrator of a program serving the elderly can subsequently evaluate the results of the program and determine whether it was successful (the control function of management). The terms "goals" and "objectives" are sometimes used interchangeably in agencies. However, most of the management literature suggests that goals establish the direction for any agency and state what will be accomplished over the long run. For example, the purpose of a transportation service may be to increase the general mobility of older people in the community or to enable them specifically to participate in the activities of a senior center. On the other hand, while objectives also establish direction, they are short range and are always measurable (Harbert & Ginsberg, 1990). There are two types of objectives that can constitute part of an agency's plan of action. The first type, impact objectives, defines outcomes in terms of change expected in project participants as a result of project activities, such as demonstrated improvement in specific health indicators among elderly patients in health care programs. Such outcomes are often difficult to measure, particularly in human service programs such as those serving the elderly. The second type of objectives, output objectives, defines outcomes in terms of the expected level of services or activities of the project, such as an increase of 20% in the number of elderly served in a meals-on-wheels program. Generally, programs serving the elderly state their objectives as output objectives, although impact objectives would clearly be more desirable. The attainment of impact objectives enables the agency to demonstrate accountability at a higher level by providing proof of effectiveness and efficiency.

When agencies serving the aging include output objectives in their plan of action, these objectives should answer the "what," "where," "who," "how," "how many," "when," and "how much" questions. That is, they should articulate (1) the types of services or activities to be undertaken, (2) the location where the activities will take place, (3) the target groups for the effort, (4) the expected level of effort, (5) the time period for the effort, and (6) the cost. For example, a transportation program for the elderly could include the following output objectives: "The program is to provide, through Title XX funds, a $40.00 monthly cash subsidy to each of 100 low-income elderly in the community in order to meet their transportation needs." Or, "the program is to provide volunteer automobile transportation three days a week for the 200 older residents living in one area of the community" (Harbert & Ginsberg, pp. 198–199).

Since the purpose of having measurable objectives is to ensure that the client's needs are being met effectively and efficiently, it is crucial that the goals and objectives of the agency be relevant to the needs of the client. To help make certain that the goals of an agency serving the aging appropriately address its clients' needs, the administrator of the agency should seek client involvement in the establishment of goals and objectives. One means of bringing about this involvement of older adults in the planning process is by including them on advisory and policy-making boards. In fact, many federal programs for older people require that they be represented on such boards.

As Wetle (1985) noted, however, there is a tendency among programs serving the elderly to assume a paternalistic approach and to exclude them from the decision-making process. Although this paternalistic approach may be due, in part, to society's wish to protect its older citizens, it may also be based on motivations that have less to do with the good of the individual than with some perception of the good of the institution, the care provider, the family, or society in general. For example, failure to involve the older person in the decision-making process may be based on the ageist assumption that to be old is to be incompetent. For both moral and practical reasons, the administrator of a program serving the elderly should seek the advice of the clientele whenever possible in establishing agency goals and objectives and developing programs aimed at achieving these ends.

Organizing

The second major function of the administrator of an agency serving the elderly is organizing. Stated in simple terms, organizing means creating a structure by establishing relationships between people, work and physical resources. The purpose of organizing is to provide a framework within which people can work together effectively, utilizing resources, to achieve common goals in an optimum manner (Eckles, Carmichael, & Sarchet, 1974).

The first step in creating the structure of an agency serving older adults is to determine which organizational pattern is most appropriate for achieving established goals and objectives. Weinbach (1990) identified three general organizing patterns of human service agencies. These include the production line organization, the linkage organization, and the custom service organization. Usually the selection is made by the individuals in the highest level administrative positions in the organization, and reflects not only the established goals and objectives of the agency, but the environment in which the agency will operate, including needs to be addressed and the availability of resources.

The *production line organization*, an organizing pattern promoted by early management theorists, involves a number of individuals performing their own rather specialized tasks in a prescribed sequence. Although this type of organization would appear to be most appropriate for product manufacturing organizations using assembly lines, such as automobile plants, it is also used in human services. For example, an organization offering medical services for the chronically impaired elderly may "process" the clientele in an assembly line fashion. The older person coming to the clinic may go through the following established sequence of events: (1) the receptionist sees the client first, gathers data such as insurance information, and completes forms; (2) the nurse then meets with the patient, gathers medical information through questioning and performing established medical procedures; (3) the physician then sees the patient, asks additional questions and perhaps performs

other tests, and either completes the diagnosis or determines if additional tests or referrals are needed to complete the diagnosis; and (4) the
physician in the clinic, or the other health provider who was brought
into the process, develops and carries out a treatment plan.

Although organizing an agency serving the elderly in a production
line manner may help promote efficiency, this pattern has its draw-
backs. As Weinbach (1990) noted, it is impossible to standardize the
treatment of individuals, families, or groups. The health and human
service needs of individuals are too diverse to be responded to through
standardized activities of staff. Furthermore, such an approach is dehu-
manizing to the client who feels treated as an object being examined,
tested, probed, and shoved about, rather than an individual with
unique needs.

The *linkage organization* involves an agency structured in such a way
that its primary function is to serve as a mediator or broker. The purpose
of this type of agency is to bring people and services together. In the
business world, for example, a stock brokerage firm links the individual
who wishes to buy a particular stock with another individual who
wishes to sell this stock. Many agencies serving the elderly, such as
information and referral services, legal services, and protective services,
are organized to function in this way. This type of agency serves as a
mediator between the elderly client and the services s/he needs.

During recent years increasing attention has been given to the concept
of "case management" in human services, and this method is now used
extensively in addressing the needs of the elderly (Beatrice, 1979; Steinberg & Carter, 1983). Case management is an approach to service delivery that attempts to ensure that clients with complex, multiple problems
and disabilities receive all the services they need in a timely and appropriate fashion. Instead of providing a specific direct service, case managers in agencies using this approach link the client to the broader maze of
direct service providers. These case managers assume ultimate responsibility for seeing that the service delivery system is responsive to all the
needs of each client. Although the range of case management functions
varies depending on contextual factors, it always entails four basic
functions: assessment, planning, linking, and monitoring.

The third way in which human service organizations can be structured is the *custom service organization* pattern. In this type of structure
the organization provides services directly to the clients rather than
brokering these services. Again, there are a variety of services for the
elderly provided through this type of structure, including respite care,
congregate meals, adult day care, homemaker services, etc. Agencies of
this type exist to respond to a specific need or needs, and these needs
should define the boundaries of the services provided. That is, the

agency must clearly identify the needs it is responding to, establish goals and objectives in relation to these needs, and structure itself specifically in relation to these needs, goals, and objectives.

In all three types of organizational structures serving the elderly administrators often find it difficult to operate within the established boundaries of the agency because they recognize and are concerned about the needs of the elderly that are not being met by their organization or any other. In some instances, it may be within the mission of the agency to assume new goals and objectives to meet these recognized needs. Often, however, the administrator must seek other means of addressing these clients' needs, such as through advocating for the development of new legislation and the creation of additional programs and services for the elderly.

Thus, in providing advocacy for the elderly the administrator of an agency serving older adults goes beyond planning and organizing within his/her own agency. That is, the administrator views the needs of the elderly within a larger context and seeks to play a role outside the organization in developing a *system* within the community that can address the total human service needs of the aging. Although many services for the elderly are available in most communities, there are significant gaps. Furthermore, services that do exist have often been developed in a categorical approach, resulting in parallel and overlapping arrangements among community mental health and retardation agencies, vocational rehabilitation services, housing, Area Agencies on Aging, hospitals, nursing homes, in-home services agencies, family service agencies, veterans services, meals-on-wheels, etc. Consequently, a major challenge facing administrators of agencies serving the elderly is to help develop a system of services in each community that will provide a continuity of care appropriate to the older persons' needs as they vary in kind, level, and intensity, and to plan and organize the services offered by his/her agency so that they constitute an appropriate part of the larger system.

Beyond developing the basic type of organization for the agency— production line, linkage, or custom service—and assuring the agency's appropriate role in a total community system of services for the elderly, organizing also includes developing appropriate departmentation within the organization. Departmentation refers to the grouping of people and their activities along some basic pattern or model so that their activities can be adequately supervised and managed. Traditional management literature has identified a variety of ways for developing departments in business organizations and Weinbach (1990) has pointed out that many of these methods can be applied to human service agencies. First, a program serving the elderly may be organized into departments based on *simple number,* or grouping those who perform the same duties under a single manager. For example, in a long-term care facility all social work activities may be organized under the direction of a single social work supervisor or manager.

A second means of organizing agencies serving the elderly is by *time.* In organizations that operate during evening and/or weekend hours, service providers may be managed in groups according to the shift during which they work. For instance, in a nursing home all nurses who are on duty during the evening shift may constitute a group that is supervised by a single supervisor on duty during that same period.

Departmentation by *territory* is a third means by which an agency serving the elderly can be structured. In this case, a large organization providing services such as adult protective services is subdivided into manageable subunits based on geographic areas. Persons working within a certain region would be supervised by the same individual.

The fourth type of departmentation, by *service,* is the antithesis of departmentation by territory in that it is based on a belief in the benefits of specialization. Persons in an organization serving older adults may offer very specialized services, such as recreational therapists within a long-term care facility, and be organized into a department and supervised based on this specialty.

Finally, an agency serving the elderly may be organized into departments based on a typology of *clients serviced* and their problems. In this approach it is recognized that a problem may require one or many related services that might efficiently be provided by the same helping professional. For example, elderly patients being seen in a counseling facility might be categorized based on their primary problem, such as loss and grief, marital difficulties, health related problems, or financial problems. Whatever the type of services needed, a staff member identified as a specialist working in the problem area would be assigned to offer treatment. This individual would work primarily, and perhaps exclusively, with clients who have this type of problem.

As Weinbach (1990) emphasized, each of these (and other) methods of departmentation has advantages and disadvantages. It is the responsibility of the manager of an agency serving the elderly to determine which type of departmentation, or combinations, best suits that particular organization.

Finally, organizing involves the development of policies, procedures, and regulations to govern the operation of the agency. Max Weber (1964), in an effort to describe the most effective and efficient organization (which he referred to as a "bureaucracy"), emphasized that there must be written rules to govern almost every activity. This, according to Weber, reduces the need for ad hoc decision-making, results in rational decisions based on the best information, and standardizes activities throughout the organization. The criticisms of "bureaucracies" notwithstanding, it is now commonly accepted in the management literature that all organizations must have formal rules of operation.

In developing policies and procedures as part of the planning process administrators of agencies serving the elderly should act on information from several sources. First, most agencies serving elderly clients are affected by numerous federal, state, and local regulations. These regulations must be followed for the agency to continue receiving funding or sanction. Second, most agencies serving the elderly are part of a larger network of similar agencies and many of these groupings have standardized procedures that apply to member agencies. Third, in going beyond externally established policies and procedures, managers of agencies serving the elderly should seek input from several sources in developing operational guidelines that will govern their respective agencies. Information should be sought from other administrators in the agency as well as staff, either informally or formally, through a system such as Management by Objectives. In recent years increasing attention has been given to the utilization of Management by Objectives as a means of utilizing staff input in managerial problem-solving and decision-making. This is a management system in which managers and subordinates engage in the process of identifying organizational goals and objectives and structuring the agency's operation around these. The process focuses attention on solving problems as a team and, as a consequence, setting mutually agreed on, measurable objectives and identifying policies and procedures that will be used to work toward the achievement of these objectives (Weiner, 1982).

It should again be emphasized that clients can also serve as an important source of information in developing policies and procedures in agencies serving the elderly. Their participation on agency boards and advisory groups can provide insights that would otherwise be missed.

Staffing

The third function of the administrator of an agency serving older persons is staffing, which has to do with the recruitment, selection, development, and appraisal of personnel to fill the roles designed into the organizational structure of the agency. The ultimate success of the agency is largely dependent on the manner in which the administrator carries out these four elements of staffing.

Responsibility for staff *recruitment* will vary among agencies serving the elderly, often depending on the size of the organization. In large agencies, such as hospitals serving the elderly, there may be a personnel department that handles the recruitment of professional and nonprofessional staff. In smaller agencies, such as an adult day care center, the administrator may carry out all recruitment activities.

As the aging population has increased the demand for human service professionals from all fields has grown dramatically. Meanwhile, in many areas such as nursing and social work, there is a shortage of trained personnel. This means that the agencies serving the elderly must actively recruit personnel, competing with other organizations that are seeking staff with the same qualifications.

There are various recruitment methods that can be used by agencies serving the elderly. Since many of these agencies are public organizations, it is necessary that they recruit personnel through the formal federal, state, or local government system of which they are a part. Such an agency may have to compete with other governmental organizations seeking similar personnel, and have limited flexibility in exercising creative recruitment methods. Insofar as agencies serving the aging have the opportunity to develop their own recruitment plans, they should explore a wide variety of methods. These include advertising in professional newsletters as well as in the general news media, sending advertisements to other human service organizations, and recruiting students who are completing their studies in the professional areas in which personnel are sought. Often, however, the best recruitment method is through informal networking, or locating people through word-of-mouth contact with others in the field.

Regardless of the method used to recruit personnel, it is essential that the qualifications of the person being sought are clearly articulated. This specificity saves time by screening out those persons who are clearly unqualified. Because of the shortage of personnel in certain professions serving the elderly, however, administrators are often fearful of defining descriptions so narrowly that they are unable to find anyone to fill the available job.

Recruitment of personnel for agencies serving the elderly should always incorporate an affirmative action plan. Given the fact that the growing aging population includes men and women and persons of all races and ethnicity, it is important to hire staff who are representative of the groups being served by the agency. Both as a social worker concerned with the problems of discrimination and social justice and as a manager seeking to comply with federal guidelines so as not to put an organization in jeopardy, the administrator of an agency serving the elderly must exercise affirmative action in recruiting and hiring staff.

Just as recruitment varies with the type of agency serving the elderly, so does the *selection* process. Regardless of the size of the agency and the type of personnel department it may have, however, the individual who will supervise the person being hired should have a voice, and preferably final authority, in the selection process. After all, it is the immediate supervisor who best knows the needs of the job and is able to assess a person's potential for meeting these qualifications.

There are usually several steps in the selection process. The first step is screening, or eliminating those candidates who clearly do not meet the stated job requirements. Second, there may be a testing process, depending on the type of position. For example, typing tests may be administered to applicants for clerk-typist positions. The third step, which is essential, is the interviewing process. Ideally, the applicant should be interviewed by the person who will be the immediate supervisor, for the reasons described above.

The purpose of the interview is to secure information, to give information, and to judge if the applicant matches the requirements of the position. Determining this "match" involves making a judgment as to whether the candidate possesses those characteristics that are especially important for persons who work with the elderly. For instance, it is important to determine if an applicant exhibits "ageist" attitudes, to assess his/her ability to relate well with the elderly, and to assess the candidate's level of interest in the job and degree of professional commitment. As Radde (1981) points out, the interview process also enables one to address expectations that an applicant may have in regard to the job. Given the short labor supply in many fields serving the aging, interviewers may be tempted to present the job and the organization in the most favorable light by promising the applicant almost anything. This seductive process may lead the applicant to accept the job based on unrealistic beliefs about the position and the organization. The interviewer needs to be honest and candid in presenting the agency, the job, and opportunities for career development. If this does not happen, and if false promises are made either explicitly or implicitly, the employee will be disappointed when his/her expectations are not met, with the result that the morale will be lowered and the employee may ultimately resign.

The next component of the staffing function entails staff *development*. The facilitation of staff growth and development is probably the most neglected area of the staffing responsibility. As new theory and information develop in the field of aging, it is important for professionals serving the elderly to be aware of this and to keep their knowledge and skills current.

There are several methods by which administrators of programs serving the elderly can facilitate staff growth and development. First, they can utilize the supervisory process to impart new knowledge. Second, administrators can provide continuing education opportunities for their staff. These opportunities can include formal education, conferences, seminars, and workshops. With the growth in the field of aging services, many professional education programs in areas such as social work, psychology, and nursing have begun to offer concentrations or specializations in gerontology. Furthermore, numerous organizations offer high quality conferences and workshops concerned with professional services to the elderly.

A third means of enhancing staff development in agencies serving the elderly is through providing opportunities for new learning on the job. This can be done through methods such as job rotation or assigning personnel to carry out special tasks that will broaden their knowledge and skills. Also, monitoring arrangements can be extremely valuable, especially for new employees in programs serving the elderly.

Although various methods such as those described above can be used to facilitate staff growth, it is important that the agency serving the elderly create a systematic program for staff development (Miringoff, 1980). Not only will an effective staff development program improve the quality of services provided to the elderly population being served, but it will also enhance staff morale and result in less job turnover.

The final component of the staffing function is that of *appraisal*, or evaluation of personnel. Although evaluation is often seen in a negative, judgmental sense, several writers (Oberg, 1972; Plunkett, 1975) have pointed out that this is a positive process when conducted properly. Evaluations should be an ongoing part of the supervisory process whereby the employee is provided regular feedback regarding his/her performance. Hence, the traditional annual evaluation should include no surprises for the employee. The feedback provided through the supervisory process and at the time of annual evaluation should be aimed at helping the employee become more effective and efficient on the job. Attention should be focused on the requirements of the job and how these are being met through the employee's work. The employee's strengths in carrying out the job should be noted and areas of weakness dealt with in a manner that is supportive and concerned with helping the employee improve performance.

There are many types of employee evaluations. Perhaps the most common type used in agencies serving the elderly are "trait" evaluations. These entail rating scales that require the supervisor to score the individual on the basis of specific criteria such as "job knowledge," "ability to plan and organize work," "ability to express self in writing," and "interest in work." There are many problems with such evaluations, as pointed out by Koontz et al. (1986). For example, such evaluations often assess personal traits rather than work-oriented characteristics. Also, trait evaluations are not objective, and managers do not like to use subjective judgment on a matter so important. Finally, the basic assumption of trail appraisals is open to question. That is, the connection between the employee's performance and that person's apparent traits is dubious; what the supervisor thinks of an employee is substituted for what that person actually does.

The manager of an agency serving the elderly should go beyond trait evaluations, even when these are required by the larger organizational structure of which the agency is a part. In the spirit of assisting employees to improve their performance, the manager should consider using written narrative evaluations that articulate in detail how effectively the employee is meeting job requirements and can improve performance. Also, the manager should consider implementing a system of "evaluation by verifiable objectives." In this system employees are appraised in terms of the establishment and accomplishment of specific, meaningful, actionable objectives. For example, a social worker in a program providing foster care services for the elderly may be responsible for accomplishing the following objective (among others): "By June 30, 1991 develop 25 approved new foster care placements within Richland County." The social worker's annual evaluation would include an examination of whether 25 placements were developed, and an analysis of the strengths and weaknesses of the worker's professional activities in relation to accomplishing this objective. Ideally this type of appraisal should be part of a larger management system, such as Management by Objectives, in which employees participate in the identification, with their administrator, of objectives they need to achieve in their work. Each employee is measured in terms of what he/she has done, compared to what was agreed on as a reasonable target.

This process enhances objectivity in evaluation and promotes a positive, facilitative relationship between administrators and staff (Koontz et al., 1986).

Directing and Leading

The fourth function of administrators of agencies serving the elderly is that of directing and leading the agency employees. Directing and leading are the interpersonal aspects of managing by which employees are helped to understand and contribute effectively and efficiently to the attainment of the organization's objectives. This function has to do with establishing the proper relationship with employees, communicating effectively with them, supervising them appropriately, motivating them, and helping them work toward the achievement of the agency's objectives. Given the nature of the field of social work, administrators with graduate training in this discipline generally have a good grasp of this function.

The administrator of an agency serving the older adults will likely relate to employees on the basis of his/her assumptions about human nature and behavior. McGregor (1960) identified two opposite orientations of administrators based on their assumptions about human beings. Theory X managers assume that people have an inherent dislike for work; they must be coerced, controlled, directed, and threatened to get them to pursue organizational goals; and the average person prefers to be directed, wishes to avoid responsibility, has little ambition, and wants security above all.

For example, a nursing home administrator with a Theory X orientation would tend to mistrust subordinates. Such a manager would tend to use tangible reward and punishment (or the threat of it) to get nurses, social workers, and others to do what is needed. This manager would also adopt a "we/they" attitude and employ coercion from time to time. This Theory X administrator would institute an oppressive, controlling collection of rules and procedures for the operation of the nursing home, all of them designed to enforce compliance. There would be an emphasis on maintaining tight schedules, documentation of one's work, and close adherence to agency regulations. Insofar as such a manager's orientation would affect others working in the organization, they would respond, in turn, by having similar attitudes toward the residents and treating them with little dignity and respect.

Given the mission of organizations serving the elderly, one would hope that the administrator of such agencies would not manifest a Theory X approach to management, but a Theory Y approach instead. According to McGregor (1960), an administrator with a Theory Y orientation assumes that physical and mental work is as natural as play or rest, people are self-directed and will strive to achieve objectives to which they are committed; people not only accept but seek responsibility, and most people have high degrees of imagination, ingenuity, and creativity they will use to solve organizational problems if given the opportunity. The administrator with this orientation will seek to maximize human growth and development and will do so by creating an organizational environment in which individuals realize that they can achieve their goals by directing their efforts toward the achievement of the organizational goals.

A nursing home administrator with a Theory Y orientation, for example, would not make policy decisions arbitrarily and use power to enforce these; rather, the Theory Y administrator would involve nursing home staff in decision-making as much as possible, encourage staff to establish their own objectives, and allow them to assist in evaluating their own effectiveness. This administrator would act in ways that communicate trust and belief in the good intentions of the staff to work toward the attainment of the nursing home's goals. This administrator would create an environment in which the focus would be on the residents, rather than on bureaucratic policies and regulations. It is likely that the staff would reflect this Theory Y orientation, and would treat the residents with similar warmth, respect, and trust.

There has been substantial research in social work and other disciplines to support the relationship between the administrator's supervisory style and the response on the part of the persons supervised. It has been well documented that an autocratic style of leadership results in poor morale and, generally, inefficient work among employees. Furthermore, laissez-faire type leadership produces frustration among employees, poor commitment to organizational goals, and poor quality work. The democratic style of leadership, on the other hand, typically results in more effective and efficient work performance and greater job satisfaction among employees (Austin, 1981; Odiorne, 1970).

Although these findings generally apply to most management situations, the administrator of an agency serving the elderly should realize that different circumstances call for different types of leadership. For instance, the administrator of a program providing home health services to the elderly may find it necessary to shift from the usual democratic style of leadership to a more autocratic style of supervision to implement new federally required practices in an abbreviated period of time. Or the same administrator may find it necessary to be autocratic with certain staff who simply do not perform well under any other supervisory approach. Other home health staff, on the other hand, may function better under a laissez-faire type of leadership. In other words, while the democratic-participative style of management is generally the most effective and efficient, the administrator of an agency serving the elderly should maintain flexibility, gearing his/her style to the specific situation and the individuals involved.

The administrator of a program serving older adults should also pay attention to those factors that produce the greatest motivation among staff. Perhaps the best known research on this topic is that of Herzberg (1968). Herzberg made a distinction between two types of factors related to motivation. The first type of factors, called "maintenance" or "hygiene" factors, includes such things as agency policy and administration, supervision, working conditions, interpersonal relations, salary, status, and job security. Herzberg found that the presence of these factors will not motivate people in an organization; yet they must be present or dissatisfaction will arise. The second group of factors, called "motivators," relate to job content and include such things as achievement, recognition, challenging work, advancement, and growth on the job. The presence of these factors will yield feelings of satisfaction and they are, therefore, true motivators.

Since many agencies serving the elderly are public funded organizations, administrators of these agencies may have relatively little control over some of the "maintenance" factors. That is, policies, salaries, fringe benefits, working conditions, and so on may be established at higher levels of authority. Nonetheless, through exercising an appropriate leadership style, the administrator of an agency for the elderly can ensure the presence of true "motivators" in the organization. For example, the administrator of a program providing housing assistance to the elderly can formally recognize the accomplishments and achievements of agency staff. Also, this administrator might be able to rotate agency personnel to give them the opportunity to learn new tasks and experience growth on the job. Or, this administrator can develop a plan to move staff into areas of increased responsibility based on their demonstrated competence in previous roles, thus manifesting recognition for their previous accomplishments and presenting them with new, challenging opportunities.

It is important to recognize, however, that not all people are motivated by the same things. Social work administrators, by virtue of their professional training, should be attuned to the individual differences among employees. In seeking to motivate staff, agency administrators should consider these differences and endeavor to structure the job situation to maximize the motivation and job satisfaction of each employee.

McClelland (1953, 1955, 1961) identified three distinct motives that affect people's work-related behavior: the need for achievement, the need for power, and the need for affiliation. The successful administrator should be able to determine which type of need tends to motivate each employee and then structure the work situation to capitalize on this motivation.

The goal of the *achievement-motivated* person is to experience success in a situation that requires superb or improved performance. This individual is concerned with excellence and wanting to do his/her personal best. Such a person likes to take personal responsibility for finding solutions to problems and enjoys achieving unique accomplishments. He/she is restless and innovative, takes pleasure in striving, and desires concrete feedback on a regular basis.

The goal of the *power-motivated* person, on the other hand, is to have an impact or influence on others. This individual is greatly concerned about reputation or position, often gives advice, and wants his/her ideas to predominate. This individual has intense feelings about status and prestige and has a strong need to influence others and change their behaviors. Such people are often fluent, sometimes argumentative, and are seen by others as being forceful, outspoken, and even hard-headed. This power motivation can be either personalized, wherein the individual is primarily concerned with personal dominance over others, or socialized, wherein the person exercises power for the benefit of others to attain group goals.

Finally, there is the *affiliation-motivated* person whose goal is being with others and enjoying mutual friendship. This individual is primarily concerned with being liked and accepted and has a great need for warm, friendly relationships and interaction. This type of person is well attuned to personal feelings and the feelings of others and often enjoys consoling or helping other people.

By recognizing the predominant motivational pattern in individual employees, the administrator of an agency serving the aging can place them in positions or structure their jobs so as to respond to their individual needs. For example, the director of a multipurpose senior center might recruit paid and volunteer staff who tend to be affiliation-motivated to work in congregate meals programs. At the same time, this director might assign a (socialized) power-motivated employee to a position of responsibility for public relations of the center. Again, the director may select an employee who tends to be achievement-motivated to develop and implement a new program such as transportation service for seniors who are served by the center. In each of these instances, the administrator has responded to the motivational needs of employees so that they will experience job satisfaction and the agency will benefit directly from their job performance.

This section on directing and leading has emphasized that the administrator of an agency serving the elderly should have a keen awareness of his/her own personality and leadership style as well as the personality and "followership" style of the staff. The administrator must endeavor to create a "mesh" between this leadership and followership. This mesh is brought about through the relationship between the administrator and employee. That is, the administrator who is self-aware, agency-aware, self-secure, and job-secure should have no problem in communicating openly and honestly with employees. Such open communication and genuine relationships form the basis for successful interaction between the administrator and employee. Through such relationships and consequent administrator–staff interaction, the performance of each individual and the agency itself is maximized.

Controlling

The final function of administrators of agencies serving the elderly is that of controlling. Although the term "controlling" may have negative connotations for social workers, given their commitment to the value of client self-determination, its use in management literature is benign. Controlling is the measurement and correction of organizational and individual activities in order to make sure that the agency's objectives and the plans devised to obtain them are being accomplished. For this function to be performed, it is necessary that the agency have clearly stated objectives, measurable outcomes, an adaptable organizational structure, and a data system that can assess the effectiveness of the various program components. Unfortunately, some agencies serving the elderly have lacked these four requisite components so that it has been impossible to know if the agency is "on target" in achieving its mission.

In recent years, however, several events have caused administrators of agencies serving the elderly to give more serious attention to the function of control. First, the dramatic growth of the field of services for the elderly has caused the general public and, in particular, those persons responsible for allocation of resources to programs, to scrutinize how these funds are being spent. Given the limited money available for human services, agencies serving the elderly have found it necessary to demonstrate accountability in order to justify their demands for resources. Taxpayers, faced with higher taxes at a time when the value of the dollar is decreasing, are demanding to know if social programs for which their tax dollars are being spent, including programs for the elderly, are worthwhile.

The elderly being served are also pressing for accountable programs. The past decade has constituted an era of consumerism, a time when clients have begun to demand that services they receive are of acceptable quality. The elderly, in particular, have become an increasingly vocal and powerful lobbying group, adamant in their requests for social programs that are effective and efficient in meeting their demands.

Finally, personnel in agencies serving the elderly, partly in response to the influence of the environment and client demands, have developed a greater commitment to agency accountability. They have become increasingly aware of the need for programs that are responsive to the needs of the elderly and that are of demonstrable quality. The personnel in these agencies, including administrators, have begun to shift their focus to ends rather than means, or to the "what" instead of the "how."

These external and internal developments have led administrators of agencies serving older adults to seek ways to become more accountable and to demonstrate through empirical means that the services offered by the agency are optimally effective and efficient. Carrying out this purpose is the "control" function of management.

For the administrator of an agency serving the aging to carry out the control function, it is necessary that several criteria be met. First, it is necessary that the agency's objectives be clearly articulated in terms that are clear, specific, and measurable.

Designing such objectives for control purposes occurs during the planning process, as discussed earlier in this chapter. Often the objectives of agencies serving the aging are stated in such vague and general terms that it is impossible to demonstrate with certainty whether they are being attained. Examples of nebulous objectives are "to strengthen the support system of the client," "to enhance the client's social functioning," or "to improve the client's mental health." It is impossible for the administrator of an agency to control its operation to ensure success when objectives are so poorly stated that he/she cannot determine if they have been achieved. Objectives should be *clear* so that the administrator who is monitoring program effectiveness will know exactly what results are expected, *specific* so that they can be translated into operational definitions and made visible, and *measurable* so that data collection and analysis methods can be applied (Raymond, 1981).

The second necessary criterion is the establishment of outcome measures. These measures must reflect as closely as possible the changes the agency is concerned with producing, as articulated in the stated written objectives. In some agencies, such as health care organizations, outcome measures can focus on changes in the elderly clients being served. In other agencies, such as transportation services, the measures may address the extent to which services are implemented. In some organizations, such as advocacy programs, the measures may be concerned with the development and implementation of new services or programs.

Often a program's success cannot be adequately assessed by analyzing a single outcome measure. It is then useful to employ multiple measures. For example, a health care program concerned with improving the health of a group of elderly outpatients might use several outcome measures, such as rates of illnesses, levels of functioning of specific organs, and self-reports from patients regarding how they feel. Each of these is a partial measure of a larger concept, but no single measure would be an adequate indicator of the program's success. By combining these criteria, the administrator can achieve a more complete and accurate picture of the program's outcome (Raymond, 1981).

The third criterion that must be met for the administrator of an agency serving the aging to carry out the control function is that he/she must be able to develop an organizational structure that has the greatest potential for achieving the stated objectives of the organization. That is, the administrator should be able to create the necessary work units, development appropriate policies and procedures, and design and implement programs aimed at achievement of the agency's objectives. As stated earlier in this chapter, this effort comprises the "organizing" function of the administrator. Unfortunately, in organizations providing services to the elderly factors such as staff size, case load size, and legal mandates occasionally militate against the creation of an organization that can fulfill the agency's objectives in an optimum manner. Nonetheless, operating within these constraints, the administrator must seek to achieve maximum agency effectiveness and efficiency through designing what appears to be the "best" program structure and continually modifying it as needed based on feedback as to achievement of objectives.

The fourth criterion is an adequate information system. The administrator of an agency serving older adults must ensure that the agency's information system can provide accurate, detailed data that can be rapidly procured and is specifically related to decision-making requirements, planning requirements, and measurement of agency objectives. Recent developments in technology have made it possible for agencies serving the elderly to develop sophisticated computerized information systems capable of providing a variety of information that can be used to monitor performance. This information can include measures of total program performance, program component performance, and performance of individual staff members. In each instance, effectiveness is measured in terms of the attainment of state objectives, and efficiency is measured in terms of the cost of attaining these objectives.

When the "control" function of management relates to the performance of the individual employee, this becomes part of the "staffing" function discussed earlier. At this level the administrator may employ a variety of techniques to influence employee behavior. Weinbach (1990) refers to the methods that can be used to influence employees as the "control menu." These methods include plans, formal guides for action, training, performance review, advice and information, directives, sanctions, loyalties, idealism, professional values, and example. Each of these methods can be used to influence the behavior of employees to make them more effective in meeting established standards. It should be noted that some of these methods involve the "directing and leading" function of managers.

It can thus be seen that the "control" function of managers is related to the other management functions discussed earlier—planning, organizing, staffing, and leading and directing. In fact, these other management functions contain elements of control. These functions enable the manager to shape, constrain, and direct the activities of the staff in such a way that they will contribute to the attainment of the group and organizational objectives.

Conclusion

The role of the administrator of an agency serving the elderly is multifaceted and is becoming increasingly complex as a result of several factors. As federal, state, and local policies and regulations change, agencies serving older citizens must be restructured accordingly. The goals and objectives of agencies must shift in response to the needs of the times, and the methods of agency operation must be altered in order to address the new directions taken by the organization. Changes in the funding of programs serving the elderly also require organizational restructuring. Systems must be developed to implement newly funded programs and existing systems must be modified in response to reduced funding for various services.

The role of the administrator of an agency serving the elderly is also made more complex by the changes in the population being served. As the elderly citizens in our society increase in number most programs serving the elderly must expand in size to accommodate new clientele. Furthermore, as the types of needs of the elderly population continue to change, a broader variety of services must be provided in response. These trends are likely to continue as the increasing numbers of older citizens become more vocal and skillful in their advocacy efforts. Health and human services for this group will continue to expand in size and scope as policy makers and agencies respond to the requests of the elderly.

Because of the growing complexity of programs serving older persons, it is now more important than ever that the managers of these agencies have a sound knowledge base in administration. An administrator who lacks this theoretical foundation and who tries to learn the job through trial-and-error will soon be overwhelmed and unable to manage the organization successfully. Furthermore, it is also important that administrators of programs serving the elderly have a philosophical orientation that is humanitarian in nature and that places paramount importance on the good of the client rather than the good of the organization. Such an orientation enables the manager to respond to the increasing environmental complexity with less equivocation in establishing new goals and objectives and planning appropriate programs of service. It is for this reason that a manager with an educational background in macro social work is well-qualified to administer programs serving the elderly.

Although administrators need such a theoretical grounding, it has been stressed in this chapter that there is no unique body of knowledge specific to the management of agencies serving the elderly. It is possible, however, to apply principles of management of organizations in general to the administration of programs serving the elderly. In this chapter it has been suggested that an appropriate framework for understanding and applying these principles of management is the "operational" approach, which integrates and synthesizes principles of management in terms of the major functions that all managers perform: planning, organizing, staffing, directing and leading, and controlling. This chapter has also stressed the utilization of a contingency perspective, which examines the application of administration principles in the context of the environment, the organization, and the particular parties involved rather than prescribing "the best" ways of managing organizations. Within this operational framework and contingency perspective, principles of management have been presented in this chapter as they apply specifically to organizations serving the elderly.

References

Abels, P., & Murphy, M. J. (1981). *Administration in the human services: A normative systems approach.* Englewood Cliffs, NJ: Prentice-Hall.

Austin, M. J. (1981). *Supervisory management for the human services.* Englewood Cliffs, NJ: Prentice-Hall.

Beatrice, D. F. (1979). *Case management: A policy option for long-term care.* Washington, DC: Health Financing Administration, Department of Health, Education and Welfare.

Bresnick, D. A. (1983). *Managing human services in hard time.* New York: Human Services Press.

Carlisle, H. M. (1973). *Situational management: A contingency approach to leadership.* New York: American Management Association.

Eckles, R. W., Carmichael, R. L., & Sarchet, B. R. (1974). *Essentials of management for first line supervision.* New York: John Wiley.

Evashwick, C., Ney, J., & Siemon, J. (1985). *Case management: Issues for hospitals.* Chicago: Hospital Research and Educational Trust (American Hospital Association).

Harbert, A. S., & Ginsberg, L. H. (1990). *Human services for older adults: Concepts and skills.* Columbia, SC: University of South Carolina Press.

Herzberg, F. (1968). One more time: How do you motivate employees? *Harvard Business Review, 46,* 53–62.

Koff, T. H. (1988). *New approaches to health care for an aging population.* San Francisco: Jossey-Bass.

Koontz, H., O'Donnell, C., & Weihrich, H. (1986). *Essentials of management,* 4th ed. New York: McGraw-Hill.

McClelland, D. C. (1953). *The achievement motive*. New York: Appleton-Century-Crofts.

McClelland, D. C. (1955). *Studies in motivation*. New York: Appleton-Century-Crofts.

McClelland, D. C. (1961). *The achieving society*. Princeton, NJ: Van Nostrand Reinhold.

McGregor, D. (1960). *The human side of enterprise*. New York: McGraw-Hill.

McQuillan, F. L. (1974). *Fundamentals of nursing home administration*, 2nd ed. Philadelphia: W. B. Saunders.

Meenaghan, T. M., Washington, R. O., & Ryan, R. M. (1982). *Macro practice in the human services*. New York: Free Press.

Miller, D. B. (1969). *Extended care facility: A guide to organization and operation*. New York: McGraw-Hill.

Miringoff, M. L. (1980). *Management in human service organizations*. New York: Macmillan.

O'Berg, W. (1972, January-February) Making performance appraisal relevant. *Harvard Business Review, 50*, 61–67.

Odiorne, G. S. (1970). *Training by objectives*. London: Macmillan.

Plunkett, W. R. (1975). *Supervision: The direction of people at work*. Dubuque, IA: William C. Brown.

Radde, P. O. (1981). *Supervising: A guide for all levels*. San Diego: University Associates.

Raymond, F. B. (1981). Program evaluation. In R. M. Grinnell, Jr. (Ed.), *Social work research and evaluation* (pp. 419–428). Itasca, IL: F. E. Peacock.

Rogers, W. W. (1980). *General administration in the nursing home*, 3rd ed. New York: Van Nostrand Reinhold.

Steinberg, R. M., & Carter, G. W. (1983). *Case management and the elderly*. Lexington, MA: Lexington Books.

Taylor, F. (1947). *Scientific management*. New York: Harper & Brothers.

Weber, M. (1964). *The theory of social and economic organization* (A. M. Henderson & Talcott Parsons, Trans.). New York: The Free Press of Glencoe. (Original work unfinished at time of Weber's death in 1920.)

Weinbach, R. W. (1990). *The social worker as manager: Theory and practice*. New York: Longman.

Weiner, M. E. (1982). *Human services management: Analysis and applications*. Homewood, IL: Dorsey Press.

Wetle, T. T., (1985). Ethical aspects of decision making for and with the elderly. In M. B. Kapp, H. E. Pies, & A. E. Doudera (Eds.), *Legal and ethical aspects of health care for the elderly* (pp. 258–267). Ann Arbor, MI: Health Administration Press.

11

Evaluating Programs for Older People

NANCY LOHMANN

Why Evaluate Programs?

This chapter deals with the evaluation of programs for older people. Before reviewing the processes and techniques of program evaluation, it may be helpful to examine a very basic question about evaluation: Why evaluate programs for the aged or, for that matter, for any other segment of society? Human service workers are interested in evaluating programs largely because they wish to know which interventions are effective and with what persons or groups they are effective. Such knowledge enables human service workers and others to use the most effective intervention for a given problem, and to use that intervention with the group or population with which it is most likely to achieve maximum effectiveness. The results of program evaluation are often one of the factors used to determine which intervention(s) will be used in human service practice.

Those funding human service interventions are interested in evaluation as a means of assuring that social programs and agencies are accountable. Funding organizations want to assure that their funds are being put to good use. Program evaluation, which can help assess the effectiveness and impact of programs, is one means of establishing accountability.

Human service workers and other social scientists are also interested in the contributions program evaluation can make to knowledge building. The results of program evaluation contribute to the pool of knowledge about program effectiveness and the groups at whom programs are directed. They help those serving the aging and aged, for example, to make distinctions among subgroups of the elderly and better understand the meaning of such distinctions.

The Growth of Interest in Evaluation

The last few decades have seen an increased emphasis on program evaluation. Interest in program evaluation is not new, however. Rossi and Freeman (1985) indicate that social experiments and their evaluation have been identified as far back as the 1700s. Contemporary interest in program evaluation has its origins largely in efforts to evaluate social programs in the 1930s, the time of New Deal programs, many of which represented large scale social experiments. Some social work studies even predated this time period. Zimbalist (1977) describes Sophie van Senden Theis' report on *How Foster Children Turn Out* in 1924 as an example of some early social work research that embodied some of the characteristics of evaluative research.

An even greater interest in evaluation occurred in the 1940s and 1950s, which Rossi and Freeman (1985) describe as the "boom period" in evaluation research, with programs on delinquency prevention, public housing, and community organization among the programs evaluated. Zimbalist (1977) identifies the Cambridge-Somerville Youth Study, which was an experiment in the prevention of juvenile delinquency, as one of the more important studies of this period for social workers.

With the growth of social programs during the time of President Lyndon Johnson's "Great Society," there was an accompanying growth of interest in program evaluation during the 1960s and 1970s. Many federal grants and other funding sources required program evaluation as a condition of award, several significant books on the topic were written (for example, Suchman, 1967; Caro, 1971; Weiss, 1972), and firms specializing in program evaluation were created. This general emphasis on program evaluation was accompanied by an emphasis on preparing social workers to engage in evaluation.

The preparation of social workers who could conduct evaluative research was initially focused on doctoral and master's level social workers and was characterized by an increase emphasis on research courses in social work curricula. By the 1980s, however, there was increasing recognition that all social workers, including baccalaureate level persons, needed to be prepared to evaluate social programs and their own practice. This belief was expressed in the "Curriculum Policy for the Master's Degree and Baccalaureate Degree Programs in Social Work Education" adopted by the Council on Social Work Education (1984) for accredited programs. That statement indicated that both BSW and MSW students should be exposed to content on the "use of research and of program evaluation" and should be prepared to "evaluate their own practice systematically" (p. 127).

Much of the following discussion uses program evaluation as the context for describing the elements of evaluation. Within the last decade, there has been increased emphasis on the evaluation of direct clinical practice, which is not always thought of as a "program." Although from the agency's perspective, the services all its clinicians are delivering represent a program, the individual practitioners probably do not think of their efforts with a given client as a "program." As a result, clinicians may think a discussion of program evaluation not relevant to their activities.

Such discussion is relevant, since, for the purposes of designing research, the activities of individual clinical practitioners could be thought of as a "program." The same principles of framing the research question, designing the research, collecting and analyzing data, etc., apply to the evaluation of clinical interventions with an individual and to the evaluation of a social program. The growth of a body of literature on single-subject design in clinical practice has served to emphasize the differences between the interventions of a single clinical practitioner and the large program in which those interventions take place, rather than the similarities. Although much of the discussion that follows focuses on programs, it is applicable to the practice evaluation that might be undertaken by a clinical practitioner.

What Is Program Evaluation?

Carol Weiss (1972), in a text that is regarded as one of the classics in evaluative research, defines the purpose of evaluation research as that of measuring "the effects of a program against the goals it set out to accomplish as a means of contributing to subsequent decision making about the program and improving future programming" (p. 4). As this definition indicated, program evaluation has several components and requirements.

1. It requires the measurement of the effects of a program, which means the evaluator must both know what effects are anticipated and have a means of measuring them.
2. It requires that the effects be measured in comparison with the goals that were set in advance for the program.
3. It requires that the results of the evaluation have an impact on decision making, which means that those making decisions about the program must be informed of the results.
4. It requires that the results contribute to future programming, which means that the outcomes must be disseminated to those involved in this program as well as more broadly so they can impact on program design and development.

The methods and techniques of program evaluation come largely from experimental research, with attention paid to the research design and controls necessary for such research. However, since program evaluation occurs in applied settings, where programs and their services are being delivered to clients, rather than in the more traditional laboratory setting of an experiment, adaptations of the experimental model are required. Even with those adaptations, evaluation research is still attempting to find out what interventions work and with whom. Sometimes one may take his/her interest even further, and attempt to determine why the intervention works. Finding the answers to research questions, however, starts with the traditional research process, aspects of which are described below.

Framing the Research Question

The first step in the process of evaluating a program or intervention is to identify the research question(s) that the researcher wishes to answer. The research question expresses hypotheses about the elements of the program that have an impact. The research question will deal with the goals of the program, since it is those goals that describe the impact that human service intervention is expected to have. The following are examples of the questions that might be asked:

1. Does the homemaker program my agency provides meet the needs defined by our clients? Does it deliver a cost-effective service? Does it delay institutionalization among its older clients?
2. Does my agency's adult day care program, which includes older persons and children, reduce the stress experienced by their family members? Does it produce increased interaction and alertness on the part of the older persons participating? Is it more cost effective than in-home care would be? Does it reduce the expected rate of institutionalization?
3. Does my agency's education and training program for older workers result in job placements? Does it result in increased life satisfaction among the older participants? Does it result in satisfaction among employers with the knowledge and skills of the older workers?
4. Does my agency's counseling services reduce the depression experienced by older persons after the loss of a spouse? Are the number of sessions with a client related to the effectiveness of the service? Is the level of education of the therapist related to the effectiveness of the service?

It is likely that not all of these questions would be asked in the evaluation of any specific program. The questions illustrate the range of goals a program may have, and thus the range of research questions we might want to ask.

In framing the research question, some attention needs to be paid to whether the research results are intended to be formative or summative. "Formative research" is research that is intended to be completed while the program is on-going, and to impact immediately on program design and delivery. The results of formative research on homemaker's services, for example, might produce relatively immediate changes in the way the program is designed and delivered to ensure that the program better meets the needs identified by clients. Additional services might be offered, or the way in which the services are offered might be changed.

"Summative research" is research that is intended to be completed as the program ends, and that is expected to impact on future programs rather than the program being studied. The older worker education and training program, for example, might be intended to run for only a year and the summative results of its evaluation would not influence its activities but might affect the design of programs like it elsewhere.

Another factor that needs to be considered when framing the research question(s) is whose question or questions are to be answered. Are the questions those that are asked by the agency executive, who want to evaluate a program to improve its effectiveness? Are the questions ones that need to be asked to meet a contractual obligation with a funding agency? Are the questions being asked by a board of directors as a means of deciding where to direct scarce agency resources? The person or group asking the research questions and the use they plan to make of the answers may also have an impact on the design of the evaluation.

The source of the questions may indicate how detailed or broad ranging the evaluation should be, the time frame in which answers are needed, and the form in which answers to the research questions will be most useful. A supervisor or worker may want immediate feedback on highly specific issues in a matter of days on a crucial evaluative question. A funding source may have very general questions about program effectiveness, while an agency executive may want answers to detailed questions to help him/her make programmatic decisions. The board of directors may need answers within 3 months for their review, which could limit the kinds of questions that could be asked, while the funding source may want answers in 2 years. The information about program impact may be intended for a sophisticated research consumer, and so can be very detailed and specific, or may be intended for a less sophisticated consumer who will not understand or care about any complex statistical analyses.

Identifying the Sample

The sample for the program evaluation consists of those persons who will be studied in conducting the evaluation. Given the limitations present in many practice settings, the sample is often predetermined. The sample will often be all those persons participating or scheduled to participate in a given program. The program participants probably will not have been randomly selected from all older people in a given geographic area. They will likely have been admitted to the program after having been through an intake procedure that evaluated their eligibility for the program.

In other forms of research, such as research sampling public opinions, great attention must be paid to the representativeness of the sample studied. Methods of random selection are often used to ensure representativeness. Although such methods are equally appropriate for evaluative research, their application is often not possible. Thus, the range of sampling alternatives present in other research forms is less likely to be available in program evaluation.

The samples used in evaluation are most like a "purposive" sample. The persons in the sample were chosen because they had certain characteristics. The characteristics are often more related to eligibility for the social intervention than the purposes of the research. Such characteristics may include an income that is below a certain level, the presence of a social, emotional, or physical condition requiring intervention, or other factors that determine eligibility for the program. Such samples are nonrandom, and thus generalizations from those studied in the evaluation to a larger population of older people should be made with care.

Designing the Evaluation

Once there is clarity about the research questions that are to be asked, the human service worker can focus on how to design research that will answer those questions. The design must be one that will permit the development of answers to the questions that are of interest. If, for example, the research questions deal with the cost effectiveness of one service as compared to others, the evaluation design must be one that will collect information on the cost and effectiveness of all of the services. The design must also be one that will control for extraneous factors that may influence the intervention's impact. Practitioners need to use the most rigorous design possible, given the limitations posed by the practice setting. Research design represents an effort to control threats to validity or those things other than the intervention that might explain the changes being observed.

Program evaluation design is still heavily influenced by a book by Donald T. Campbell and Julian C. Stanley, *Experimental and Quasi-Experimental Designs for Research* (1963). In that book, the authors categorize research design into three categories: preexperimental design, quasi-experimental designs, and true experimental designs. Differences among designs in the three categories deal with the amount of control one is able to exert over factors other than the intervention that might influence the outcome. The intervention, in the designs, is designated as "X." The factors other than the intervention that might explain the results are designated as threats to the internal validity of the design. Other factors that might limit the generalizability or the ability to apply the results of the program evaluation in other settings are designated as threats to the external validity of the design.

True experimental designs are characterized by random assignment of subjects or clients to a group(s) being exposed to the intervention and a group(s) that is not exposed to the intervention. [Random assignment to an experimental or control group differs from random selection of a sample. Random selection helps control for the extent to which those in the experiment (the sample) are like the larger universe from which they are drawn. As a result, random selection helps control for some of the threats to the external validity or generalizability of the study.] Such experimental designs are possible in laboratory settings. However, in the applied settings in which programs operate and services are delivered, such experimental designs often cannot be used.

The pre- and quasiexperimental designs that often can be used in practice settings do not provide the same level of control over internal and external threats to validity as do true experimental designs. Thus, in practice settings where program evaluations are to be carried out, the researcher sometimes has difficulty establishing that it is the program's intervention that had an impact on the clients rather than some other factor such as the previous experiences of clients or the nature of the clients selected. In spite of these limitations, the information gained from program evaluation is useful.

There is insufficient room here to discuss in detail all of the possible research designs or the meaning of all of the threats to internal and external validity. A complete discussion may be found in Campbell and Stanley (1963), and most standard research texts discuss some aspects of the designs. This discussion will be limited to the designs most often used when evaluating programs for the aged.

One-Shot Case Study

One of the more common designs is the one-shot case study. In this design, the impact of the intervention is observed or measured after an intervention has been introduced. In fact, many of the published evaluations of program effectiveness are of the case study type. This design is often graphically displayed as below, with an "x" representing the intervention and "o" representing the observation or measurement of the impact of the intervention.

X O

An example of a one-shot case study would be an evaluation of an agency's day care program, which is already in place with a full complement of older clients who have been in the program for some time. The experiment or "x" would be the day care program, since it is the program that is the intervention. The research question might be whether the day care program had an effect on the amount of interaction and level of alertness of the older clients. Accordingly, measurement or observation would be of the amount of interaction among older clients and the alertness of older clients.

The lack of control provided by this design makes it difficult for the researcher to be certain that observations are the result of the intervention. Although older client's interactions and alertness can be measured, the case study design does not provide much control over other variables (or the threats to internal validity) that might explain what the researcher observes. It may be, for example, that the clients have always had high levels of interaction and alertness, and that the day care program had no impact on either of those variables. In spite of these limits, the design is often used in human service program evaluation.

One-Group Pretest–Posttest Design

A design that is slightly more sophisticated than the one-shot case study is the one-group pretest–posttest. This design, with "x" representing the intervention and "o" the observations, would be graphically displayed as

O X O

In this design, the evaluator would have an observation both before and after clients were introduced to the intervention. The observation before the experiment is the pretest, and the observation after the intervention has been introduced is the posttest.

Using the day care example, the evaluator might measure the amount of interaction and level of alertness of an older client before he/she started in the day care program and then measure interaction and alertness after 2 months in the program. If the program achieved its goal, a higher level of interaction and alertness would be expected after clients had been in the program for 2 months. Although this design would help eliminate the issue posed by the one-shot case study—that these older clients have always had high levels of interaction and alertness—other threats to validity remain. It may be, for example, that the posttest observation occurred immediately before lunch was served, and the interaction and alertness were due more to hunger and the anticipation of lunch than the general services provided by the day care program.

It would often be very easy to use this design to evaluate the effects of a program or intervention. Since clients typically go through some kind of intake or assessment procedure before being admitted to a program, there is an opportunity to conduct a pretest. Some planning for evaluation is required to ensure that the measuring instruments to be used have been identified and are ready for use during intake. The use of pretests as part of an intake interview or similarly early in the assessment process can be a simple yet powerful tool in the evaluation of clinical practice.

Static-Group Comparison

The static-group comparison design is a preexperimental design that involves the comparison of two groups of persons. One group is exposed to the intervention and the other group is not. Both groups are given posttests only. The design is graphically displayed as the following:

$$X \quad O$$
$$O$$

With this design, it is assumed that the difference between the two groups is due to the intervention. With the day care example, the evaluator might measure the amount of interaction and alertness of older people enrolled in the program and older people not in the program. If those enrolled are found to be more alert and interactive, one would argue the program produced that difference.

Of course, one cannot be certain the program produced all of the difference because there are factors other than the intervention that may account for some of the differences. It may be, for example, that those who chose to enroll in the day care program were more interactive even before their enrollment, and thus the differences between the two groups would have been present even without the program.

Time Series

The quasiexperimental design called "time series" is an expansion of the one-group pretest–posttest that controls for some additional threats to validity. The time series design is graphically displayed in the following manner:

O   O   O   O   X   O   O   O   O

As with the above preexperimental designs, the time series design involves only one group—the group exposed to the intervention. Unlike the one-group pretest–posttest design, however, that group is observed or measured several times before begin exposed to the intervention or program, and several times after exposure.

With the day care illustration, the evaluator might measure the interactions of the older persons who wished to enroll in the day care program several times before they started the program. Multiple measurements would help control for the effects that might be the result of tiredness or medication, for example, and that might be present in only one pretest observation. The same measures after the older persons were enrolled in the program would also provide greater control over the threats to internal validity.

Multiple measures before admission to a program or service are often more difficult to accomplish than the single observation found in the one-group pretest–posttest design. However, as is discussed below, a single pretest in combination with multiple posttests can often yield useful information.

Nonequivalent Control Group Design

By adding a pretest to the static group comparison design one would get a nonequivalent control group design. This quasiexperimental design would be sketched as

O   X   O

O   O

The use of the pretest helps control for differences that may have existed between groups even before one group was exposed to the intervention. In the day care illustration, one might measure the level of interaction and alertness of older people who wish to be admitted to the program and of other older people who have not applied for admission. The pretest would help determine if those admitted to the program had higher levels of interaction and alertness even before intervention. The posttest enables the evaluator to determine if there are differences in interaction and alertness among those in the program.

Some important gerontological studies have used the nonequivalent control group design. Tobin and Lieberman's study of the impact of institutionalization (1976), for example, compared an institutionalized sample of older persons with a sample of persons on the waiting list for nursing homes and a sample of "community" older persons not thought to be at imminent risk of institutionalization. The pretests and posttests of these three groups enabled them to assess the effects of the institutional environment.

Single-Case Study

The single-case study applies the *basic elements* of research design to an individual rather than to a group of individuals. As a result, these designs are often associated with clinical practice. Single-system methodology was first developed in behavior modification, where the effects of various interventions and reinforcements over time would be assessed. It has since been applied to a wide range of other therapeutic interventions. Bloom and Fischer (1982) indicate that single system designs can be especially useful when the practitioner wishes to evaluate his/her own practice, when control groups and some of the other characteristics of classical experimental design are not possible, and as a means of formative research and hypothesis generation. As will be noted, these designs do not differ significantly from the designs described by Campbell and Stanley (1963).

The basic single system design consists of an observation period and an intervention period with observation continuing during the intervention. This design is graphically displayed as follows:

A   B

"A" represents the observation of the client and of the incidence of the problem or behaviors he/she wishes to alter. This observation is referred to as the "baseline" observation. "B" represents the practitioner's intervention with the client as well as the observations of the problem/behaviors after the intervention has been started.

This design is similar to the one-group pretest–posttest design (O X O). In the AB design, the observations that occur after intervention are not graphically displayed, but they are present. Thus, although the graphic representations of the designs may differ, the basic preexperimental approach of the two designs is the same.

To illustrate this design with the day care example, a practitioner might observe the level of interaction and alertness in a given older person before he/she enrolled in the day care program. After enrollment, that same older person might be observed periodically to assess the level of interaction and alertness.

The same kinds of threats to validity that were discussed above are present in single-system designs. Changes that are observed, for example, might not be due to the intervention but to some characteristic of the client that was present even without the intervention.

One variation on the basic single system design is the following:

A   B   A

In the ABA design, "A" again represents observation of the behaviors. "B" represents the intervention phase with the accompanying observations. The second "A" represents the withdrawal of the intervention while behaviors are observed. If the intervention is the cause of the changes observed during the "B" phase, the practitioner would expect the original behaviors to return during the second "A" phase.

With the day care illustration, during the first "A" phase stage we would again observe the level of interaction and alertness in an older person before he/she were admitted to the day care program. During the "B" phase the practitioner would enroll the older person in day care and observe his/her interaction and alertness while in the program. During the second "A" phase, the older person would be withdrawn from the day care program while observations continued. If the day care program had the hypothesized effect, the practitioner would expect the level of interaction and alertness during the second "A" phase to be much like that observed during the first "A" phase.

Another variation on the basic single-subject design is the designs referred to as "multiple baseline designs." Multiple baseline designs focus on several behaviors and several interventions at the same time. They are often graphically displayed as follows:

A_1 B_1

A_2 B_2

A_3 B_3

With the day care illustration, A_1 might represent observations of interactions and alertness with B_1 the day care program and as well as its effect on interaction and alertness. A_2 might represent observation of physical flexibility and B_2 could represent an intervention of daily physical exercise and the observation of its impact on flexibility. A_3 could represent an observation in the form of client-reported incidences of insomnia. B_3 could represent an intervention of relaxation exercises and the clients reports of insomnia during that intervention.

Other variations on the basic single-system case design are possible and are often used. Review of a text in this area, like Bloom and Fisher's (1982), will provide more information about the range of designs and special features to be considered with each design.

Research Design and Older Persons

Research design represents an effort to control threats to validity or those things other than the intervention that might explain the changes being observed. There are two particular threats to validity that are difficult to control when working with the aged unless a true experimental design with its random assignment to groups is used. Those threats are the threat of "maturation" and the threat of "mortality."

The threat of maturation refers to "all of those biological or psychological processes which systematically vary with the passage of time, independent of specific external events" (Campbell & Stanley, 1963, pp. 7–8). With older people, the biological process that occurs with the passage of time is the loss of physical strength and stamina since aging is marked by physical decrements. Because of these changes, the evaluator may be inclined to think a program or intervention is less successful than it actually is because older clients' conditions or behaviors remain the same or decline, rather than improving. It may also be true that observed declines are due to the effects of aging, not the program/intervention, and that the intervention is actually slowing the rate of decline that would be present were the program not available.

The threat of mortality, which may be present when the evaluator is comparing groups, is "differences in groups due to the differential dropout of persons from the groups" (Campbell & Stanley, 1963, p. 12). When the program is designed for the frail elderly or the very old, the evaluator may find a relatively high rate of mortality because the older persons either become too ill to participate or die. This rate of mortality may also be taken to mean the program is less successful than it actually is.

These threats can be controlled by random assignment of clients to an experimental condition and a control condition. However, since such random assignment is often not possible in practice settings, we often find maturation and mortality uncontrolled. It is important for the practitioner to consider the natural effects and consequences of the aging processes on his/her interventions with the aged, and to factor those consequences into the interpretation of the results.

A Final Word on Design

The area of research design often seems very complicated to beginning and even experienced practitioners. That sense of complication sometimes comes from the efforts of research methodologists to further elaborate on what, to the practitioner, appear to be the esoterica of design. Practitioners are well served by keeping in mind the basic purpose of design: To control for factors other than the intervention that might explain observed changes. Practitioners ought to consider the timing and order of the observations and interventions they use, and attempt, to the extent feasible, to limit the chances that something other than their intervention produced the result they observe.

Measuring Intervention Effects

The interest in program evaluation stems from questions about whether a practice intervention has the effect that it is intended to have. The research question expresses what the intervention is and what effect the intervention is expected to have. The design allows evaluators to better determine whether the behaviors they observe and changes in those behaviors are the result of the intervention or of other factors. Another important element of the evaluation research process is the method of measurement (through the collection of data) of the changes experienced by older clients. Those measurements represent the observations appearing in the graphic representations of design.

The measurement or data collection process can take several forms. Among the methods of collecting data are the following:

1. *An interview*, which may range from being very structured, with the same questions asked of all persons, to relatively unstructured, with the questions asked varying by the issues that emerge during any given interview.
2. *A questionnaire*, which may be closed, with respondents checking their response, or open-ended, with respondents writing a response. Students are very familiar with closed and open-ended questionnaires, since a multiple-choice test is a closed questionnaire and an essay test is an open-ended questionnaire.

3. *A projective or other indirect technique,* like a Rorschach test, that does not measure directly the attitudes or characteristics that are of interest, but makes use of responses to items that are related to those attitudes or characteristics.

4. *Observational methods,* which may range from the practitioner observing activities and behaviors and recording his/her observations to the practitioner acting as a participant-observer, and participating in activities while also observing the actions of others.

5. *The analysis of data collected* for other purposes, but that can provide some information about the characteristics of interest to the researcher. The results of medical examinations, for example, can tell the evaluator something about the physical flexibility of the older people in the day care program, although the exam may not have been conducted as a part of the data collection about the program.

Space in this chapter is too limited to permit a thorough discussion of the advantages and disadvantages of each method of data collection, and of the way the human service practitioner proceeds to use each method. Standard research texts, e.g., Babbie (1983), which are often used in undergraduate and graduate social work programs, provide information on these topics that should be consulted by the practitioner when designing a program evaluation.

Regardless of the method of measurement used, the researcher's interest is that the measurement be a valid and reliable indicator of the characteristic he/she is measuring. A *valid indicator* is one that is measuring what the researcher believes it to be measuring. If a questionnaire, for example, asks questions about social interactions, its questions, if it is valid, should deal with social interaction and not with some other topic, such as physical mobility or the client's level of verbal articulateness. A *reliable measure* is one that produces the same results time after time no matter who is using the measure. A measure of alertness, for example, should always measure the same levels of alertness in the same way and should produce the same results, no matter which practitioner uses it.

A significant amount of attention has been paid to measurement in social gerontology, and inventories of measures as well as their levels of validity and reliability are available for practitioners (See, for example, Kane & Kane, 1981.) The validity and reliability of measures of life satisfaction among the aged have been established (see, for example, Lohmann, 1980, 1989) and have often been used in intervention evaluations with the aged to determine if a given program has increased the level of life satisfaction. Gerontological sources often provide detailed information about the validity and reliability of various measuring instruments (see Morris et al., 1990).

Measures specific to clinical social work (or other human service) practice have also been developed. Walter Hudson (1982) developed a series of indexes for use with situations social workers often encounter, some of which, such as the "Index of Self-Esteem" and "Index of Marital Satisfaction," may be helpful in the evaluations of interventions with older people. Other collections of measuring instruments contain still other scales and devices that may be useful in program evaluations (see, for example, Miller, 1977). Although existing measuring devices may be helpful, because their validity and reliability have already been assessed, such devices are sometimes used in conjunction with or replaced by measuring instruments constructed by the practitioner. The advantage of a practitioner-designed instrument is that it can be made specific to a given program and its evaluation. The particular questions about the program can be answered very directly by such instruments. The disadvantages of practitioner-designed instruments include the fact that their validity and reliability are often unknown.

When designing an instrument—questionnaire, interview, etc.—for use in an evaluation, the practitioner should attempt to establish its validity and reliability to the greatest extent possible. Questionnaires, for example, should be pretested on persons like the clients they will be used with so confusing or unclear questions may be identified and revised. At a minimum, several persons should review the questionnaire to assess whether it is really measuring the characteristic it is supposed to measure. More sophisticated methods of establishing the instrument's validity and reliability should be applied, as time and the practitioner's talents allow.

Regardless of the method of data collection used or the specific measuring instruments used, the human service practitioner should not lose sight of the goal for measurement in program evaluation: obtaining valid and reliable indicators of changes that may have been produced by the practice intervention. The practitioner should use the most appropriate measuring devices for the given intervention situation, given this goal.

Analyzing the Data

Once the characteristics of interest have been measured, the data collected need to be analyzed. During a program evaluation, data analysis will likely occur at several points. Pretest or baseline data, if collected, may be analyzed before the intervention occurs or while the intervention is underway. After the intervention has been introduced, posttest data may be analyzed, either as they are collected or once the intervention has ended. Thus, although data analysis is often described as one of the final steps in the research process, it may actually be occurring at several points during the process.

The methods of data analysis may be quantitative and/or qualitative in nature, depending on the kind of information collected. Quantitative analysis involves the application of statistical techniques to the data. Qualitative analysis involves the description and analysis of the data without the use of numbers to represent the data.

The statistical techniques used may range from descriptive statistics to inferential statistics. Descriptive techniques could include summaries of the number of clients giving a specific response, the average or mean response given, the median response (half the responses are above that one and half below it), and the modal response (the response occurring most often).

More sophisticated data analysis may range from the use of "chi square," which allows comparison between groups or samples, to regression analysis, which allows us to determine how much influence a given variable had on the outcome. With the development of relatively inexpensive statistical packages for personal computers, the application of sophisticated statistical techniques is no longer dependent on the computational skills of the practitioner or access to a large computer.

In determining the statistical techniques to be used, it is important that the practitioner focus on the questions to be answered and the kind of data collected. The disadvantage of easy access to sophisticated statistical computing is that it is tempting to apply a complicated statistical test to data that do not meet the assumptions of that test. The test, for example, may be appropriate only for data collected from a random sample, and the practitioner could not randomly select the persons participating in the program. Or the test may be appropriate only for data collected with an interval measurement, on which the distances between points on a scale are equal, and the questionnaire used does not represent an interval measure.

Blalock's classic book on *Social Statistics* (1972) can help the practitioner determine the type of measurement appropriate for the data collected. For a practitioner whose familiarity with statistics is limited, this text may be too complicated and a source such as Weinbach and Grinnell's *Statistics for Social Workers* (1987), with its clear explanations, may be of greater help. Regardless of the sources consulted, the practitioner should remember that statistics are intended to be tools to help answer the research question and, as such, should be subordinate to the purpose of the research.

Qualitative data techniques may range from using the reports of observations to illustrate themes emerging from the evaluation to content analyses, some of which may include descriptive statistics, to analyze the data. Qualitative analysis depends on the skills of the practitioner to see meaning and relationships in the data. Glaser and Strauss (1967) have written the classic book in this area: *The Discovery of Grounded Theory*.

Whether quantitative or qualitative methods of data analysis are used, it should be remembered that the methods of analysis are tools intended to help answer questions. The method of analysis used should be determined by the nature of the questions to be answered and the nature of the data collected. The precision with which the research question has been asked, the amount of control provided by the research design used, and the validity and reliability of the measuring instrument(s) are as critical, if not more critical, than the method of data analysis used. It can be easy, however, to become infatuated by the statistical manipulations that are possible and to ignore the more critical elements of the research while focusing on statistics.

Conclusion

The interest of human service workers in program and practice evaluation comes from the need to determine which interventions are effective with what group(s) of clients. The techniques and methods of evaluative research provide evaluations with ways to better determine that it was the intervention, and not some other factor(s), that produced changes in clients.

In evaluating human service programs and practice, practitioners need to use the most rigorous research methodology feasible, given the practice setting. Human service workers need to pay particular attention to the following elements of the research process:

1. The framing of the research question(s) asked about the intervention.
2. The kind of sample selected for the research.
3. The rigor of the research design applied and the controls provided by that design.
4. The validity and reliability of the measuring instruments used.
5. The appropriateness of the methods of data analysis selected, given the assumptions of the analytic methods.

A focus on evaluative research by human service workers will help ensure the human service worker that he/she is providing the best possible intervention, contribute to the profession's accountability to the clientele and funding agencies, and add to the knowledge base of the human service profession.

References

Babbie, E. (1983). *The practice of social research.* Belmont, CA: Wadsworth.

Blalock, H. J., Jr. (1972). *Social statistics.* New York: McGraw-Hill.

Bloom, M., & Fischer, J. (1982). *Evaluating practice: Guidelines for the accountable professional.* Englewood Cliffs, NJ: Prentice-Hall.

Campbell, D. T., & Stanley, J. C. (1963). *Experimental and quasi-experimental designs for research.* Chicago, IL: Rand McNally College Publishing Company.

Caro, F. (Ed.) (1971). *Readings in evaluation research.* New York: Russell Sage Foundation.

Commission on Accreditation. (1984). *Handbook of accreditation standards and procedures.* Washington, DC: Council on Social Work Education.

Glaser, B. G., & Strauss, A. L. (1967). *The discovery of grounded theory: Strategies for qualitative research.* New York: Aldine.

Hudson, W. W. (1982). *The clinical measurement package.* Homewood, IL: The Dorsey Press.

Kane, R. A., & Kane, R. L. (1981). *Assessing the elderly.* Lexington, MA: Lexington Books.

Lohmann, N. (1980). A factor analysis of measures of life satisfaction, adjustment and morale. *International Journal of Aging and Human Development, 11,* 35–43.

Lohmann, N. (1989). Service providers and the concept of life satisfaction. *Journal of Applied Gerontology, 8,* 8–17.

Miller, D. C. (1977). *Handbook of research design and social measurement,* 3rd ed. New York: David McKay Company.

Morris, J. N., Hawes, C., Fries, B. E., Phillips, C. D., Mor, V., Katz, S., Murphy, K., Drugovich, M. I., & Friedlob, A. S. (1990). Designing the national resident assessment instrument for nursing homes. *The Gerontologist, 30,* 293–307.

Rossi, P. H., & Freeman, H. E. (1985). *Evaluation: A systematic approach,* 3rd ed. Beverly Hills: Sage.

Suchman, E. A. (1967). *Evaluative research.* New York: Russell Sage Foundation.

Tobin, S. S., & Lieberman, M. A. (1976). *Last home for the aged.* San Francisco, CA: Jossey-Bass.

Weinbach, R. W., & Grinnell, R. M., Jr. (1987). *Statistics for social workers.* New York: Longman.

Weiss, C. H. (1972). *Evaluation research: Methods for assessing program effectiveness.* Englewood Cliffs, NJ: Prentice-Hall.

Zimbalist, S. E. (1977). *Evaluative research in social work: The Background.* Historic themes and landmarks in social welfare research. New York: Harper & Row.

12

Program Consultation

R. O. WASHINGTON

Introduction

The purpose of this chapter is to present a paradigm by which the consultant and the client can measure the extent to which the goals of consultation in some phase of gerontology practice have been met. It will present in specific details suggestions for determining what kind of feedback mechanisms can be set up so that the consultant and the client can (1) assess whether the consultation is meeting benchmarks and requisites, (2) revise/reaffirm a definition of the problem, and (3) establish objectives for meeting consultation goals.

Such a strategy also will require some elaboration of goal setting as well as a discussion of operational problems related to establishing success criteria in observable and measurable terms. The paradigm to be presented is derived from the premise that *goal setting* is a basic prerequisite to any productive consulting relationship. Without a clear understanding of the goals to be sought, it is impossible for the consultant either to specify possible courses of action or evaluate the desirability or feasibility of the options open to the client.

Frame of Reference

Practitioners in the field of gerontology use consultants in a variety of ways. Frequently, however, they do not agree among themselves about what is and is not consultation. Without an agreement in operational terms on what constitutes consultation, then practitioners are hopelessly lost in any attempt to measure its impact. Consultation serves several needs of a client. Consultants bring fresh ideas to the organization. They serve as catalysts for change, they save time in dealing with complex problems by providing ready expertise, and they approach problems with a solution orientation.

Working Definition

Bell and Nadler (1979) define consultation as "the provision of information or help by a professional helper (consultant) to a help-needing person or system (client) in the context of a voluntary, temporary relationship which is mutually advantageous." (p. 2) Consultants offer assistance by *intervening*—that is, by taking some action to help a client solve his/her problem. The interventions involve much more than simply telling a client what to do or applying "common sense" remedies to a situation (Blake & Mouton, 1976). According to Bell and Nadler (1979), the consultation process involves five phases.

Phase 1: Entry

The entry phase begins with some contact of one by the other. Problems are jointly explored, perceived needs and symptoms are discussed, relationships are clarified, goals and roles are defined, resource parameters are identified, methodology is clarified, and ultimately a contract is negotiated.

The time that elapses during entry may range from a brief telephone call to numerous meetings. Throughout the entry phase, both parties are seeking to ascertain the degree to which the consultation will be a potentially advantageous relationship.

Phase 2: Assessment

After a consultant has accepted a request for consultation, his first responsibility is to define the problem. This is necessary in order to understand the problem and to lay the groundwork for mutual understanding of the help that the client wants, arriving at a rational assessment and developing a plan to try to give the client the help he/she wants. In some instances, the consultant's more objective view may result in a picture that differs to some extent from the problem as seen by the client.

This phase of the consulting relationship also focuses on the identification of the issues of concern and specification of problems. These areas may be clear or ambiguous. In some instances, the initial events are symptoms of larger, deeper issues. Whichever case dominates, there are organizational or programmatic situations that are deemed problematic, in need of change, elimination, or amelioration. In the initial phase

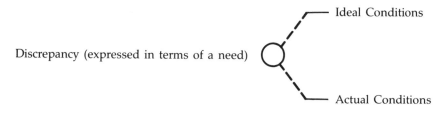

Figure 1. Depiction of a need.

of the consulting effort, the process should seek as much precision as possible about what the desired changes are. Without clear goals, without clarity of targets, and without some sense of direction, the change effort will lack focus or aim.

As stated, an assessment and evaluation process begins with a definition of the problem. In most instances, the problem will be stated in the form of a need, which is defined as a problem that exists because of a discrepancy (point A in Figure 1) that can be observed between an ideal condition (point B) and an actual state (point C).

The advantage of describing needs in terms of a discrepancy is that consultants can then generate measurable goals by stating them in terms of reduction of need within some time frame. Needs, therefore, may be expressed in the form of client dissatisfactions, discrepancy between what is and what ought, and necessary conditions for social well-being ("best practice" standards). Once both the consultant and the client view the problem from the same perspective, they can begin to collaborate on a statement of the goal.

A *goal* is a statement that represents in general terms an end to which the consultation is directed. It should also state the actual changes in the problem that the consultation will attempt to produce. It specifies the outcome behavior of the client and/or a desired state or condition once the planned course of action is completed. The goal-setting process should begin first by identifying the target(s) for change, which may be classified as (1) persons or groups who are regarded as either deviants or problem individuals, or persons affected by problem individuals, or persons or systems who are objects of undesirable activities or conditions; (2) clients or other individuals who are functionaries of the aging delivery systems; (3) physical objects or territorial units such as housing conditions, recreational facilities, or neighborhoods. If the target for change is the client or other individuals, then the goal statement should also specify the *desirable behavior changes* the client is expected to demonstrate at the conclusion of the consultation. Once targets for change are clearly identified, objectives can be stated in terms of rates of change, direction of change, nature of change, and/or amount of change. Rates and amounts of change are expressed in quantitative terms. Directions and the nature of change are concerned with changes in classification, quality, or kind rather than magnitude, and are usually expressed in qualitative terms.

The next step involves the development of an inventory of resources (i.e., personnel having appropriate expertise, available facilities, etc.) available for use in meeting the needs defined as the problem. The last step in this phase involves a series of comparisons among needs in order to determine which needs will be met and in what order and within what time frame.

Phase 3: Response

The response phase includes the planning and engagement of structured activities or interventions to correct the problem or improve the situation that was spelled out in the consultation agreement. Bell and Nadler (1979) are unclear about when assessment stops and response begins. They note that many models of consulting place a planning phase between the two to separate them more distinctly.

The response or action phase also includes the selection of a course of action, redefinition of the consultative goals, and identification of appropriate objectives. An objective is defined as a state of the intended outcome stated in terms of the precise behaviors that will be manifested before the objective can be said to have been attained. There are two reasons the consultant should be able to specify objectives in measurable terms: (1) it facilities communication, and (2) it ensures accountability and quality control—to know when the criterion level of performance has been met.

Objective setting involves specifying sequentially a set of performances that must be performed by the consultant and the client in order to advance toward the goal. They constitute criterion tasks, and are operationally defined in terms of a beginning point and an end point; therefore, the completion of a criterion task may be viewed as a performance episode. Objectives also represent *approximations* toward the goal. The completion of a performance episode signifies that the goal has been met to some degree in terms of some defined event. Therefore, either the existence or nonexistence of a desired site or the movement toward this state can be either qualitatively or quantitatively measured. When all the objectives have been met, the goal is considered to have been achieved.

Once the consultant and the client have agreed on a set of operational and sequential performances, they must project in advance which of these performances are viewed as critical benchmarks toward the achievement of the consultation goal. This presumes that certain objectives are more critical to goal attainment than others. This assessment can be accomplished by inferring a causal relationship between the performance episode and advancement toward the goal.

The identification of critical benchmarks in light of new and unintended outcomes should be repeated at the completion of each performance episode. The importance of measuring the impact of each performance episode is that such a procedure serves as a cybernetic process that can be used to validate or revise the definition of the problem or to modify consultation goals and objectives. Another advantage of such a feedback system is that the outcome data from the preceding performance episode become the baseline data (input) for the implementation of the next set of performances (objectives) or for the set of modified activities (alternative objectives).

Phase 4: Disengagement

The disengagement phase includes the evaluation of results conducted to determine not only if the consultation has been successful and is progressing as planned, but also whether there is a need for response revision or additional resources.

An effort is made to decrease the client's dependence on the consultant and develop within the client the ability to use self-generated data by involving the client in monitoring progress and evaluating results. Change can be sustained only if the client attains sufficient growth during the consultation.

Phase 5: Closure

Presuming the consultant has taken steps during disengagement to ensure continuity and internal support, he or she should be ready for a mutually satisfying termination of the consultation. Termination may mean leaving the client or may mean ceasing one effort and starting another. The challenge of the consultant is to bring the client to a point at which a consultant is no longer necessary (Bell & Nadler, 1979).

Case Study

To illustrate these five phases, let us construct a fictitious scenario and see how each phase is played out.

The Rosa Lee Jones Adult Day Care Center conducted a program evaluation of its agency and the Executive Summary of the report concluded that "the agency was poorly organized and structured, its budget and accounting procedures needed to be revised and the agency's mission was unclear."

After reading the evaluation report, members of the Board of Directors became alarmed and held a meeting to determine what position the Board should take relative to the report. The Board eventually decided that it would hire a consultant to work with the Board and the Executive Director. The Board selected an Advisory Committee to the consultation process and selected Mr. Simmons from the consulting firm of Simmons and Associates.

Entry Phase

The chairman of the Advisory Committee called Mr. Simmons and asked him to meet with the Committee to explore the parameters of the proposed consultation. Two weeks later, the Committee met with Mr. Simmons to discuss details of the consultation. It was agreed that the consultant would work with the Board in three specific areas: (1) preparation of a mission statement, (2) development of an organization structure, and (3) installation of a fiscal information and budgeting system. The Committee concluded its initial meeting by requesting that the consultant prepare a formal proposal to be submitted to the Advisory Committee within 2 weeks.

Two weeks later, Mr. Simmons presented a prospectus to the Advisory Committee that included the goals and objectives of the consultation. The goal statements were rephrased from the three general parameters presented to the consultant during the initial meeting.

The goals of the consultation shall be:

1. To improve the skill and abilities of the Board and staff of the Rosa Lee Jones Day Care Center to make, implement, and evaluate policies and programs of the Center.
2. To arrive at an effective organizational structure through engaging Board and staff in a series of discussions and analyses of job functions.
3. To achieve an efficient and effective management information system that serves the center's fiscal and budgetary as well as its operational needs.

The statements regarding the consultation objective were rewritten to read as follows:

1. A 1-hour workshop over a 6-month period will be conducted each month prior to the regular board meeting. It will cover content on policy development, policy analysis, and program management.

2. Six workshops will be devoted to strategic planning
3. Two workshops will be devoted to the implementation of a management information system
4. Individual consultation sessions will be provided to the Executive Director and the Board President on call.

The committee agreed on the goals and objectives of the consultation, specified what was expected of the consultant in terms of amount of time to be devoted to the consultation, method of consultation, and expectations of the consultant regarding the committee's tasks. The consultant then prepared a working agreement (contract) that was formally signed by both parties.

Assessment Phase

A major task of the consultant during this phase was to facilitate a reevaluation of the organization and its goals. This phase also included articulating the present problems, the surface symptoms, and the underlying historical causes, as well as identifying strengths of the organization and the opportunities and potential for change. At this stage, the mission and goals of the organization, its structure, communication patterns, and leadership were also evaluated.

The consultant began his work by collecting and reviewing all pertinent histories and records of the Jones Adults Day Care Center. This enabled him to answer the aforementioned general questions and the following eight specific questions:

1. What are the current problems, issues, or areas of concern that prompted this request for consultation?
2. How has the client's organization attempted to cope with this situation in the past?
3. What were the consequences of these previous actions, and how do they influence current efforts?
4. Why is the client requesting help at this time?
5. What are the client's expectations of the consultant?
6. What are the consultant's expectations of the client?
7. What other individuals, groups, or organizations should be involved in formulating the focus of this total consultation project?
8. What is the desired outcome or resolution of these problems or issues?

The next step the consultant undertook was to conduct an interview with selected members of the staff and the Board. The purpose of this step was to ascertain, in the case of the staff, their perception of organizational goals, resources, organizational values, and beliefs and other factors that may have a bearing on organizational performance. In the case of the Board, the attempt was to ascertain the organization's willingness to commit its resources to the resolution of its problems.

Phase 3: Response

After reviewing the assessment data, the consultant concluded that the most efficient way to carry out the goals and objectives of the proposed consultation process was to engage the Board and staff in a strategic planning process. Since strategic planning was entirely new to the majority of the Board and staff, the consultant began by preparing the group for an extended process. He asked the Executive Director to arrange for a 1-day retreat of Board and staff in order to orient the group to the strategic planning process.

The 1-day retreat was set for a Saturday. The agenda for the retreat was set to accomplish one goal: to reach consensus on the mission of the agency. The consultant considered this an important first step because the mission statements usually state the organization's ethical, philosophical, and ideological tone as well as its commitment. In other words what is its reason for being. A mission statement also serves as the basis for establishing the policies and priorities for program operation and policies in turn define how the program's resources will be allocated. The consultant began the retreat by presenting the following prepared statement:

> The Amherst H. Wilder Foundation defines strategic planning as the process of determining *What* an organization intends to be in the future and *how* it will get there. It is finding the best future for your organization and the best path to reach that destination.

Such planning involves fundamental choices about the future:

1. The mission or goals you will pursue.
2. The programs, services or products you will offer to accomplish this mission.
3. How you will attract and utilize the resources you need: people, money, expertise, facilities, etc.

A distinction is sometimes made in the planning literature between long-range planning, which focuses on what an organization intends to look like at the end of a given period of time, and strategic planning, which focuses on the action plan for how the organization will get there. In practice, however, the two go hand in hand. Therefore, for our discussion today, we shall use the terms strategic planning and long-range planning interchangeably to refer to the process of determining both where you want your organization to be and how you will get there.

Strategic planning is also distinguished from another kind of planning—operational or short-range planning. Operational planning is what many organizations do when they develop yearly objectives, program plans, and budgets. Operational or short-range plans focus on a shorter time period than strategic plans, for example, 1 year instead of 5 years. Operational plans show in specific terms how, in the coming year, an organization will move toward the future described iñ its strategic plan.

The relationship between strategic planning and organizational change is fairly straightforward. That is to say, the result of a strategic plan is to anticipate change for improvement. In other words, strategic planning can be described as developing a vision for the future. This involves two tasks:

1. Developing the best vision you can of what your organization should look like in the future, usually 2–5 years from now: its mission, services, staffing, finances, and so on.
2. Determining how you will move your organization toward the desired change.

To accomplish these two tasks you must find a fit between three sets of forces:

1. The mission of your organization—what you intend to accomplish.
2. Opportunities and threats your organization faces—what is needed and feasible.
3. The strengths and weaknesses of your organization—what you are capable of doing.

What this suggests then is that change should not be initiated simply for the sake of change. Many practices, customs, and values in organizations are worthy of retention. Therefore, change should occur only if it will enhance human values, and the attainment of the economic and social goals of the organization.

Following a discussion of the prepared statement, the group began a discussion of the mission of the agency. By the end of the day, the group concluded that the retreat had been successful. Not only had the group arrived at a revised mission statement, it also had formulated new organizational goals, identified unmet needs of the target group, and set forth new program strategies.

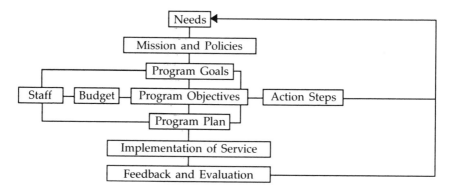

Figure 2. Conceptual scheme used by the consultant.

Consultant's Role

The consultant's role in this process was that of facilitator helping the group to identify those organizational and environmental variables that influence the mission. Figure 2 depicts the conceptual scheme used by the consultant to arrive at the mission statement and to establish further discussions by the group.

Figure 2 shows that the planning process begins with an assessment of needs, and mission and policy statements are statements of intent— intent to reduce needs to zero.

The mission statement provides the basis for program goals that reflect program objectives, budget, staff, and action steps. Program plans and their constituents, staff, etc., constitute the organization's program plan and provide the basis for program implementation and eventually program evaluation.

When working with a client group, there are several things a consultant must remember.

1. The consultant must not let his prejudice and bias get in the way of good judgment and the accurate interpretation of facts.
2. The consultant must avoid engaging the group in a debate. His role is to present both sides of the issues and assist the group in arriving at its own conclusion.
3. The consultant must remember that he is the guest in the "home" of the host. All courtesies generally accorded a guest is expected by the client. Therefore, consultants must avoid know-it-all attitudes and condescending behaviors.
4. Since the aim of most consultant relationships is change, consultants frequently find themselves advocating changes that affect the status quo. Wise consultants remember that all change is

painful for someone and therefore should be implemented with sensitivity and care.

5. In making recommendations, consultants should offer no more than the facts support, avoid speculations and guesses, and remember that consistently unsound recommendations destroy credibility.

The 1-day retreat proved so successful that members of the Board and staff agreed to meet the following week to continue the planning process. One week later, the group met. Since a specific goal of the consultation process was to assist Board members in improving their skills to implement and evaluate program goals, the second gathering was devoted to introducing the group to the five major steps in the strategic planning process and the interrelationship and interdependence of the steps as a holistic process. The five steps are depicted in Figure 3.

Figure 3 shows that all typical strategic planning processes involve (1) articulation or reaffirmation of a mission statement, (2) environmental scanning—review of internal and external forces that may have a facilitating or debilitating impact on program goals, (3) stated goals and objectives, (4) testing of goals, and (5) analysis of feedback data.

After the second gathering of the group, the consultant decided the group was now ready to address the problem of organizational structure. Several sessions were devoted to this topic.

This phase of consultation began first by understanding the history and work ethos of the agency. It also involved examining worker performances, grouping performance activities into logical work units, establishing reporting relationships, and defining lines of authority and responsibilities. The principal goal of this phase of consultation was to achieve a smoother running organization.

As Figure 4 shows, human service organizations should be examined by looking at four aspects of its organization:

1. *Organization goals*—as indicated in goal-settling action, goals represents a reduction in the discrepancy between the *is* and the *ought*. When the goal is met, the discrepancy is reduced to zero, goals are multiple and even changing.
2. *Operational processes*—are those subsystems that make up the "actions and activities" of the organization. They represent those activities that facilitate system maintenance.
3. *Organizational resources*—include the technical knowledge base, technology, materials, machines and equipment, and financial resources.
4. *Administrative processes*—includes such processes as organizing, controlling, and coordinating procedures that constitute the facilitating systems of an organization.

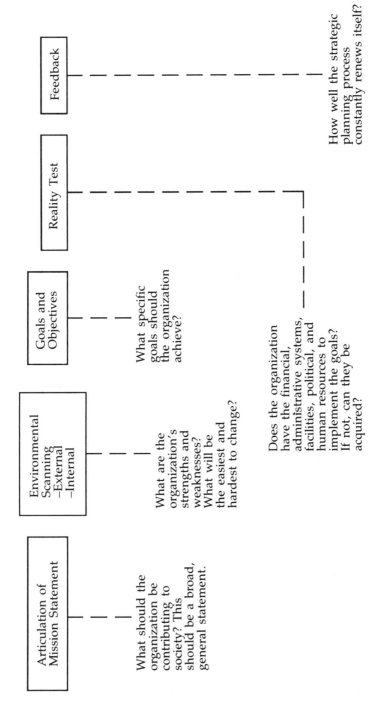

Figure 3. Five steps in the strategic planning process.

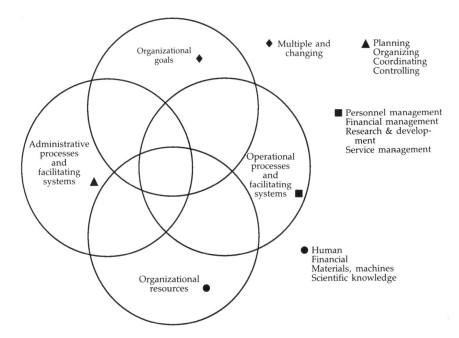

Figure 4. Aspects of human service organizations.

After completion of the sessions on organizational structure, the group began its work on the Management Information System (MIS). The first session was devoted to a discussion of the three types of information systems:

1. *A client information system* designed to provide the organization with information related to clients. It focuses on data pertaining to tracking the client through the service system; it includes data about needs, service provision, unmet needs, client satisfaction, continuity, and availability of services.
2. *An organizational operating information system* designed to facilitate basic administrative functions such as planning, budgeting, and reporting. It produced a variety of reports, regarding client management, staff activity, and statistical analyses for cost centers, agency personnel, and funders.
3. *A performance information system* designed to support improved decision making and include data required for measuring program effectiveness.

Other sessions were devoted to the functions of an MIS, assessing information requirements, planning the MIS, developing work plans, identifying date elements, designing forms, and installing the MIS.

Usually, the response phase is completed when recommendations are presented or when the series of task has been demonstrated. However, there are circumstances in which the consultant's help is needed in putting plans into practice. In fact, some consultants will not accept an assignment unless it includes an opportunity to implement the recommendations.

The consultant's assistance is especially useful when implementing recommendations that involve changes in organization and the ways in which individuals or departments interact to accomplish their tasks and/ or work methods and procedures. It is often useful for the consultant to hold work sessions with the employees concerned to demonstrate how the changes will affect the way they perform their duties and to illustrate with problem-solving examples. Such meetings also provide an opportunity to assess employee reaction to the recommendations and the impact of their implementation. In some cases, on-the-job coaching may be needed, followed by periodic checks to make sure that the plans are being properly carried out. The consultant may use these work sessions to revise recommendations to better suit the situation if need be and still maintain their objectives. The consultant may also be helpful when the recommended changes cut across departmental or divisional lines. The company's chief executive is likely to be too busy to oversee the implementation himself, and lower level executives may encounter political difficulties (Golightly, 1985)

Preventing and Handling Resistance to Change

Change is always difficult to accept. Resistance to change is frequently expressed by those with vested interest in the status quo, those who fear losing privileged positions, or those who feel that their jobs may be in jeopardy of elimination. Consultants must have the skill to abate these fears. Consultants as outside "firemen" are frequently placed in the position of advocating or implementing changes that management wants but finds difficult to implement.

A central fact of organizational life is that organizations find it easier to keep busy with routine tasks than to take on new functions or to change accustomed modes of behavior. The reasons for resistance to change are many. For example, resistance to change is strongest when members feel pressured into change that may result in some loss of face or loss of stature. Supervisors and middle mangers often resist change because it disrupts the management process. Change may require learning new skills or modifying accustomed ways of doing things. Some members may feel that change will result in the erosion of standards.

Large organizations such as the Jones Adult Day Care Center tend to drift toward what is frequently called organizational inertia. Over a period of time, procedures, regulations, activities, and attitudes become routine, habitual, and cemented. Gardner (1963), in his book *Self-Renewal, the Individual and the Innovative Society,* warns us that

> When we talk about revitalizing . . . an organization we tend to put exclusive emphasis on finding new ideas. But there is usually no shortage of new ideas, the problem is to get a hearing for them. And that means breaking through the crusty rigidity and stubborn complacency of the status quo. (p. 43)

Frequently, defenders of the status quo do so because of what they believe is the public interest. Distinguishing between self-interest and what is in the public interest is sometimes very difficult. It is perhaps important to acknowledge that there are significant psychic costs to change. For some members of the organization, changing established patterns of practice or adding new functions may mean starting all over again. In addition, there are other factors that are endemic to the organization that also inhibit change (Ingalls, 1976).

1. *Conflicting perception of the situation.* If agency staff view a problem under discussion in different ways, no effective decision will be made until the differing perceptions are explored and understood by all.
2. *Fear of consequences.* The possible outcomes of an impending decision may overwhelm the staff. The ambiguity of fear may have a paralyzing effect on the staff's ability to come to a decision, unless the fear is encountered openly and dealt with effectively.
3. *Conflicting loyalties.* Individuals usually have memberships in several groups at a time. Multiple memberships may serve as hidden agendas that create pressure within the staff. Often such agendas need to be identified for free choice to occur.
4. *Interpersonal conflict.* Personal differences, interpersonal conflict, or role ambiguity within the agency can provoke defensiveness, antipathy, and biased discussion, preventing full clarification of the issues.
5. *Methodological rigidity.* Staff action can be so frozen by a method or style of decision making that free and open discussion of a problem and its various related elements is limited.
6. *Inadequate leadership sharing.* When the agency does not share leadership functions and relies too heavily on a designated or self-appointed leader to tell them what to do, a decision may be made that lacks staff commitment and acceptance of respon-

sibility for carrying it out. The rule should always be: Those who are affected by the decision should participate in the decision making.

Developing an appreciation for each of these obstacles to change makes it easier to deal with resistance. For example, instead of asking: "What's wrong with those members who resist my proposed changes," the consultant may be more successful by asking: (1) What is wrong with my proposed changes? (2) Have the changes been properly explained so that they are understood? (3) What is wrong with the methods used to bring about the changes? (4) What is wrong with the relationships between those promoting change and those who resist? (5) Is the price of change too high (economically, socially, or psychologically) given the benefits to be derived? (6) What are the possible secondary consequences of the proposed changes?

What these questions suggest is that the kinds of changes people frequently resist are changes that are not clearly understood, changes that they had no part in bringing about, changes that threaten their vested interest and security, changes advocated by those whom they do not like or trust, and changes that do not fit into the values and ethos of the agency. The lesson to be learned from all of this is that organizational change must be viewed as progress; otherwise it will be seen as a threat to the status quo.

Organizations that succeed in implementing changes and reducing resistance show the following characteristics and/or initiate the following activities (Gerbert, 1984).

1. The organization is under intense internal and external pressure for improvement. Performance and morale are low and management and organization members sense a need for examining the present status of the organization. There may be a sense of groping for solutions.
2. A group (Advisory Committee) is formed within the organization, either as an ad hoc committee or task force, and is brought together to produce the improvement within the organization.
3. The organization's leaders are actively involved in the process of reevaluation.
4. The consultant and the organization's leaders work with members of several levels of the organization to collect data to be used in diagnosing problems.
5. Potential solutions are generated through a process of group participation. The solutions may include revising the mission statement and goals, restructuring the organization, improving communication, and changing hiring and promotion proce-

dures. This stage is most effective when members are open to accepting a wide range of alternatives.

6. As the group moves toward selecting solutions, it must be noted once again that involvement of members at all levels will increase the likelihood of success.
7. Small pilot projects are used to demonstrate the efficacy of the proposed solution. Adequate pilot testing will ease the diffusion process, decrease resistance, and conserve resources. If small-scale implementation succeeds, then a broader application can be undertaken.
8. The change effort is diffused throughout the entire organization.
9. The organization is stabilized, and the means are created for continued self-evaluation.

Disengagement

By the end of the fourth month, the consultant had held a series of meetings with the Board and staff regarding the mission statement, submitted the statement to the Board of final adoption, submitted to the Board a new organizational chart, and installed a new management information system. All that was left was the refinement of the MIS and the training of the staff to implement the budgeting and accounting phase of the new MIS.

To ensure that the staff had mastered the new procedures, the consultant devised a series of hypothetical situations to be solved by the members of the board and staff. The series continued until the consultant was satisfied that all new procedures had been well mastered.

A formal evaluation of the consultation process was conducted by the consultant. The following basic questions were reviewed by the consultant:

1. Did the consultation do what we wanted it to do?
2. Were the consultation objectives met?
3. Could more desirable outcome(s) have been achieved by reshaping or redirecting the current program inputs? adopting some previously suggested, but rejected, alternative(s)? or substituting some wholly new alternative(s)?

Closure

Having completed all the tasks specified in the contract, Mr. Simmons began to bring the consulting relationship to closure. Separate exit interviews with the Executive Director and the Advisory Committee were conducted to ascertain satisfaction with the consultation process as well as outcome.

Positive responses to the questionnaire yielded a positive rating for the consultation. The next step was to prepare a final report to be submitted to the Board. Most consultants prefer to prepare both an oral and written report of their activities. An oral report enables the consultant to present all aspects of the findings without "washing all the dirty linen in the public." On the other hand, the written report is likely to be around for a long time and the writing must be more explicit and thorough because a written document lacks the expressiveness and visual advantages of a spoken dialogue. Following are a few tips on good report writing.

1. Clarity and simplicity should be the hallmark of good report writing. Every word that serves no function, every long word that could be a short word, every adverb which carries the same meaning that is already expressed, every passive construction that leaves the reader unsure of who is doing what weakens the strength of the sentence.

2. The report should seek to achieve a balance between strong points and weaknesses. A report that is completely negative is likely to turn the reader off before he gets too far. A report that is too glowing tends to lose its credibility.

3. Be sure you have prepared the reader in the body of the report through examples and illustrations for the new ideas, directives, or recommendations for changes you have offered. Recommendations offered without a context lose their credibility. In other words, the more change, uncertainty, and/or threat, the more carefully you should prepare your readers.

4. If some members of the agency are likely to disagree with some of your recommendations and ideas, be sure to present both sides of the argument in your report. Remember, your credibility affects your ability to implement recommendations.

5. In the social sciences literature on persuasion, there is something called the "primacy-recency" issue. The argument presented first is said to have primacy; the argument presented last, recency. Although experiments and studies on topic have failed to produce conclusive findings regarding which is most effective for what situation, most social scientists advise that the most controversial aspects of the report and those recommendations that are likely to receive the most support should be left for the latter part of the report. The idea is that when you end with your strongest point, you do not let your readers down.

Some Concluding Comments

This chapter sets out to define consultation and to provide the reader with rules about how the client can assess the success of a consultation experience. It emphasized the significance of goal setting in consultation and the five principal phrases of the consultation process. The chapter also sought to inform the reader that the end product of consultation is change and the difficulty of advocating organizational change. It also attempted to provide the reader with "tips" that can be used by the consultant to successfully effect change and minimize resistance.

Generally, no one calls in a consultant until there is a problem. First and foremost, a consultant is a problem-solver. Therefore he/she must have command over a body of knowledge and competence to define and analyze the problem properly. An experienced consultant knows the importance of defining his/her role at the beginning of the consultation process and adapting his/her problem-solving methods to the individuality of the client. He/she must bring professionalism to the assignment and maintain confidentiality.

References

Bell, C. R., & Nadler, L. (Eds.). (1979). *The client-consultant handbook.* Houston, TX: Gulf Publishing Co.

Blake, R. R., & Mouton, J. S. (1976). *Consultation.* Reading, MA: Addison-Wesley.

Gardner, J. W. (1963). *Self Renewal.* New York: Harper & Row.

Gerbert, B. (1984). Planned change and the future of the dental education. *Journal Dental Education, 50,* 687–688.

Golightly, H. (1985). *Consultants: Selecting, using and evaluating business consultants.* New York: Franklin Watts.

Ingalls, J. D. (1976). *Human energy: The critical factor for individuals and organizations.* Reading, MA: Addison-Wesley.

13

Grant Writing and Fund Raising

PAUL K. H. KIM

Introduction

A number of literary works about ancient China, Egypt, and the early Christian era (the Old Testament in particular) suggest the importance of the human spirit in caring for fellow human beings who are in need of help. Examples of terminology signifying such human acts of kindness are "charity" or "philanthropy." A positive attitude about caring for one's fellow man was a pervasive social ethos and thus established public acceptance in ancient societies with the first organized structure, Plato's Foundation, dating back to 347 B.C. in ancient Greece. In Greek, "philanthropia," meaning man's love and concern for his fellow man, was patronized by the ruler who primarily supported only selected friends, relatives, and allies for their civil and cultural activities; the Roman "beneficium" allowed Emperors to give soldiers, friends, and churches portions of land for their services; Byzantine philanthropy emphasized "selfless love"; and in the middle ages, the "concession" method prevailed, a type of franchise, contract, or grant (in England) (White, 1975).

In the mid-seventeenth century, Benjamin Franklin founded the American Philosophical Society. Ever since, foundations and foundation-type societies have been burgeoning in the United States, i.e., the appearance of the Magdalen Society of Philadelphia in 1800 (became the White-William Foundation in 1918) and the Smithsonian Institute in 1835, the famous Carnegie and Rockefeller Foundations in 1886 and 1889, respectively, and the Rhodes Trust in 1902, with many more following since the 1920's, resulting in an excess of 24,000 foundations in existence today.

The federal government was never idle in grant activities. In 1803 the U.S. Congress granted $30,000 to Professor Samuel F. B. Morse to test

299

possible public use of an electromagnetic telegraph system. Like private foundations, Congress authorizes the federal government to solicit, screen, and fund grant applications for the implementation of scientific and human services research and demonstration projects. Thus, combining both private and public funds, American grantsmanship has become a privilege of American citizens, scientists, and human service professionals in particular, and amounts to a multibillion dollar enterprise.

Unlike *charitable gifts* given on the basis of specified need as presented by potential beneficiaries, *grants* are by and large determined by donors' concern and interest and based on two implications—faith (to believe) and obligation (to promise). Namely, the grantor shall believe and trust that grantees will perform agreed on activities and subsequently meet expectations of the benefactor, the grantor (White, 1975). Both private and public grantors have become very well organized and systematically administer funds through a number of different means and in accordance to their own preferential priorities.

Professionals in the field of gerontological and geriatric research and services have been on the bandwagon of American grantsmanship and fund-raising. Funding is pursued because (1) problems facing older Americans today are insurmountable with only the current level of governmental fiscal authorization and appropriation, (2) through almost all government departments, offices, agencies, and commissions (even NASA) more public funds are made available, on a competitive basis, for the development and sustenance of new or existing gerontological research and service programs, and (3) because of responsive private funding support through foundations, corporations, and concerned individuals.

In view of this demand, challenge, opportunity, and even professional privilege, this chapter is designed to discuss (1) sources and kinds of grants, (2) a typical structure of a grant proposal, and (3) guidelines (or tips) for successful proposals. Nonetheless, in the interest of professionals in the field of gerontological human services, the tone and content of the chapter are related to service grants and contracts including research and demonstration.

How to Find Funding Sources

Public Funding Sources

A good work habit of agency administrators, managers, and staff who are responsible for program planning, development, maintenance, and evaluation is devoting 15–30 minutes daily to reading such publications as "The Federal Register," "The Commerce Business Daily," and "The Catalog of Federal Domestic Assistance." These publications contain the most updated information about grants and contracts administered by the federal government and/or through state and local governments at any given time. Such publications can be subscribed to through the Superintendent of Documents, U.S. Government Printing Office, Washington, DC 20204; or one can easily find them through public libraries and the grants office of local colleges and universities.

"The Federal Register" is a daily publication that reports regulations and legal notices issued by various federal government agencies, offices, and commissions. One can read announcements on the availability of grants and contracts (RFP—Request for Proposal, or RFA—Request for Application) about 60 days before the application deadline. It is imperative for grant writers to fully understand the statutory mandates pertaining to entitlement projects, for the administrative branch of federal government responsible for the interpretation and administration of the law has to closely adhere to the mandate. The knowledge gained by reading "The Federal Register" will be most helpful in developing grant ideas, initiating necessary groundwork, constructing and asking intelligent questions to the designated federal office, and, finally, writing a grant or contract proposal within the scope of the legislative mandate. One should carefully review the Contents page, looking for announcements from agencies of his/her interest, and collecting some prospective grant or contract ideas that are in the making. "The Federal Register" costs about $340 for an annual subscription through the Office of the Federal Register, National Archives and Records Administration, Washington, DC 20408.

"The Commerce Business Daily" (CBD) is another daily publication by the government. Unlike "The Federal Register," one reads a list of federally initiated grants and contracts, as well as the name of the federal agency responsible for administration, the address, the name of the contact person, the telephone number of that agency, the title of the proposed project and its objective, the RFP/RFA number, and the deadline for application.

Another valuable publication for grant writers is "The Catalog of Federal Domestic Assistance." This annual publication includes rather detailed information about all federally funded programs through different federal departments, agencies, commissions, and offices. For example, 1176 assistance programs administered by 52 federal agencies are being reported in the 1990 publication. It contains a list of programs by agencies, functions, and subjects, as well as definition, eligibility, and objectives of federal assistance.

Besides these three publications, one can find still more public funding sources for research and service programs for the elderly. He/she

may contact various government offices at state, regional, and federal
levels to learn about possible grants and contracts initiated by the government even before the announcement through "The Federal Register"
and "CBD." (Frequent cries heard from grant writers attest to the reality
that they did not learn about grant or contract possibilities until almost
the last minute and could not fully prepare themselves to be competitive
applicants.)

Although almost all federal administrative units administer grants
and contracts relevant to gerontological research and service programs,
one should be in close contact with the staff of the Administration on
Aging of the Department of Health and Human Services (DHHS), the
State Unit on Aging (usually housed in the Governor's Office or the
State's Department of Human Resources), local Area Agencies on Aging
(AAA), the National Association of State Units on Aging (NASUA), and
the National Association of Area Agencies on Aging (NAAAA—N4A) in
Washington, DC. The National Institute of Health of DHHS and its
separate units such as the National Institute of Aging (NIA) and Mental
Disorders of the Aging Research Branch of the National Institute of
Mental Health (NIMH) are some important federal government units
that serve gerontological and geriatric researchers and service providers
as well as older persons. The U.S. Departments of Agriculture, Transportation and Labor, Housing and Urban Development (HUD), AC-
TION Office in the White House, and their counterparts at state and
local levels are all valuable sources for information. In addition, professional organizations nationally advocating on behalf of older Americans
(i.e., the Gerontological Society of America, the American Society of
Aging, the National Council on Aging, the American Association of
Retired Persons, and organizations representing ethnic elderly groups)
profusely divulge funding information through personal contacts and
publications of their respective organizations.

Kinds of Federal Funding Assistance. Gerontological researchers and
service providers may be primarily interested in the following three
types of public funding assistance:

1. *Grant*: A public office/agency and a normally not-for-profit organization enter into an agreement that the former provide funds mutually
confirmed (including direct and indirect costs) in order for the latter to
perform the activity specified by the benefactor. Grant activities normally involve research, training and education, conferences, and travel
that are relevant to physical and social sciences, and health and human
services.

Public grants are sanctioned by respective public laws and administered by government administrative units at federal, state, and local

levels. Specific guidelines for application and the process of review are widely publicized by the grantor agency. Such grants are designed to be responsive to public agenda identified in the specific law and normally support innovative, original, and exploratory ideas. Grant programs thus allow grantees an extensive freedom in performing designated activities.

2. *Contract*: Public agencies announce activity needs that can be better performed by private sectors. Government administrative units normally employ competitive bidding systems for specified works. For example, offices of Federal Medicare and State Medicaid Programs announce the availability of service contracts with private health care providers to implement home health care for the elderly and enter into a contractual agreement, on which the latter provides a specified service and the former reimburses. Thus, it is in a way a third-party payment system.

Governments use one of the following contractual agreements: (1) a *Fixed Price Contract*, based on a reasonable cost estimate of required activities; (2) a *Cost Reimbursement Contract*, paying all allowable costs for activities; (3) a *Cost plus Fixed-Fee Contract*, a combination of (1) and (2); and (4) a *Cost Sharing Contract*, which is partial reimbursement by the grantor.

3. *Fellowship and Scholarship*: This program is designed to support advanced and continued education of individuals. Although these programs may be subsumed by training grants and contracts, a unique stipulation of this type of funding mechanism is limited to specified scientific disciplines and human service professions, age, gender, and/or ethnicity. National Defense Fund, Government Guaranteed Student Loan, and Postdoctoral fellows are some examples.

Other federal grants include block grants (to award states for flexible human service planning and implementation), capitation and formula grants (awarded on the basis of the number of people served rather than the task to be performed), categorical grants (for a certain field of interest—mental health, handicaps, maternity and children, etc.), construction grants (for construction, renovation, and expansion of buildings), project grants (given to individuals and organizations on their established merits), etc.

Private Funding Sources

In addition to public appropriation of funds, America proudly maintains her unique character as a "Country of Giving" as demonstrated by registered foundations and concerned individuals who faithfully and generously give funding support to American ventures that are designed to improve the quality of life of Americans as well as people abroad. Many U.S. automobiles display and celebrate this spirit on their bumpers saying "Think Giving, Thank Love." American giving exceeded $87 billion in 1986 for research and human service programs through grants, awards, and fellowships, for an increase of more than $7 billion over the previous year. The most active givers are larger foundations, big corporations, small business sectors, religious organizations, and individuals. Furthermore, Americans proudly observe the third Friday of the month of November as "The Philanthropy Day."

Foundations. "Foundation" is defined as follows:

> A nongovernmental, non-profit organization with funds and programs managed by its own trustees or directors, and established to maintain or aid social, education, charitable, religious or other activities serving the common welfare, primarily through the matching of grants. (Buckman, 1975, p. xi)

Foundations may be classified into two general categories: an *operating foundation*, which uses general revenue for the foundation's own activities including its programs or institutions, i.e., research institutes, museums, etc.; and *nonoperating foundations*, of greatest interest to grant writers, which award a variety of grants to organizations and individuals. There are more than 24,000 grant-making foundations in the States.

Nonoperating foundations are further divided into five types depending on purposes and/or organizational structures as follows:

1.   National Foundations or General Purpose Foundations: These are large and well-known foundations that are operated by a professional staff under broad charters. They are indeed grant-makers: for example, the Ford Foundation receives more than 30,000 proposals annually and funds about 2,000. The Lilly Endowment and Rockefeller Foundations belong in this category.

2.   Special Interest/Purpose Foundations: Like national foundations, Special Interest Foundations are national in scope and managed by professional staff. Nonetheless, these foundations have set forth a specific field of activity, i.e., health (an interest of the Robert Wood Johnson Foundation), mental retardation (specified by the Joseph P. Kennedy Foundation), and policy agenda for the aging and aged (expressed by the Viller Foundation). The Kresge Foundation is interested in building, repairing, and/or renovating buildings that are to be used for education and human services.

3.   Family Foundations: These foundations have been set up and controlled by living family members whose assets range from a few thousand dollars to over $100 million. Their grants more or less reflect

the family's wishes and interests and usually fund activities in cities and locations in which the family resides and/or accumulated its wealth. Thus, one may consider this kind of foundation as big individual givers. Memberships of its board are primarily family members or immediate associates, i.e., Rockefeller Brothers Fund.

4. Community Foundations: These foundations are established with gifts and/or bequests of multiple donors, and are professionally managed, normally by local bankers. They are public charities that collect money from the public and direct grants within the community. Funds are to be used only for the improvement of community life; examples include the Cleveland Foundation, New York Community Trust, New Orleans Foundation, and San Francisco Foundation. Most of them are named after the location that the respective foundation is expected to serve.

5. Company Sponsored or Corporate Foundations: More than 400 companies with nationwide operations have established their own foundations. Through the corporate endowment, which is built on corporate profits, grants are awarded to not-for-profit organizations including human services agencies. These foundations favor programs that are in the line of corporate interest. They also generously give support to education, United Way, minority enterprises, and local social services that particularly benefit its employees as well as the community at large. Exxon Education Foundation, Sears-Roebuck Foundation, and the Motorola Foundation are examples.

The grant writer can locate foundation funding sources by reviewing the *Foundation Directory*, the *Annual Register of Grant Support*, and other publications issued by the Foundation Center, 79 Fifth Avenue, 8th Floor, New York, NY 10003. The Foundation Center provides information about local libraries that hold the Foundation Center collections. The Taft Foundation Reporter is another good source.

Foundation Directory: This annual publication contains about 6600 major foundations with assets of more than one million dollars and/or those that award grants in excess of more than $100,000 a year. Those listed (about one-fourth of all American Foundations) together account for more than $106 billion or 96% of the total foundation asset, and in 1987 awarded $6.3 billion (93% of the total foundation giving). The directory contains names and addresses of foundations, their financial data (wealth or assets), purposes, the most recent record as well as types of grants awarded, limitations, application procedures, etc. The grant writer should comprehend a foundation's purposes and track record of granting research and program activities in the field of gerontology and geriatrics. In the early 1980s there were more than 300 foundations that awarded grants for gerontological activities at home and abroad.

Annual Register of Grant Support: This publication of the Foundation Center contains information as others above. However, the index column of this volume will guide the reader to foundations that support aging.

Another valuable source of information on foundation support is the *Foundation Center Source Book Profiles*. This is a quarterly and semiannual publication containing names and addresses of about 500 national foundations (granting projects nationwide), contact persons, application procedures, purposes, grant types, and activity areas. Those foundations normally award more that $200,000 annually. *Foundation Grants to Individuals* is being published by the Foundation Center every other year, containing application information for individuals who are primarily looking for scholarships, fellowships, and travel grants. *Foundation News* is being published by the Council on Foundations in Washington, DC, but its cumulated index is published by the Foundation Center. This publication includes foundation grants over $5,000, indexed by states, subject areas, recipients, and specific grant activities. The reader may be able to identify foundations that favor and/or have established a track record of awarding gerontological programs.

In addition, the *Taft Foundation Reporter* published by the Taft Foundation Information Service in Washington, DC will educate the prospective grant writer with information about contact person(s), financial data, foundation philosophy, application review process, recent grants awarded, etc.

Corporations. In 1986 American corporations awarded grants that totaled more than 4.5 billion dollars (National Register Publishing Company, 1987). Many corporate foundations are national in scope, but some limit themselves to funding programs in geographic areas in which their own branches are located. For example, the Levi Strauss Foundation, which is a foundation friend supporting programs for the elderly, entertains only grant proposals from the states in which the Levi company has its plant(s).

Contacts with the local corporate branch of respective company sponsored foundations can never be overemphasized. Information about particular corporate foundations is available through local corporate branches/offices. The grant writer who is able to solicit local corporate support will be most successful, for the respective Foundation Headquarters looks favorably at proposals having a strong recommendation and/or deliverance from a local counterpart. In fact, some such foundations *require* a letter of support from the highest echelon of the corporate branch.

Business Sectors. Besides big foundations and corporations, there are numerous small businesses, some of which are locally and/or regionally chained, i.e., hardware stores, clothing stores, supermarkets, automobile dealers, dry cleaning businesses, and all kinds of shops and stores for merchandise. Although local owners do not advertise availability of and interest in funding, many give their time, energy, and money for local causes. Those businesses can be found through direct contact with them or "mouth to mouth" means. An effective introduction would be through personal visitation, albeit short, during which period the fund raiser explains who he/she is, what organizations/ agencies are being represented, what the issue/purpose of activities is, and how much funds are needed to launch the program by when, and then answers other questions that the business person being visited may have.

A simple yet successful fund raising scenario, for example, occurred as follows: Being employed by a small regional state university that had rather limited funds for research activities, a professor was not able to test out a research idea that was potentially large and national in scope. Frustrated, he randomly selected a store in a shopping mall, called, set up an appointment, and visited the owner on the way home from work. The visitation lasted about 10 minutes during which they talked about his research idea and some predicaments being associated with a small academia. At the end of this incidental meeting the owner of the store verbally promised that she would deliver $5,000 (the amount that the professor requested) to him through the university. Needless to say, this is a "one-of-a-kind" story, but one can read and hear about the same stories through local mass medias. One may argue that this case is sheer "luck," but the lesson lies in the fact that there are a number of silent business people who are ready to give monies for good causes, preferably locally relevant, and also appreciate the fund raiser's ingenuity and commitment to the community. One should remember, however, that timing, appearance, formats of problem presentation, etc. should be individually designed and planned. Nonetheless, a trial-and-error method is a good place to begin, with nothing to lose in the asking.

Individuals. In addition to those individuals who are owners of small businesses, the fund raiser should not overlook ordinary individuals who would like to donate monies and usable goods. According to the *Annual Register of Grant Support: A Directory of Funding Sources* (National Register Publishing Company, 1987), donations by American individuals amounted to about $72 billion in 1986, accounting for about 84% of the total private awards, including foundations and corporations.

Some interesting and valuable information about individualized giving is related to *who* they are, *what* they give, and *how* they give. First, as indicated earlier, "entrepreneurs" are interested in supporting local religious, educational, social, and cultural activities. Widows give more than married individuals; persons over 55 years of age give more than their younger age counterparts. Some donations are larger in size, such as wills, annuities, deferred gift annuities, and memorial giving/honor gifts (Crow, undated).

Many, if not most, individual givers may be effectively motivated to support local activities through personal contacts, direct mail, fund-raising activities (i.e., radiothon, telethon, dinner, dancing, recreation, etc.), product sales, membership drives, etc. Thus, successful methods in effectively reaching out to potential individual givers are unlimited and again dependent on the fund raiser's ingenuity and commitment to the program of which he/she is a part. Nonetheless, a word of caution: fund raising activities should be situational, and locally and culturally relevant. (Princess Diana's reception party cost more than $3,000 per guest, which may be acceptable in Washington and political culture, but may never be appropriate for most, if not all, American cities and towns.) American people are ready to give. Present opportunities for them to support.

A Typical Structure of Grant Proposal

The structure or outline and the content of a grant proposal should be in compliance with the application requirement. Requirement for government grants and contracts may be different from those issued by private foundations; different government agencies require different proposal contents and different foundations do likewise. Some proposals are very simple and easy to comply with, short in length, and brief in content; others require extensive details and specifications on all proposal prospectives.

In most cases, proposal contents are clearly delineated by the benefactor and thus the grant writer should follow those guidelines explicitly in writing. Nonetheless, the most important underlying message that should be pervasive (albeit implicitly) throughout the text of the proposal is the writer's appreciation of and responsiveness to the statutory mandates, the state-of-the-art knowledge and programs relevant to the issue, and the capability of key personnel. Passages such as "I/We are very knowledgeable" and "Key Project staff are very competent" are less convincing than any clear demonstration or proof of the same in the text. Grant reviewers are extremely mindful of such information.

According to one of the most recent reports of the Bureau of Health Professions (1989), strengths of approved geriatric education center grant applications (as indicated by grant reviewers) include the following:

Categories	Reviewers (%)
Appreciation and Responsiveness to RFP/statutory mandates	
Objectives	80
Understanding	66
Writer's knowledgeability	
Documentation of issue	78
Staff capability	66
Complete protocol: well written	71

On the other hand, the most serious weaknesses of disapproved proposals are (1) a lack of understanding and responsiveness to RFP/ objectives of the grant program, which unfortunately resulted in the development of inadequate protocols (almost 9 of 10 proposals), and (2) questionable staff capability, detected in about 60% of such proposals. Knowledgeability about the issue and quality of presentation were not mentioned by the reviewers in this group. It is speculated that such elements were not even included in the proposal text.

The following section provides structure and content that grant proposals should typically contain.

Summary or Abstract

The purpose of this section is to briefly introduce the nature and procedure of the proposed grant project: **Who** you are, **why** and **what** you are proposing to do, **who, how,** and **when** you are going to do it, **how** you are going to evaluate the project, **how much** it will cost, and **why** you should be the one to do it. The summary or abstract of the proposal is the first and the most powerful introduction of the "Project Self"; it should be the equivalent of a photograph. It is the impression-setting, attention-gathering, and stimulus-provoking opportunity presented to grant reviewers. Accordingly, all reviewers read this section, understand the nature of the proposal, and frame their mind as to what is expected of the proposal. In many cases, this portion of the proposal is the sole basis for initial screening and perfunctory decision by reviewing staff of the grant office. This section therefore includes who addresses what issue, goals and objectives of the project, how the project is to be implemented, how much money is being requested, and how an evaluation is to be performed. Concluding remarks should include the benefit of project outcomes as well as the impact on American society and on the quality of life of American people.

An average length of a proposal summary is about 200–250 words, no more than one typewritten page double spaced. When the grant writer solicits support from individuals who express their interest in monetary supports, or who may be influential and advocate on behalf of the project, the proposal summary is the part to be distributed.

Do's and Dont's

- Do write at least one sentence about your identification (who you are), creditability, issues or problems, project objectives, methodologies, cost, and possible impacts on the quality of life of Americans.
- Don't write more than one page, 200–250 words.
- Do write clearly in plain English, jargon free.
- Don't repeat any sentences or thoughts.

Introduction

The purpose of this section is to introduce the applicant's "self" (organization, agency, or individual) in terms of who and what you are, and how the proposal is organized in terms of structure and outline.

This section of the proposal can certainly be longer than the summary or abstract, but should not exceed two or three pages. The introduction may begin with a preamble of the organization requesting grant support, in the form of its identity, credentials, organizational mission and goals, and its established service record in the area designated by the RFP. One should avoid, however, a lengthy presentation about the philosophy and history of the organization, an intricate description of organizational structure, and any simple listing of previous grants and contracts awarded. Instead, it is suggested that the focus be on providing evidence of the organization's capability and credentials, extant program(s), and the number of clients being served, etc. Authentication of such can be supported by letters from former clients, authorities in the field, or public documents that attest to the organization's record. Other organization(s) that may be included in the grant project should be simply described. Also, the grant writer should not fail to cite relevant quotes and statistics that support the organization's qualifications and promote why it deserves the grant. Relevant supportive documents mentioned in this section could be appended in the end of the proposal.

Although the next section of the proposal, "documentation," will elaborate the scope and seriousness of the issue that the grant project is designed to address, it is wise to indicate reasons why the proposing organization intends to undertake the project for the specified time period as opposed to another time. Imminence of the project must be clarified.

Another component of this section is a brief description of the structure or outline of the proposal. The grant writer is urged to follow the RFP instruction in the proposal outline, but it does not imply that he/she has no freedom to change or modify the presentation, and certainly one can. But, when altered, a brief explanation on specific changes and modifications should be included in the introduction. Lastly, it is very important to indicate where the reviewers are to look for some evaluation criteria in the proposal (i.e., implementation activity on recruitment is explained in pp. 43–47; budget justifications are set forth in p. 35; etc.)

Do's and Don'ts

- Do describe your organization in terms of its mission, purposes, goals, and programs (activities).
- Don't present any case studies on clients that you have served.
- Do indicate precisely what you have accomplished with empirical data.
- Don't be remiss with evidence of your credibility, supplemented by statistics, letters of support/appreciation from clients and influential persons, public recognitions, and publications.

Documentation of Issue

The purpose of this section is to present the issue/problem to the grantor and/or grant reviewers: what problem is to be attacked, why is it an issue, and its imminence and seriousness.

This section is primarily a statement of the problem based on empirical facts. It is designed to discuss the problem to be tackled by the applicant in terms of (1) the identification and history of the problem, pervasiveness or scope of the problem, (2) number of people affected by the problem, and (3) status of extant service programs addressing the problem.

An empirical documentation of the problem should include such pertinent information as statistical data, research reports, theoretical concepts, relevant authorities, and, most importantly, potential clients' testimonials. Having stated the problem as the field of aging services, i.e., poor health and mental health, substandard housing, a lack of intangible services, a lack of trained professional manpower, etc., the reality of the problem should be presented with facts. Furthermore, a cause–effect relationship should be discussed, based on research reports and/or theories. When the applicant is interested in helping Alzheimer's victims and their caregivers, for example, he/she should cite the number of victims and clients to be served (nationally and/or locally), followed by a discussion of possible causes of the disease, behavioral characteristics of the clients, social and health service needs facing the victims, etc. This discussion will set the tone of a goal, objectives, and implementation methods to follow.

The second component of this section of the proposal is a description of state-of-the-art service programs nationally and locally available (or not available for that matter), nature and costs, availability and accessibility of such program(s), as well as programmatic deficiencies. Where programs are already operational, a level of adequacy should be discussed. Having presented programs as such, unavailability, unaffordability, inaccessibility, and other deficiencies not only become the basis for the project goals and objectives, but also build a case for grant support.

Do's and Don'ts

- Do document the issue based on research, published theories, and vital statistics.
- Don't forget to provide citations.
- Do remember this section is the "brain" of your project from which the rest will unfold almost mechanically.
- Don't be a name-dropper.

Goals and Objectives

The purpose of this section is to illustrate project actions to be taken relevant to the issue documented previously, namely, to list and briefly explain what the applicant is going to do—the project goals and objectives.

A "goal" refers to a brief statement on a **chosen/wanted state of affairs** (the situation or condition) that the applicant wishes to be in or to have. Such a statement is written in broad, general, and immeasurable terms, i.e., to provide, improve, establish, develop, etc. An "objective," on the other hand, is an interpretation or an operationalization of a goal with specifics, such as a time period (when), an action (to do what), a target population (who), a degree of change (how much), an intervention (how). Therefore, one goal may have several objectives. Unlike a goal statement, however, all objective statements should be written with directional and empirical (or behavioral) terms, i.e., increase, decrease, to do (action terms), etc. An example of a statement of a goal and relevant objective statements follows:

Goal: To provide high quality health care for the elderly.
Objectives: 1. By the end of (month/year), (number) of caregivers for the elderly in "xyz county" who receive respite care service will increase to "a number" (or by "x%").

2. During the life of the grant, the project will have (a number) elderly who are under the triage clinic care.

Objective 1 includes the following:

1. Time period (by the end of month/year)
2. Action/movement (to increase the number of service recipients)
3. Target population (caregivers for the elderly living in "xyz" county)
4. Change/final outcome from (number) elderly to (number) or by x% of caregivers for the elderly
5. Intervention (respite care).

As implied in the second objective, once the target population has been defined one may omit subsequent definitions from objective statements, i.e., in the goal statement: to provide high quality health care to the elderly *living in xyz county.* Nonetheless, the most important aspect of this section is that goal statements should be broad and inclusive, and objective statements should be specific and measurable.

The use of "objective" in the previous paragraph is intended to mean "process objective," which implies nothing but what is intended to be achieved during the specified period. Unfortunately, however, some grant proposals contain what is called "outcome objectives," which are in principle related to the benefits generated from process objectives, namely, impacts of products. For example, the applicant predicts (and even guarantees, albeit implicitly) what will happen to primary caregivers (i.e., becoming employees, movie-goers, etc.) or how they will use their free time (i.e., traveling, participating in recreation, dancing, etc.). Although outcome objectives can be written with all specificities as required in process objectives, this type of objective is extremely difficult to measure, simply because no one can control or force service recipients to act in a particular way. In other words, how service recipients use their free time is not under program governance. What the grant project has set out to do and can control is to increase the number of primary caregivers for the elderly who receive respite care. It cannot and should not purport to increase the number of movie-goers among caregivers or pledge that caregivers be gainfully employed as the result of receiving project services. Thus it is imperative for applicants to write process objectives (in numerical terms) rather than outcome objectives.

Another caution relevant to phrasing process objectives is that the statement should be related to the issue as indicated in the section on Documentation. For example, if the problem documented was substandard housing occupied by older persons, the grant writer should not state a goal and objectives related to health care. In other words, the issue documentation will dictate goal and objectives statements.

Do's and Don'ts

- Do list goals and respective objectives one by one.
- Don't write long goals and objectives more than 20–25 words.
- Do write measurable objectives.
- Don't stray from the issue.
- Do emphasize that you are offering the grantor an opportunity to serve humanity.
- Don't forget the fact that you are merely a human being and cannot solve all human miseries, only a few.

Implementation Methods

This section of the proposal is related to goals and objectives, and its purpose is to describe all project activities relevant to respective objectives including **what, how, why, when,** and **who,** as well as a **time frame** projected in a graph.

The **What** aspect names and describes *one* or more comparable activities relevant to a project objective. Needless to say such activities should be related to a specific objective. For example, Objective 1 above is to increase the number of caregivers for the elderly who receive respite care; then, relevant activities could be (1) staff recruitment and training, (2) client recruitment, (3) service procedure, (4) payment policy, etc. The **How** explains all implementation strategies of the activity. For example, relevant to (1) staff recruitment and training: (a) number of respite care workers to be recruited, (b) identification of potential trainees in terms of geographic areas, organizations such as churches, institutions of higher education, social club, etc., (c) means of reaching out to potential recruits, (d) training methods, i.e., didactic, experiential, mentorship, etc., (e) qualification and identification of trainers, and (f) the required number of hours for training, etc.

Immediately following How's it is appropriate, however brief, to point to reasons why such particular strategies are selected or preferred over others, namely, **Why's**. For example, why "xx" number of trainees, why "xx" organizations for outreach, why "xx" training curricula, why experiential learning, why "xx" trainer is selected, etc. In addition to strengthening an applicant's implementation methods, those Why's will implicitly convey to the grant reviewers the applicant's state-of-knowledge.

When is related to implementation time schedule, i.e., how long staff recruitment will take, when the training will begin, when actual service will begin, etc. A detailed explanation of timings (1) to (4) above should be included. One exception to the explanation of timing is that some grant writers opt to use a graphic description (as described later). Nonetheless, it is more appropriate and effective if one presents verbalization, articulation of time scheduling and graphing.

Lastly, the applicant is expected to assure the grantor **Who** will be responsible for each implementation activity. Successful proposals include the name of such persons and his/her qualifications, although that person is yet to be recruited. "To be named" is not sufficient, because the applicant is not demonstrating his/her knowledge about prospective staff. In this case, the applicant's plan for staffing is weak, because the prospective grantee is not positively convincing the grantor as to what he/she will do when/if the quality person that the applicant is looking for is not available. However, when/if one or more staff are to be recruited, it is highly recommended (1) to indicate names and abstracts of their qualifications in the text, and (2) to append their vita with a letter of agreement or intent to joint the project on approval.

One example of a neatly organized structure of this sort including what's, when's, who's, how's, and why's is as follows:

Methods or Implementation Strategies

Objective 1: Respite Care (Note: This serves to remind the reviewers of Objective 1, and thus the grant writer does not have to repeat the objective statement, but rather can use a few key words highlighting the statement.)

Method 1:	Staff Recruitment and Training
	Explain in detail How's, Why's, When's, and Who's.
Method 2:	Client Recruitment
	Explain in detail How's, Why's, When's and Who's.
Method 3:	Service Process
	Explain the same as above.
Method 4:	Payment Policy
	Explain the same as above.

Objective 2: Triage Clinic Care

Method 1:	Name the Activity
	Explain in detail How's, Why's, When's, and Who's.

Methods 2, 3, 4, . . . , n per objective are to follow.

Objective 3: (Name a program.) and 4, 5, 6, . . . , *n* to follow.

Methods 1, 2, 3, 4, . . . , n per objective are to follow.

A graphic presentation of the proposed time schedule could be included last, possibly on a separate page with one of following charts: TIME, GANTT, or PERT (Program Evaluation Review Technique).

A time chart (or calendar chart) contains the list of all activities and indicates, normally by "month(s)," when a particular activity will occur and repeat, and/or be complete. Thus, this kind of presentation can be used for both continuous and interrupted activities (Table 1).

A GANTT chart (or bar chart) is to indicate what and how long activities occur over time. This chart is normally used for continuous rather than interrupted activities. In other words, once ended, that particular activity does not restart. Thus, bars indicate when activities start and terminate (Table 2).

A PERT chart (or Web chart) is normally used with a series of interdependent activities in order to follow a proper sequence, namely, at the completion of one objective and/or method activity, the others to follow (Table 3).

The nature of the project will dictate which charting method is most appropriate. In most cases of human service grants and contracts, however, the time (calendar) chart or GANTT chart is usually most practical. However, some research grants and contracts may need to adapt a PERK chart.

Do's and Don'ts

- Do relate to goals and objectives.
- Don't be overly ambitious.
- Do use paragraphic headings.
- Don't create any redundant activities.

Evaluation

The purpose of this section of the proposal is to express the intent to appraise project activities as often as needed and/or required. It proposes an evaluation design including data collection and analysis.

Continuous evaluation activities are an integral component of the service project, and thus most, if not all, grantors require that an evaluation plan be included in the proposal. This process is not only to assist project managers and administrators to frequently review and assess the progress that the project has made, but also to reinforce staff efforts and heighten their decision making and morale. Further, through evaluation the project can earn the trust of clients as a result of their being well informed in terms of effectiveness of the project. This section of the proposal, therefore, contains matters related to "Who," "What," "How," "Why," and "When." A detailed evaluation process is discussed in Chapter 11.

The **Who** describes the person or persons who will be responsible for the project evaluation. Positively stating the persons' name and their

Table 1. Activity Time Schedule

	Month											
Activities	2	4	6	8	10	12	14	16	18	20	22	24
Objective 1: Respite Care												
1. Staff recruitment	x	x	x					x^a	x			
2. Client recruitment	x	x	x	x	x			x	x	x	x	
3. Service process		x	x				x^a					
4. Payment policy		x	x				x^a					
Objective 2: Triage Clinic												
1.	(Repeat above as appropriate)											
2.												
•												
•												
•												

[a] As needed.

Table 2. Activity Schedule

	Month												
Activities	2	4	6	8	9	10	12	14	16	18	20	22	24
Objective 1: Respite Care													
1. Staff recruitment	──────────────────												
2. Client recruitment	──────────────────────												
3. Service process	────────────												
4. Payment policy	────────────												
Objective 2: Triage Clinic													
1.	(Repeat above as appropriate)												
2.													
•													
•													
•													

Table 3. Activity Schedule

	Month												
Activities	2	4	6	8	9	10	12	14	16	18	20	22	24
Objective 1: Respite Care													
1. Staff recruitment	──												
2. Client recruitment	──												
3. Service process	──												
4. Payment policy	──												
Objective 2: Triage Clinic													
1.						────────							
2.						────────							
•						────							
•													
•													

qualifications can only strengthen the proposal. **What** is limited to project goals, objectives, and implementation activities. Any activities or project components not stated in the previous two sections should not be included. Nonetheless, in general, evaluation criteria involve (1) effort (staff and resources put into the project), (2) efficiency (flow of efforts, or effort over effect), (3) effect (end outcomes, or function of efforts and efficiency), (4) adequacy (relative level of meeting the need, or effect over need), and (5) process (causal relationship of effects). Depending on the nature of the project and/or the requirement mandated by the grantor, the applicant is expected to perform one or more evaluation criteria. Human service grants normally focus on project effects, while R and D (Research and Demonstration) grants most likely encompass all criteria.

The **How** involves evaluation methods. It calls for detailed evaluation process and design, as well as methodologies of data collection, organization, and analysis. Specific design(s) should be discussed, sampling strategies and evaluation instrument(s) described (and included in an Appendix), and statistical tools elaborated. Necessary measurement tools (or instruments) to be used should be fully developed and articulated in terms of reliability and validity. If such instruments are not readily available at the time of submission of the proposal, the grant writer should describe their nature and content. In addition, some rationalizations and justifications (i.e., **Why's**) of selecting **How's** should be explained. For example, why the applicant proposes an evaluation performed by external or internal evaluator(s), why the applicant selected a particular method of sampling and instrumentation, etc. **When** is the frequency of evaluation activities, namely, how often the evaluation is to be completed—monthly, quarterly, semiannually, and/or annually, and why that particular interval.

In general, grantors require both formative and summative evaluations. Formative evaluation is designed to primarily assess organizational changes as a partial consequence of having the grant project implemented, i.e., alterations in organizational and/or project goals and objectives, resource allocation, staff personnel, service programs as well as delivery strategies, etc. Summative evaluation is designed to enumerate the project's end products, nothing but vis-à-vis goals and objectives. Whereas the former is more or less a qualitative systems approach, the latter is primarily a quantitative measure of relevant project performances. Both evaluations are mutually reinforcing, in that changes in the organization, agency, and/or project itself are based on the summative evaluation, while the formative evaluation facilitates the project process to maximize project production. Formative evaluation normally

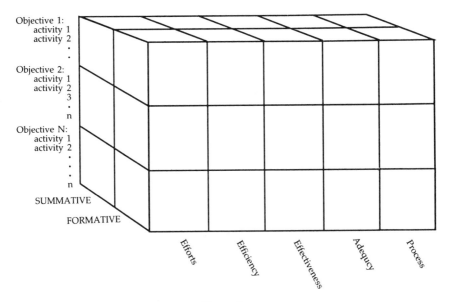

Figure 1.

focuses on project efforts, efficiencies, and processes; summative evaluation customarily concentrates on effects and adequacy of the project. One should not propose an "esoteric" evaluation design and "profound" or unnecessary statistical analysis. Avoid research jargons. Stay within the scope of evaluation.

In summary, one may think about project evaluation conceptually as depicted in Figure 1.

The evaluator will find $n \times m \times r$ number of evaluations in toto. But, in reality, evaluations are to be completed only with a number of those cubics as related to the goals and objectives of the project and/or to comply with the grantor's interests and mandates. It is the evaluator's prerogative to decide which smaller cubics are to be appraised within the stipulation established between the grantor and grantee.

Do's and Don'ts

- Do include all activities in either summative or formative evaluation.
- Don't forget to define evaluation criteria.
- Do use plain English words.
- Don't assume the reviewers are knowledgeable in evaluation processes.

Budget and Its Justification

The purpose of this section of the proposal is to present an itemized budget for the project. In most cases the grantor provides applicants a uniform format for budgeting, which is usually divided into two major categories: personnel and nonpersonnel. Each category is further divided into *requested, contributed* (or matching), and a *total*. A typical layout of this section is shown in Table 4.

Budget justifications are normally required and are included in a designated place or immediately following the budget section of the proposal. Justifications for personnel categories primarily include the designated person's functions and/or responsibilities in the project. A basis for determining salaries and wages should be explained on the basis of a local or regional norm. Needless to say, names of such individuals should be mentioned once or more earlier in the section of goals and objectives and/or implementation methods. Fringe benefits that the hosting organization normally grants to employees can be included with a specific rate. Consultants' wages may be calculated on a hourly or daily basis, or on the predetermined rate during the life of the grant. In short, all justification should be done based on creditable references, i.e., publicized norms for salaries by disciplines and professions, competitive bids for contracts, etc.

Items of nonpersonnel categories should also be justified in detail with relevant information, i.e., a unit cost, rate, time period, etc. Particulars of this classification are unlimited, but one needs to be creative in that no more than seven or eight items should be listed.

In addition to allowable budget items listed above, most grantors permit applicants to request what is called "indirect" costs. One way to comply is to compute it based on a prearranged agreement between the grantor and the applicant's organization. Normally, the federal government has an established individualized rate for social, health, and educational organizations. Or else, the RFP/RFA clearly indicates an allowable rate for indirect costs. A rate of indirect costs as determined by many foundations can usually be obtained by contacting the grantor as the grant develops.

Do's and Don'ts

- Do list all personnel needed for the project, including what percentage of time they will be devoting to the project.
- Don't inflate budget by item, salaries and wages in particular.
- Do explain each item clearly and precisely.
- Don't cloud budget columns with wordy explanations.
- Do organize columns neatly.
- Don't overbudget for contributions.

Table 4. Layout for an Itemized Budget

		Personnel			
Name	Title	% Time	Requested	Contribution	Total
Salaries					
B. Smith	Director	100	25,000	25,000	50,000
C. Doyle	Associate	75	30,000	10,000	45,000
xxxx	Secretary	100	25,000	0	25,000
xxxxx					
xxxxxx					
xxxxxxx					
Fringe Benefits					
FICA or institutional retirement at xx%			xx,xxx	xx,xxx	xx,xxx
Health insurance at x%			xx,xxx	xx,xxx	xx,xxx
Disability insurance at x%			x,xxx	x,xxx	xx,xxx
Sick leave at x%			x,xxx	x,xxx	xx,xxx
Others (explain)					
Consultants and Contracts					
D. Mills	Consulting Psychiatrist		x,xxx	x,xxx	xx,xxx
S. Sturges	Program Consultant		x,xxx	x,xxx	xx,xxx
xxx					
xxxx					
xxxxx					
	Subtotal		$xxx,xxx	$xx,xxx	$xxx,xxx
	Nonpersonnel				
Project office					
xxxx ft^2 at $xx/ft/year			xx,xxx	xx,xxx	xx,xxx
Rentals and equipment purchases					
Items: 1.				x,xxx	x,xxx
2.				x,xxx	x,xxx
3.				x,xxx	x,xxx
Supplies (consumable)					
Items: 1.					
2.					
3.					
Staff travel					
Where to and when					
How many times					
Trainee travel					
Where to and when					
How many times					
Local and long distance telephone					
Mailing cost					
Reading materials					
etc. etc.					
	Subtotal:		$xx,xxx	$xx,xxx	$xx,xxx
	Grand total		$xxx,xxx	$xxx,xxx	$x,xxx,xxx

- Do request equipment in the first year.
- Don't forget to include service costs for equipment.

Institutional/Organizational Capability

The purpose of this section of the proposal is to demonstrate the applicant's capabilities that ensure successful performance of project activities. It is designed to point out organizational resources and a record of collaborative activities, particularly the qualification and capability of the project director.

The grantor clearly indicates some qualifications for application, normally one of which is that the applicant should be a not-for-profit organization. Organizational resources required include a physical facility, library, staff, and other particulars that are needed for the project. One can include organizational structure in that the place of the proposed project is specified and project autonomy is assured. In addition, the most important function of this section is to highlight the project director's qualifications and capabilities. It is not suggested, however, that the grant writer elaborate each qualification and capability of the director in any undue detail. Although his/her vitae and sample publications may be abstracted and included in the proposal text, it is implied that such materials may be appended (see Appendix below).

Do's and Don'ts

- Do relate the director's capabilities to the goals and objectives.
- Don't xerox and paste organization's brochures for inclusion.
- Do try to write this section as a supplement to the Introduction.
- Don't try to glorify the director.

Future Funding Plans and Prospects

Although many grant projects may not be able to continue their activities after funding support expires, many if not most grantors would like to have the project sustained, especially when the project has positively demonstrated its effectiveness in promoting the quality of life and in alleviating human misery. Therefore, some grantors are interested in learning about applicant's plans for maintaining the same or modified project activities, albeit smaller in scope.

Therefore, the applicant may propose one or all of the following funding prospects included in permanency plans:

1. Fee for service, based on a sliding scale.
2. Establish organizational status to qualify for available third party payments.

3. Fund raising plans including more grants and contracts, and activities previously listed in this chapter under *How to Find Funding Sources.*

A detailed activity plan for future funding can be one of the most important standards that the grantor may impose on the applicant. Accordingly, it is highly recommended that grant writers carefully study the grantor's expectation in this respect.

Do's and Don'ts

- Do use established records in fund raising.
- Don't promise too much.
- Do present realistic plans.
- Don't forget to include in the proposal, if applicable, promissory notes or statements made by potential givers.

Conclusion

The purpose of this section of the proposal is to conclude the proposal with two reminders: One is to remind the reviewer that the applicant is responding to the specific RFP/RFA, and the other is to point to the pages and/or sections where the reviewer can read the applicant's compliances with evaluation standards.

The conclusion should not be the same as the Summary or Abstract as discussed earlier in this chapter. Instead, as a part of the first reminder, one may "philosophize" the issue constructively and present it to the reviewer as the applicant's commitment. What and how the project significantly touches the lives of human beings suffering misery can be briefly reemphasized.

The second part of this section is designed to assist the reviewer to find passages in the proposal text that are responsive to evaluation criteria. Although one may successfully rearrange the proposal text in accordance with evaluation criteria (which is normally publicized by the grantor), it is not only tedious but also repetitious without inordinate care. Nonetheless, by virtue of the required proposal outline, which is different from the evaluation criteria in terms of the respective order of sequence, the reviewers are naturally bound to struggle in locating passages relevant to specific evaluation criteria. Subsequently, if they fail to identify these criteria, the applicant stands to lose. Therefore, the grant writer should utilize this section to clearly point out pages and paragraphic headings that contain compliance with evaluative standards. Having done so, the reviewers are able to reread the important text and quickly direct their thoughts to the right direction and, hopefully, to approval for funding.

At the end, if required, the Director's Assurance can be included. A Director's Assurance is a promissory statement to the effect that the Project Director will comply with the grantor's mandates and timely perform all activities of the project as proposed. This kind of statement is usually given by the grantor and bears the Director's signature.

Do's and Don'ts

- Do write very briefly.
- Don't repeat the Summary or Abstract.
- Do write with pride that you are offering the grantor an invaluable opportunity to serve humanity.
- Don't forget to indicate page(s) and paragraphic headings relevant to reviewers' evaluation criteria.

References

This section of the proposal is designed for the grant writer to demonstrate his/her state-of-the-art knowledge relevant to the proposed project. It does not imply, however, that one must provide a lengthy bibliography, much of which is irrelevant to the proposal. It is strongly suggested that one include all references cited in the text and use one system (or style) of manual, preferably APA (American Psychological Association) style. In view of the complexity of the APA style and the limited space for this chapter, the grant writer is encouraged to be familiar with the system.

Appendix

One function of appending materials relevant to the proposal is to simplify the proposal text and to make it neat, precise, and less cluttered by too much "stuff." Only relevant materials mentioned in the narrative proposal text should be included in this last section of the proposal.

One interesting way to append hefty material is to develop an abstract and include it in the appendix. Some grant writers submit a separate volume of Appendix along with the proposal text. The second method, however, requires special attention so that the volume(s) do not get lost in mailing and shuffling, which are also unavoidable parts of grant application and review process.

Tips for Potentially Successful Proposals

Interesting yet important tips for someone who hopes to be successful in grant and/or contract writing include the following:

1. Educate yourself through reading publications relevant to funding sources. Attend national conferences and tap resources and grant ideas.
2. Keep in close contact with individuals who might have some funding information in your area of interest. Try to combine your official trips with "grant shopping trips" normally during early spring and fall.
3. Write the first proposal with an experienced and successful grant writer and learn the trade, or consult with such persons.
4. Persevere. Do not easily give up though you fail and fail and fail again. You will be successful sooner than you expect.
5. Be sure you have complete information about and understanding of RFP/RFA. Feel free to ask any number of questions to the person who is in charge of granting and/or contracting processes.
6. Be aware of the fact that you are not begging for monies. Be proud of yourself, for you are the one who is giving the grantor a golden opportunity to fulfill its duties most efficiently and effectively.
7. Present your proposal as interesting and easy to read. Have your friend(s) read the proposal and raise questions.
8. Make your proposal brief, just long enough to precisely respond to all required items by the grantor; no more, no less.
9. Write your proposal with plain English, no jargons.
10. Organize your proposal neatly with the same typesetting. Avoid any xeroxed passages in the text.
11. Do not forget paging including appended materials.
12. Bind the proposal tightly in one booklet. Make sure it is not torn or will separate easily.

Therefore, the final proposal product includes the following:

1. Cover letter
2. Required cover page, project summary, budget summary (justification may be attached), abstracts of personnel vita, etc. (whatever is provided by the grantor)
3. Table of Contents
4. Summary/Abstract of the Project
5. Introduction
6. Documentation of Issue—Presentation of Problem
7. Goals and Objectives of the Project
8. Implementation Methods
9. Project Evaluation
10. Project Budget (and Justification)

Summary

Grant writing and fund raising activities on behalf of the elderly are certainly an American privilege. Public and private resources for human services are generous and open to every concerned professional in the field of gerontological and geriatric research and services. Skills in grant writing entering into contracts are unique yet develop with experience.

Grant writing is an effective means to better serve the elderly, particularly in times of prevailing fiscal austerity imposed by the government on human services. Foundations, corporate and business sectors, and many individuals are out there to help researchers and professional service providers endure financial stringency. *What* to do *when* and *how* to do by *whom* and *why* are integral parts of grant and contract proposals. Happy Grantsmanship! "Try it. You'll like it." For sure.

References

Buckman, T. R. (1975). Analytic Introduction. In M. O. Lewis (Ed.), *The Foundation Directory* (p. xi). New York: Columbia University Press.

Crow, M. R. (Undated). *Creative funding for private agencies*. A paper presented at a National Assoc. of Christians in SW, Cincinnati, OH.

Executive Office of the President. (1990). *Catalog of federal domestic assistance 1990*. Washington, DC: U.S. Government Printing Office.

Foundation Center. (1989). *Foundation directory*. New York: Author.

National Register Publishing Company. (1987). *Annual register of grant support*. Wilmetter, IL: Author.

Taft Foundation Information Service. (1989). *Taft foundation reporter*, 20th ed. Washington, DC: Taft Group, Inc.

White, V. P. (1975). *Grants: How to find out about them and what to do next*. New York: Plenum Press.

Index

A,B,C Model of New Life
    Experiences, 144–145
A,B,Cs of healthy human emotion
    A,B,C Model of New Life
        Experiences, 144–145
    attitude model of habits, 148–151
    belief model of habits, 147–148
    description of, 143–144
    and habitual beliefs, 146–147
    originator of, 143
AAA (Area Agencies on Aging), 197,
    209, 218, 237
AARP (American Association of
    Retired Persons), 6, 197
Achievement-motivated person, 251
Activity theory, 5–6
Administration on Aging (See AoA)
Administrators of programs, 233,
    256–257 (See also Management
    of services)
Affiliation-motivated persons, 252
Age stratification theory, 9–10
Aging
    and autonomy, 175
    and change, 74
    and control, 2
    and cultural diversity, 2
    and death, 72, 137–138
    and dependency, 175
    and drug-induced illness, 137
    and isolation, 175–176, 180
    mental health needs of, 36–37,
        174–175
    moral economy of, 15–18
    needs of, 174–175
    Network, 209, 218
    organizing activities for, 198–199
    and physiology, 2
    political economy of, 13–18
    and reminiscing, 68–69, 71
    and research design of program
        evaluation, 271–272
    and self-government, 171
    social planning for, 199–202
    and social problems, 194
    and social relationships, 52–53, 75

theories of
    evolution of, 3–4
    first generation, 4–7
    second generation, 7–10
    third generation, 10–18
    and transportation, 175
Aging Network, 209, 218
Aging planning, 214 (See also Social
    planning)
Alanon, 57
Alcoholics Anonymous, 57
American Association of Retired
    Persons (See AARP)
American Philosophical Society, 299
Analyzing data, 274–276
Annual Register of Grant Support: A
    Directory of Funding Sources,
    306, 307
AoA (Administration on Aging), 215
Applied behavior analysis, 120
Appraisal of staff, 247–248
Area Agencies on Aging (See AAA)
Assertiveness Training, 43
Assessment
    in counseling process, 39–42
    in life review, 73
    needs, 198–199, 222–224
Assessment phase, 280–282, 285–286
Attitude model of habits, 148–151
Attitudes, 144, 147
Attitude-triggered emotional feelings,
    148–151
Autonomy, 175

Behavior, 119
Behavioral analysis and therapy (See
    also Behavioral gerontology)
    concepts of, basic, 117–121
    and conditioning principles, 121–125
    future directions of, 130–131
    impact of, 117
    and observational learning
        principles, 129–130
    and operant learning principles,
        125–129
    term of, 120

327